Psychoanalysis in Contexts

nis boc

Psychoanalysis in Contexts provides a comprehensive overview of the central issues and debates in contemporary psychoanalytic theory. It also offers guidelines for the reformulation of social, political and cultural theory in the light of psychoanalysis.

It includes a discussion of the nature of subjectivity and its relation to the unconscious; the inter-relation of unconscious sexuality and gender; and the psycho-political dimensions of the late modern age. *Psychoanalysis in Contexts* will become a standard reference point for students and professionals in psychoanalysis and contemporary theory, and for all those in the social sciences interested in the psychoanalytic reformulation of contemporary social thought.

Anthony Elliott is Research Fellow in the Department of Political Science at the University of Melbourne. He is the author of *Social Theory and Psychoanalysis in Transition* (1992), and *Psychoanalytic Theory: An Introduction* (1994). **Stephen Frosh** is Senior Lecturer in Psychology at Birkbeck College, University of London, and is Consultant Clinical Psychologist at the Tavistock Clinic. He is the author of *Identity Crisis: Modernity, Psychoanalysis and the Self* (1991), and *Sexual Difference: Masculinity and Psychoanalysis* (1994).

Psychoanalysis in Contexts

Paths between Theory and Modern Culture

Edited by
Anthony Elliott and Stephen Frosh

London and New York

First published 1995
by Routledge
11 New Fetter Lane, London EC4P 4EE

Simultaneously published in the USA and Canada
by Routledge
29 West 35th Street, New York, NY 10001

Typeset in Times by
NWL Editorial Services, Langport, Somerset

Printed and bound in Great Britain by
Mackays of Chatham PLC, Chatham, Kent

British Library Cataloguing in Publication Data
A catalogue record for this book is available from the British Library

Library of Congress Cataloguing in Publication Data
A catalogue record for this book has been requested

ISBN 0–415–09703–7 (hbk)
ISBN 0–415–09704–5 (pbk)

For Albert (A.E.)
For Arieh (S.F.)

Contents

Contributors

Jessica Benjamin is a practising psychoanalyst in New York City, and is on the faculty of New York University Postdoctoral Psychology Program in Psycho-analysis and the New School for Social Research Program in Psychoanalytic Studies. She is author of *The Bonds of Love: Psychoanalysis, Feminism and the Problem of Domination* (1988).

Cornelius Castoriadis is Director of Studies at the Ecole des Hautes Etudes en Sciences Sociales in Paris and a practising psychoanalyst. He was the founder and principal theoretician of the *Socialisme ou Barbarie* group and magazine (Paris, 1949–65). He is the author of many works in social theory and psychoanalysis, including *Crossroads in the Labyrinth* (1984), *The Imaginary Institution of Society* (1987) and *Philosophy, Politics, Autonomy* (1991).

Nancy J. Chodorow is Professor of Sociology at the University of California, Berkeley and a psychoanalyst in private practice. She is the author of *The Reproduction of Mothering: Psychoanalysis and the Sociology of Gender* (1978), *Feminism and Psychoanalytic Theory* (1989), and *Femininities, Masculinities, Sexualities: Freud and Beyond* (1994).

Peter Dews is Senior Lecturer in Philosophy at the University of Essex. He is the author of many papers in modern European thought, and of *Logics of Disintegration* (1987).

Anthony Elliott is Research Fellow in the Department of Political Science, University of Melbourne. He is the author of *Social Theory and Psychoanalysis in Transition: Self and Society from Freud to Kristeva* (1992) and *Psychoanalytic Theory: An Introduction* (1994). His research interests include the changing meaning of identity in the context of the global political system and the relations between psychoanalysis and postmodernity. These interests are set out in a forthcoming work, *Subject To Ourselves*.

Stephen Frosh is Senior Lecturer in Psychology at Birkbeck College, University of London, and Consultant Clinical Psychologist in the Child and Family Department at the Tavistock Clinic, London. He is the author of many papers in the areas of psychoanalysis and psychology, and of several books, including *Identity Crisis* (1991), *The Politics of Psychoanalysis* (1987), *Psychoanalysis and*

Psychology (1989), and, with Danya Glaser, *Child Sexual Abuse* (1993). His most recent book is *Sexual Difference: Masculinity and Psychoanalysis* (1994).

Joel Kovel trained as a psychiatrist and psychoanalyst, graduating in the latter in 1977 from the Institute at Downstate Medical Center, Brooklyn, New York. He was Professor of Psychiatry at the Albert Einstein College of Medicine and is now Alger Hiss Professor of Social Studies, Bard College, New York. His books include *White Racism* (1984), *History and Spirit* (1991) and *Red Hunting in the Promised Land* (1994).

David Macey is a translator and the author of *Lacan in Contexts* (1988) and *The Lives of Michel Foucault* (1993). He is currently working on a biography of Frantz Fanon.

Michael Rustin is Professor of Sociology at the University of East London and a Visiting Professor at the Tavistock Clinic. He is the author of *The Good Society and the Inner World* (1991), and, with Margaret Rustin, *Narratives of Love and Loss* (1987).

Janet Sayers is Professor of Psychoanalytical Psychology at the University of Kent, where she teaches psychoanalysis to psychology, social work, probation and women's studies students. She also works as a psychoanalytic psychotherapist, both privately and in the National Health Service. Her previous books include *Mothering Psychoanalysis* (1991). She is currently completing a collection of case histories provisionally entitled *Freudian Tales*.

Hanna Segal was born in Poland in 1918. She was analysed by Melanie Klein and qualified as a psychoanalyst in 1947. She is also a child analyst and was one of the pioneers in the psychoanalysis of psychotics. She was twice President of, and is a practising psychoanalyst and teacher at, the British Psycho-Analytical Society. She is a Fellow of the Royal College of Psychiatrists. Her books include *Introduction to the Work of Melanie Klein* (1973), *Klein* (1979), *The Work of Hanna Segal* (1981), *Dream, Phantasy and Art* (1991), and numerous papers, mostly published in the *International Journal of Psycho-Analysis*. Her research interests include psychoanalytic contributions to the understanding of art and the creative process, as well as of the psychodynamics of social processes.

Madelon Sprengnether is Professor of English at the University of Minnesota. She is the author of *The Spectral Mother* (1990).

Acknowledgements

Many people have provided guidance and encouragement in the process of assembling this volume. We should like to thank David Stonestreet at Routledge for commissioning the book. Many thanks also to Brad Scott and Craig Lonsdale for their invaluable help. We owe particular debts to Nicola Geraghty, Albert Paolini, Nick Stevenson and Simon Prosser for their advice and support.

The contributors have been especially responsive to the many queries and administrative questions that we raised about earlier drafts of their essays. We thank them for their attention to detail.

Many of the essays appear for the first time in the present volume. However, some of the essays have been published, or are forthcoming, in journals and anthologies: they are reprinted here with permission. Details of original presentation and/or publication are as follows.

Cornelius Castoriadis, Chapter 1: 'Logique, Imagination, Reflexion', text of a lecture presented to a colloquium on 'The Unconscious and Science' held March 5 and 6 1988, at the University of Paris-X (Nanterre). With slight changes, this text was published in *L'Inconscient et la science*, ed. R. Dorey (Paris: Dunod, 1991): 9–36; and *American Imago: Studies in Psychoanalysis and Culture*, vol. 49, no. 1, 1992: 3–33 (trans. David Ames Curtis).

Anthony Elliott, Chapter 2: The essay was first delivered as a lecture in April 1994 at the Psychoanalytic Institute of Northern California, San Francisco. A modified version will be published in *American Imago: Studies in Psychoanalysis and Culture* (forthcoming).

Peter Dews, Chapter 3: A shorter version of the essay first appeared in Harry Kunneman and Hent de Vries (eds), *Enlightenments: Encounters between Critical Theory and Contemporary French Thought* (Kampen, The Netherlands: Kok Pharos 1993).

Nancy J. Chodorow, Chapter 5: From her *Femininities, Masculinities, Sexualities: Freud and Beyond* (The University Press of Kentucky, 1994).

Jessica Benjamin, Chapter 6: This essay is to appear in a volume *Like Subjects and Love Objects: On Recognition, Identification and Difference* (London and New Haven: Yale University Press).

Stephen Frosh, Chapter 9: An edited version of the essay first appeared in his *Sexual Difference: Masculinity and Psychoanalysis* (London and New York: Routledge, 1994).

Anthony Elliott and Stephen Frosh
Melbourne and London

Introduction

Anthony Elliott and Stephen Frosh

During the last decade and a half, psychoanalytic theory has undergone dramatic changes. The Freudian theoretical tradition has become revitalized and examined with new interest; the predominance of the post-structural psychoanalytic approach developed by Lacan has come under fire in many quarters of the social sciences; and approaches in the object-relational school, especially the Kleinian, have diversified and in turn given rise to a plurality of methodological positions. Among other problems, the following issues have emerged as central in contemporary psychoanalytic debate: the status of the unconscious, especially as concerns the nature of human subjectivity; the connection between the pre-Oedipal and Oedipal phases in the constitution of identity; the structure of sexual and gender difference; and the relationship between psychical creation on the one hand and imaginary and symbolic experience on the other.

At the same time, there has been a profound reappraisal of the grand schemas of contemporary cultural, social and political theory. The 1970s and 1980s witnessed important critical evaluations of the sweeping, universal pretensions of discourses such as humanism, liberalism and Marxism. Post-structuralist and postmodernist critics raised serious issues about the basic assumptions of modern theory, opting for the local, specific and particular over the general and universal (which were considered anxiety-provoking). These developments accompanied the emergence of notions of the dissolution of subjectivity, of identity, of human action and agency. In its place there appeared a baffling variety of critical terms – power, discourse, difference, the text – which were subsequently deployed in the contemporary debates on modernity and postmodernism.

The essays contained in this volume represent an attempt to examine these important changes taking place in psychoanalysis and social-theoretical discourse over recent years. Many of the essays in *Psychoanalysis in Contexts* assess the relevance and importance of psychoanalysis as concerns the proliferation of approaches in social-theoretical thinking, as well as exploring the relationship of psychoanalysis to theory *per se*. New directions in psychoanalytic thinking that have previously been little known or neglected are introduced, including the work of such authors as Castoriadis and Laplanche. Older traditions of psychoanalysis, such as Freudian and object-relational approaches, are examined from new and/or different theoretical perspectives. Moreover, theoretical approaches which have undergone a revival of interest and/or reconceptualization are also reviewed, such as the post-Lacanian writings of Kristeva, Irigaray and Žižek and the contemporary Anglo-American writings of Benjamin, Kovel, Segal and others.

In preparing this book we have endeavoured to create a dialogue between competing psychoanalytic approaches to the study of subjectivity, social action and modern societies. We believe that the volume opens new paths between psychoanalytic theory and contemporary culture. In the remainder of this introduction, we shall explore some of the key themes which have recently emerged in psychoanalysis and social-theoretical thinking. This sketch is intended as a conceptual backcloth for the critical debates which follow. Following on from this, we shall summarize the main arguments of the essays in this volume.

PSYCHOANALYSIS, REFLEXIVITY AND THE OTHER

Psychoanalysis has always revolved around an ambivalent encounter with otherness. For Freud, faced with the inexhaustible passion of his female hysterical patients, there was an attempt to colonize, to take over what was other and make it amenable to the demands of rationality. This procedure was not only an instance of the occluding of nature by science, a common nineteenth-century strategy for dealing with the terrors induced by the unknown; it also spanned the polarity of femininity versus masculinity, translating the former into the latter by making women's hysterical discourse the possession of the male expert. But alongside this imperialism, familiar to this day in the practice of reductionist psychoanalysis, there was also a recognition of something outside the control of the analyst, an acknowledgement that these strange women were presenting an otherness which could also be found within the man of science – indeed, right inside Freud himself, in the heart of his self-analysed unconscious. Put in the literary terms that offer the most compelling contemporary metaphor for the analytic process, this recognition of the other within the self becomes an instance of intertextuality: 'The discovery of the unconscious was Freud's discovery, within the discourse of the other, of what he was actively reading within himself' (Felman 1987: 60).

There is an infinite regress here of great importance: psychoanalysis analyses – that is its function. But it can never fully encompass its object in its analysis, because one of the principles of psychoanalysis is the unending nature of the unconscious dynamic. The analytic attitude, as Rieff (1966) and others have famously portrayed it, is characterized by a relentlessly deconstructive urge that allows no end points or perfect solutions – no cures, just living with ailments. On and on goes analysis, striving to domesticate an otherness, a wildness, which it knows to be untameable. Psychoanalysis is, in this sense, a both/and phenomenon: it attempts to make sense of otherness and recognizes the essentially irrational way the sense-making process operates. It is both hermeneutic and epiphanous, both mechanistic and ecstatic. It argues that all mental phenomena can be explained by reference to unconscious impulses, but also says that the explanations themselves are in part constituted by these same impulses – that they are motivated and hence available to analysis themselves. Again it is Freud who offers a clear instance of this self-reflexive conundrum from which psychoanalysis can never escape. In *The Interpretation of Dreams*, Freud (1900) presents his famous 'Specimen Dream' of Irma's injection, concluding from it that dreams are constituted as wish-fulfilments – the discovery which he believes will make his name. However, as Anzieu (1975: 140) comments, 'Freud noted subsequently that thoughts which follow on from dreams are still dream-thoughts. So the thought that dreams are wish-fulfilments is an integral part of the dream content.' Analysis of the dream produces the generalization that dreams are wish-fulfilments, but this too is a wish-fulfilment, the wish being that Freud should unravel the mystery of dreams. More generally, psychoanalysis is itself constituted within the structure of irrationality – of the unconscious – and all its operations bear that mark.

The self-referential nature of the psychoanalytic enterprise is particularly well-attuned to a postmodern cultural context in which meaning is continually dislocated and dispersed. The quintessential awareness here is of the subjective strain of immersion in a cultural setting in which images and surfaces dominate – in which 'seduction' is the primary force – and in which the capacity of individuals to hold onto meaning is constantly undermined. But as Žižek (1991) points out, from the slippery vantage-point of a deconstructing Yugoslavia, what is starting to become terrifying about postmodernity is not so much the gaps and absences in people's lives, but the way everything is wrapped up together into a space that denies distance. In the modernist tradition of which Freudian psychoanalysis is a part, the importance of struggling to create distance is accentuated – that critical distance that enables judgement and understanding to be achieved. So when Freud presents dreams, mostly his own, as the founding act of psychoanalysis, it is to show how they are interpretable, intelligible, as the dis- course of the unconscious. They are irrational in their content, but not in their form. Similarly with hysteria; listening to the word of the woman, Freud colonizes it to create a kind of science, to make sense of what is in other contexts thought unreachable. The 'cure', such as it is, consists in this: to draw a boundary so that what is irrational is nevertheless known, so appearing in the arena of that which is symbolizable, and can be contained. The project of most therapy is of this kind: through symbolization, making meanings out of what appears not to be meant.

Postmodernism, however, recognizes something different. The Real is the moment of failure of symbolization, what is left behind when all interpretation is over. Under postmodern conditions, it is with this that we come face to face. What might seem to be an empty space is full to overflowing with contradictory impulses, producing both the dread of what Kristeva (1983) terms 'abjection', and the life and energy of the semiotic. The law and its corruption are bound up together, they live side by side, entangled one with another. The relativity of this version of postmodernism derives not, as many critiques of postmodernism suggest, from its failure to take up an ethical position (see Bauman 1993), but from its recognition that the appalling elements in its experience can be the same as the most sublime.

What makes psychoanalysis so attractive under cultural conditions of this kind is the remarkable fluidity of its encounter with subjectivity. The Freudian emphasis on that underlying truth which can be unearthed, given a good enough detective process, has proved unsustainable in the face of modernist and postmodernist deconstruction. Every time a truth appears, another, different one lurks inside it – the discourse of the other, reading the reader as she or he reads. Kleinians have recognized this with their emphasis on the potentially psychotic nature of the encounter between the unconscious phantasies of analyst and patient: somehow one is inserted into the other, all mixed up, never to be fully the same again, never completely distinguishable. Object-relational and self theorists, with their focus on the development of intersubjectivity, are struggling with something similar: to have a 'self' one has to have an other – and this other has in some way to be incorporated, thus de-essentializing and destabilizing the self. Mapping the developmental processes through which this intersubjectivity arises is both a humanistic endeavour – mental health lies in a certain pattern of supportively constructive relationships with others – and a realization of the impossibility of ever coming to the end of the penetration of one individual by another. Lacanians are always slipping about on this same issue, rendering obsolete everyone who claims to know or have authority, including the authority of the master of psychoanalysis him- (always him-) self. The otherness of the other is just another imaginary fantasy; it always lies within.

It is in the realm of imagination that so much of this comes to fruition. For some time, the Lacanian reading of the imaginary as a mode of false consciousness – a necessary but specious fantasy structure – has dominated psychoanalytic cultural theory. As a consequence, the structuralist emphasis on the determination of individuality by external forces – here, relentlessly, language – has relegated imagination to the domain of romance. But the pessimism of this perspective is too hard to bear, and itself can be interrogated as a political phenomenon (see Elliott 1992). The structural determination of the symbolic makes it impossible to conceive of alternatives – to create, for example, a culture of resistance; yet this is precisely what seems to happen whenever power operates, as Foucault (1979) demonstrated aeons ago. Within psychoanalysis, whenever the analyst speaks, it sparks off some new struggle for autonomy and self-definition in the patient. When Lacan pronounces that all there is is the symbolic and that this wears the phallic veil of the name-of-the-Father, a space is created into which others rush, saying no, this is not so, we can imagine something else within which your imagined structure looks arbitrary and oppressive. How, if everything is known so fully, can it also be true that there is no complete knowledge or truth? And if the knowledge is not full, then creating a new imaginary is not so fantastic a task.

Much of the work on imagination has been couched within feminist psychoanalytic concerns. For Irigaray (1989), to take a particularly powerful example, maternal space, in the absence of a symbolic account of the mother which is not constructed from the masculine position – that is, which is not constructed from within the Lacanian symbolic – is an untheorizable space always threatening to turn into engulfment. Her focus is on the significance of the early, pre-Oedipal mother–daughter relationship, but her argument is that this cannot be symbolized properly under patriarchy, given the way the phallic nature of the symbolic order intervenes. That is, the mediation of all symbolic activity by the lens of phallic discourse wipes out the mother as woman, contributing to misogyny and distorting the account of the pre-Oedipal imaginary so that it becomes impossible to discover the meaning of the feminine in its own terms. As Wright (1989) points out, this is true of psychoanalysis itself, which tends to examine the mother in terms of whose property she is – whether of the child or the father – but not in terms of her own positive content. Grosz (1990: 174) makes a characteristic point about the place of the woman in the masculine symbolic.

> As the sexual other to the One sex, woman has only been able to speak or to be heard as an undertone, a murmur, a rupture within discourse; or else she finds her expression in a hysterical fury, where the body 'speaks' a discourse that cannot be verbalised by her.

This idea of an undertone, a murmur, connects with Kristeva's (1983) notion of the semiotic; it suggests something alluring and threatening, something holding the possibility of overturning the dominant order of things.

It is in this realm, at the intersection of psychoanalysis and politics, that the imagination is most clearly at work in contemporary culture. Since Freud's abandonment of the 'seduction' theory, psychoanalysis has taken fantasy as its main, and perhaps its sole, legitimate focus. Sometimes, this has been done in order to reduce the space for fantasy to operate – to introduce a little bit more reality. But there has always been a strand opposed to this, from the early writings of Wilhelm Reich, through the libertarian Freudians of the 1950s, and now in the work of contemporary psychoanalytic feminists and social theorists (see Frosh 1987; Elliott 1994). This strand sometimes flirts with a romantic and ideological advocacy of imagination for its own sake, sometimes linked with a crude caricature of the unconscious as a haven for pure, unsullied passion.

However, in recent times, the sophistication of theorization of the imaginary has increased, so that it is now possible to explore the gap between the external structures of society, culture and language and the inner life of each individual subject. Contemporary psychoanalytic thinking emphasizes the creative, inventive aspects of the imaginary and psychical organization. But where, exactly, are the psychic resources for imaginary creation derived from? What psychic, affective, or representational sources of creativity must we attribute to human subjects? According to Enid Balint (1993), psychoanalysis is the discovery of 'imaginative perception', that realm of unconscious representation and affect through which the subject creates its world. In Balint's gloss, 'the first imaginative perception can only arise out of a state of eager aliveness in two people, the infant with the potential for life and the mother alive inside herself and tuning in to the emerging infant' (1993: 102). Extending this point, Cornelius Castoriadis argues that psychical imagination is creation *ex nihilo*. The unconscious is pure imaginary creation, the making and remaking of psychical forms in and through which men and women image themselves, and each other, in day-to-day social life. 'The imagination', as Castoriadis argues in this volume, 'gives rise to the newly thinkable'. Whether at the level of individual fantasy or global social transformations, self and society interlock through this structuration of imaginary representations. Although self-generated, however, these same imaginary creations necessarily escape the memory, control and conduct of human subjects. From this angle, social organization always outstrips the self-referential representational activity of human subjects; or, to put the matter slightly differently, the social imaginary always exceeds the domain of unconscious fantasy. What is involved here is the social, political and historical binding of desire; the instantiation of repression, intersubjectivity and cultural forms. And intersubjectivity, as Elliott notes in this volume, entails a 'representational wrapping' of unconscious desire, primary repression and identification. In this context, the goal of reflexivity, in both psychoanalysis and social life, is to promote emancipation from self-incurred, intersubjective distortion.

TRANSITIONAL THINKING: PATHS BETWEEN PSYCHOANALYSIS AND MODERN CULTURE

The foregoing discussion of current trends of development in psychoanalysis and social thought provides a backcloth for the essays contained in this volume. The chapters that follow can be regarded as a series of alternative constructions of this psychoanalytic imagination. Each deals with fantasy in connection with cultural and social structures, and each creates a new space for thinking about 'the other', both outside and within. Psychoanalysis is being pushed to its boundaries here, self-reflexive and outward-looking at one and the same time. The issues and concerns raised throughout the volume are offered by highly distinguished practitioners in the field: by psychoanalysts, psychoanalytic critics, and social and cultural theorists. The book is divided into three parts. Part I offers a series of psychoanalytical perspectives on issues of subjectivity and intersubjectivity. Part II deals with issues of sexuality, sexual difference and gender hierarchy. Part III examines contemporary psychoanalytic debate on culture, society and politics. Together they form a broad and comprehensive overview of contemporary psychoanalytic debates on subjectivity, theory and culture.

In Chapter 1 the European psychoanalyst and social theorist Cornelius Castoriadis offers an analysis of psychoanalysis in relation to imagination, logic and reflection. Castoriadis points out that, in the writings of Freud, the nature of the unconscious is characterized, not only as imagination, but as 'unbridled imagination' – a self-generated stream of imaginary representations or images which can become the source of radically novel social significations. Castoriadis suggests that the psychical apparatus is the ontological site of phantasmatic and fantastic creations; what he calls the 'radical imagination'. Taking aim at the fashionable claims of the French Lacanian psycho-Heideggerians, Castoriadis rejects the view that representation can be traced to the real (lack, absence, trauma and the like). On the contrary, the original *Ur-Vorstellung*, that is, proto-representation, is a 'phantasmatic scene' that is realized as a wish or desire of a sexual nature. Thus, Castoriadis argues that the human psychical world is afunctional: an unlimited, unmasterable unconscious representational flux.

The relationship between unconscious representation and intersubjectivity is further examined by Anthony Elliott in his essay 'The affirmation of primary repression rethought' (Chapter 2). Examining recent debates in Anglo-American and European psychoanalysis, Elliott traces the complex, contradictory links between the unconscious and creativity, representation and the human imagination. In this respect, Elliott focuses on four key psychoanalytic issues as concerns the constitution of identity: the profoundly imaginary dimensions of the unconscious, primary repression, identification, and the pre-Oedipal phase of development. He contends that primary repression, the bonding of the drive to psychical representation, is not merely a preparatory step for the negotiation of the Oedipus complex, but is essential to the establishment of an elementary form of subjectivity itself. Pointing to the impasse in contemporary debates about the intertwining of subjectivity and intersubjectivity, Elliott advances new psychoanalytic terminology to overcome the deadlock. He proposes the concept of 'rolling identification', the psychical basis of the shift from self-referential representational activity to an elementary form of intersubjectivity. Rolling identifications, which entail what the author calls a 'representational wrapping of self and others', permits identity to emerge as a relation to the self-as-object and pre-object relations. Elliott concludes the essay with a consideration of the significance of primary repression, and the politicization of identification.

In 'The crisis of Oedipal identity: The early Lacan and the Frankfurt School' (Chapter 3), Peter Dews offers an analysis of psychoanalytical accounts of subjectivity and intersubjectivity, with special emphasis on Lacanian psychoanalysis and its relation to the tradition of critical theory. Dews points out that, in the writings of Lacan, the Oedipus complex is abstracted as a 'transcendental' structure constitutive of subjectivity as such. In doing so, Dews says, Lacan rationalized the social and political dimensions of patriarchy. Through a careful reading of Lacan's writings of the 1930s, however, Dews suggests that this abstraction can itself be seen as a response to a specific *historical* crisis: the chaotic multiplicity of social forms constitutive of identity-formation. In this connection, Dews reinterprets Lacan's concepts of the 'symbolic phallus' and the 'name-of-the-Father' as ahistorical fictions: concepts aimed at shoring up a patriarchal ideal of subjectivity. Building on this line of analysis, Dews then reconstructs how recent developments in psychoanalytic theory attempt to come to terms with this familial and social identity crisis in modernity.

The concept of subjectivity in Lacanian theory is further considered in David Macey's essay 'On the subject of Lacan' (Chapter 4), which takes up some important psychoanalytic and political issues in a distinctive way. Macey traces Lacan's theory of the subject as refracted through classical psychiatry, phenomenology, surrealism, Kojève's interpretation of Hegel, the linguistics of Saussure and Jakobson, and other theoretical currents. Mapping Lacan's rereading of Freud, Macey contends that Lacan's mastery of psychoanalysis lies in his capacity to effect a radically new interpretation of established doctrine. But this mastery, says Macey, also has the effect of displacing psychoanalytic categories into general philosophical ones. Thus the technical language of 'libido', 'drive', 'representation' and the like is translated into a philosophically-charged discourse in which the category of desire-as-lack reigns supreme. Not only does this lead to a neglect of the manifold intersections of conflicting desires and powers in the contemporary epoch, according to Macey, but significantly it also produces a radically asexual and affectless theory of psychoanalysis.

Nancy J. Chodorow's essay, 'Individuality and difference in how women and men love' (Chapter 5), opens the discussion on sexuality and gender hierarchy in this volume. Chodorow emphasizes the way cultural stories about love influence and structure male–female relations, and how this affects different unconscious and conscious senses of identity and gender. Chodorow argues, however, that psychoanalytic theory itself has tended to overgeneralize and universalize the role love plays in the constitution of masculinity and femininity. In an attempt to overcome this limitation in contemporary psychoanalysis, Chodorow suggests that it is necessary to reframe the relations between personal identity, gender and culture, thus raising the question of the gendering of love as a personal appropriation and transformation of cultural stories and fantasies. For Chodorow, the problem of gender asymmetry is a problem of how to analyse gendered subjectivity, as embedded in contexts of power, without eradicating individually created and particular differences. Chodorow concludes by suggesting that we must attend to the individual psychobiographical history of any individual in order to understand the complex cultural patternings of love.

The issue of difference as it relates to the feminist critique of the contemporary gender system is examined by Jessica Benjamin in 'Sameness and difference: Toward an "over-inclusive" theory of gender development' (Chapter 6). Benjamin concentrates on the implicit assumption in differentiation theory that acknowledging sexual and gender differences is central to the constitution of modern identity. However, the central problem with this model, according to Benjamin, is that it occludes the creative tension – necessary to human subjectivity – between difference and likeness, otherness and sameness. By contrast, Benjamin maintains that the difficulty lies in assimilating difference without rejecting likeness; that is, in holding a space between opposites. To explicate this, Benjamin traces four central psychoanalytic phases in early gender development: core gender identity; the early differentiation of identifications in the context of separation–individuation; the pre-Oedipal over-inclusive phase; and the Oedipal phase.

The issue of how feminists engaged with psychoanalysis have dealt with the place of the father is taken up in Janet Sayers' essay, 'Consuming male fantasy: Feminist psychoanalysis retold' (Chapter 7). Sayers argues that despite the centrality of fantasies about masculinity and patriarchal power in constructing political realities, feminists have tended to adopt those psychoanalytic approaches that emphasize mothering. One consequence of this is that feminist psychoanalysis has not been able to throw much light on the impact of aggrandizing fantasies about men and (particularly) their absence, at either the individual or a social level. Sayers describes how the Lacanian tradition in psychoanalysis, which seems to offer a corrective to this maternal bias, has also generated a good deal of hostility and confusion amongst feminists because of its apparently wilful obscurity. Sayers then uses a series of four case histories of women with eating disorders to demonstrate the mode of operation of defences which sustain patriarchal fantasies in the face of absence and deprivation. These case histories not only illustrate the workings of particular defences, but introduce a preliminary programme for deconstructing traditional images of masculinity. Recognizing and grieving for 'the man who never was' is a necessary first step.

In 'Mourning Freud' (Chapter 8) Madelon Sprengnether focuses on the relationship between psychoanalysis and feminism on the one hand, and the founding concept of the Oedipus complex on the other. Sprengnether returns to the original formulations of Oedipus in Freud's writing, and then critically traces its elaboration in terms of Freud's personal history, family network and self-analysis. This emphasis on the biographical ground of Freud's formulation of the Oedipus complex allows her to raise alternative psychoanalytic constructions. According to Sprengnether, the Oedipus complex has enjoyed a central role in psychoanalytic culture, and also in feminist readings of Freud, because of the ease with which it explains and rationalizes the current gender system. One important consequence of this, Sprengnether says, has been the failure in both psychoanalysis and feminism to critically interrogate Freud's Oedipal construct. For though post-Freudian trends in object-relations and Lacanian theory have focused on areas that Freud neglected, such as the pre-Oedipal period and female sexual development, they have generally served to supplement, rather than to displace, the theoretical primacy of Oedipus and the holy phallus. In this context, Sprengnether argues that Freud's Oedipal construct was a way of covering over the traumatic impact of maternal loss in his emotional life, and thus suggests that Oedipus in his writings represents an attempt to legitimate patriarchal ideals of autonomous male subjectivity. Against such defensive thinking, Sprengnether concludes her essay by re-examining the role of mourning and melancholia in the constitution of human subjectivity, and argues that this originary, non-violent separation between self and other makes a more useful starting point of inquiry for psychoanalytic feminism than does Freud's Oedipal construct.

Stephen Frosh's essay on 'Masculine mastery and fantasy, or the meaning of the phallus' (Chapter 9) also takes up the question of what has happened to the Oedipus complex, but in a different way. Frosh argues that psychoanalysis has always played out the ambiguities of sexual difference in its own theories. These theories have consistently expressed the idea that sexual difference is a fundamental subjective position, but they have also exposed the fluidity of gender identifications and transferences. Frosh focuses on one particular paper by Lacan, 'The meaning of the phallus', as an exemplary instance of this ambiguous position. He argues that Lacan presents himself as an 'authoritative' voice on the nature of sexual difference, full of arrogantly masterful declarations on the nature of masculinity and femininity – and on the 'meaning' of the phallus. However, Lacan also exposes the emptiness of phallic mastery and the ways in which idealized and denigratory images of the woman – both of which he shares – are used to bolster the otherwise empty category of 'masculinity'. Frosh suggests that Lacan's slippery and convoluted paper expresses the struggle of masculine psychoanalytic theory to come to terms with otherness – and as such reveals some of the underlying structures of masculinity and of psychoanalysis itself.

Hanna Segal's essay, 'From Hiroshima to the Gulf War and after' (Chapter 10) opens the discussion on the contribution of psycho-politics to the study of contemporary culture in this volume. After locating her analysis of the socio-political field in the context of Freud's cultural writings, from *Totem and Taboo* to *Civilization and its Discontents*, Segal elaborates Freud's psychoanalytic conception of the complex, contradictory relations between self and society. She then links this to a broader discussion of post-Freudian psychoanalysis, especially as concerns the phenomena of psychosis, splitting, and destructiveness in group functioning. In the second section of the essay, Segal uses psychoanalytic theory to interpret and question the potential risks of nuclear conflict or disaster in the late modern age. She contends that modern societies, with their technological and industrial forms, generate intense anxieties as regards the wishes and terrors of people's self-destructive drives. Following Klein and Bion, she suggests that splitting and projection have become institutionalized in modern nation-states and the industrialization of war. This, in turn, has led to a global spread of psychic dehumanization (the other as enemy) and denial (the failure to treat the danger of nuclear war seriously). Against this psychoanalytic backdrop, Segal develops a series of interesting and innovative interpretations about the role of anxiety and guilt in the reproduction of massively destructive warfare this century, and concludes by considering the possibilities for collective disinvestment from these life-threatening institutional dangers.

In Chapter 11, entitled 'On racism and psychoanalysis', Joel Kovel takes up the question of 'otherness' in a detailed and provocative way. Using the notion of the 'primitive', he argues that by recognizing the 'polycentric' nature of mind, psychoanalysis has reconnected Western thought with pre-modern experiences of interconnection and ego-boundedness. Racism, he contends, is an affliction of the modern psyche in its systematic character and its reliance on an abstract essence ('race') to become the point of splitting between people. Kovel offers a careful reading of the way this process operated in American slavery and its construction of black people, showing particularly clearly how images of animality and sensuous energy were projected into the black 'other'. Kovel suggests that, by undermining the claims of the ego to total superiority over id-centred irrationality – and hence by resurrecting the polycentrality of the mind disavowed by Western rationality – psychoanalysis breaks with the imperialist process of silencing the other.

The final essay of the book (Chapter 12), Michael Rustin's 'Lacan, Klein and politics: The positive and negative in psychoanalytic thought', returns to the question of the way forward for psychoanalytic encounters with social and political theory. Rustin explores the contributions of Lacanian and British School traditions to ways of confronting politics. In both traditions can be found a radical impulse, but expressed in different ways and with differing implications. Rustin concentrates particularly on how the focus of the Lacanian tradition on negativity compares with the British School's willingness to articulate a 'positive' core of ideas about human nature and human needs. In developing his argument, Rustin provides succinct critical overviews of the use of psychoanalytic ideas by European political thinkers, notably Althusser, Laclau and Žižek. The deconstructive thrust of all this work, including in particular its revelations concerning the workings of language and ideology, have proved attractive in political applications of psychoanalysis. However, Rustin suggests, the bleakness of the values implicitly articulated by Lacanian-inspired theories – with the possible exception of Žižek's work – is likely to be less productive than the moderately positive emphasis to be found in British School theory. In particular, Kleinian and post-Kleinian work has not neglected negative experience and has continued the Freudian tradition of making everything available to inspection and critical analysis, but has also been willing to examine the question of what conditions might allow people to develop alternative futures.

Thus, at the end of this book – just as at its beginning – the issue is raised of how possible it is to imagine something different, to use psychoanalysis as a critical space for reflection, innovation and progress.

REFERENCES

Anzieu, D. (1986) *Freud's Self-Analysis*. London: Hogarth Press.
Balint, E. (1993) *Before I was I: Psychoanalysis and the Imagination*. J. Mitchell and M. Parsons (eds), London: Free Association Books.
Bauman, Z. (1993) *Postmodern Ethics*. Oxford: Blackwell.
Elliott, A. (1992) *Social Theory and Psychoanalysis in Transition: Self and Society from Freud to Kristeva*. Oxford: Blackwell.
—— (1994) *Psychoanalytic Theory: An Introduction*. Oxford: Blackwell.
Felman, S. (1987) *Jacques Lacan and the Adventure of Insight*. Cambridge, Mass: Harvard University Press.
Foucault, M. (1979) *The History of Sexuality, Volume 1*. Harmondsworth: Penguin.
Freud, S. (1900) *The Interpretation of Dreams*. Harmondsworth: Penguin, 1976.
Frosh, S. (1987) *The Politics of Psychoanalysis*. London: Macmillan.
Grosz, E. (1990) *Jacques Lacan: A Feminist Introduction*. London: Routledge.
Irigaray, L. (1989) 'The Gesture in Psychoanalysis'. In T. Brennan (ed.) *Between Feminism and Psychoanalysis*. London: Routledge.
Kristeva, J. (1983) 'Freud and Love'. In T. Moi (ed.) *The Kristeva Reader*. Oxford: Blackwell.
Rieff, P. (1966) *The Triumph of the Therapeutic*. Harmondsworth: Penguin.
Wright, E. (1989) 'Thoroughly Postmodern Feminist Criticism'. In T. Brennan (ed.) *Between Feminism and Psychoanalysis*. London: Routledge.
Žižek, S. (1991) *Looking Awry*. Cambridge, Mass: MIT Press.

Part I

Subjectivity and intersubjectivity

1 Logic, imagination, reflection

Cornelius Castoriadis

INTRODUCTION

I have elected to speak today about the following three notions: logic, imagination, reflection. Before doing that, however, permit me a few words concerning the title of this colloquium.

'The unconscious and science' can be read in two ways. I will not be speaking about the unconscious as an object of science; I will touch upon it, in fact, only indirectly. But there is another aspect, which we can formulate as follows: how, generally speaking, is a science possible, if human beings are essentially defined by the existence of the unconscious, if they are, as Roger Dorey has recalled, split? How, under these conditions, is a science of the unconscious possible – that is to say, how is psychoanalysis itself possible?

The classic response to the question concerning the possibility of science is this: the fact that man is a logical animal (he has or is *logos*, understanding, reason, etc.) is what makes science possible. Man is *zoon logon echon*. And Freud himself, in a celebrated passage, evokes 'our God *Logos*', which would be, perhaps, for him, the ultimate culmination of a phylogenetic process – that is, a biologically acquired property.

My response will be entirely different. Perhaps it would have aroused Freud's indignation, but I believe it is faithful to the nerve centre of his inspiration and research. First let me summarize it so as to provide a guiding thread through the labyrinthine intricacies of what will follow. Simply put, logic is what we share with animals – even with living beings in general. Yet animals have no science. True, we are separated from them by consciousness. But, as I will show below, consciousness as such does not lead to science, either. Man's distinguishing trait is not logic, but imagination, and, more precisely, unbridled imagination, defunctionalized imagination. As radical imagination of the singular psyche and as social instituting imaginary, this sort of imagination provides the conditions for reflective thought to exist, and therefore also for a science and even a psychoanalysis to exist.

FREUD AND THE IMAGINATION

Freud's contribution to the question of the imagination's relation to reflective thought, or reflection, is riven by a deep antinomy. In German, imagination is *Einbildung*, a quite honourable word, especially since the time of Kant, who made it into a central concept of the *Critique of Pure Reason*. Now, if one checks the *Gesamtregister* of the *Gesammelte Werke*, the general index to Freud's complete works in German, one will find that the term *Einbildung* appears only twice,[1] and both times in contexts of no great import, for they concern the 'Imaginings' of the neurotic. ('Imagination' does not appear in the index to the *Standard Edition*.) By way of contrast, one will note that the terms *Phantasie* and *phantasieren*, which appear very early in Freud's writings (the letters to Fliess are full of them), cover four and a half pages of the *Gesamtregister*.

At the start these terms possessed a very narrow acceptation. As Freud says in a letter to Fliess (1897a: 247), phantasy – *Phantasie* – and phantasying – *phantasieren* – 'are derived from things that have been *heard* but understood [only] *subsequently*'; and, he adds deliciously, 'all their material is of course, genuine'. There is nothing in *Phantasie*, in phantasy, that the subject has not already perceived beforehand; here phantasy is a matter of reproduction. The goal of phantasies is defensive, and they 'arise from an unconscious combination . . . of things experienced and heard' (Freud 1897b: 248; 1897c: 252; 1897d: 255, 258). Later on will come the idea that *Phantasien* are 'detached fragments of thought processes' (1911: 222).[2]

Everything happens as if these 'phantasies' were only the product of a recombinative activity, and therefore in no way originary or creative. And when Freud is confronted with the problem of 'originary phantasies' which have no 'actual' real source (in life), he will seek a mythical 'real' source for them, in phylogenesis. What we have here is the old conception, in psychology, of imagination as pure combinatory of elements with which the psyche has already been furnished from elsewhere; that is, by the perceptual apparatus or, as Freud says in his *Project For A Scientific Psychology* (1895), by the system of psi neurons.

What we call imagination thus turns out in fact to be lacking in psychical status, it being referred back to a derived and secondary activity. We have here an enormous paradox, for it could be said, on the other hand, that Freud's entire life's work deals with nothing but the imagination. The patriarch of the movement, one of whose mouthpieces is the review entitled *Imago* (founded in 1912 by Hans Sachs and Otto Rank), the man whose work would be incomprehensible if in the imagination one did not see a central, constitutive power of the psyche, does not want to know anything about it. There should be something surprising about this, but this sort of misrecognition, this veiling (of the imagination) is far from unprecedented. What we witness here is the repetition of a gesture, more than two millennia old, which had already been made by the first discoverer of the imagination himself, Aristotle (in his treatise *De Anima*), and which was reproduced by Kant, whose *Critique of Pure Reason* places the productive imagination (*produktive Einbildungskraft*) near the centre of the faculties of the psyche in his first edition (1781), but whose second edition, published seven years later, curtails the role of the imagination, subordinating it to the understanding (see Castoriadis 1986/1978).

In fact, a book could be written about this antinomy in Freud's thought as well as about the history of the battle which rages between, on the one hand, those terms which at first appear to him indubitable and which become increasingly problematic – namely this sort of trinity or trinomial of reality, logic, pleasure, the psychical apparatus operating more or less logically *vis-à-vis* a reality given to it, so as to avoid displeasure (this is the first formulation of the pleasure principle as found in the 1895 *Project*) or to maximize pleasure – and, on the other hand, the imagination; that is to say, the elaborations, perhaps even the phantasmatic and fantastic *creations*, of the psychical apparatus. An assessment of this battle cannot be drawn up in a few lines, but one of its results is already certain: Freud, who from the beginning to the end of his work in fact spoke of nothing but the imagination, of its works and its effects, obstinately refused to thematize this element of the psyche. Moreover, the motive for this covering up (of the imaginary element) seems evident to me. To take the imagination into account seems to Freud incompatible with the 'project for a scientific psychology' or, later, with a 'scientific' psychoanalysis – as for Aristotle, perhaps, and certainly for Kant, the imagination ultimately had to be put in its place, a place subordinate to that of *reason*. And Freud's last arguments against (physicalist or behaviourist) scientism in matters psychological, as true as they are, could be endorsed without hesitation by a rationalist philosopher. Such a scientistic psychology, he had said, would be incapable of explaining 'the property of being conscious or not' (1923: 18), this 'fact without parallel, which defies all explanation or description – the fact of consciousness'. Quite justified sarcastic remarks rain down upon the proponents of American behaviourism, who 'think it possible to construct a psychology which disregards this fundamental fact!' (Freud 1938: 157). Let it be noted in passing that, while psychoanalysis does accord and has to accord the 'fundamental fact' of consciousness its place, psychoanalysis is far from being able to 'explain' it.[3] As I will try to show, it will not even be up to the task of elucidating this fact so long as it also ignores the fact that consciousness implies imagination.

Appearances to the contrary, there is for Freud a strict logic of the unconscious. The appearances in question relate, among other things, to the celebrated statements that the unconscious knows nothing of time and contradiction ('There are . . . no negation, no doubt, no degrees of certainty [in the Unconscious]. . . . Reference to time is bound up . . . with the work of the Cs system' (1915a: 186, 187)) and that dream-work 'does not think, does not calculate or judge in any way at all' (1900: 107). It is this logic, which is supposed to preside over the operations of the unconscious in themselves, that, in the abstract, psychoanalytic theory and, concretely, psychoanalytical interpretations during therapy aim at restituting. We need only recall the formidable deployment of arguments and syllogistic (even arithmetic) reasoning present, like an effective midwife, each time dreams, slips and parapraxes are interpreted.

When one considers not only Freud's ('scientific') point of departure and horizon but also, as we shall see, certain inherent necessities of the thing itself, there is nothing surprising about this fact. Let us recall *The Project for a Scientific Psychology* (1895) – which, I have always thought (and recent studies have shown quite clearly), provided, right to the end (even though Freud disowned it), the invisible skeletal structure for his work, and, in a sense, rightly so. Now, ontologically speaking, the model of *The Project* reduces the entire psychical world to the following equation:

psyche = (1) infrastructural network (neurons) +
          (2) energy +
          (3) 'traces' (stored or actual representations) +
          (4) physiological laws regulating the circulation, etc. of these
               traces as well as of their energy 'charges'.

Clearly, elements (1), (2) and (4) could not escape the empire of logic. The status of element (3) ('traces') will be discussed below.

Introducing 'psychical instances', each one acting on its own account as well as in conflict with the others, changes nothing. It even tends to efface the 'contradictions' of the unconscious; these contradictions become mere conflict and opposition between instances, each one aiming at 'its own' ends but all of them obeying the same logic. If the psyche furnishes us with alogical products, it is that we almost always observe mixtures, compound products, '*compromises*', as is said in *The Unconscious* (Freud 1915a: 186),[4] dreams providing us with the most dazzling example of all this. At the limit, and ideally, the multiple 'contradictions' between the attributes of an element of a dream, or between the significations of an image or an oneiric story, seem to dissolve when each atom of meaning is imputed, through a one-to-one correspondence, to the conflicting instances which have necessarily cooperated in the production of the dream and which have concluded in the dream-text their strange compromise. It would no longer be the unconscious, then, that would be contradictory; now the subject, or the psyche *in toto*, would become merely the place where the battle of desires and mutually incompatible prohibitions is engaged. It is important to note in passing that this (scientific strategy of) reduction, even (of) trivialization, of necessity forms the major part of the work of interpretation (which, in the case of a mindless analyst, risks becoming nothing but that).

Obviously, Freud would not have been Freud if he had remained there. What lies beyond is introduced by the invasion into his schemata – and already into *The Project* – of an element, the radical imagination of the psyche or the psyche as radical imagination, whose implications, as we have said, he will resist throughout his life and whose character he will never make explicit. I must limit myself here to indicating, without any logical or chronological order, a few of the breaches by means of which the imagination invades the reality/pleasure/logic trinomial and explodes it from the inside out. Logical expository order here would be, in any case, impossible to achieve since the elements I am now going to treat in succession are closely imbricated each within the others.

Let us begin with dreaming. A dream is a group of representations, the interpretation of which passes by way of associations between representations. The associative path is *inevitable* but it is not *determinable*. This fact may be expressed by the absence of a one-to-one (biunivocal) correspondence between the 'signifiers' of the dream (the representations of its manifest content) and its 'signifieds' (its latent representations and the desires they make real). I am leaving aside here, as secondary, the problem of 'symbols' *stricto sensu*. The result is a multivocal (and, truly, indeterminate) correspondence between 'signifier' and 'signified', one of whose sides Freud has brought out: the overdetermination of what represents 'something', of what is there for something else; at the same time, he leaves us in the dark as to what must be called the symbol's *underdetermination* and even about the *oversymbolization* and *undersymbolization* that always exists in a dream. There is always a signifier for several signifieds (overdetermination), but this signifier as well is not the sole one possible for these signifieds (under-determination); a signified can be indicated by several signifiers (oversymbolization) or can be indicated only 'in part' (undersymbolization) (see Castoriadis 1984/1968: 23). Clearly, the *Rücksicht an Darstellbarkeit*, the taking into account and even the exigency of figurability, which is constitutive of dreaming, not only does not close the questions thus raised but constitutes their condition. (The situation is in fact analogous to the delegation of the drive via representation, the *Vorstellungsrepräsentanz des Triebes*, which we will discuss on p. 21.) That which cannot be made into a figure must become figurable and be made into a figure. But how? By the creative – and indeterminable, because creative – work of the imagination as instaurator of symbolism, of the quid pro quo.

This creative character of the imagination may remain masked when we stay within the circle of representations and the representable. I note once again that the term 'representation', *Vorstellung*, is of absolutely cardinal importance for Freud; there is, so to speak, not a single page of text written by Freud where one fails to encounter it. This should put the French psycho-Heideggerians, who have spent the past quarter-century making fun of it, in their proper place. If one holds to the traditional view, which Freud himself seems to have adopted most of the time, these representations themselves appear to be reducible to the simple combination of elements, already furnished by the perceptual apparatus, by means of tropic processes – metaphor, metonymy, antonymy, etc. – and 'symbolization' in the narrow sense. Psychical work, and notably dream-work, thus appears reducible to a combinatory – indeterminate perhaps in its results, but not in its components – of *already given* representational elements, culminating in other, more complex representations and in these bizarre stories recounted in our dreams. But two questions immediately arise and force themselves unavoidably upon Freud: this combinatory operates with a view to what? And, starting from what – from what initial or ultimate components – is the edifice built?

We know the response to the first question: it leads to the wish (or desire) realized by the dream, a wish or desire of a sexual nature. But human beings would not be human beings if they dreamed interminably of sexual satisfaction through canonical copulation (in fact, they practically never dream about that). Next appear the jungle world of phantasies and the monsters populating this jungle, which themselves are manipulated by other, still more monstrous and totally invisible monsters, the *Ur-phantasien*, the originary phantasies whose prehistorical and phylogenetic 'reality' Freud will try to reconstitute on the basis of a few scattered vertebrae. But what is truly at issue here is the psyche's originary capacity to posit and to organize images and scenes that are a source of pleasure, independent of all 'reality' and of all canonical representation corresponding to organ pleasure.

The second question leads to even more dizzying enigmas. Even if one were to grant that all psychical work is reducible to the insipid combination of a few unchanging elements, one would still be compelled to ask: where do these elements come from, and how are they constituted? Freud encounters this question on two levels.

The first level goes well beyond the terrain of psychoanalysis; this is undoubtedly why, after a few interrogatory notes jotted down in *The Project*, he will come to abandon it. This level of capital importance in every respect concerns the capacity for the human psyche – and this it shares with every living being, in any case certainly with the animal psychism – to create images and to bring them into relation to each other (*mettre en relation*), starting from 'stimuli' having no qualitative connection with these images. In *The Project* this capacity appears in the form of a mystery: the psychical apparatus transforms what for science are mere quantities – 'masses' and 'movements', says Freud (and the kind of science to which he is referring knows only of masses and movements) – into *qualities*; bound up with this is the mystery of another quality, of a quality of these qualities, consciousness (and the 'ego') – for which a specific class of neurons, omega neurons, will be postulated. There is therefore this creation of images and of their relation. Here we must consider a banal point, but we have to insist upon it: there is no relation between wavelengths and colours any more than between vibrations in the air and sounds that are perceived. Sounds, colours and everything else that traditional philosophy relegates to the status of what it calls secondary qualities are, properly speaking, the creation of the sensorial imagination (of the capacity of the sensorial part of the psyche to set into images the X that *shocks* it, to use Fichte's term). This sensorial imagination is not only sensible, it is also categorical, for images do not exist unless they are at least minimally organized. I will return to this point, but let me note in passing that twentieth-century phenomenology, too (for example, Husserl as well as Merleau-Ponty), with the fantastic primacy it uncritically accords to 'perception' (which is supposed to 'give things in person') glides right over the central role that imagination plays for the subject in the constitution of a world.

But Freud encounters the question of the origin of the elements of the *Vorstellungen* at a second level and one much more specific to (the concerns of) psychoanalysis. This level is unexpected, yet how enigmatic and how fecund! The metapsychological writings of 1915 – especially *Drives and their Vicissitudes*, but also 'Repression' and 'The unconscious' – take up again what in 1895 was apparently the problem of the relationship of (physical) quantity to (psychical) quality and transform them into the problem of the relationship between the somatic and the psychical. A middle term, the drives (*Triebe*), is introduced, which 'are at the frontier of the somatic and the psychical'. Arising, so to speak, from the depths of the somatic organization and its functional operations, they must act on the psychism, though they do not possess the *quality* (precisely) of the psychical. In order to acquire some sort of existence for the psyche, they therefore have to become *present* in the latter, to be *presented* to it; therefore they have to be represented, they have to find a representative, a delegate, an ambassador, a spokesperson – *ein Vertreter*, as one would say in German. But nothing exists for the psyche that is not representation, *Vorstellung*. What is therefore at the start a push (*poussée*) which is of somatic origin, but which is also sufficiently 'psychoid' to be able, so to speak, to knock at the door of the psyche, has to be transformed into something representable by and for the psyche. It must find a representation, a *Vorstellung*, in order to be represented – *vertritt* – in the psyche: this is what Freud calls the *Repräsentanz*, the ambassador, one could say, and which he could have called *Vertretung* as well. This situation is expressed by the limpid term *Vorstellungsrepräsentanz des Triebes*, the delegation of the drive (into or near the psyche) by means of a representation. Freud's formulations and explanations concerning *Vorstellung* as representative of the drive, concerning the 'nucleus of the unconscious' formed by *Triebrepräsentanzen*, representations of drives, concerning the presentation of the drive by means of a representation (Freud 1915a: 177ff., 186; 1915b: 148), are as clear-cut as the reasons for the quarrels and interminable confusions which have surrounded the translation of this term in the French psychoanalytic world are mysterious. *Repräsentanz*, forged from *Repräsentant*, *repräsentieren*, belong to the class of 'Frenchoid' terms frequently found in German and especially in Viennese German: a delegation, a mission representing a government, a constituted body, etc. The second *s* in *Vorstellungs-repräsentanz* indicates a quasi-genitive which can perform a great variety of functions (subjective, objective, possessive, attributive, or instrumental 'genitive': cf. *Verpflictungsschein*, *Verrechnungskurs*, *zurechnungsfähig*, etc.). The drive is not psychical; it has to send into the psyche ambassadors which, in order to be understood, must speak a language that is recognizable and 'comprehensible' by the psychical – and they therefore must present themselves as representations. (I must leave aside here the important, complex and difficult question of 'leaning on' (*étayage* in French, *Anlehnung* in German). I have spoken about it in *The Imaginary Institution of Society* (Castoriadis 1987/1975: 289–90).)

An obvious aporia then arises: why is it only for a human being that this question, that of the delegation of the drive by representation, is posed? Why is there not for human beings – as we must presume that there is in animals – a canonical representative which would always, in the same manner, express the drive in 'psychical' terms? Why does this canonical representation, undergoing all the changes we know it undergoes, undergo them, I would not say 'in no matter what way', but, in any case, in such a way that an indefinite ('number' of) representations can be the place holder (*lieu tenant*), that which holds the place (*tient lieu*) of the drive for the psyche – from the female body as such to the fetishist's pointed boot?

We can also broach the question by taking the text on *The Two Principles of Mental Functioning* as our starting point (Freud 1911). In those functions that do not have to do with reality, the representation is formed under the aegis of the pleasure principle. Why do certain representations procure pleasure? And once again, where do they come from? And why, for example, do they not interminably reproduce scenes of 'biologically canonical satisfaction' (as is now inferred is the case in the dreams of animals)? We know that these questions preoccupied Freud for his entire life; he returns to them regularly. He begins by thinking that there always is a 'real' origin for the pleasing representation (or the traumatic one; as far as we are concerned here, the problem remains the same); the hallucination, he writes, is a repetition of agreeable perceptions (1895: 319). He will soon be obliged to abandon the thesis of the real origin of a traumatism, the famous *neurotica* (1897a, Letter No. 69: 259–61). But his long and bitter struggle to unearth a supposedly 'real' primitive scene will reappear in the 'Wolf Man' – only for him to renounce it finally in a footnote wherein he states that its 'reality' was not so important after all. At the end he will try to derive phantasies, to the extent that they cannot result from 'really' lived experiences of a subject, from certain phylogenetically constituted originary phantasies. I have already spoken briefly about this option.

What can we say, if not that Freud is wrought up by the question of the imagination throughout his entire life's work, even if he does not name it and does not recognize it as such? To the indications already given to this effect, we could add many others. For example, everything conveyed by the idea of the 'magical omnipotence of thought', and, more generally, by the set of processes described in *The Two Principles of Mental Functioning*. Also, for example, what is implied by *denial*, where, as opposed to what happens with repression or other defence mechanisms, it is the *same* psychical instance that posits something (whether an object or attribute, it matters little) both as existing and as non-existent – which certainly goes beyond the borders of any function intended to represent some sort of reality. For example, finally, the second topography, the chaos that reigns in the Id, and the need for all this to become, in one way or another, representable.

LOGIC AND IMAGINATION

I have just spoken of the reality/pleasure/logic trinomial – the indubitable basis for *The Project* (1895). The model presented in *The Project* functions with a reality that is divided into the 'external' and the 'internal' (the network of neurons, 'charges'), qualities (above all, pleasure/displeasure), and a principle of avoidance of 'internal' displeasure via *discharge*, which tacitly presupposes for its operation a yes/no – therefore the kernel of a logic, the discrimination of two mutually exclusive terms, the affirmation of the one and the negation of the other.

This logic will, for Freud, remain at work in the psychical processes (that he will describe later on). This is evident for conscious processes, for the Ego; but it must also be said, for lack of a more detailed discussion, that contrary to certain formulations found in the 1915 text on the unconscious, which have not yet been adequately interpreted, there is a certain logic of unconscious processes, provided that we do not thereby mean diurnal logic.

A brief explanation of the content of the term 'logic' as I am using it here is required. I simply intend thereby ordinary logic, what I also call 'ensemblistic–identitary' – or briefly, 'ensidic' – logic, because, once purified, this is what presides over the constitution of set theory, or in any case the so-called naive theory of sets (ensembles), which is at the basis of modern mathematics. These terms should not scare anyone off: this logic concerns everything that can be constructed and built up starting from the principles of identity, contradiction, the excluded third or *n*th (*n* here being finite) and from the organization of anything given, by means of univocally defined elements, classes, relations and properties. (The paradoxes to which this logic can lead when one introduces infinite sets on the one hand, self-reference on the other, cannot detain us here.)

Let me postulate here three theses, only the third of which I can argue in favour of to any extent at this time.

1 That which is – the totality of existing-being (*l'être-étant total*) – is, in itself, intrinsically regulated, one of its strata (i.e. the first natural stratum), by ensidic logic – and it is so, undoubtedly as well, though with lacunae, and fragmentarily, in all its strata.
2 The institution of society always and necessarily reconstitutes and recreates a logic which adequately corresponds to this ensidic logic – thus allowing it to survive *qua* society – and it does so under the aegis of the social imaginary significations instituted each time – thus allowing it to create a world endowed with *meaning* (which, each time, is different). Like the imaginary significations instituted each time, this 'social' ensidic logic is *imposed* upon the psyche during the long and painful process of fabricating the social individual (see Castoriadis 1987/1975: 221–72).
3 Quite evidently, this logic also dominates that essential constituent of the first natural stratum which is *the living being* in general – therefore also, human beings *qua* simple living beings. Cells, plants and dogs function, first and foremost, according to a vast network of yes/no, attraction/repulsion, acceptance/rejection, and according to an interminable process of categorizing 'the given' in terms of what we would call mutually exclusive attributes. Like contemporary neurophysiology, molecular biology is a working application (*mise en oeuvre*) of this logic, a logic which it rediscovers, or which it introduces, as you wish, into its objects of inquiry. To this extent, a simple living being can be qualified as, for the most part, a sort of ensemblistic–identitary automaton. This expression is to be taken with many grains of salt, for the image (one thereby conjures up) appears much too simple when one thinks of the truly complex functions performed by living beings; for example, the jumble that contemporary scientific research is now untangling at the frontier between the central nervous system, the endocrine system and the immune system. The idea of living beings as ensemblistic–identitary automatons must be taken as a working idea which serves to organize what, in our knowledge of living beings, relates to ensidic logic, and to distinguish as well as to display what resists or outstrips this logic. Let me recall, too, that the word 'automaton' originally did not signify 'machine'. Automaton, *autos-matos*, is that which moves *of itself* – quite the contrary of what modern languages and peoples have come to consider as automatons.

Nevertheless, even viewed in this way the living being is also, as immunologists know, a *self*. And it is also and especially, as good philosophers have always known, a *for-itself*. As such, it must possess (otherwise it would not exist as a living being) the three essential determinations that are the intention, the affect and representation. Obviously, there must be at least the minimal intention of conservation/reproduction, with the consequences that this pair entails. At minimum, the affect is pleasure/displeasure ('signal' of attraction/repulsion). For present purposes, however, what matters is *representation*.

For the living being, 'representation' does not mean, and *cannot* mean, a photograph or carbon copy of an 'outside world'. Recalling here what we said above about 'qualities', sounds and colours, etc., we should say that it is a matter of a *presentation* by and for the living being, by means of which the living being – starting from what are for it only mere *shocks*, to take up again Fichte's term (*Anstoss*) – creates its own world.

Information theory is now fashionable. We are told that the living being gathers informational data in nature and processes them in various ways. This sort of language should be pitilessly condemned. No one has ever seen 'information' sprouting in spring fields, or in autumnal ones. The living being *creates* information *for itself*. Nothing is information except for a *self* – which can transform, or not transform, the X of an outside shock into information. Radio waves offer no information to terrestrial living beings, and the Weierstrass-Stone theorem offers no information to my local baker, who would look at me askance if, upon entering her shop, I should announce to her that the space of polynomials is everywhere dense in the space of continuous functions. This same theorem would offer no information to René Thom, who would ask, 'So, what else is new?' The conditions under which a statement constitutes a piece of information for someone depends essentially on what that someone already is. Every piece of 'information' in the usual sense presupposes a high degree of subjective structuration and depends on the latter for its being information. But originarily, this subjective structure first has to *give form to* – to *inform* – the X of the shock and render it present for itself. 'X' is Kant's term for the transcendental object; and these are also those 'masses' and 'movements' of Freud's 1895 *Project*. We never know them as such, but only by means of those 'qualities' that the 'neurons' bring into being. The self therefore has to posit this X as form, make it be as form, which means it has to make an image of it, in the largest sense of the term. Now, there is no image without a bringing into relation (*mise en relation*). No 'atom'-like images exist. The most basic Gestalt, a bright point on a dark background, already contains an indefinite ('number' of) relations: it implies the unending network of relations that we call 'an object in space'.

Let us take up again for an instant the Kantian problematic and its terminology. Sensibility must organize, and without organization there is no sensation. In the *Critique of Pure Reason* Kant writes: '*Imagination* is the faculty of representing an object even *without its presence* in intuition' (1966: 88). But this presupposes that the object is already given, that it has already been formed as an object. The imagination in question here is the *secondary imagination*. We, on the contrary, would say: the imagination is the faculty of positing an object, of presenting it for the subject originarily, of making it be an object, starting from X, starting from a shock coming from X or starting from nothing. Kant continues: 'As all our intuition is sensuous, the faculty of imagination belongs to sensibility.' Quite obviously, it is the inverse that is the case: beyond an excitability lacking form (*informe*), sensibility belongs to the imagination, as the power to make 'images' be for a subject.

Now, such sensibility cannot operate without organizing, therefore without an elementary logic – an application of categories (*catégorialité*). The first, the originary, the radical imagination, the power of presentation, is thereby power of organization. The formation, *ab ovo*, of an 'image' is, *ipso facto*, the positing of 'elements' and the bringing of these 'elements' into relation, the two occurring straight off 'at the same moment', the one being made by the other.

Before going further, let us face up to an objection that would come from Freud himself. It comes from the famous passage in *The Interpretation of Dreams* where Freud rejects the idea that thought plays a part in dream-work. Let us recall that Freud is talking all the time about unconscious thought processes (*unbewusste Denkprozesse, ubw. Denvorgänge, ubw. Denkakte*, etc.). Apropos of dream-work, which transforms the thoughts of the dream into its (manifest) contents, he writes, however, that this work 'does not think, calculate or judge in any way at all; it restricts itself to giving things a new form' (1900: 107). For Freud, and I believe he is right, this work consists in displacements and condensations and culminates in such displacements and condensations, and these affect the psychical intensities and parts of dream thoughts; it is always subject (*soumis*) to the exigency of figurability and is productive of this figurability. Likewise, in *The Unconscious* (1915a), Freud insists upon the fact that the essential characteristics of the primary processes are displacement and condensation. Now, dream-work does not actually think, if by thinking we intend either thoughts handling abstractions ('concepts') or else thoughts wholly subject to the rules of the usual logic. In the main, dream-work *images*, figures, presentifies, and it does so under known constraints and with the means at its disposal. Yet can we go so far as to say, with Freud, that it 'does not think, calculate or judge in any way at all, it restricts itself to giving things a new form'? The phrase is ambiguous. In certain respects, dream-work does not think, calculate or judge; in other respects, it does think, calculate and judge, for one cannot transform without thinking, calculating and judging. Dream-work is, it is true (as I just said about the representations which give shape (*figurant*) to a drive), indeterminable – but it does not transform just anything into just anything else. Likewise, the inversion of psychical intensities, which is for Freud the main feature of displacement, bears the trace of a calculation as well as its result, as is clear in this very characterization: *inversion* of *intensities*. There certainly is, therefore, in dream-work, a setting into images (*mise en images*), this being the central dimension of dreaming – *das Wesentliche am Traum*, as Freud quite rightly claims; that is to say: the creative work of the imagination, the presentation and presentification as visible and possibly audible of that which is in itself neither visible nor audible (the ultimate X being, here again, the drive). But in this work, as in all work of the imagination, we again find present a certain ensemblistic–

identitary logical element, both in the organization and the fibration of each image in and for itself as well as in the arrangement, composition and sequencing of the group of images forming the dream. Without the support of these logical elements, the work involved in dream interpretation quite obviously could not even begin. No more than one could, even with the greatest amount of inspiration, write or even improvise music without making calculations, neither could one displace and condense without the use of certain elementary, non-conscious and, of course, non-explicit logical operations, without what Hobbes considered the essential attribute of reason, that is to say, calculating, making computations, 'reckoning'.

All this is to say that we have suffered from a little too much abstraction (or from misguided abstraction), both in the history of philosophy and in psychoanalysis. At its root, the imagination is the capacity to posit an image starting simply from a shock and even – here we part ways with Fichte, and this is our most important point – starting from *nothing at all*: for, after all, the shock concerns our relations with 'something' *already given*, whether 'external' or 'internal', whereas the imagination moves autonomously. Yet one must not truly be reflecting if one says that this capacity is simply the positing of an image. An image must hold together, it brings together 'determinate' elements, presentable elements; and these elements are always found caught up in a certain organization and in a certain order; otherwise there would be no image, but simply chaos.

Let me return one last time to Kant. As we know, Kant distinguishes and contrasts the 'receptivity of impressions' and 'the spontaneity of [pure] concepts'. In fact, beyond, once again, mere excitability, spontaneity – imaging spontaneity – is already there from the start. It is responsible for the form of impressions and for their being brought into relation; it is, in other words, responsible for the first *representation*. In the constitution of the latter – what Kant called, in the first edition of the *Critique of Pure Reason*, the 'synthesis of apprehension in intuition' (1966: 100) – we can recognize the work of the radical imagination of the subject, which already contains within itself the germs of logic since every formation implies multiple bringings into relation according to rules. We do not need to linger on the second synthesis distinguished by Kant, the 'synthesis of reproduction in imagination', what is in fact memory. But a few remarks are necessary concerning the third synthesis, the 'synthesis of recognition in concepts'. Kant writes that 'without our being conscious that what we are thinking now is the same as what we thought a moment before, all reproduction in the series of representations would be vain' (1966: 103). What is at stake is the consciousness that we are thinking the same thing. How can we be assured of this consciousness? Here Kant introduces the concept. But the concept, in its proper sense, is unnecessary. A dog probably does not have what we call the concept of a rabbit, yet it knows quite well that it is the same rabbit that it is chasing along a trajectory (which is, moreover, the solution to a differential equation, that of the curve of pursuit, which minimizes at each instant the space which remains to be covered in relation to the moving prey). This sameness of the representation through the successive acts of the subject must lean on something, and this can only be the 'image' or the representation as *generic*, namely the capacity of the subject – whoever or whatever it may be here, whether man or even animal – to see, in this changing representation within the Heraclitean flux of the given, *the same*; to neglect secondary elements (for example, already simple differences of time and space); and to preserve that which is essential, *as far as need and usage are concerned*, as the same image. But neither is the concept sufficient; *consciousness* of this sameness must lean as well – and here we enter the human domain – on something that is there *for* the image and the representation, something for something else, the *quid pro quo*. In the psyche that something may be variable, it may be stable: fixation upon an image as representative of such and such a thing which 'transcends' (*dépasse*) it. But for us others, as waking and speaking human beings, this is the sign – the word. Without words, how could I assure myself of the *sameness* of the concept?

Consciousness of sameness leaning on the mere generical character of the image is the elementary degree of psychism one must postulate as already existing within animals. Consciousness of sameness leaning on signs or words is what is proper to the human psyche. The latter presupposes a decisive turning point in the history of the imagination: the capacity to see a thing in another thing which bears no relation to what it 'represents'. But it also presupposes something other which neither the psyche as such nor any transcendental subject is capable of producing: language, as creation of the social-historical imaginary. Let us note finally that words (or, more generally, linguistic expressions), which provide a support for thought, do not generally correspond in actual social-historical reality to what a philosopher would call concepts. Even as 'empirical concepts', their signifieds are vague and approximative; and above all, they are decisively codetermined by the imaginary significations instituted each time in each particular society.

The living being therefore possesses an 'elementary' imagination which contains an 'elementary' logic. By means of this imagination and this logic it creates, each time, *its* world. And the property characteristic of this world is that it exists, each time, in *closure*. Nothing can enter into it – save to destroy it – except in accordance with the forms and laws of the 'subjective' structure, of the *self* in each case, and in order to be transformed in accordance with these forms and these laws. In the case of simple living beings, however, this imagination and this logic are, on the one hand, fixed and, on the other, subject (*asservies*) to its functioning. And here we have the line of cleavage (separating them from human imagination and logic).

THE HUMAN IMAGINATION

We must postulate that a break in the psychical evolution of the animal world occurs when human beings appear. The biological foundation for this break cannot detain us here; undoubtedly, it has to do with the overdevelopment of the central nervous system, but above all with a different organization of this system. The main thing is that, by means of a monstrous development of the imagination, this psychical neoformation, the human psychical world becomes *a-functional*. Hegel said that man is a sick animal. We must say much more than that: man is a mad animal, radically unfit for life. 'Whence' – not as 'cause', but as condition of that which is – the creation of society.

This a-functionality manifests itself in the inadequacy and, properly speaking, in the *breakdown* of the 'instinctual regulations' – whatever meaning one might give to this term – that dominate animal behaviour. It is founded upon two characteristic features of the human psychism:

1 The autonomization of the imagination, which is no longer enslaved to functionality (*fonctionnellement asservie*). There is unlimited, unmasterable representational flux, representational spontaneity without any assignable end, disconnection of 'image' and 'shock = X' or, in the sequencing of images, disconnection of the representational flux and what would be a 'canonical representative' of biological satisfaction.

2 The domination, in man, of representational pleasure over organ pleasure. The disconnection of sexuality from reproduction is one of its clearest consequences – the most banal as well as the heaviest of consequences, as we know from psychoanalysis. (Cases of masturbation and occasional homosexuality among certain higher mammals remain exceptions and in any case never challenge the reproductive functions of sexuality.)

There is therefore a bursting of man's animal psychism under pressure from the inordinate swelling of the imagination. This certainly allows large elements of the animal psychobiological organization to remain intact – for example, key elements of the 'sensorial imagination' (generally speaking, we never depart from a certain biological canonicity in the formation of elementary images of the 'external world' that are shared by the entire species and no doubt shared, too, though in an imprecise sense, with those of higher mammals) – but also a considerable amount of debris from the ensidic logic regulating the psychism as an animal psychism. These elements would be completely inadequate for the purpose of keeping this strange biped alive, but they will serve as support for society's fabrication of the social individual, humans such as we know them. This fabrication presupposes, in effect, that the sensorial imagination remains more or less identical across the various singular specimens of the human species and that the imposition of a social logic, of the ensidic logic recreated each time by society and reinstituted by the latter, finds points of support in the psychism of singular human beings. But also, and above all, the social fabrication of individuals on the basis of this raw material that is the psyche of the newborn already presupposes in this newborn the domination of representational pleasure over organ pleasure. Without such domination, no sublimation, and therefore no social life, would be possible. As has been said since antiquity, man is a being of language. To speak presupposes that the pleasure of speaking, of communicating and of thinking (which could not be done without words) has become much stronger than that of sucking a breast or a thumb. In the act of speaking we already have the essentials of sublimation, that is to say, the replacement of organ pleasure by a pleasure that has only to do with representation.

Society, in its turn, is instituted (*s'institue*) each time in (a state of) closure. Closure of its logic, closure of its imaginary significations. Society fabricates individuals by imposing both of these forms of closure on them; it therefore fabricates, first and foremost – and exclusively, in the overwhelming majority of societies – closed individuals, individuals who think as they have been taught to think, who evaluate likewise, who give meaning to that which society has taught them has meaning, and for whom these manners of thinking, of evaluating, of imposing norms and of signifying are *by the psychical construction* unquestionable. Even among us, this closure is an essential part of the singular human beings we meet in clinical situations; it is expressed through repetition.

All this means, too, that, through this social fabrication of the individual, the institution subjugates the singular imagination of the subject and, as a general rule, lets it manifest itself only in and through dreaming, phantasying, transgression, illness. In particular, everything occurs as if the institution had succeeded in cutting off communication between the subject's radical imagination and its 'thought'. Whatever it might imagine (whether it knows it or not), the subject *will think* and will make/do (*fera*) only what it is socially obligated to think and to make/do. We see here the social-historical side of the process that, psychoanalytically speaking, is called repression.

SUBLIMATION, THOUGHT, REFLECTION

Sublimation – a term which received little elaboration from Freud, who said that 'we will have to return to it' – is the process by means of which the psyche is forced to replace its own or private objects of cathexis, including its own image of itself, with objects that exist and have value in and through their social institution, and to make them for itself 'causes', 'means' or 'supports' of pleasure (see Castoriadis 1987/1975: 311–20).

Here we encounter again the massive conversion that characterizes the emergence of humanity, that is to say, the substitution of representational pleasure for organ pleasure and the appearance, through the works of the social imagination, of the institution, therefore the creation of what are, properly speaking, *invisible objects*. (In their social capacity, objects are invisible. One may see vegetables and cars, one never sees the commodity 'vegetable' or 'car'; the commodity is a social imaginary signification.) And we encounter a primordial fact: disconnected from the drive, the singular imagination becomes capable of offering the psyche public objects as objects of cathexis.

As we know, the term 'thought' was utilized by Freud to designate groups of representations (or even the representation itself) as well as the processes through which these representations are connected. For my part, I prefer to speak of representations and their connection, whether such connection be near-obligatory or almost random.

If, however, we take the term 'thought' in the sense of simple conscious functioning – and then, for Freud, it is basically a matter of a function of the ego – it is clear that this thinking, this functioning, is carried out first and foremost in (a state of) *closure*, which is an expression of the need for the *self* to exist as self and which, within its boundaries, its categories and the main lines of its content, is the form of closure that happens to be imposed upon the individual through the process of its social fabrication. It therefore unfolds under the sign of repetition, though this repetition cannot, in general, be qualified as 'pathological': we need only think of archaic or simply traditional societies (or even our own!). The specific details of such 'social' repetition are to be found in 'individual' repetition. But such individual repetition is, so to speak, without significance for psychoanalysis.

An additional explanation of the term 'closure' is required here. Closure means that what is thought cannot be put into question in its essential features. Now, starting from the moment that there is language, it becomes possible in every human society to pose questions. Nevertheless, what is characteristic of the immense majority of societies is that these questions always remain limited in import, and cannot go beyond (*dépasser*), or even attain, or intend, that which for society, for the tribe, are what we might metaphorically call the axioms of its social institution, its rules of inference and its criteria for making deductions. It is inconceivable that one would be unable to ask, in any language whatsoever: Was it X or Y who did this? Was there really a lion yesterday on the outskirts of the village? The other person will respond yes or no, and she or he can lie or be mistaken. But all this takes place within closure. No one can ask: Does the earth really lie on the back of a great tortoise? That must remain unquestionable. To take an example much nearer to us, in a consistent Hebrew society, no one can ask: Is the Law just? To pose the question would be just as absurd as to say, in Orwell's 1984: 'Big Brother is ungood', which was to become, in the final, perfect phase of Newspeak, a pure and simple grammatical absurdity. Now, it happens that, in the *Old Testament*, Justice is one of God's names. God has given the Law. How, psychically *and* linguistically, could one say that the Law is unjust? These are the ultimate axioms which are neither questioned nor capable of being questioned.

We are no more intelligent than the Hebrews, still less so than primitive persons. We could even say that we are much less intelligent than the latter, for who among our scientists today would be capable of inventing weaving, for example, or calculating the length of the year if she or he did not know it already? But this (primitive) intelligence, this (primitive) thought, moves within an instituted closure; and – otherwise there would be no history – in an extremely slow fashion, over thousands of years, something percolates up, either from the creativity of the singular psyche or from the collective, in the form of changes in pebble-tool work, then, abruptly, in the form of the Neolithic revolution, and then the rest.

Briefly speaking, taken in this way this sort of thought is strictly functional at another level; no longer the level of satisfaction of the individual's drives, but rather, to use entirely Freudian terms, the level at which equilibrium is attained between reality – which is never anything but social reality, as Freud says in *Totem and Taboo* – and the individual's drives. This equilibrium has been attained in a thousand and one ways, through monogamy, polygamy, the patriarchal family, the patrilineal or matrilineal system, with Jahveh, the Egyptian gods, the Greek gods, the human sacrifices of the Aztecs, etc.; in short, an equilibrium established somehow or another. In relation to such an equilibrium, there is always the possibility of transgression – but the latter is codified. There is illness, but it is not uninteresting to note that this is always considered a *sign* of something else, and it is codified and treated in a corresponding fashion (shamans, sorcerers, etc.). And, of course, there are dreams – which are equally subjected to codified interpretation. And that is all.

It is useful to stop here for a moment and examine Freud's 'drive for knowledge' (*Wisstrieb*). This strangely named 'drive' (at least in the light of Freud's subsequent determination of the drive as the 'frontier between the somatic and the psychical') is in truth the form of the singular human being's search for meaning from as early as the breakup of its original 'autistic' or monadic state (see Castoriadis 1975: 273–339). We need not worry here about the 'objects' upon which it places privileged concern ('Where do children come from?' = What is my origin, who am I?), nor with the imaginary (phantasmatic) constructions which satisfy it at the start (infantile sexual theories). What is striking is that this *Wisstrieb* almost always *is saturated* by its absorption of social sexual theory (and of social cosmic theory). (The retention in the unconscious of phantasies connected with infantile sexual theories does not concern us here.) In general, the search for meaning is gratified by the meaning offered/imposed by society – that is, by social imaginary significations. This gratification of its search goes hand in hand with a halt to interrogation: for every question there are canonical responses or social 'functionaries' (magicians, priests, mandarins, theoreticians, general secretaries, scientists) who possess them. The psychoanalytic outlook cannot in itself and by itself account for the fact that there is a *Wisstrieb* which stops and a *Wisstrieb* which does not stop – any more than for the difference between Scythian sublimation and Greek sublimation.

This is to say that consciousness (*conscience*) does not mean science (*science*), and thought does not mean reflection. Reflection appears when thought turns back upon itself and interrogates itself not only about its particular contents but also about its presuppositions and its foundations. Based on everything that has just been said, however, it may be affirmed that these presuppositions and these foundations are not something that belongs to it, they have been furnished to it by the social institution – for example, among other things, by language. Genuine reflection is therefore, *ipso facto*, a challenging of the given institution of society, the putting into question of socially instituted representations, of what Bacon called the *idola tribus*, an expression to which we must give a much broader sense than the one he gave to it. This putting into question of the representations of the tribe occurs, for example, when Thales and others begin saying that what the Greeks tell are nice stories, but what *truly is* is; when Heraclitus accuses the (mythological) poets of not knowing what they are saying; and this is what Freud himself was saying when, upon his arrival in the United States, he said, they do not know that we are bringing them the plague. The psychoanalytic plague involves the putting into question of all instituted representations concerning the marvellous innocence of the child, the sexual life of man, his altruism and his goodness, his unalloyed and clearly defined belonging to one or the other sex, etc. And representations concerning sexuality are obviously a cornerstone of the edifice of the social institution.

Since the appearance of reflection implies the simultaneous and reciprocally conditioned emergence of a society where no sacred (revealed) truths exist any longer and where it has become psychically possible for individuals to put into question both the foundation of the social order (possibly to reaffirm it, should that be one's response) and their own thought – *that is to say, their own identity* – this appearance of reflection can therefore only take place when accompanied by an upheaval in, and a fundamental reshaping of, the entire social-historical field.

On the part of the subject, reflection implies much more than what Kant calls 'transcendental apperception', that is to say, 'this pure, original, and unchangeable consciousness' of the unity of consciousness, the 'consciousness of a necessary unity of the synthesis of all phenomena according to concepts, that is to say, according to rules' (1966: 105). It implies the work of the subject's radical imagination. For there to be reflection, first of all there must be something that the radical imagination alone can provide: one must be able to represent *oneself* not as an object but as *representational activity*, as a non-object object; it is a matter of seeing double and seeing *oneself* double, and of oneself acting as acting activity. Next, the subject must be able to detach itself from the certitude of its own consciousness. This implies the capacity to place in suspension the ultimate axioms, criteria and rules which found thought as simply conscious activity, with the supposition that others (other axioms, criteria and rules), not yet certain, perhaps not yet known, might replace them. It is a matter, then, of seeing *oneself* and positing *oneself* as this purely imaginary being, in all senses of the term: an activity which, while having possible contents, has no determined and certain content. At the moment true interrogation takes place, I have already put into question what had, by others and by myself, hitherto been taken for granted, and this concerns not trivial objects but matters essential to my thought; I envisage – or do not envisage – other possibilities, and during this phase I tend to be a pure activity suspended between the refusal of something, of that which I am henceforth led to reject, and the expectation, the possibility of another thing that in no way is certain. I tend to be pure activity, open like interrogation, or rather I must posit myself as such. Of course, it always is also I that I posit as subject of this activity – and I posit *myself* as subject *qua* this interrogative activity, and I thereby posit myself as 'consciousness of a necessary unity' as well; but at this level, this unity is not that of a connection between 'all phenomena according to concepts' or rules; it is the unity of the *intended aim* of a meaning that *is to be made to be*, of syntheses and rules which *remain to be found* at the end of a process that places in suspense the very rules of its own unfolding. Of course, all the contents and rules (of thought) can never be put into question simultaneously; but all of them can be posited as, each in their turn, provisionally suspended.

The second way in which the work of the radical imagination is, *vis-à-vis* reflection, fundamental is the contribution it makes to the content of reflection and of theory. This contribution consists in the creation of *figures* (or of *models*) of the thinkable. All theoretical work, all work of reflection, the entire history of science show that the creative imagination is at work positing figures/models which are not fixed once and for all, which in no way could be considered as empirically inferred but which are, on the contrary, conditions for the organization of empirical knowledge or, more generally, of the object of thought. This is seen most clearly and most strikingly in the development of mathematics. The mathematical imagination (which Kant wanted to confine to the pure, 'ordinary' intuition of space and time) is an incredible accumulation of nonintuitable figures – spaces of n-dimensions, or of infinite or fractional dimension, not to speak of other, still more 'unrepresentable', and yet imaginable creations. The connection with 'words', that is to say, with mathematical symbols, is evident and irrecusable, but combinations of 'words' do not create mathematical thought; mathematical thought must, on the contrary, construct the various symbolisms that convey it. But more generally speaking, we may say that everywhere there is thought there is positing of figures of some sort, figurations of an idea or vaguely intuitable models of a theory in the process of being made explicit as such. Thus, the imagination gives rise creatively to the newly thinkable. The history of science provides us with innumerable examples. Let me mention here the story of the discovery of the formula for benzene by Kekule, the great organic chemist of the last century, who had a dream one night and the next day finally found, with the help of this dream, what he had been looking for in vain for many years: the hexagonal stereochemical formula for the benzene molecule. It would be more appropriate, however, for us to end here with two examples taken from Freud himself. In rereading the 1895 *Project*, we are led to ask: What is this *Project*, then, if not an imaginary *constructum* of Freud's, one by which he renders the psychical realm thinkable? There are diagrams – but there are not just diagrams; there is also the circulation of 'charges', barriers, the proximity or distance of neurons, etc. Freud fabricates a mental image for himself, a figure, a model; he fabricates it for himself because he is engaged in the process of reflection but it is also starting from this image that he reflects, and he could not reflect without it.[5]

The second example I wish to take from Freud is the celebrated passage from 'Analysis terminable and interminable' (1937). At the end of his tether, he bursts out with this declaration: 'We can only say: *So muss denn doch die Hexe dran!* [We must call the Witch to our help after all!] – the Witch Metapsychology. Without metapsychological speculation and theorizing – I had almost said "phantasying" – we shall not get another step forward' (1937: 225). (As Serge Viderman has noted, Freud's first French translators suppressed this sentence, no doubt due to a filial sense of propriety.)[6] Let it pass that metapsychology might be an old witch cooking up God knows what magic philtres; but to confess that theorization turns out to be a 'phantasying', that is to say, the imagination, the mad woman in the house, would ruin forever the theoretical respectability of psychoanalysis. One has to, in effect, 'phantasy' something about the psychical apparatus – as about all else – in order to be able to think something about it. That does not mean that this 'phantasying', that is to say, the activity of the imagination, is out of control. Here is not the place to enter into a discussion with Popper and the Popperians; let us note, simply, that what we are able to imagine and, on that basis, to theorize about the psychical apparatus is certainly not refutable, 'falsifiable' in Popper's sense; but stating that point is a far cry from abolishing the distinction between truth and falsehood. An infinity of stupid statements can be made about the apparatus of the psyche, and these stupidities can be shown to be stupidities. The number of theoretical constructions which can hold up is quite limited and very rare; and without any possible doubt, something distinguishes, and would distinguish even for the most obtuse Popperian, someone – Freud, for example – who produces a plausible model of the psychical apparatus and someone who would say: all that happens because red-currant jelly travels along the neuronal pathways. Demonstrable stupidities exist as such, and they are infinite in number, but there are very few ideas which hold up at a first glance and can even withstand critical examination. More generally, we may say that an important new theory – that of Newton, Einstein, Darwin or Freud himself, not to mention those of philosophers – is never a simple 'induction', no more than it is the mere product, 'by subtraction', of the 'falsification' of previously existing theories. It is, *under constraint of the data* (this is what in fact empirical knowledge as well as 'falsification' amount to), the positing of a new imaginary figure/model of intelligibility.

Reflection is therefore definable as the effort to *break the closure* in which we are each time necessarily caught up as subjects, whether such closure comes from our personal history or from the social-historical institution which has formed, i.e., humanized, us.

As I hope to have shown, in this effort the imagination plays a central role, since the putting into question of established truths does not occur, and can never occur, within a void, but is always paired with the positing of new forms/figures of the thinkable, which are created by the radical imagination and are subject to the control of reflection, all of this under the aegis of a new 'object' of psychical investment, a non-object object, an invisible object, the truth. I speak of truth here not as the adequation of thought to the thing but as the very movement that tends to open breaches in closure, where thought always tends to shut itself up again.

Now, reflection is not only what renders psychoanalysis possible, since psychoanalysis is ultimately the return of the subject upon itself and upon the conditions for its functioning, but it can also serve as an element in the definition of the *end* of the analysis (in the two senses of the word 'end'). To go beyond repetition is to allow the subject to get out of the framework which its settled organization has fixed it in once and for all and to open it to a genuine history of which it will be able to be the co-author.

The same goes for the analyst. His work will remain vital and fruitful only to the extent that, beyond the patient's defences, resistances and armouring, he succeeds in glimpsing something of the singular radical imagination of this singular human being before him. And this reflects back on the analyst himself, if he is ready to let his own frameworks budge, to listen to something else, to think something new, and to let the patient, via interpretation, find himself again in this something new, understanding that he had always been there and that he does not have to remain there.

Once again, we may state that, unless one remains engaged in empty interrogation, all successful thought certainly establishes a new closure in its turn, as we know from experience, including the thought of Freud, at least with some of his successors. But it is also true that, among the forms thus created, some possess a mysterious and marvellous permanency. And the truth of thought is this very movement in and through that which has already been created as permanent finds itself placed otherwise and illuminated in a different light by new creations of which it has need, so as not to sink into the silence of the merely ideal.

NOTES

1 Freud, *Gesammelte Werke* V: 296–8, S.E.7: 288–90; G.W. XI: 381–3, S.E.16: 367–8.
2 A translation of Castoriadis's original French translation of the citation. S.E. reads: 'thought-activity was split off'.
3 In the beginning, Freud believed it even possible to 'construct' or 'produce' language. But an abyss separates what he was describing from genuine language, and, still more so, theoretical reflection.
4 Contradiction between (conscious and unconscious) psychical systems: ibid., 186ff.
5 This is such a powerful image, moreover, that some of its key elements can still be found in the famous article by McCulloch and Pitts some fifty years later. See W.S. McCulloch and W. Pitts, 'A logical calculus of the ideas immanent in nervous activity', *Bulletin of Mathematical Biophysics*, 5 (1943): 45–133.
6 As n. 2 on this page of the *Standard Edition* explains, the quotation comes from Goethe's *Faust*, Part I, Scene 6. Cf. Serge Viderman, *La Construction de l'espace analytique* (Paris: Denoel, 1970): 323–4.

REFERENCES

Castoriadis, C. (1984) 'Epilegomena to a theory of the soul' (1968), in *Crossroads in the Labyrinth*, trans. Martin H. Ryle and Kate Soper. Cambridge, Mass: MIT, and Brighton: Harvester.
—— (1986) 'La Découverte de l'imagination' (1978) in *Domaines de l'homme. Les Carrefours du Labyrinthe II*. Paris: Seuill.
—— (1987) *The Imaginary Institution of Society* (1975), trans. Kathleen Blamey. Cambridge, Mass: MIT, and Oxford: Polity.
Kant, I. (1966) *Critique of Pure Reason*, trans. F. Max Muller. New York: Anchor.
Freud, S. (1893) 'Some points in a comparative study of organic and hysterical paralyses'. S.E.1.
—— (1895) *The Project for a Scientific Psychology*. S.E.1.
—— (1897a) Letters to Fliess. S.E.1.
—— (1897b) Draft Letter. S.E.1.
—— (1897c) Draft Ms. S.E.1.
—— (1897d) Draft Note. S.E.1.
—— (1900) *The Interpretation of Dreams*. S.E.5.
—— (1911) 'Formulations on the two principles of mental functioning', S.E.12.
—— (1915a) 'The unconscious'. S.E.14.
—— (1915b) 'Repression'. S.E.14.
—— (1916) *Introductory Lectures on PsychoAnalysis*. S.E.16.
—— (1923) *The Ego and the Id*. S.E.19.
—— (1937) 'Analysis terminable and interminable'. S.E.23.
—— (1938) 'An outline of psychoanalysis'. S.E.23.

2 The affirmation of primary repression rethought

Anthony Elliott

In this chapter I shall offer some critical reflections on the state of the self in its unconscious relational world. The principal issue I shall be concerned with is that of connecting a conception of the human subject as self-representing, self-symbolizing and self-reflective with socio-symbolic, intersubjective explanation in psychoanalysis. The forging of such a connection, I argue, involves attention to the following: the question of unconscious representation; the nature of intersubjectivity; and their mutual imbrication with the structuring properties of modern institutions and culture.

In the first section, the chapter unpacks a variety of psychoanalytical assumptions or understandings concerning the developmental genesis of unconscious representation. It is suggested that there are a number of important problems with traditional psychoanalytic accounts of the representational psychic space of the human subject. It is also suggested that we need to probe further in order to understand the crucial links between the unconscious and creativity, representation and the human imagination. Throughout, it will be one of my objectives to trace the rapprochements and realignments between Anglo-American and continental traditions of psychoanalysis that now appear to be taking place.

In the second section, I examine the structuration of representation with reference to primary repression and identification. It is argued that primary repression is not merely a preparatory step for the negotiation of Oedipal identity, but is rather essential to the establishment of an elementary form of subjectivity itself. In this connection, the recent psychoanalytical work of Kristeva and Laplanche on primary repression is examined, and subjected to critical analysis.

The final sections of the chapter are more reconstructive and innovative in character. For existing psychoanalytical accounts I suggest we should substitute the concept of *rolling identification*, the psychical basis of the shift from self-referential representational activity to an elementary form of intersubjectivity. Rolling identifications are defined as a representational flux which permits human subjects to create a relation to the self-as-object and pre-object relations. Such primal identification, it is suggested, operates through a *representational wrapping of self and others*. The chapter concludes with a consideration of the significance of primary repression, and the politicization of identification.

REINSTATING REPRESENTATION: FANTASY AND CREATION, IMAGINATION AND SELF

First, then, the question of unconscious representation. This relates directly to some of the deepest problematics of subjectivity.

In *The Interpretation of Dreams*, Freud boldly proclaims that 'nothing but a wish can set our mental apparatus at work' (1900: 567). From the perspective of classical Freudian theory, the work of the psyche functions via the pleasure principle, a principle which operates through a repetition of desired fantasies. What kind of fantasies lead to psychical pleasure? Freud argued that they might be sexual, or destructive, or derived from self-preservative needs for security.

For Freud, representation, drive and affect are the fundamental conditions structuring unconscious fantasy (1915a: 177; 1915b: 148). Unconscious fantasy, to be sure, is constituted as representation, and is the moment of creation *par excellence* of the psyche (on the creative nature of the unconscious see Ricoeur 1970; Castoriadis 1984; and Elliott 1992). This is expressed in Freud's formulation that the psyche must submit the drive to a delegation through representation *(Vorstellungsrepräsentanz des Triebes)*. What this means is that psychical functioning depends upon somatic drives passing into psychic representational space, which in turn constitutes itself as a *fantasy fulfilment through a forming of images*. Freud makes clear that he regards representation as the 'most general and the most striking' characteristic of the unconscious, through which 'a thought, and as a rule a thought of something that is wished, is objectified . . . is represented as a scene, or, as it seems to us, is experienced' (1900: 37).

Freud's thinking about unconscious representation takes us to the heart of some of the most crucial questions about self and object formation. Yet, as Greenberg and Mitchell (1983) point out, there are fundamental inconsistencies in Freud's doctrines. On the one hand, Freud can be said to uncover the constitutive imaginary dimensions of self-organization and unconscious relational experience (Castoriadis 1987; Elliott 1992). Fantasy, hallucination, omnipotence of thought: these are, for Freud, central unconscious dimensions of the human imagination. From this angle, creation for Freud is understood in terms of the fantasy registration of drives. On the other hand, however, Freud (at various points in his work) displaces these profoundly imaginary dimensions of self-organization. These displacements range from attempts to locate the 'real', objective events of trauma (1895) to the search for an original, collective Oedipus complex (1913).

Many psychoanalytic theorists in recent times have recognized, though they have not forcefully acknowledged, the problem of unconscious representation. In Anglo-American psychoanalysis, one general approach focuses upon representation in *developmental* terms. In this perspective, self and object representations are understood as emerging across time and, through intersecting with the interpersonal field, develop into richer, more complex impressions of the external world. Broadly speaking, Anglo-American post-Freudian theories have underscored the role of interpersonal relations in the constitution of psychical structure and the self. From this perspective it is *human relatedness* that generates a sense of selfhood, with relational processes being understood as lying at the heart of self-organization and development. In object relations theory and related variants, the psychic economy is never merely an internal affair, the regulation of unconscious drive conflict alone. Instead, the gratifications and frustrations of psychical life are seen as fundamentally structured by the dynamics of human interaction. Significantly, such a recognition of the intersubjective foundation of the self has led psychoanalytic debate away from issues of Oedipal conflict and sexual repression to a concern with the earlier pre-Oedipal period and disturbances in ego-formation.

In a detailed elaboration of Freudian theory, Greenberg (1991) argues that the representational world of the self grows out of a complex interplay of desires for safety and effectance. Greenberg suggests that feelings of certainty and excitement are forged and reproduced through acting on the world, through productivity and industry. Similarly in contemporary object relations theory, Sandler (1989), echoing Ferenczi, contends that representation is primarily propelled by engagement with early attachment figures especially via maternal responsiveness – which in turn generates feelings of safety. And so too, Benjamin's (1988) intersubjective psychoanalysis posits the erotic component of unconscious representation as bound up with a dialectic of dependence and interdependence.

However, the problem with all of these gradualist perspectives is that they bypass the question of representation – and its affective driveness – altogether. We find here a generality about psychic representation and a lack of detail as to how the unconscious intersects with the self's relational landscape.

If object relational theorists have too narrowly defined representational forms, they have compounded the problem by failing to examine the self-instituting, material conditions of fantasy itself. This is certainly true of the Kleinian tradition, which divides the internal world between paranoid anger and personal despair. From the Kleinian standpoint, internal fantasy processes are causative of the fundamental contradictions and deformations of intersubjectivity – with such processes being installed in the external world through projective identification and thus institutionalized. However, the view that social life is distorted by fantasy leaves the question of what is being 'distorted' here entirely open. How does fantasy inherently distort the social world in the act of constructing it? How might political conditions affect and determine the systematic distortion of fantasy formations which underpin social life? What seems to happen to the concept of fantasy in Kleinian theory is that, while it is correctly seen as the crucial psychic underpinning of all social activity, it is not recognized as being inseparably bound up with the material conditions of its making (see Elliott 1994). Instead, fantasy as the ground of intersubjective distortion is closed off from the social world and rounded back upon the human subject itself.

French psychoanalysis offers another perspective on the structuring conditions of self-organization and unconscious representation. In Lacan's theory, the concept of the unconscious is tied directly to organized signifiers, it is conceived as a language, but it relates the organization of desire only to secondary repression as symbolic law (see Castoriadis 1984; Macey 1988; and Elliott 1992 for critical discussions of Lacan's linguistic reconceptualization of Freudian psychoanalysis). More significant, for our purposes, is Lacan's dramatization of self-constitution as a primary relationship to otherness. 'The human ego', says Lacan, 'establishes itself on the basis of the imaginary relation' (1975: 133). Yet the imaginary in Lacan's work refers only to the specular. Lacan's 'mirror stage' is a kind of archaic realm of distorted and alienating images, a spatial world of indistinction between self and other, from which primary narcissism and aggressivity are drawn as key building blocks in the formation of self. Lacan's account of specular self-formation, however, does not stand up to close examination. The argument that the mirror distorts fails to specify the psychic processes interior to the individual subject which makes such misrecognition possible. For example, what is it that leads the subject to (mis)recognize itself from its mirror image? How, exactly, does the individual cash in on this conferring of selfhood, however deformed or brittle? The problem is that surely for an individual to begin to recognize itself in the 'mirror' she or he must already possess a more rudimentary sense of subjectivity. For to take up a reflected image as one's own must no doubt require some general capacity for affective response. I have discussed these problems of Lacan's doctrine in some detail in *Social Theory and Psychoanalysis in Transition* (Elliott 1992: 138–58).

In French theory, the general response to this impasse in Lacanianism involved a return to the issue of fantasy itself. Imaginary misrecognition as the basis for Oedipal repression was displaced in favour of a thoroughgoing investigation into the pre-history of the subject, notably the question of primal fantasies and inherited memory traces. Among analysts, Laplanche and Pontalis (1968) directly addressed the issue of primal fantasy and repression as the condition for unconscious psychical productions. Laplanche and Pontalis argued that Freud's notion of primal fantasies – seduction, castration, primal scene – refers to the symbolic transmission of the conditions of possibility for unconscious representation.

Echoing Lacan's structuralist tendencies, Laplanche and Pontalis contend that Freud's postulation of an external event in subjective pre-history grants a determining role to a symbolic reality that has 'an autonomous and structural status with regard to the subject who is totally dependent upon it'. Significantly, the question of the origin of representation is thus raised. This symbolic reality, as a force outside and other, acts as a template for the fantasy world of the individual subject. Yet fantasy, Laplanche and Pontalis caution, cannot be reduced to a mere hallucination of the object of desire. On the contrary, fantasy is itself a realm of interchangeable places, plural identifications, multiple entry points. As Laplanche and Pontalis put it,

> Fantasy is not the object of desire, but its setting. In fantasy the subject does not pursue the object or its sign: he appears caught up himself in the sequence of images. He forms no representation of the desired object, but is himself represented as participating in the scene.
>
> (1968: 16)

Such representational multiplication is therefore one of the central dimensions of unconscious fantasy, and Laplanche and Pontalis offer a series of important specifications in this respect. A number of questions, however, are prompted by their formulation of primal fantasy, that is, unconscious representation. What are the conditions for the *emergence* of fantasy? What emergent capacities should be attributed to the psyche in this respect? How are unconscious fantasies elaborated?

The difficulty in pursuing these issues, as Borch-Jacobsen (1988) points out, is that the human subject has been cast principally outside of the domain of representation in most versions of psychoanalysis. That is, while unconscious representation is seen as a necessary condition for the development of subjectivity, it has been reduced to little more than a 'stage' or 'screen' for disguising the functioning of desire. As Borch-Jacobsen notes:

> we are left viewing fantasy as a spectacle represented to a subject who remains outside the drama, outside representation. . . . [However] we have to leave the visible (the imaginary, the specular) behind and dismantle the theatre, we have to stop placing the subject in a position of exteriority *(sub-jacence)* with respect to representation.
>
> (1988: 44)

A plausible position on the status of unconscious representation, I believe, can be found in the writings of the continental psychoanalyst Cornelius Castoriadis. Castoriadis argues that Freud's 'primal fantasies' are not genuinely originary fantasies because they involve a relatively developed articulation of 'contents' and 'relations' between the self and others. Originary fantasy for Castoriadis, by contrast, involves a *'lack of distinction between the subject and the non-subject'* (1987: 286). Originary fantasmatization, or what Castoriadis terms the 'radical imaginary', is a primal architecture of representations, drives and passions in and through which the subject creates a world for itself. 'The originary psychical subject', says Castoriadis, 'is this primordial "fantasy": at once the representation and the investment of a Self that is All' (1987: 287). Unconscious representation, according to Castoriadis, is creation *ex nihilo*. Human imagination is pure creation, the making and remaking of images and forms as self-production. This does not mean, absurdly, that human beings are unconstrained in their representational activity, that is, the making of self and object representations. On the contrary, Castoriadis argues that the self-creating nature of representation 'leans on' biological properties of the individual, and is bound up with the symbolically structured character of the social-historical world.

To speak of 'originary representation' is certainly at odds with the bulk of contemporary theory; and it is usually from this angle that Castoriadis is criticized in post-structural psychoanalysis and postmodern circles. Such critics argue that the whole concept of representation, the idea that some transcendental signified automatically assigns a set of stable meanings to the subject, has seriously come to grief since the linguistic turn in modern philosophy. This kind of criticism, however, reflects a fundamental misunderstanding of what Castoriadis means by 'originary fantasmatization'. The concept of unconscious representation for Castoriadis does not denote an organic bond between image and thing, idea and object. Rather, Castoriadis suggests that the unconscious comprises a fantasmatic flux, a representational magma of significations, which is strictly unthinkable within the confines of western rationality and logic.

Castoriadis (1989), following Freud, further reminds us that originary fantasy and representation underlies the capacity of the subject for critical self-reflection and autonomy. As he says of psychoanalysis itself: 'the possibility of representing *oneself as* representational activity and of putting oneself in question as such is not just a philosophical subtlety; it corresponds to the *minimum* we require of every patient when we try to lead him/her to discover that X is not Y but that it is very much so for *his/her* own representational activity and that there may be reasons for this' (1989: 27). Representation, unconscious flux, originary fantasmatization: these are, says Castoriadis, necessary conditions for the possibility of reflectiveness in the individual human subject.

This focus on representational activity, as an essential source for explicating subjectivity, has also received attention in recent Anglo-American psychoanalysis. Many accounts stress the representational and affective driveness of subjectivity, highlighting that the individual subject generates a sense of personal agency in and through the medium of unconscious forms (Schafer 1983; Mitchell 1988). Here the individual subject is understood as constituting and reconstituting agency in the course of imaging itself and other people. Such a focus suggests attention to the nature of unconscious early representations and internalizations, the meshing of these representational forms with object-relatedness, experiences of personal continuity and fragmentation, and also the level of a person's felt agency. Lear (1991) has argued that human autonomy depends upon the individual reflecting upon unconscious feelings and representations as the product of *their own creation and elaboration*. Similarly, Spezzano contends that psychoanalysis aims at 'translating the vocabulary of blame into a vocabulary of responsibility for disturbing and painful affective experience' (1993: 123).

Let me sum up so far. I think it necessary that psychoanalysis and contemporary theory accept this underlining of the profoundly imaginary dimensions of human subjectivity. The imaginary tribulations of the self, it is suggested, are rooted in the relations between originary representation, unconscious flux, fantasy, and affect. That is to say, the 'subject' begins life as representation, no more and no less.

FREUD AND HIS FOLLOWERS: ON THE CONCEPTS OF REPRESSION AND IDENTIFICATION

The psyche, then, as representational flux, is closed in upon itself, an initial self-sufficiency. This is the psyche's original monadic or auto-erotic organization (see Castoriadis 1987; Elliott 1992). As Freud writes of this psychical state:

It will rightly be objected that an organization which was a slave to the pleasure principle and neglected the reality of the external world could not maintain itself alive for the shortest time, so that it could not have come into existence at all. The employment of a fiction like this is, however, justified when one considers that the infant – provided one includes with it the care it receives from its mother – does almost realize a psychical system of this kind.

(1911: 220n)

Yet the following questions immediately suggest themselves: What is it that breaks up the self-sufficiency of this psychical state? How does the psyche open itself to a world of structured intersubjectivity? Where does this psychical capacity come from?

Freud thought that the creation of the human subject occurs in and through repression. Primary repression, Freud wrote, 'consists in the psychical (ideational) representative of the drive being denied entrance into the conscious' (1915b: 148). The outcome of primary repression, which arises from the non-satisfaction of infantile needs, is the bonding or fixing of drives to representations (see Elliott 1992: 27–9). But Freud stops short of spelling out the precise implications of primary repression for the structuration of subjectivity. Instead, his own theoretical and clinical accounts of the development of subjectivity centre upon the concept of secondary repression, or 'repression proper', as formulated in the Oedipus and castration complexes. In Freud's scheme, it is the paternal breakup of the imaginary child/mother dyad which initiates 'repression proper', and constitutes the development of identity and culture.

However, Freud's construction of Oedipal repression as constitutive of identity obscures as much as it illuminates. The view that the small infant (re)presents or discovers *itself* through Oedipal identifications implies that subjectivity is a given, and not a phenomenon to be explicated. The inconsistency here is that the infant surely cannot identify with Oedipal presentations unless it already has a more rudimentary sense of identity. Moreover, it seems that this problem is only compounded if we reverse the logic in operation here, as Lacan does, and trace the imaginary ego as modelling and misrecognizing itself in specular images. For, as previously noted, the specular relation is only constituted as a *relation* to the extent that it is shaped by psychic space itself. And in Lacan's account, this (mis)copying is linked to further alienation through the constitution of the subject via a phallocentrically organized structure of language and culture.

By contrast, the psychoanalytic direction of contemporary theory involves a renewed emphasis upon primary repression and identification. Kristeva (1987, 1989) and Laplanche (1987, 1992) provide detailed treatments of the topic. Here it is suggested that the dynamics of primary repression and identification involve an elementary gap between self and other, a gap which is the very condition for the arising of the subject. Primary repression is thus not merely a preparatory step for the constitution of Oedipal identity. Rather, primary repression is considered as elementary to the establishment of subjectivity itself. In what follows, I shall critically examine some of the central theoretical issues on primary repression as discussed by Kristeva and Laplanche. Following this, I shall attempt to sketch an alternative account of primary repression as linked to the dynamics of subjectivity and intersubjectivity.

In her recent writing, Kristeva connects the constitution of subjectivity to the imaginary tribulations of the pre-Oedipal phase rather than to the Oedipal, symbolic process alone. According to Kristeva, the primary identifications of narcissism already represent an advancement over the affective, representational flux of auto-eroticism. She describes primary identification as the 'zero degree' that shapes psychic space itself, and links this arising of the subject to Freud's notion of a 'father in individual prehistory'. In this 'prehistory', the child forges an initial identification, prior to sexual division, with a maternal-paternal container. As Kristeva explains this *pre-Oedipal* identification:

> Freud has described the One with whom I fulfill the identification (this 'most primitive aspect of affective binding to an object') as a Father. Although he did not elaborate what he meant by 'primary identification', he made it clear that this father is a 'father in individual prehistory'. . . . Identification with that 'father in prehistory', that Imaginary Father, is called 'immediate', 'direct', and Freud emphasizes again, 'previous to any concentration on any object whatsoever'. . . . The whole symbolic matrix sheltering emptiness is thus set in place in an elaboration that precedes the Oedipus complex.
>
> (1987: 26–7)

And again, on the sexual indistinction of primary identification:

> The archaeology of such an identifying possibility with an other is provided by the huge place taken up within narcissistic structure by the vortex of primary identification with what Freud called a 'father of personal prehistory'. Endowed with the sexual attributes of both parents, and by that very token a totalizing, phallic figure, it provides satisfactions that are already psychic and not simply immediate, existential requests; that archaic vortex of idealization is immediately an other who gives rise to a powerful, already psychic transference of the previous semiotic body in the process of becoming a narcissistic Ego.
>
> (1987: 33)

Note here that the reference to an *other* ties the emergence of identity to the intersubjective field. Note too that this identification with the imaginary father (which is less a partial object than a pre-object) *constitutes* primary repression; it 'bends the drive toward the symbolic of the other' (Kristeva 1987: 31).

Kristeva argues that primary identification arises, not from the child's desire for the pre-Oedipal mother, but from an affective tie with the *mother's desire for the phallus*. Echoing Lacan, she contends that the child comes to realize that the mother herself is lacking, incomplete. In this connection, the child encounters the desire of the other: that the mother's desire is invested elsewhere, in the imaginary phallus. For Kristeva, identification with the imaginary father functions as support for the loss of the maternal object, and provides an imaginary lining to subjectivity which guards against depression and melancholia. Thus:

> 'primary identification' with the 'father in individual prehistory' would be the means, the link that might enable one to become reconciled with the loss of the Thing. Primary identification initiates a compensation for the Thing and at the same time secures the subject to another dimension, that of imaginary adherence, reminding one of the bond of faith, which is just what disintegrates in the depressed person.
>
> (1989: 13–14)

Yet, because the investment in this imaginary father comes from the inside, the emergence of identity is itself a precarious, fragile process.

Like Kristeva, Laplanche is also concerned with reconceptualizing the conditions of primal identification and repression, with the purpose of mapping the inaccessible, unconscious significations between the individual subject and the intersubjective realm. Laplanche suggests that an elementary form of subjectivity is constituted when the small infant enters into an identification with certain 'enigmatic signifiers' in the pre-Oedipal phase, a phase which initiates the binding of unconscious drives through primal repression. The concept of the enigmatic signifier refers to the intervention of the other into psychic interiority, prior to the establishment proper of the signifying character of the symbolic order. This initial relation to the other, says Laplanche, occurs in and through seduction, transmitted via parental messages to the child. As Laplanche puts this: 'The *enigma is* in itself a *seduction* and its mechanisms are unconscious. . . . The "attentions of a mother" or the "aggression of a father" are seductive only because they are not transparent. They are seductive because they are opaque, because they convey something enigmatic' (1987: 128). Signifiers are constituted as enigmatic for Laplanche since adult messages both outstrip the child's capacity for affective response and because they are shot through with parental unconscious signification. From this angle, what is on the outside, parental or adult (sexual) messages, constitutes an inaccessible field of significations on the inside, the repressed unconscious. In the words of Laplanche, the implication of this is that there 'is no initial or natural opposition between the instinctual and the intersubjective, or between the instinctual and the cultural' (1987: 137).

As an example of the seductiveness of enigmatic signifiers, Laplanche points to the role of the maternal breast in infant development. He argues that the breast is a carrier of maternal fantasy which transmits opaque sexual significations within the mother–child relation. As Laplanche puts this:

> Can analytic theory afford to go on ignoring the extent women unconsciously and sexually cathect the breast, which appears to be the natural organ for lactation? It is inconceivable that the infant does not notice this sexual cathexis, which might be said to be perverse in the same sense in which that term is defined in the *Three Essays*. It is impossible to imagine that the infant does not suspect that this cathexis is the source of a nagging question: what does the breast want from me, apart from wanting to suckle me, and come to that, why does it want to suckle me?
>
> (1987: 126)

The child thus receives a sexually distorted message from mother, a message which it is emotionally unable to comprehend.

There is, I believe, much that is of interest in Kristeva and Laplanche on the constitution of the unconscious through primary repression. Both Kristeva and Laplanche, in differing theoretical ways, underline the importance of primary repression as the support for the arising of an elementary form of subjectivity, which is subsequently secured through the Oedipus and castration complexes.

However, there are also serious theoretical difficulties arising from their work. Kristeva has been much criticized, in both psychoanalytic and feminist circles, for linking the moment of identification with the imaginary father. For feminists such as Cornell (1991: 69–71), this has the effect of reinscribing gender stereotypes within the pre-Oedipal phase, and thus results in a denial of woman's imaginary. For, according to this critique of Kristeva, to deny the power of the imaginary father is to risk depression, melancholia and, possibly, death. From a different angle, Laplanche's work has also been criticized for its neglect of the more creative dimensions of sexual subjectivity. As Jacqueline Rose has pointed out, Laplanche's reinterpretation of primary repression means that the 'child receives everything from the outside', desire being inscribed within the repressed unconscious via the deformations of parental sexuality itself (Laplanche 1992: 61). In my view, these criticisms are indeed valid. The standpoints of Kristeva and Laplanche are flawed in respect of the power accorded to the other (imaginary father/seduction) over psychic interiority, or the outside as constitutive of desire itself. By contrast, I suggest that we must develop a psychoanalytic account of subjectivity and intersubjectivity which breaks with this inside/outside boundary.

PRIMARY REPRESSION/IDENTIFICATION RETHOUGHT: REPRESENTATIONAL WRAPPINGS OF SELF AND OTHER

For these accounts I suggest we should substitute the delineation of an elementary dimension of subjectivity formed in and through primary intersubjectivity – a mode dependent upon the fixation of primal repression and identification. In the constitution of primary intersubjectivity, the small infant actively enters into the push-and-pull of object – or, more accurately, pre-object – relations. This is less a phenomenon of the other 'breaking in' from the outside than one of ordering psychic interiority within intersubjective boundaries of shared, unconscious experience. The organizing of shared, unconscious experience occurs through a process that I call *rolling identification*. Derived from the representational flux of the unconscious, rolling identifications provide for the insertion of subjectivity into a complex interplay between self-as-object and pre-object relations. Rolling identifications literally spill out across libidinal space, with representational flux passing into objects, and objects into psychical life, in a ceaseless exchange. Here the rudimentary beginnings of pre-self experience arises from factors such as sensory impressions of autistic shapes and objects (Tustin 1980, 1984; Ogden 1989), which form feelings of warmth, hardness, coldness, texture and the like; a primitive relation to bounded surfaces (Ogden 1989), such as the child's own body, the body of the mother as well as non-human substances; and from maternal rhythmicity (Kristeva 1984), including tone, breath and silences.

Rolling identifications veer away in erratic directions, and their elaboration is plural, multiple, discontinuous. Before the differentiation proper of self and other, this modality of psychic organization is basic to the wealth of images, fantasies and feelings that circulate within intersubjective communication. To capture the nature of rolling identification, we must connect the auto-erotic indistinction between the self and the nonself of which Castoriadis speaks with the concept of primary repression. Now primal repression, as expressed by Freud, involves the fixation of the drive to a representation, the registration *(Niederschrift)* of which constitutes the repressed unconscious. Such a relation, the fixation or bonding of libidinal drive and psychic representation, is closely bound up with primary identification, the 'original form of emotional tie with an object' (Freud, S.E. XVIII: 107). My argument is that, pursuing Freud's logic concerning primal repression and identification, it is possible to establish dialectically related connections between basic aspects of self-organization and intersubjective settings. That is, the experience of subjectivity and intersubjectivity presuppose one another. In this respect, rolling identifications are an imaginary anchor connecting subjectivity and the object world.

Now primary identification 'does not wait upon an object-relationship proper' (Laplanche and Pontalis 1985: 336). It is constituted, rather, through a process of incorporating a pre-object; or, as Kristeva says, primary identification 'bends the drive toward the symbolic of the other' (Kristeva 1987: 31). But how, exactly, is the drive 'bent' in the direction of the other? How does the subject make this shift from self-referential representational fulfilment to primary intersubjectivity? How, in any case, does the presentation of otherness enter into the construction of the psyche? Several factors suggest themselves on the basis of the foregoing observations. To begin with, the infant's subjectivity – marked by representational flux – can be thought of as becoming *internally split* once the emergent relation to the pre-object is established. Primary identification, and the general narcissism which it ushers in, is therefore closely bound up with loss. Loss here is understood as a result of the preliminary dissolution of basic representational self-sufficiency. As Castoriadis expresses this:

> Once the psyche has suffered the break up of its monadic 'state' imposed upon it by the 'object', the other and its own body, it is forever thrown off-centre in relation to itself, orientated in terms of that which it is no longer and can no longer be. *The psyche is its own lost object.*
>
> (1987: 296–7)

The subject, simply, suffers the loss of self-referential representational fulfilment, and it substitutes a relation to pre-objects and self-as-object as the basis for creating 'a place where one lives' (Winnicott 1971).

To be sure, the possible adaptive reactions must register basic relational connections. Indeed, this is the outlook described by Kristeva and Laplanche – the subject is referred beyond itself via an imaginary anchor in parental significations. This standpoint, while more sophisticated than most, is still inadequate however, since its conception of the subject and the unconscious is too simple. Here we must return to certain threads in my argument about unconscious representation. The relation between the rudimentary beginnings of subjectivity and primary intersubjectivity – the psychical registration of self-as-object and pre-object relations – cannot be understood outside of the representational dynamics of desire itself. According to the view I am proposing, there is a *representational wrapping of self and other* achieved through primal repression and identification. By this I mean that the subject establishes a preliminary ordering, to use a kind of shorthand, of pre-self experience, otherness and difference as the basis for the elaboration of psychic space itself. Such representational wrapping does not just 'register' other persons and the object world, but is the central mechanism which makes their humanization possible. It is when Freud speaks of the pre-Oedipal child having '*created* an object out of the mother' (1926: 170) that we come close to capturing the 'wrapping' accomplished through representational activity. *Representational wrapping spirals in and out of intersubjective life, ordering and reordering both psychical imagination and the social process of which it is part.*

We can explore some possible connections here by means of an example. Let me briefly concentrate on the dream of Irma's injection, the dream that Freud takes in *The Interpretation of Dreams* as a paradigm for his thesis that dreams are wish-fulfilments:

> *A large hall – numerous guests, whom we are receiving. – Among them was Irma. I at once took her on one side as though to answer her letter and to reproach her for not having accepted my 'solution' yet. I said to her: 'If you still get pains, it's really your own fault.' She replied: 'If you only knew what pains I've got now in my throat and stomach and abdomen – it's choking me' – I was alarmed and looked at her. She looked pale and puffy. I thought to myself that after all I must be missing some organic trouble. I took her to the window and looked down her throat, and she showed signs of recalcitrance, like women with artificial dentures. I thought to myself that there was really no need for her to do that. – She then opened her mouth properly and on the right side I found a big white patch; at another place I saw extensive whitish grey scabs upon some remarkable curly structures which were evidently modelled on the turbinal bones of the nose. – I at once called in Dr M., and he repeated the examination and confirmed it. . . . Dr M. looked quite different from usual; he was very pale, he walked with a limp and his chin was clean-shaven. . . . My friend Otto was now standing beside her as well, and my friend Leopold was percussing her through her bodice and saying: 'She has a dull area low down on the left.' He also indicated that a portion of the skin on the left shoulder was infiltrated. (I noticed this, just as he did, in spite of her dress.) . . . M. said: 'There's no doubt it's an infection, but no matter; dysentery will supervene and the toxin will be eliminated.' . . . We were directly aware, too, of the origin of the infection. Not long before, when she was feeling unwell, my friend Otto had given her an injection of a preparation of propyl, propyls . . . propionic acid . . . trimethylamin (and I saw before me the formula for this printed in heavy type). . . . Injections of that sort ought not to be made so thoughtlessly. . . . And probably the syringe had not been clean.*
>
> (Freud 1900, S.E.4: 107)

The Irma dream, among other things, bears directly on the place and role of representations in unconscious wish-fulfilment. Indeed, Freud's 'specimen dream' powerfully underlines the representational constitution and structuring of unconscious pleasure itself. What is the pleasure represented in this dream? According to Freud, the dream released him from 'responsibility for Irma's condition by showing that it was due to other factors' (Freud 1900, S.E.4: 118). The representational architecture of the dream casts Dr M., Leopold and Otto at fault; a responsibility issuing from their medical incompetence (the thoughtless injection, the dirty syringe and so on). Significantly, the dream also transfers responsibility to the patient herself. Interpreting the dream as a wish-fulfilment of 'professional conscientiousness', Freud says of this fantasy scenario: 'I was not to blame for Irma's pains, since she herself was to blame for them by refusing to accept my solution. I was not concerned with Irma's pains, since they were of an organic nature and quite incurable by psychological treatment' (Freud 1900, S.E.4: 119).

But this is only the tip of the iceberg. The Irma dream, being Freud's own dream, has been continually revised and transformed within psychoanalytic lore: a dream problematic, a lesson in the limits of self-analysis, a source for speculation about Freud himself. Significantly, in this way, the articulated representations – Irma's resistance to opening her mouth, her injection with a dirty syringe, and the like – have been read as symptomatic of Freud's sexual fantasies (see Gay 1988: 83).

Undoubtedly the dream of Irma's injection reveals much about Freud's fantasy world, but the point that calls for our attention is somewhat different. The representational space of the dream, and of Freud's associations to the dream, can best be grasped only in the movement of its own production. We plunge, at this point, into the representational flux – the rolling identifications and wrappings of self and other – of fantasy itself. It is possible to trace the indistinction and reversibility which characterizes Freud's fantasy scenario at a number of levels, of which I can only mention one or two here. Firstly, behind Irma, as many commentators have argued, we find Emma Eckstein, a central figure in the origins of psychoanalysis itself. Emma Eckstein offers a particularly clear instance of Freud's alarm at the thought of male medical practitioners maltreating their female patients. In December 1894, Freud arranged for his friend and medical mentor, Wilhelm Fliess, to operate on Emma's nose in order to alleviate her distressing hysterical symptoms. The operation backfired: Fliess had left a half-metre of gauze in Emma's nasal cavity which, when later extracted, led to a massive haemorrhage and the near death of the patient. The dream of Irma's injection is rife with the guilt that Freud experienced over Fliess's bungled operation upon Emma Eckstein. As Freud notes of Fliess in his self-analysis of the Irma dream: 'Should not this friend, who plays such a large role in my life, appear further in the dream's context of thought?' It is certainly arguable that Fliess did play a larger role in the dream than Freud imagined. Indeed, the dream of Irma's injection is itself a massive displacement of Freud's anxiety about Fliess himself (see Gay 1988: 82–7); and thus, by extension, of Freud's wish to be absolved from medically irresponsible behaviour.

Secondly, this collapsing of self–other boundaries and representational recycling of primary intersubjectivity is perhaps even clearer in the feminine identifications registered in the Irma dream. For the women who figure in the dream are women after whom Freud's own daughters were named. (There is now little doubt about the identity of the three women: Irma is Anna Hammerschlag-Lichtheim; her friend is Sophie Schwab-Paneth; and the third woman, who Freud associates with his wife Martha, is Mathilde Breuer.) As Freud commented to Abraham about the dream: 'Mathilde, Sophie and Anna ... my daughters' three godmothers, and I have them all!' (Quoted in Appignanesi and Forrester 1992: 127). It could be argued that Freud's sense of surprise – 'I have them all!' – goes to the heart of glimpsing, not only his sexual megalomania, but the representational depth of wish-fulfilment itself. There is a kind of infinite regress here: sexual desire leads to a falling into the 'other', which reactivates the unending nature of unconscious desire. Rolling identifications thus fall, not only within the self–other split, but within the familial, social network itself. As Appignanesi and Forrester comment: 'It is not sexual megalomania in the sense of quantity that is most striking in this dream, but the different sorts of women who are possessed. Not three, so much, as patient, widow, godmother, friend – and daughter' (1992: 129). Significantly, the fantasy staged in and through the dream permits the obtaining of pleasure; desires which deconstruct identity and differentiation, which realize the rolling indistinction between self and other, which repeat 'what occurred and what continues to occur in the manufacture of the so-called primal phantasm' (Lyotard 1989: 19).

SUMMARY: THE REPRESENTATIONAL DYNAMICS OF SUBJECTIVITY AND INTERSUBJECTIVITY

We are now in a position to sum up the argument thus far. I have suggested that there is a connecting track between the representational activity of the subject on the one hand and the dynamics of intersubjectivity on the other. These connections are forged, I suggested, through rolling identifications and representational wrappings of self and other. The emergence of subjectivity, according to this view, can be represented as follows:

1 In the shift from self-referential representational fulfilment to primary intersubjectivity, the infant's subjectivity is organized through *rolling* identifications. In this context, *representational wrappings of self* and *other* are the constitutive means for the child's sense of 'going on being' (Winnicott 1956).

2 These mechanisms provide the ontological backdrop for psychic space itself and the ordering of imaginary experience. To the extent that representational wrappings are articulated, the subject can negotiate the imaginary tribulations of 'potential space' (Winnicott 1971) and the 'semiotic' (Kristeva 1974).

3 What puts an end to the child's fantasied world without differentiation is the constitution of the individual as subject through the impact of 'social imaginary significations' (Castoriadis 1987). The intertwining of representational wrapping, imaginary and socio-symbolic forms is the means through which human beings establish a psychical relation to the self, others, received social meanings, society and culture.

THE SIGNIFICANCE OF PRIMARY REPRESSION, AND THE POLITICALIZATION OF IDENTIFICATION

How far does the notion of primary repression lead us to rethink the constitution and/or positioning of the subject in terms of socio-symbolic signification? Do rolling identifications and representational wrapping, as a grounding feature of subjectivity, offer a non-violative relation to otherness and difference? Do they promise a release from the constraint of identity, gender and power in their current institutionalized forms?

The insights of Freud, and of modern psychoanalysis more generally, should of course lead us to caution in this respect. Whatever the radicalizing possibilities of primal repression and identification, identity requires meaning, and therefore symbolic law, which constitutes subjectivity in its socio-cultural dimensions. The transition from a fantasy world of representation to socio-symbolic signification refers the individual subject beyond itself. It establishes a relation to the other, and therefore to cultural, historical and political chains of signification. The entry of the subject into socially constituted representations secures the repetition of the law. Thus, imaginary representations are pressed into the service of the current social order, gender hierarchy, power relations and the like.

For these reasons, it makes little sense to understand the psychical processes organized through primal repression as signalling a 'beyond' to symbolic law. The signifying process of any given social order depends upon the repetition of common, symbolic forms – a phenomenon which in part explains the relative closure of social systems and modern institutions.

However, none of this means that human subjects can be reduced to mere 'supports' of symbolic law. Contrary to Lacanian and related deterministic theories, 'history' is not fixed once and for all, and offers no guarantees with regard to the organization of power. Thus the connection between law and desire, ideology and the affective, is not a fixed reality instituted by the symbolic. Freud's account of Oedipus, as Kristeva comments, 'was not, as he has been too easily accused of, to respect the paternal law of taboos that sketch our social interplay ... [but rather] to sort out the types of representations of which a subject is capable' (1987: 9–10).

In this respect, representational forms, I have suggested, are shaped to their core in and through pre-Oedipal processes of repression and identification. As an elementary elaboration of pre-self experience and pre-object relations, primal repression permits the *representational splitting of the subject*, which is bound up with the contradictions of the intersubjective network itself. This elementary organization of psychical space will be repressed with entry to the socio-symbolic order, thus cementing the reproduction of 'social imaginary significations'. However, these elementary, representational wrappings of self and other are never entirely repressed. They cannot be shut off from identity and culture, and remain present within social imaginary emotions and images of every kind. The interaction of representational self–other forms and socio-symbolic significations, primary and secondary repression, is thus central to the constitution and reproduction of subjectivity.

From this angle, then, what is the socio-cultural significance of primal repression and identification? What is at issue here is the interlacing of those fantasmatic images and feelings attained through rolling identification and socially instituted representations. If we understand that social significations are unconsciously organized within the matrix of former pre-Oedipal experience, we can see that there is a wealth of fantasies, images and feelings available to the subject as it creatively engages with cultural forms. Early fantasmatic images provide not only a support for identity, but also the identificatory basis on which to re-imagine our world. Representational wrappings of self and other – constituted in and through primal repression – infuse the power of the radical imagination and help to contest, question and destabilize our relation to the symbolic. This is easily demonstrated by reference to social movements. The women's movement in recent decades, for example, has pioneered attempts at reordering repressed arenas of love, intimacy and sexuality within new social frames of gender.

The political and ethical importance of these rudimentary representations of self and other, primary intersubjectivity, lies in their ordering and reordering of social imaginary significations. Representational intersubjective wrapping, prior to sexual division and socio-cultural identity, infuses the radical imagination in its ongoing search for the care, love and emotional relatedness of others. The way beyond oppression and exploitation lies in retracing the shared representational and affective conditions which link us ineluctably together. It is here, in the politics of solidarity and difference, that contemporary appeals to national, race, class and gender difference explore the fantasmatic dimensions of identity and culture.

The politics of difference require creativity, innovation, reflectiveness, in order to enact the different itself. In pursuit of the new, the different, beyond the constraint and domination of the current social order, there are values and affects embedded in the subject's relation to primal identification which are of vital importance. Primal identification, and the repression which consolidates it, opens a preliminary distance between the self and others, and is thus a foundation for human autonomy and all genuine social relationships. For this link to the other, prior to mirror asymmetry and the imprint of social significations, can offer a prefigurative image of a cultural condition in which relatedness, fulfilment and creativity are more fully realized. The role of unconscious representation in dreaming the new lies precisely in this connection to the other, primary intersubjectivity, a condition from which we might imagine the self, society, politics and ethics anew.

REFERENCES

Appignanesi, L. and Forrester, J. (1992) *Freud's Women*. London: Virago.
Benjamin, J. (1990) *The Bonds of Love*. London: Virago.
Borch-Jacobsen, M. (1988) *The Freudian Subject*. Stanford, California: Stanford University Press.
Castoriadis, C. (1984) *Crossroads in the Labyrinth*. Cambridge, MA: MIT Press.
—— (1987) *The Imaginary Institution of Society*. Cambridge: Polity Press.
—— (1989) 'The state of the subject today'. *Thesis Eleven*, 24: 5–43.

Cornell, D. (1991) *Beyond Accomodation: Ethical Feminism, Deconstruction and the Law*. New York: Routledge.

Elliott, A. (1992) *Social Theory and Psychoanalysis in Transition: Self and Society from Freud to Kristeva*. Oxford: Blackwell.

—— (1994) *Psychoanalytic Theory: An Introduction*. Oxford: Blackwell.

Fletcher, J. and Stanton, M. (eds) (1992) *Jean Laplanche: Seduction, Translation, Drives*. London: ICA.

Freud, S. (1900) *The Interpretation of Dreams*. S.E.4 and 5.

—— (1911) 'Formulations on the two principles of mental functioning'. S.E.12.

—— (1913) 'Totem and Taboo'. S.E. XIII, pp. 1–161.

—— (1915a) 'The unconscious'. S.E.14.

—— (1915b) 'Repression'. S.E.14.

—— (1921) 'Group psychology and the analysis of the ego'. S.E. 18, pp. 69–143.

—— (1926) *Inhibitions, Symptoms and Anxiety*. S.E.20.

Gay, P. (1988) *Freud: A Life for our Times*. London: Dent.

Greenberg, J. (1991) *Oedipus and Beyond*. Cambridge, MA: Harvard University Press.

Greenberg, J. and Mitchell, S.A. (1983) *Object Relations in Psychoanalytic Theory*. Cambridge, MA: Harvard University Press.

Kristeva, J. (1984) *Revolution in Poetic Language*. New York: Columbia University Press.

—— (1987) *Tales of Love*. New York: Columbia University Press.

—— (1989) *Black Sun: Depression and Melancholia*. New York: Columbia University Press.

Lacan, J. (1975) *Le Seminaire, Livre I, Les Ecrits techniques de Freud*. Paris: Seuil.

Laplanche, J. (1987) *New Foundations for Psychoanalysis*. Oxford: Blackwell.

—— (1989) *Jean Laplanche: Seduction, Translation and the Drives*. London: ICA.

Laplanche, J. and Pontalis, J.B. (1968) 'Phantasy and the origins of sexuality', *International Journal of Psycho-Analysis*, 49, 1: 1–18.

—— (1985) *The Language of Psycho-Analysis*. London: Hogarth Press.

Lear, J. (1991) *Love and Its Place in Nature*. New York: Farrar, Straus & Giroux.

Lyotard, J.F. (1989) *The Lyotard Reader*, edited by A. Benjamin. Oxford: Blackwell.

Macey, D. (1988) *Lacan in Contexts*. London: Verso.

Mitchell, S. (1988) *Relational Concepts in Psychoanalysis*. Cambridge, MA: Harvard University Press.

Ogden, T. (1989) 'On the concept of an autistic-contiguous position'. *International Journal of Psycho-Analysis*, 70, 1: 127–40.

Ricoeur, P. (1970) *Freud and Philosophy: An Essay on Interpretation*. New Haven, Yale.

Sandler, J. (1989) 'Toward a reconsideration of the psychoanalytic theory of motivation' in A. Cooper, O. Kernberg and E. Person (eds), *Psychoanalysis*. New Haven, CT: Yale University Press, pp. 91–110.

Schafer, R. (1983) *The Analytic Attitude*. New York: Basic Books.

Spezzano, C. (1993) *Affect in Psychoanalysis: A Clinical Synthesis*. Hillsdale, NJ: The Analytic Press.

Tustin, F. (1980) 'Autistic objects'. *International Review of Psycho-Analysis*, 7: 27–40.

—— (1984) 'Autistic shapes'. *International Review of Psycho-Analysis*, 11: 279–90.

Winnicott, D. (1956) 'Primary maternal preoccupation', in *Through Paediatrics to Psycho-Analysis*. New York: Basic Books.

—— (1971) *Playing and Reality*. New York: Basic Books.

3 The crisis of Oedipal identity
The early Lacan and the Frankfurt School

Peter Dews

INTRODUCTION

Perhaps we do not find it surprising enough that the thought of Jacques Lacan should have come to function as a major point of reference for feminist theory in the English-speaking world. Lacan's best-known work, dating from the inception of his *Seminar* in 1953, is characterized by an almost obsessive concern with the relation between language and subjectivity, but Lacan shies away from connecting his formal conception of language to any historical, let alone ideological, dimension of meaning. Rather, in his reformulation, psychoanalysis is focused on the simultaneous relation of dependency and non-identity between the subject and language *as such*: Lacan is unequivocal that in psychoanalysis 'it is not a question of the relation of man to language as a social phenomenon'.[1] To this extent, the appeal of his work for feminists derives not from its historical or sociological insights, but sheerly from its emphasis on the symbolically structured character of subjectivity in its gendered dimension, an emphasis which undermines any naturalistic conception of the opposition between the psychology of the two sexes.

At the same time, however, the political advantage which this emphasis might be considered to bring is profoundly elusive, since, in his later work at least, Lacan gives little reason to assume that such symbolic structuring might be alterable. Even those feminists most sympathetic to Lacan have found themselves struggling with the dilemma that his thought appears to establish an intrinsic relation between phallic primacy and the symbolic order. Thus, Jacqueline Rose has written:

> For Lacan, to say that difference is 'phallic' difference is to expose the symbolic and arbitrary nature of its division as such. It is crucial . . . that refusal of the phallic term brings with it an attempt to reconstitute a form of subjectivity free of division, and hence a refusal of the notion of symbolization itself.[2]

However, if refusal of the phallic term is equivalent to the absolute refusal of symbolization, then the role of the phallus can hardly be considered as 'arbitrary'. Rose recognizes this, for she goes on to defend her position by suggesting that:

> While the objection to . . . [the] . . . dominant term [i.e. the phallus] must be recognized, it cannot be answered by an account which returns to a concept of the feminine as pre-given, nor by a mandatory appeal to an androcentrism in the

symbolic which the phallus would simply reflect. The former relegates women outside language and history, the latter simply subordinates them to both.[3]

It is difficult to understand, however, why the grounding of phallocentrism in androcentrism should subordinate women to language and history, unless this androcentrism itself is considered to be immutable. Conversely, if the symbolic role of the phallus in the unconscious formation of gender identity is entirely detached from the question of the actual relations, including power relations, between men and women, it is hard to perceive where the interest of psychoanalysis for feminists might lie.

In the light of these difficulties, it might appear that other intellectual traditions, both psychoanalytically informed and committed to social critique, might offer better starting points for a feminist theorization of sexual difference. The tradition which inevitably springs to mind here is that of the Frankfurt School, which has in general been much more sensitive to the intersections between psychoanalysis and social theory than Lacanian approaches. The earlier Frankfurt School, in particular, appreciated the need to introduce a dimension of historicity into even the most fundamental psychoanalytic categories, arguing – against Freud himself – that there can be no purely timeless unconscious, since 'concrete historical components already enter early childhood experience'.[4] Until recently, however, this tradition has had little to say about the specific question of women's oppression – indeed, the issue is more present, though scarcely prominent, in the work of the earlier Frankfurt School than in the contemporary critical theory of Habermas. Furthermore, although there are now the beginnings of a feminist reception of critical theory, particularly in North America, this reception has not – on the whole – been particularly sensitive to the psychoanalytic dimension of earlier Critical Theory, or tried to make use of it to any significant extent. Rather, its principal aim has been to modify the gender-insensitive universalism of Habermasian social and moral theory.[5]

On the one hand, therefore, we find the powerful influence of a form of *psychoanalytic* theory within Anglo-American feminism which appears remote from sociological and historical concerns; on the other, a tradition of *critical* theory, now being adapted and developed by feminists, which has lost the psychoanalytical emphasis on the complex internal structure of subjectivity, in its shift to an investigation of the normative structures of *inter*-subjectivity. However, a consideration of the early – now almost forgotten – phases of Lacan's thinking opens up possibilities of at least modifying this dichotomy. For Lacan's first forays in psychoanalytic theory, prior to the inception of the *Seminar*, were by no means as hostile to historical and sociological perspectives as his later thought appears to be. Furthermore, the account of the crisis of the modern family which Lacan developed during the 1930s, and which is most fully presented in a lengthy encyclopedia article of 1938, *Les complexes familiaux*, evinces many striking similarities with the contemporaneous work of the Frankfurt School on the same issue. Against the background of these affinities, the question of why Lacan's work evolved as it did can be posed in a new way. Indeed, as we shall see, the later Lacan's apparently 'transcendental' model of a phallocentric symbolic order can itself be understood as a response to a specific *historical* crisis. Simultaneously, the possibility opens up of comparing Lacan's later work, as a response to the familial and social crisis which he diagnoses, with recent developments in psychoanalysis which attempt both to build on, and to respond to, the earlier thought of the Frankfurt School from a critical, feminist perspective – most notably the work of Jessica Benjamin.

I

Perhaps the most striking feature of *Les complexes familiaux* is the manner in which Lacan insists, against Freud himself, that the Oedipus complex is at the centre of a historically specific type of identity formation which emerges within the context of the patriarchal family. Lacan makes clear that marriage and the family are two distinct social institutions, and argues that the modern form of the family, centred on the 'matrimonial' relation between the parents, should not be confused in its psychological effects with earlier familial structures, even where these seem to overlap in terms of personnel. Indeed, Lacan specifically criticizes Freud, on the grounds that he 'presents this psychological element (of the Oedipus complex) as the specific form of the human family and subordinates to it all the social variations of the family'.[6] By contrast, Lacan claims, 'The methodological order proposed here, both in the consideration of mental structures and of the social facts, will lead to a revision of the complex which will allow us to situate contemporary neurosis in the history of the paternalistic family, and to cast further light on it'.[7]

In the account which Lacan then develops, the specific virtue of Oedipal identity formation consists in the extreme psychological tension which is generated by the role of the father, as both 'the agent of prohibition and the example of its transgression'.[8] As Lacan writes,

> It is ... because it is invested with the power of repression that the paternal imago projects its original force into the very sublimations which are to surmount it; it is from binding together the progress of its functions in such an antinomy that the Oedipus complex derives its fecundity.[9]

In other terms, the paradoxical paternal injunction, 'be and do not be like me', which confronts the child in the Oedipal situation, makes possible a form of identification which fuses emulation and difference in an advanced form of individuation. As Lacan states,

> If, as a result of their experience, both the psychoanalyst and the sociologist can recognize in the prohibition of the mother the concrete form of primordial obligation, they can also demonstrate a real 'opening up' of the social bond in paternalist authority and affirm that, through the functional conflict of the Oedipal situation, this authority introduces into repression a promissory ideal.[10]

Elaborating this general characterization, Lacan gives three principal reasons for the superiority of Oedipal identity formation over other corresponding processes. Firstly, because authority is incarnated in a familiar form by the nearest generation, it is more readily open to creative subversion. Secondly, because the psyche is formed not simply by the constraint of the adult but by his positive image (Lacan considers the father–son relation to be the pre-eminent example here), there occurs a 'positive selection of tendencies and gifts, and a progressive realization of the ideal in the character'.[11] Thirdly, the evidence of sexual life on the part of those imposing moral constraints 'raises the tension of the libido to the highest degree, and increases the scope of sublimation'.[12] On these grounds, Lacan has only the highest praise for the achievements of the modern family (by which he means the type of family, based on the free choice of partners, which began to emerge in Europe from the fifteenth century onwards):

> It is by realizing in the most human form the conflict of man with his most archaic anxiety, it is by offering the most loyal closed domain where he can measure himself against the profoundest figures of his destiny, it is by putting the most complete triumph over his original servitude within his grasp, that the complex of the conjugal family creates superior successes of character, happiness and creation.[13]

By contrast with this view, Lacan is unequivocal about the 'stagnation' which is implied by non-patriarchal patterns of socialization. In such forms the repressive social instance and the social ideal are separated: Lacan cites Malinowski's accounts of societies in which the first of these roles is played by the maternal uncle, while the father has a more companionate relation to the child. Because of this separation, such forms are unable to rival the dialectical, sublimatory tension generated by the Oedipal model. Commenting caustically on the Melanesian idylls evoked by Malinowski, Lacan remarks that 'the harmony of these societies contrasts with the stereotypical quality which marks the creations of the personality, and of art and morality in such cultures'.[14]

Despite his paeans to the patriarchal family, however, Lacan is extremely sensitive to the fact that this social form is caught up in a fateful historical dialectic. Up to a certain point a positive cycle occurs, in which the 'normative ideals, juridical statutes and creative inspirations' made possible by Oedipal identity-formation react back onto the family, thereby helping to concentrate even further within it the conditions of the Oedipal conflict, and 'reintegrating into psychological progress the social dialectic engendered by this conflict'.[15] However, this self-reinforcing cycle eventually reaches a crisis point, where the level of individuation achieved begins to undermine the now highly compacted conditions of Oedipal identity formation itself. According to Lacan, the progress of culture is manifested in the increasing demands which are imposed on the ego with regard to 'coherence and creative *élan*', with the result that 'the accidents and caprices of this [Oedipal] regulation increase step by step with this same social progress which, in making the family evolve towards the conjugal form, submits it more and more to individual variations'. And Lacan concludes:

> This 'anomie', which made possible the discovery of the complex, gives rise to the degenerated form in which the analyst recognizes it: a form which we could

define in terms of an incomplete repression of the desire for the mother, with a reactivation of the anxiety and curiosity inherent in the birth relation; and a narcissistic debasement of the idealization of the father, which causes the emergence, in oedipal identification, of the aggressive ambivalence immanent in the primordial relation to the counterpart.[16]

Against the background of this deeply historical account of structures of subjectivity, Lacan's later thought appears in a new light. On one plausible interpretation, proposed by Mikkel Borch-Jacobsen, the later Lacan attempts to shore up the Oedipus complex by transforming it into a 'transcendental' structure constitutive of subjectivity as such, while haunted by the awareness that the Oedipal norm no longer corresponds to the socially predominant processes of identity formation. Indeed, Lacan himself suggests in *Les complexes familiaux* that the emergence of psychoanalysis itself, in the melting-pot of turn-of-the-century Vienna, with its chaotic multiplicity of family forms, from the most traditional to the most irregular, can be explained in terms of the incipient crisis of Oedipal identity formation. The 'true' Oedipus complex, one might say, can be recognized only privatively, through the psychoanalytic inventory of the effects of its distorted and degenerating forms.

II

Before examining in more detail Lacan's own later response to this situation, however, I would like to highlight further the distinctive features of his account of the crisis of the bourgeois family by comparing it with the approach of the Frankfurt School at the same period. Significantly, Max Horkheimer's classic essay on 'Authority and the family' was written only two years before *Les complexes familiaux*, in 1936. Unlike Lacan, however, Horkheimer grounds his analysis from the normative standpoint of an anticipated society devoid of institutionalized relations of force and their internalized equivalents. From this point of view, the psychic apparatus is understood as serving primarily to 'interiorize, or at least to rationalize and supplement physical coercion'.[17] Horkheimer does not deny the historical advance represented by the modern patriarchal family, whose emergence he dates – as does Lacan – from the fifteenth century:

At the beginning of the bourgeois age the father's control of his household was doubtless an indispensable condition of progress. The self-control of the individual, the disposition for work and discipline, the ability to hold firmly to certain ideas, consistency in practical life, application of reason, perseverance and pleasure in constructive activity could all be developed, in the circumstances, only under the dictation and guidance of the father whose own education had been won in the school of life.[18]

However, Horkheimer argues, the function of authority can change from being progressive to regressive, relative to the goals of 'self-development and happiness' which are internal to his normative standpoint.[19] As the capitalist organization of society is consolidated, the role of the family increasingly becomes that of inculcating an adaptive and submissive attitude to authority, which is now reified and depersonalized in the form of the economic system itself. Within the family, the authority of the father, based on superior physical strength and economic power, comes to embody that irrational facticity of the social in the face of which individuals would be 'irrational' to do anything other than submit.

In Horkheimer's account, the dialectic thus set in motion eventually leads to the undermining of the role of the father. Horkheimer argues:

> The education of authority-oriented personalities, for which the family is suited because of its own authority structure, is not a passing phenomenon but part of a relatively permanent state of affairs. Of course, the more this society enters a critical phase because of its own immanent laws, the less will the family be able to exercise its educational function. . . . The means of protecting the cultural totality and developing it further have increasingly come into conflict with the cultural content itself. The father as an arbitrary power no longer offers possibilities of identification, and the child instead identifies with repressive social instances.[20]

The result of this direct identification with social power is the spread of the malleable narcissistic personality type, lacking those inner capacities for self-direction which the buffer of paternal authority once provided, ostensibly well-adapted but inwardly cold and emotionless, inclined to power worship and masochistic submission.

In considering the validity of this analysis and its political consequences, it is instructive to compare the reasons which Lacan and Horkheimer supply for the fateful dialectic of the bourgeois family. In Horkheimer the essential mediating role is played by the capitalist economy, on the assumption that 'The idealization of paternal authority, the pretense that it comes from a divine decision or the nature of things or reason proves on closer examination to be the glorification of an economically conditioned institution.'[21] However, as the development of the economy moves beyond its private, entrepreneurial phase into an era characterized by increasing monopolization and bureaucratic intervention, the individual becomes increasingly dependent on processes which lie beyond his or her control, and capacities for personal initiative become ever more redundant. In this context, the father is no longer able to provide a model of authority in the traditional sense, with its inextricable interweaving of rational and irrational dimensions. Rather, 'The fullest possible adaptation of the subject to the reified authority of the economy is the form which reason really takes in bourgeois society.'[22] The family, while not being abolished, is hollowed out, instrumentalized: the dialectic of the universal (society), the particular (the family), and the individual, as envisaged by Hegel, begins to split apart.[23]

Against the background of Horkheimer's views, it becomes apparent that there are two strands of diagnosis in Lacan's text. Lacan, too, lays considerable emphasis on the failure of the father as the crucial factor in contemporary character disorders. In his view, these disorders find their 'principal determination in the personality of the father, who is always lacking in some way, absent, humiliated, divided, or fake.'[24] Furthermore, his description of the results of this failure converges strikingly with the Frankfurt School account of the narcissistic personality:

> Like sinister godmothers installed at the cradle of the neurotic, impotence and utopianism enclose his ambition, so that he either smothers within himself the creations awaited by the world in which he appears, or misrecognizes his own impulse in the object against which he revolts.[25]

Lacan also admits that the decay of the paternal imago is in part at least the result of social and economic factors. It is a

> decline conditioned by the rebounding against the individual of the extreme effects of social progress, a decline which in our time is most pronounced in the collectivities which have been most tested by the effects of such progress, namely: the concentration of economic power and political catastrophes.[26]

Horkheimer makes the comparable claim that 'The cell of society is no longer the family but the social atom, the solitary individual. The struggle for existence consists in the resolution of the individual, in a world of apparatuses, machinery and manipulation, not to be annihilated at any moment.'[27] Unlike Horkheimer, however, Lacan detects another – perhaps deeper – reason for this decline, which he connects not with the lack of genuine individuality in mass society, but rather with the dialectic of individuation as such. In Lacan's view, Oedipal socialization requires what he calls a 'typical quality in the psychological relation between the parents';[28] in other words, well-defined maternal and paternal roles. However, in the ever more predominant 'conjugal marriage', dominated by the personal choice and interaction of the partners, this typical quality tends to disappear. What Lacan terms 'matrimonial demands' of the modern conjugal family, generated by the very conception of marriage as a relationship between equals, one might say, leads to the 'social decline of the paternal imago'.[29] At this level, Lacan's diagnosis could be said to run in the opposite direction to that of Horkheimer. For the latter, the crisis of individualization occurs at the point at which the tendencies towards concentration and bureaucratization of the capitalist economy begin to eliminate the need for individual creativity, judgement and conscience. For Lacan, however, working in an intellectual tradition profoundly influenced by Durkheim, it is individualization as such which poses the fundamental problem. The very 'coherence and creative *élan*' which modern culture demands of individuals produces a degree of *anomie* which destroys the minimum of typicality in the relation between the parents necessary for the functioning of the Oedipus complex. Once this historical turning point is reached, then personalities characterized by a 'narcissistic deviation of the libido' will begin to be formed.

III

As I have already indicated, a thought-provoking interpretation of the shift from the Lacan of *Les complexes familiaux* to the later and better-known Lacan has been provided by Mikkel Borch-Jacobsen. In his book, *Lacan: The Absolute Master*, and in a paper on 'The Oedipus problem', Borch-Jacobsen suggests that, in *Les complexes familiaux*, Lacan sets out to resolve a difficulty which had already troubled Freud: how can the identificatory rivalry of the Oedipal complex be resolved precisely through a *further* identification with the rival? Borch-Jacobsen argues that Lacan attempts to resolve this problem by drawing a much more rigorous distinction than Freud between the super-ego and the ego-ideal, the former forbidding rivalrous identification, and the latter encouraging a sublimatory identification.[30] As we have already seen, for the Lacan of *Les complexes familiaux* the contemporary crisis of Oedipal identity formation consists in the fact that this distinction is breaking down: both the 'lacking' father and the arbitrarily authoritarian father fail to sustain the delicate equilibrium between idealizing identification and repression.

On Borch-Jacobsen's reading, Lacan's later work, with its strict distinction between imaginary and symbolic registers, represents an attempt to shore up a form of identity formation which has already fallen into decay. The Lacanian concept of the 'name-of-the-Father', equivalent to the totem of 'primitive' societies in its function as the pole of identification which allows a symbolic resolution of the Oedipal crisis, and the concomitant distinction between the 'imaginary' and the 'symbolic' phallus, are in fact *normative* concepts and distinctions, vain attempts to sustain an ideal of subjectivity which no longer maps on to the actual social processes of identity formation. As Borch-Jacobsen writes:

> how is it possible to prevent the identification with the symbolic father-phallus from being confounded with the rivalrous and homosexualizing imaginary father-phallus? . . . it does absolutely no good whatsoever to invoke the *rightful* difference between the two identifications, since that difference, far from being a fundamental, *a priori* structure of every society, turns out actually to be bound solely to the 'elementary structures of kinship'. Our societies, on the other hand, are defined by a general crisis of symbolic identifications – 'deficiency of the paternal function', 'foreclosure of the name of the father', perpetual questioning of the symbolic 'law' and 'pact', confusion of lineage and general competition of generations, battle of the sexes, and loss of family landmarks.[31]

Borch-Jacobsen's own attitude to these social developments, however, is curiously insouciant. He believes it possible simply to 'stop treating the Oedipus complex as a *problem*', and to accept the accelerating symbolic breakdown of our societies.[32] But this response seems far too sanguine: Lacan was among the first twentieth-century thinkers to have grasped the significance of the rise of what he calls, in *Les complexes familiaux*, 'an introversion of the personality through a narcissistic deviation of the libido', [33] and in his diagnosis of the social consequences of this introversion he concurs to a considerable extent with other traditions of social critique. As a number of commentators have argued, the 'postmodern' dismantling of subjectivity and celebration of symbolic fragmentation, which view themselves as transcending such a standpoint of critique, in fact often result in an even more exaggerated form of subjectivist voluntarism.[34] One cannot simply brush aside Lacan's claim that 'the promotion of the ego, consistent with the utilitarian conception of man which reinforces it, culminates today in an ever more advanced realization of man as individual, that is to say, in an isolation of the soul ever more akin to its original dereliction'.[35] Thus the question must be posed of possible alternative patterns of identity formation, which would be opposed to the 'deregulation' to which Borch-Jacobsen seems resigned, but which would also bridge the impossible gulf between the *pays réel* and the *pays légal* which appears to open up in later Lacanian theory.

Understandably, it is above all feminist psychoanalysts, and psychoanalytically-informed feminist theorists, who have tried to address the issue of possibilities of post-Oedipal identity formation. For such identity formation, even if accepted as having been relatively 'successful' during a certain historical phase, suffers from an intrinsic gender disequilibrium and distortion. Indeed, it is fascinating to observe that, in the final pages of *Les complexes familiaux*, Lacan himself describes the crisis of Oedipal identity formation as inevitably arising from the historical suppression of the feminine principle. In a further dialectical twist, the progressive individualization which Oedipal socialization promotes leads to the rejection by women of their predetermined familial role. Thus, Lacan suggests, 'One may perceive in the virile protest of woman the ultimate consequence of the Oedipus complex.'[36] Lacan fully admits that 'the origins of our culture are too connected to what we willingly describe as the adventure of the paternalist family, for it not to impose, upon all the forms whose psychic development it has enriched, a prevalence of the male principle',[37] and he is aware that, in the long historical run, this social and cultural bias must generate an unstable situation. The occultation of the feminine principle by the masculine ideal, as he calls it, has resulted, in contemporary society, in an 'imaginary impasse of sexual polarization', in which are 'invisibly engaged' the 'forms of culture, morals and the arts, struggle and thought'.[38] Significantly, it is with this thought that *Les complexes familiaux* – somewhat abruptly – concludes: contemporary feminist theoreticians working within a psychoanalytic framework can be seen to be addressing precisely that 'social antinomy' which Lacan had presciently described, and found himself unable to circumvent, in 1938.

IV

In the concluding part of this discussion, I shall take the work of Jessica Benjamin as the primary example of an attempt to address the issues raised in *Les complexes familiaux* from a feminist perspective. Benjamin's work is of special interest in the present context because it seeks to build on and transform the heritage of the earlier Frankfurt School, which – in her view – leads to the same 'social antinomy' which we have just found evoked in Lacan. She considers that the Horkheimer view of individual capacities for non-conformity and critical resistance as grounded in the internalization of paternal authority fails to acknowledge the distorted form of identity produced by Oedipal socialization, which is based on an autarkic separation of the self from others and an instrumental relation to objects, at the cost of capacities for reciprocity and empathetic communication.[39]

The core of Benjamin's argument consists in the contention that symbolic *exclusivity* of the phallus, although not its *primacy* as the unconscious embodiment of agency and desire, is the result of an androcentric social structure.[40] Identifying with the father as bearer of the phallus allows the male child to separate from the mother, although to an excessive extent which involves a *repudiation* of femininity, while this identification is not adequately available to the female child, who nevertheless has no alternative route to independence. Benjamin's contention is that a more nurturing father and a more socially autonomous mother could provide *two* poles of idealizing identification, replacing the classical counter-position of progressive, individuating father against regressive mother.

Benjamin notes that theorists who lament the decline of the paternal imago rarely foreground the ambivalence of the father figure. Drawing on Freud's account of the genesis of the incest taboo through the overthrowing of the father of the primal horde in *Totem and Taboo*, Bejamin argues that:

> Paternal authority . . . is a far more complex emotional web than its defenders admit: it is not merely rooted in the rational law that forbids incest and patricide, but also in the erotics of ideal love, the guilty identification with power that undermines the son's desire for freedom.[41]

She suggests that it is not possible to make a hard and fast distinction between Oedipal and pre-Oedipal figures, and that it is misleading to do so in order to defend the notion of the rational, progressive father. To this extent, her account seems to focus on the crucial problem for Lacan highlighted by Borch-Jacobsen: Oedipal identity formation can only be defended as an ideal, on the normative assumption that ego-ideal and super-ego can and should be held apart, even though embodied in the same person. In Borch-Jacobsen's account, this has *never* been possible:

> For what mysterious reason should the hate identification with the rival *necessarily* be transformed into a respectful identification with the bearer of authority? Identification *is* precisely the reason for the rivalry and, even more essentially, for 'affective ambivalence', so there is every reason to believe that the post-Oedipal identification should, instead, perpetuate that ambivalence.[42]

In response to this problem, Benjamin contends that the pre-Oedipal identificatory love for the father cannot simply be equated with a rivalrous, homosexual identification. Rather,

> To explain what Freud called the 'short step from love to hypnotism', from ordinary identificatory love to bondage, we must look not merely to the distinction between oedipal and pre-oedipal, but to the fate of the child's love for the father in each phase . . . the idealization of the pre-oedipal father is closely associated with submission when it is thwarted, unrecognized.[43]

The importance of this argument is that, in Lacan's account, there is no equivalent *idealizing* identificatory love. Lacan, prior to the entry into the symbolic order brought about by the Oedipus complex, knows only the jealousy and rivalry of narcissistic identification, which – in *Les complexes familiaux* – he theorizes in terms of the child's relation to the intruding sibling. It is this rivalry which is ultimately broken by the identification with the paternal ego-ideal. Thus Lacan states:

> The identification, which was formerly mimetic, has become propitiatory: the object of sado-masochistic participation detaches itself from the subject, becomes distant from it in the new ambiguity of fear and love. But, in this step towards reality, the primitive object of desire [i.e. the mother] seems to vanish.[44]

However, if one distinguishes this process from that of an initial idealizing paternal identification, then a reinterpretation of the roles of the sexes also becomes possible. Benjamin stresses that the result of the Oedipus complex is that the male child must abandon not only his incestuous, but also his identificatory love for the mother. This is because, even more than in the case of the father, such identificatory love is taken to be regressive. In Lacan's early theory, for example, the maternal imago is described as embodying 'the metaphysical mirage of universal harmony, the mystical abyss of affective fusion, the social utopia of a totalitarian guardianship, all emerging from the haunting sense of the lost paradise before birth, and the more obscure aspiration towards death'.[45] Lacan is undoubtedly justified in pointing out that the interference of 'primordial identifications' will mark the maternal ego-ideal, and perhaps also in contending that the father presents the ego-ideal in its purest form, but he provides no explanation for his assertion that the maternal ideal must 'fail', leading to a feeling of repulsion on the part of the female child, and – presumably, by extension – in the case of the negative male Oedipus complex.[46] One might conclude that this failure, as in the paternal case, which Lacan himself – in part, at least – attributes to the pressure of social and economic factors, derives from the general lack of recognition of the autonomy of the mother. Benjamin herself is far from suggesting that the role of the father, and indeed of the phallus, in the process of separation and individuation can be superseded, but she argues nevertheless that the possibility for separation without rupture would be opened up by a different relation to the mother. In this case, the father might also be able more readily to accept the female child's phallic identification, since this identification would not be driven by the desperation of the need to break away from an engulfing mother.

It will be apparent that the key to Benjamin's revision of the Oedipus complex, which she wishes to view as 'only a step in mental life, one that leaves room for earlier and later levels of integration',[47] consists in her conception of the identificatory love which she associates with the pre-Oedipal *rapprochement* phase, in which the child seeks an initial balance between unity and separation. It is significant therefore that the French psychoanalyst Julia Kristeva should also be concerned with this type of love in her attempt to break down the rigidities of the Lacanian conception of Oedipal identity formation. Like Benjamin, Kristeva is engaged in a re-evaluation of narcissism, in an attempt to circumvent the aporia which she formulates in the observation that '[T]o seek to maintain, against the winds and tides of our modern civilization, the exigency of a severe father who, through his name, bestows on us separation, judgement and identity is a necessity, a more or less pious wish'.[48] Kristeva's more detailed investigations of the character of pre-Oedipal identificatory love may therefore provide a useful corroboration and substantiation of the perspective Jessica Benjamin seeks to propose.

Kristeva's essay, 'Freud et l'amour: le malaise dans la cure', in her book *Histoires d'amour*, is fundamentally an attempt to retheorize the notion of narcissism, so that narcissism no longer appears as constituting an inevitable block to the achievement of individuation. Kristeva seeks to show, contrary to Lacan's account, that the emergence of the subject cannot be connected exclusively with the Oedipal crisis, with the breaking apart of the mother–child dyad through the intervention of the father. In Kristeva's account narcissism already represents an advance over an undifferentiated auto-eroticism; it implies an initial gap between self and other before the intervention of the symbolic order, or rather before its intervention in its purely signifying aspect. Kristeva does not deny that the symbolic order is always already in place, but she suggests that there are diverse 'modalities of access' to the symbolic function. In imitating and, at the same time, libidinally investing the speech of the mother, the child is already entering into an identification which constitutes an elementary form of subjectivity. However, the other with whom the child identifies is not the purely symbolic other of Lacanian doctrine: 'Finally', Kristeva writes,

> by virtue of being the pole of a loving identification, the *Other* appears not as a 'pure signifier', but as the space of metaphorical movement itself: as the condensation of semic traits as well as the unrepresentable heterogeneity of the drives which subtends them, exceeds them and escapes them . . . Lacan situates idealization in the field of signifiers and of desire alone, and has detached it clearly – even brutally – both from narcissism and from the heterogeneity of the drives and their hold on the maternal container.[49]

However, for Kristeva, this initial identification does not take place with the mother figure alone. Here she agrees with Benjamin, who suggests that during the rapprochement phase the distinction between male and female identifications has not yet consolidated. Developing a suggestion of Freud, Kristeva describes an 'imaginary father', a 'coagulation of the mother and her desire', which allows the mother to function as lack and plenitude simultaneously, thereby making possible an initial distanciation *prior to* the entry into the Oedipal situation. The immediacy of the relation to this 'father–mother conglomerate', Kristeva suggests, has an important consequence: 'the term "object" like that of "identification" becomes *inappropriate* in this logic. A not-yet identity [of the child] is transferred, or rather is displaced, to the locus of an Other who is not yet libidinally invested as an object, but remains an Ego Ideal.'[50]

It is fascinating to observe how the concerns of Benjamin, emerging from and reacting to the Frankfurt School, and those of Kristeva, similarly related to Lacanian thought, converge in this respect. This convergence should not be taken to imply a strict parallelism between the traditions which they oppose, however. For if one looks more closely at Horkheimer's position, it appears that Horkheimer did not simply attribute individuation and a capacity for resistance to the role of the father, as Jessica Benjamin frequently claims. In his 1960 essay, 'Autorität und Familie in der Gegenwart', Horkheimer wrote:

> Earlier, the mother provided the child with a sense of security, which made it possible for it to develop a certain degree of independence. The child felt that the mother returned its love, and in a certain way drew on this fund of feeling throughout its life. The mother, who was cut off from the company of men and forced into a dependent situation, represented, despite her idealization, another principle than the reality principle.[51]

Horkheimer goes on explicitly to affirm that the sustaining of the child's relation to the mother can help to prevent too rapid an adaptation to reality, at the cost of individuation.

This conception might appear to be nostalgic, despite the fact that, in its emphasis, it coincides with, rather than contradicts, the tenor of Jessica Benjamin's account. The difference of orientation – bourgeois past, rather than feminist future – derives from Horkheimer's conviction that, with the increasing incorporation of women into the rationalized extra-familial world, the distinctive structure and emotional quality of the family is being destroyed: 'The equality of women, their professional activity, the much quicker emancipation of the children alters the atmosphere of the home. . . . Like existence in general, marriage is tending to become more rational, more purposive, more sober.'[52] Nevertheless, Horkheimer is in general critical of the separation of the sensual and the ideal in the traditional image of the mother, and in the father's attitude towards her. He argues that 'under the pressure of such a family situation the individual does not learn to understand and respect his mother in her concrete existence, that is, as this particular social and sexual being . . . the suppressed inclination towards the mother reappears as a fanciful and sentimental susceptibility to all symbols of the dark, maternal and protective powers'.[53] Thus, against Lacan's view, Horkheimer suggests that it is precisely the *repression* of identificatory love that would tend to transform the imago of the mother into a focus for the longing for regressive fusion. Furthermore, Horkheimer does not assume that, on logical grounds, a different orientation of social development might not be possible, in which, instead of rationalization transforming the mother into a mere relay of social authority, the specific positive capacities which women have developed because of their historical exclusion from the public realm might contribute to the transformation of the instrumentalized structures of society: '[The woman's] whole position in the family results in an inhibiting of important psychic energies which might have been effective in shaping the world.'[54]

V

At this point, however, it might appear plausible to object, from a Lacanian standpoint, that Horkheimer misunderstands the fundamental concepts of psychoanalytic theory, insofar as he equates 'repression' with a putative suppression of the corporeal, a renunciation of drive-satisfaction (*Triebverzicht*). It is striking, for example, that at the beginning of 'Authority and the family' Horkheimer quotes not Freud, but Nietzsche's *On the Genealogy of Morals*, in order to substantiate his view that 'the whole psychic apparatus of members of a class society, in so far as they do not belong to the nucleus of the privileged group, serves in large measure only to interiorize or at least to rationalize and supplement physical coercion'.[55] Psychoanalysis, on this view, explores the effects within the individual psyche of the general structures of social power. However, one could argue that this direct articulation of society and the psyche elides the complex relation between anxiety and phantasy in the formation of the '*urverdrängt*', the pre-social core of the repressed.

Lacan, by contrast, begins from the assumption that the process of weaning, the traumatic series of breaks with the mother which is the precondition of independent subjectivity, is always culturally structured, and that the subject can only transcend this trauma by internalizing and repeating it. In this interpretation, castration is not a threat in which real paternal authority is embodied; rather, it is a phantasy by means of which the subject both masters through repetition the anxiety of separation from the mother, and sets up a barrier against the regressive, indeed deathly, tendencies which the maternal imago embodies. The phantasy of castration, Lacan suggests,

> represents the defence which the narcissistic ego, identified with its specular double, opposes to the resurgence of anxiety which tends to overwhelm it, in the first stage of the Oedipus complex: a crisis which is caused not so much by the irruption of genital desire in the subject, as by the object which it reactualizes, namely the mother. The subject responds to the anxiety awakened by this object by reproducing the masochistic rejection through which it overcame its primordial loss, but it does so according to the structure which it has acquired, that is through an imaginary localization of the tendency.[56]

Thus from his early work onwards it was Lacan's view that the prohibiting father functions as the *support* of the phantasy of castration, which allows the child to master the trauma of separation from the mother. Furthermore, he suggests that in order for the child to achieve a measure of psychic independence, to come to *be* as a subject at all, the father's status must appear inexplicable and ungrounded, a sheer *social fact* to be accepted, like the facts of birth and weaning themselves. Such an account seems to entail that the need for authority finds an ultimate anchoring point in the unconscious, and – as such – is ineradicable.

There can be little doubt that Lacan's position corresponds more closely to the mature insights of Freud, as expressed – for example – in 'Inhibitions, symptoms, anxiety' (1926). Here Freud definitively abandons the view, recurrent throughout his earlier work, that repression is a form of defence against impulses which are incompatible with the social and ethical norms which have shaped the personality, and that it is the cathexis of the repressed idea which is transformed into anxiety. He now argues that 'It was anxiety which produced repression and not, as I formerly believed, repression which produced anxiety.'[57] In other words, it is the attempt to escape the feelings of helplessness arising from separation, first unavoidably experienced at birth, and later focused on the threat of castration, which becomes the core motive for the formation of neurotic symptoms of whatever kind. At the same time however, Freud also emphasizes that the ego learns to use modified 'doses' of anxiety – which he defines as 'a reaction to the danger of a loss of an object'[58] – in order both to master the emotion and to signal the need to ward off unwanted impulses. The only major alteration which Lacan introduces into this account is to deny Freud's assumption that the threat of castration which emerges in response to the impulse is in any sense 'real'.[59] On the contrary, as we have seen, the phantasy of castration, supported by the imputed authority of the father, protects the subject against the dangers of symbolic de-differentiation and merger. At the same time, however, the subject refuses this acknowledgement of radical insufficiency at the level of consciousness, falling victim to the narcissistic illusion of autonomy which is the core of the ego. Lacan summarizes this process, in *Les complexes familiaux*, with his reference to 'these inherent properties of the human subject, the miming of its own mutilation, and the seeing of itself as other than it is'.[60]

It is important to note, however, that by the time he came to co-author *Dialectic of Enlightenment* in 1944, Horkheimer had developed a conception of the 'primal history of subjectivity' that was far more complex than that of 'Authority and the family', and indeed far more 'psychoanalytical' in its interweaving of the themes of traumatic separation, law and sacrifice. In the Odysseus chapter of *Dialectic of Enlightenment*, the violence of the break between self and nature, which cannot help but take place in the interests of self-preservation, gives rise to a demand for restitution: 'The self wrests itself free from dissolution in blind nature, whose claim is always re-asserted by sacrifice.'[61] However, the more the self attempts to evade this demand, as Odysseus does through trickery in his repeated encounters with the mythic powers, the more the very form of its subjectivity becomes sacrifice: the denial of the superiority of nature leads merely to an illusion of independence from nature. 'The self-identical self, which originates in the overcoming of sacrifice, is indeed once again an unyielding, rigidified sacrificial ritual that men and women celebrate upon themselves by setting consciousness in opposition to the nexus of nature.'[62] In contrast to the assumptions of 'Authority and the family', this opposition, and its disastrous consequences, seems to follow inevitably from the emergence of the self as such, suggesting a convergence with Lacan's con- ception of irreducible trauma and illusion. There remains one important distinction between the two accounts, however. Despite their lack of any coherent alternative, non-repressive model of the self, Horkheimer and Adorno seek to suggest that the trauma of separation and its sacrificial repetition are not absolute preconditions of subjectivity, that 'the institution of sacrifice is the scar of an *historical* catastrophe, an act of force that befalls humanity and nature alike'.[63] Only in this way can they defend the validity of the 'urge for total, universal and undiminished happiness',[64] despite the evidently deathly features of the imago of nature-as-mother, which emerge – for example – in their commentary on the Sirens episode.

The comparison with Lacan makes clear that Horkheimer and Adorno can only cling to their extravagant ideal of reconciliation because of a primordial lack of differentiation between mother and father figures. It is the power of nature which is 'mythically objectified' in the form of legal relationships, of the archaic contracts which Odysseus seeks to evade, so that the 'remembrance of nature in the subject' which the book famously invokes would presumably also bring about the dissolution of legal form. In *Dialectic of Enlightenment* this form is no more than a normative cosmetic for the brute facticity of superior power. By contrast, Lacan's conception of submission to a symbolic law which originates elsewhere than from the mother, and which is essential to the subject as precondition of its existence as lack of desire, undermines any antinomian utopia. It does so, however, at the cost of instating an essentially 'alienated' subject – capable of sustaining its being only by bowing to an authority whose prototype is that of the father, and which must ultimately remain inscrutable.

Is there any way out of this impasse? I would suggest that at least the direction in which a solution could be sought may emerge if we read a certain response to Horkheimer and Adorno, within the Frankfurt School tradition, *against the grain* of its own intentions. It is well known that Jürgen Habermas has criticized *Dialectic of Enlightenment* for continuing the type of totalizing critique initiated by Nietzsche, which strives for an ultimate revelation of the intertwining of genesis and validity, power and reason, rather than accepting that their disintrication can only be an ongoing, dialogical process.[65] At the same time, however, it could be argued that Habermas himself seeks to play down the traumatic features of the separation between genesis and validity which his own account of the quasi-transcendental norms of dialogue presupposes. Thus, on the one hand, Habermas repeatedly refers to the 'Janus-face' of validity claims, to the fact that they are torn between particularity and universality, immanence and transcendence, and he describes their effectivity in violent terms, as a force which 'bursts every provinciality asunder', indeed which '"blots out" space and time'.[66] Yet, on the other hand, Habermas wishes to deny that his position implies any problematic tension or split between empirical and transcendental, factual and normative dimensions, which would endanger the general project of a reconciliatory 'de-sublimation' or naturalization of reason.[67]

Yet perhaps we should read Habermas against himself. Such a reading might make apparent that entry into the normative dimension of human communication and social regulation does indeed involve a traumatic break with the bond we can think of as maternal. But at the same time the acceptance that the *normative* as such, the symbolic law in Lacan's terms, emanates neither from one nor from a collectivity of subjects, should not be equated with submission to specific, contingent social norms. There is indeed a painful decentring and wounding of narcissism contained in the realization that – as Habermas puts it – 'we are exposed to the movement of a transcendence from within which is no more at our disposal than the actuality of the spoken word makes us masters of the structure of language (or logos)'.[68] Yet this realization need not entail the acceptance of an authority which is ultimately exempt from requirements of legitimation, as Lacan's notion of the paternal function as support of the 'law' often seems to imply. At the same time, however, it is clear that feminist attempts to think beyond the impasse of Oedipal identity cannot simply shift the emphasis to the continuities between the emerging self and its environment, in order to combat the traditional 'masculine' stress on forms of rupture and radical division. Such attempts must also explore new ways of figuring the inevitable anguish of loss and self-dispossession. Significantly, whereas Lacan insists that 'castration anxiety is like a thread which runs through all the stages of development', [69] Freud himself was more circumspect, sometimes allowing that the castration complex was merely one of a series of encounters with 'the danger of psychical helplessness'.[70] Thus the founding texts of psychoanalysis leave open the space for a rethinking of individuation and autonomy, one which could acknowledge an irreducible core of dependency while relativizing the gender-skewed images of separation as mutilation which are still so centrally embedded in our culture.

ACKNOWLEDGEMENT

Thanks are due to Joel Whitebook for a helpful discussion of some of the central issues raised.

NOTES

1 Jacques Lacan, 'La signification du phallus', in *Ecrits*, Paris: Editions du Seuil, 1966, p. 688.
2 Jacqueline Rose, 'Feminine sexuality – Jacques Lacan and the école freudienne', in *Sexuality in the Field of Vision*, London: Verso, 1986, p. 80.
3 Ibid., p. 81. Other feminist defences of Lacan's theory of sexual difference are even less reflective. Ellie Ragland-Sullivan, for example, simply asserts that 'culture paradoxically crowns the male with the empty signifier of difference itself as standing in for limit or law', without offering any account of why this 'paradox' should arise. Cf. 'The sexual masquerade', in Ellie Ragland-Sullivan and Mark Bracher (eds), *Lacan and the Subject of Language*, New York and London: Routledge, 1991, p. 75. It should be added that Rose's more recent shift from Lacan towards Klein has not altered her somewhat simplifying conviction that feminist revisions of traditional psychoanalytic doctrine are invariably based on 'the idyll of early fusion with the mother'. Cf. 'Negativity in the work of Melanie Klein', in Jacqueline Rose, *Why War?*, Oxford: Blackwell, 1993, p. 140.
4 Theodor Adorno, 'Psychology and sociology', *New Left Review*, 47, January–February 1967, p. 90.
5 See, for example, the essays by Nancy Fraser, Iris Marion Young and Seyla Benhabib, in Seyla Benhabib and Drucilla Cornell (eds), *Feminism as Critique*, Oxford: Polity, 1987.
6 Jacques Lacan, *Les complexes familiaux* (1938), Paris: Navarin, 1984, p. 49.
7 Ibid.
8 Ibid., p. 50.
9 Ibid., pp. 66–7.
10 Ibid., p. 68.
11 Ibid., p. 70.
12 Ibid., 71.
13 Ibid.

14 Ibid., p. 66.
15 Ibid., p. 67.
16 Ibid., pp. 95–6.
17 Max Horkheimer, 'Authority and the family', in *Critical Theory: Selected Essays*, New York: Continuum, 1972, p. 56.
18 Ibid., p. 101.
19 Ibid., p. 71.
20 Ibid., p. 127.
21 Ibid., p. 123.
22 Ibid., p. 83.
23 Ibid., p. 128.
24 *Les complexes familiaux*, p. 73.
25 Ibid.
26 Ibid., p. 72.
27 Max Horkheimer, 'Venunft und selbsterhaltung' (1942), in *Traditionelle und kritische Theorie*, Frankfurt am Main: Fischer Verlag, 1992, p. 288.
28 *Les complexes familiaux*, p. 103.
29 Ibid., p. 72.
30 Cf. Mikkel Borch-Jacobsen, 'The Oedipus problem in Freud and Lacan', in *Critical Inquiry*, 20 (2), winter 1994, pp. 277–82.
31 Ibid., p. 282.
32 Ibid. Cf. the comparable discussion in Mikkel Borch-Jacobsen, *Lacan. The Absolute Master*, Stanford, California, Stanford University Press 1991, ch. 1. As we shall see, Borch-Jacobsen's suggestion, in both texts, that Lacan is merely nostalgic for 'good old traditional societies, where one still knew *who* one was' (*The Absolute Master*, p. 41) fails to consider his awareness of the basic instability of patriarchal structures.
33 *Les complexes familiaux*, p. 107.
34 See, for example, Charles Taylor, 'Logics of disintegration', *New Left Review* 170, July-August 1988, pp. 110–16.
35 Jacques Lacan, 'Aggressivity in psychoanalysis', in *Ecrits; A Selection*, London: Routledge, 1977, p. 27.
36 *Les complexes familiaux*, pp. 110–11.
37 Ibid.
38 Ibid., p. 112.
39 See Jessica Benjamin, 'Authority and the family revisited: or, A world without fathers', in *New German Critique*, 13, 1978, pp. 35–58.
40 In fact, this is Jessica Benjamin's implicit, rather than explicitly stated position. At a number of points in her book *The Bonds of Love* (London: Virago, 1990), she makes the argument against the Lacanian position that 'In the pre-Oedipal world, the father and his phallus are powerful because of their ability to stand for separation from the mother' (p. 95). At the same time, however, Benjamin also admits that 'the . . . problem is that the symbolic level of the psyche already seems to be occupied by the phallus' (p. 124). Her solution is to propose a symbolization of woman's desire in terms of Winnicott's notion of 'holding space', which would not seek to rival or supplant the symbolism of the phallus but rather to co-exist with it. Cf. *The Bonds of Love*, pp. 123–32.
41 *The Bonds of Love*, p. 143.
42 'The Oedipus problem', pp. 273–4.
43 *The Bonds of Love*, pp. 145–6.
44 *Les complexes familiaux*, p. 63.
45 Ibid., p. 35.
46 Cf. ibid., pp. 64–5.
47 *The Bonds of Love*, p. 177. Benjamin has recently pushed this revision further by emphasizing the potential 'post-Oedipal' role of early cross-gender *identifications* in helping to overcome the rigidity of Oedipal *identity*. Cf. chapter 6, this volume.

48 Julia Kristeva, 'Freud et l'amour: le malaise dans la cure', in *Histoires d'amour*, Paris: Éditions Denoël, 1983 (paperback edition), p. 62.
49 Ibid., p. 53.
50 Ibid., p. 56.
51 Max Horkheimer, 'Autorität und Familie in der Gegenwart', in *Zur Kritik der instrumentellen Vernunft*, Frankfurt am Main: Fischer Verlag, 1985, p. 278.
52 Max Horkheimer, 'Die Zukunft der Ehe', in *Zur Kritik der Instrumentellen Vernunft*, p. 298.
53 'Authority and the family', p. 121.
54 Ibid., p. 120. For a further critical response to Benjamin's critique of Horkheimer, see Pauline Johnson, 'Feminism and images of autonomy', in *Radical Philosophy*, 50, Autumn 1988.
55 Ibid., p. 56.
56 Ibid., p. 61.
57 'Inhibitions, symptoms and anxiety', in Sigmund Freud, *On Psychopathology*, Pelican Freud Library vol. 10, Harmondsworth 1979, p. 263.
58 Ibid., p. 329.
59 Freud persists bizarrely, throughout this text, in speaking as though castration were a genuine danger, e.g.: 'We have also come to the conclusion that an instinctual demand often only becomes an (internal) danger because its satisfaction would bring on an external danger – that is, because the internal danger represents an external one' (p. 328).
60 *Les complexes familiaux*, pp. 93–4.
61 Theodor Adorno and Max Horkheimer, 'Odysseus or myth and enlightenment' (new translation by Robert Hullot-Kentnor), in *New German Critique*, 56, Spring/Summer 1992, p. 118.
62 Ibid., pp. 118–19.
63 Ibid., p. 116. My emphasis.
64 Ibid., p. 122.
65 Jürgen Habermas, *The Philosophical Discourse of Modernity*, Cambridge, MA: MIT Press, 1988, p. 130.
66 Ibid., pp. 322, 323.
67 Herbert Schnädelbach has skilfully highlighted the incompatibility between the Kantian structures of Habermas's theory and his attachment to a naturalistic version of reconciliation *motifs* inherited from Hegel and the Left Hegelians. Cf. 'Das Gesicht im Sand. Foucault und der anthropologische Schlummer', in Schnädelbach, *Zur Rehabilitierung des 'animal rationale'. Vorträge und Abhandlungen 2*, Frankfurt am Main: Suhrkamp Verlag, 1992.
68 Jürgen Habermas, 'Transzendenz von innen, Transzendenz ins Diesseits', in *Texte und Kontexte*, Frankfurt: Suhkamp Verlag, 1991, p. 142.
69 Jacques Lacan, *Le séminaire livre XI: Les quatres concepts fondamentaux de la psychanalyse*, Paris: Editions du Seuil, 1973, p. 62.
70 Cf. 'Inhibitions, symptoms and anxiety', pp. 299–301, and the commentary in Jean Laplanche, *Problématiques II: Castration. Symbolizations*, Paris: Presses Universitaires de France, 1980, pp. 154–61.

4　On the subject of Lacan

David Macey

> Everyone is a Hegelian without realizing it.
>
> (Lacan 1978: 93)

The notion of a 'subject' is effectively ubiquitous throughout the human sciences, where it tends to replace or displace such notions as 'individual', 'self' or even 'ego'. The term constantly migrates across semantic fields and discursive domains, and is both a grammatical and a quasi-legal category. Lacan's subject is, for instance, both a linguistic entity and the subject of (or the subject produced by) its subordination of the law of the symbolic, governed in the last instance by the prohibition of incest. It can be either active or passive: the 'I' can be the subject of a statement (but may not be identical with the subject of the utterance), or of a political formation (a British subject). Within the Lacanian field itself, usage varies from the 'speaking subject' of the 'phenomenological description of the psychoanalytic experience' of 1951 (Lacan 1966a: 82–5) to Jacques-Alain Miller's admonition 'Remember you are nothing more than a subject of the unconscious' (Auffret 1990: 373), a statement which is as irrefutable as it is intimidatory.

The ubiquity of the concept of a 'subject' sheds little light on its genealogy or archaeology. While it would no doubt be possible to find antecedents in ancient philosophy, it is conventional to regard the notion as originating in the early modern period (see, for example, Howells 1992: 318–52); most French dictionaries trace the acceptation 'an individual being or person considered as the support for an action' back to the seventeenth century. Lacan himself tends to view the Descartes of the *cogito* as the paradigm for the classical subject, and to argue that the psychoanalytic experience leads us to 'oppose any philosophy stemming directly from the *Cogito*' (Lacan 1977: 165).

Thanks largely to Lacan, a distaste for the *cogito* became one of the *topoi* of 'structuralist' writing, though the extension given to it can be almost caricatural when 'Cartesian' becomes a pejorative term applying to any philosophy of consciousness. When, in 1962 for instance, Lévi-Strauss attacks Sartre for his alleged concentration of the psychological and the individual and opines that 'by sociologising the Cogito, Sartre merely exchanges one prison for another' (Lévi-Strauss 1972: 249), he simply obscures the definitive kinship between the subject of the mirror stage and the ego described in Sartre's earliest philosophical writings

(Sartre 1936–7. For the parallel, see Macey 1988: 103–4, and Howells 1992: 362 f).

The philosophical genealogy of the subject also encompasses empiricist or sensualist descriptions of the bundles of sense perceptions that generate subjectivity. More significant, however, is Kant's reference to 'The *I think* (that) must accompany all my representations. . . . But this representation, *I think*, is an act of spontaneity . . . pure apperception . . . a self-consciousness which, whilst it gives birth to the representation *I think*, must necessarily be capable of accompanying all our representations' (Kant 1934: 94).

If Descartes and Kant represent a classic and heroic incarnation of the subject (Descartes's subject is destined to be the possessor and master of nature), much of the work of philosophical and literary modernism has been devoted to the undoing of this sovereign figure. Novelists like Proust chart the dissolution of subjectivity into uncertain mirages and crystallized memories, but it is probably Nietzsche who delivers the hammer blow when he remarks that:

> A thought comes when 'it' wants, not when 'I' want it; so that it is a *falsification* of the facts to say: the subject 'I' is the condition of the predicate 'think'. *It* thinks: but that this 'it' is precisely that famous old 'I' is, to put it mildly, only an assumption, an assertion, above all not an 'immediate certainty'.
>
> (Nietzsche 1990: 47)

Nietzsche's anti-Kantian aphorisms are an important moment in the emergence of the contention that subjectivity is an effect rather than a cause, that something – the unconscious, language – speaks through and of the individual. As Heidegger puts it, *die Sprache spricht* : 'Man acts as though he were the shaper and master of language. While in fact *language* remains the master of man' (Heidegger 1971: 146). And as Lacan might put it, the subject is an effect of the primacy of the signifier: 'It is obvious that the things of the human world are the things of a world structured as speech, that language, that symbolic processes, dominate, govern everything' (Lacan 1986: 57).

Nietzsche's 'it' (*Es*) is, it will be recalled, the ancestor of Freud's 'id' (*Es*), the link between the two being the distinctly improbable figure of Georg Groddeck, author of a psychosomatic theory that borders on the mystical (Groddeck 1935). While the notion of the id owes at least something to Nietzsche, it is tempting to see the opposite pole of the psychic personality (as described by Freud after the 'turning point' of 1920) as belonging in part to the classical tradition of the subject. The evolution of the concept of the ego in Freud's work is very complex (see Laplanche and Pontalis 1986), but in its most familiar incarnation – that described in *The Ego and the Id* – it does appear to have many of the attributes of the 'famous old "I" '. It inherits many of the characteristics of the preconscious-conscious system of the first topography. The ego controls perception and is responsible for reality testing. It is the seat of rational thought, and the agency which introduces – or attempts to introduce – a temporal order into mental processes. From this reformulation will emerge the elective object of Lacan's scorn and loathing: the ego-psychology of Hartmann, Kris and Loewenstein. Ego-psychology is viewed both as a return to a pre-Freudian psychology and as a quintessentially American form of social engineering, to the extent that it speaks of the emergence of conflict-free spheres and of social adaptation:

> The new gospel of the autonomous ego and the conflict-free sphere proclaimed to the New York circle by Monsieur Heinz Hartmann is merely the ideology of a class of immigrés worried about the prestige that ruled Central European society at the time when, thanks to the wartime diaspora, they had to settle in a society where values are sedimented around the income-tax scale.
>
> (Lacan 1966b: 8)

The return to Freud proclaimed by Lacan is intended as a critique of ego-psychology and of any attempt to promote or reinforce an instance or agency of the personality that is an imaginary construct, 'an imaginary identification or, to be more accurate, an enveloping series of such identifications' (Lacan 1966b: 8). To reinforce the ego is, in this perspective, to reinforce the very seat or focus of the resistances. The return to Freud is a return to the fundamental discovery of the unconscious, which is held to subvert conventional notions of the subject. Lacan's viperish remarks about America probably reflect an anti-Americanism that was far from uncommon in France, rather than any concern for accurate historiography: it is perfectly possible to regard Anna Freud as the mother of ego-psychology (Freud 1936). It also reflects a provocative taste for scandal. Lacan clearly identifies with the Freud who reportedly told Jung that the Americans 'do not realize that we are bringing them the plague' (Lacan 1966b: 403), in a mode that irresistibly reminds one of the surrealist frequentations of his youth.There is no independent confirmation of Lacan's claim that Jung told him of this.

Caught between the imperatives of the super-ego and the instinctual demands of the id, the ego is not, however, master in its own house and cannot aspire to Cartesian certainties, though it is perhaps worth noting in passing that it is not assailed by Cartesian doubts either. The revolution introduced by the discovery of the unconscious is akin to earlier scientific revolutions. Freud does not usually describe himself as having instigated a philosophical revolution, but as continuing a sequence of punctual scientific revolutions (see in particular 'The Question of Weltanschauung', S.E. 22). The Copernican revolution subverted geocentrism. The Darwinian revolution was a further narcissistic blow which discomfited the anthropocentric illusion; Freud demonstrates that the human psyche is not under the rational and conscious control of the ego or I. The existence of the unconscious radically decentres human subjectivity. In the matter of the ego and the subject, as in so many other areas, Freud appears to stand on the cusp between the nineteenth and twentieth centuries, between the pre-modern and the modern. It is almost as though he were describing the transition from an age marked by his own positivist certainties to the much darker future adumbrated by Nietzsche. Fittingly, *Die Traumdeutung* was published on 4 November 1899, but the title page bears the date '1900' (Gay 1989: 3).

The ego of *The Ego and the Id* is the final product of a slow process of elaboration and revision on Freud's part (Freud 1923: 1–66). In terms of Lacan's development, the key Freudian reference is to transitional texts like 'On

Narcissism' (Freud 1914: 67–104). While the very young child lives in a state of auto-eroticism (which precedes the differentiation of the ego) narcissism induces a sense of self by supplying a perceptive image, a psychical construct that exists in parallel to the real body. Narcissism underpins the jubilation of the mirror-phase, but it also generates a degree of alienation: the ego is from the outset an ego-ideal or an ideal image of narcissistic omnipotence, and therefore a self-estranged subject. It is this that provides, in metapsychological terms, the starting point for Lacan's assault on the ego and for his theory of the subject; referring to 'On Narcissism', he remarks, 'In Freud, the theory of the ego is intended . . . to show that what we call our ego is a certain image that we have of ourselves, an image that produces a mirage, of totality no doubt' (Lacan 1981: 273).

Lacan's relationship with Freud is, however, never simple and claims that, to borrow Althusser's famous phrase, 'he thinks only Freud's concepts' are simply misleading (Althusser 1971: 199. For a discussion of the 'conceptuality' at stake here, see Macey 1994). Lacan's early influences range from the classical psychiatry in which he was trained to phenomenology and surrealism – the probable source for the fascination with language that predates any reference in his work to linguistics (Macey 1988). And as a sympathetic but at times sardonic historian of psychoanalysis observes, one of Lacan's talents is the ability 'to effect a new interpretation of an original body of thought . . . to make Freud's text say what it does not say' (Roudinesco 1990: 138). If there was one master who schooled Lacan in this art, it was the Russian émigré philosopher Alexandre Kojève.

Kojève is never mentioned by name in *Ecrits*, though Lacan does acknowledge his debt to him elsewhere (Lacan 1968: 96–7). Although Lacan is notorious for his failure to supply detailed reference for his allusions, the omission of Kojève's name is probably the effect of his identification with Hegel. There is little evidence to suggest that Lacan has any great familiarity with the Hegelian system as a whole, and references to 'Hegel' are best read as metonymic allusions to Kojève. A whole generation could acknowledge the same debt. An exploration of Lacan's personal debt cannot of course explain his work; it does provide a reference without which his work remains incomprehensible.

The course on Hegel taught by Kojève at Ecole Pratique des Hautes Etudes between 1933 and 1939 is, like the surrealism in which Lacan is steeped, the cornerstone of the philosophical experience of a generation: Georges Bataille, Raymond Queneau, André Breton, Michel Leiris, Jacques Lacan, Pierre Klossowski and so on. This is a generation whose concerns seem to anticipate to a remarkable degree the concerns of so-called postmodernism or poststructuralism, so much so that it is tempting to repeat Marx's pseudo-Hegelian adage about history and farce. No reader of Bataille or Klossowski will be surprised at Lacan's dialectics of death and desire, at references to the fading or dissolution of subjectivity or at the contention that the object of desire is always-already a lost object. No one familiar with Leiris's *L'Age d'homme* will be surprised to learn that the ego is a collage of identifications, the work of a psychic *bricolage* (Leiris 1946). The collective intellectual biography of this generation has yet to be written in any detail, although we do now have important elements thereof (see, for instance, Hollier 1979; Auffret 1990; Stoekl 1990, 1992). When it is written, it will no doubt do a lot to elucidate the philosophical origins of Lacanian psychoanalysis. As matters stand, a blind tasting of some sample utterances is likely to produce some intriguing (mis)recognitions. Thus, the contention that 'Man is what is lacking in man' is not of Lacanian provenance and is not a reference to the *Spaltung*, but a note drafted by Bataille in 1930 (Bataille 1971: 419. Cf. Macherey 1990: 111). It is also a pertinent reminder that many of Lacan's formulations are not the product of a theoretical ideolect, but survivals of a specific sociolect. It is from Kojève that an intellectual generation learned to speak of the cunning of reason, of struggle for pure recognition, of the beautiful soul, the unhappy consciousness and the desire for a desire, that they learned to describe death as the absolute master, and to meditate (even before they had read Heidegger) upon being towards death.

Kojève's seminar on Hegel began in 1933, and focused on *The Phenomenology of Mind*. The text itself was not available in French – and would not become available until Hyppolite's two-volume translation appeared in 1939–41. For most academic philosophers, Hegel himself was something of an unknown quantity. As Hyppolite (born in 1907) explains, his generation had been reared on a diet of neo-Kantianism: French philosophers distrusted the post-Kantians, and especially Hegel, partly because of their Cartesian suspicion of universal philosophies of history, partly because of the lingering suspicion that Hegelianism was a thinly disguised pan-Germanism (Hyppolite 1971: 31–2). The seminar, which Lacan attended quite assiduously between 1933 and 1937, is therefore a crucial moment in the history of French Hegelianism (on French Hegelianism see Kelly 1990 and Butler 1987). Kojève would read passages from Hegel in German and translate them orally, adding a commentary as he proceeded. The result is a strange, dense text in which the voices of Hegel and Kojève mingle. Kojève's commentary generates a narrative which is not necessarily identical with Hegel's. Hegel's narrative is about the gradual emergence of absolute knowledge; Kojève's is largely about the end of history, a theme which has recently been revived in a curious coda to the alleged death of metanarratives (Fukuyama 1992). It is one of the sub-plots that was to leave its mark on Lacan.

Kojève's seminar is arguably the prototype for one of the most characteristic forms of teaching to have developed in contemporary France: the small seminar of a 'master' whose teachings are transcribed after the event but which initially circulate in almost clandestine form. The text itself, edited by Raymond Queneau, did not appear until 1947, by which time its influence had spread pervasively but silently. The parallel with Lacan is remarkable. The latter's seminar began in 1951 and initially focused on readings of the 'Dora' and 'Rat-Man' cases; no transcript survives (Lacan 1979: 289–307; 386–425). Until the publication of *Ecrits* in 1966 propelled him into an unexpected bestsellerdom, Lacan's texts circulated in small-run and specialist publications like *La Psychanalyse*, the journal of the Société Française de Psychanalyse. The seminar – a small and private gathering which eventually mutated into intellectual Paris's most spectacular moveable feast

– was the original conduit for Lacan's influence and its medium was, appropriately enough, the spoken word. ('Appropriately' in that 'Psychoanalysis has only a single medium: the patient's speech' (Lacan 1966a: 40).) The appeal of orality, as practised by both Kojève and Lacan, is well captured by Maurice Blanchot; it is a mode of reflection that is 'solicited by the non-familiar'. 'There is no recognition in what it aims at; everything begins again each time, the decision to expose oneself to the non-known' (Blanchot 1963: 736). It must be recalled that virtually all of Lacan's 'writings' (*Ecrits*) were originally oral presentations, that in many ways the open-ended Seminar was his preferred environment.

The published text of Kojève's seminar, as transcribed and edited by Queneau, opens with a commentary on Section A of chapter 4 of *The Phenomenology of Mind* ('Independence and dependence of self-consciousness: lordship and bondage'). Two narratives intertwine as Kojève begins his anthropological reading of one of the classics of the idealist tradition:

> Man is self-consciousness. He is conscious of himself, and conscious of his human reality and dignity, and to that extent there is an essential difference between man and the animal, which never goes beyond the level of a mere feeling of self. Man becomes conscious of himself at the moment when – for the first time – he says Me [*Moi*]. Understanding man by understanding his origins therefore means understanding the origins of the Ego as revealed by speech.
>
> (Kojève 1990: 11)

The development of self-consciousness is not a linear process of expansive self-realization, and requires the intervention of desire. Lost in contemplation of the object of his desire, man has to be reminded of, or recalled to, his own existence:

> It is desire that transforms the being revealed to itself by itself in the (true) knowledge an object 'revealed' to a 'subject' by a subject differing from and standing over against it. It is in and through or, more accurately, as 'his' desire that man constitutes himself and reveals himself – to himself and others – as an Ego, or as an Ego essentially different to and radically opposed to the non-Ego. The (human) Ego is the Ego of a desire or of Desire.
>
> (Ibid.)

In a sense, Kojève-Hegel here rejoins a philosophical tradition that sees desire as the human essence. Spinoza, for instance, regards *cupiditas* as 'the very essence of man in so far as it is conceived as determined to do something by some given modification of itself' (Spinoza 1910: 128). The Kojèvean-Hegelian ego or subject is not, however, simply the construct of its self-modification. Desire is less desire for an object than a movement that transcends reality (and to that extent resembles Sartre's negativity). Until such time as it is satisfied, desire is the revelation of an absence, a void. A primal dialectic of desire begins to unfold, with the ego as one pole of its development rather than its source. As desire is realised through the negation of the given, a future-oriented action is the very being of the ego: 'This

Ego will therefore be its own construct: it will be (in the future) what it has become (in the present) of what it has been (in the past), that negation having been effected with a view to what it will become' (Kojève 1990: 128).

Temporality is thus being's prime mode of existence. With some slight modification, this vision of temporality is transposed by Lacan to read: 'What is realised in my history is not the past definite of what it was, since it is no more, or the present perfect of what has been in what I am, but the future anterior of what I shall have been for what I am in the process of becoming' (Lacan 1966a: 86). The object of desire is not some physical object or function (such as nutrition), but another desire. Anthropogenic desire differs from animal desire in that it takes as its object not a real, positive or given desire, but the desire of an other:

> Thus, in relations between men and women, for example, Desire is human only if one part desires, not the body, but the Desire of the other, only if he wants to possess or assimilate Desire as desire, or in other words if he wants to be desired or loved or recognized in his human value, in his reality as a human individual.
>
> (Kojève 1990: 12–13)

The dialectic of desire and recognition eventually spirals into the master–slave dialectic. Human desire is human only if the subject can transcend the animal desire for self-preservation. Only a subject who is willing to risk (animal) life for the sake of desire is truly human. Given that desire is always desire for the desire of the other, the result is a potential struggle to the death for the recognition of one's desire. To abandon one's desire and to submit to recognize the other is to become a slave; to risk one's life in a bid for recognition is to become a master. The slave, however, is the ultimate victor who transforms (negates) nature through his labour; the master passively consumes the labour of the other in an act of futile and sterile enjoyment (*jouissance*). Through his labour, the slave will eventually achieve freedom and to that extent the master is, according to Lacan, 'the great dupe, the magnificent cuckold of historical evolution' (Lacan 1986: 21).

Kojève's reading of Hegel provides, in the immediate post-war years, a *lingua franca*. As an influential historian of modern French philosophy remarks, 'it became the place where the multiple references of the period converged . . . the desire for a *common language*, which it seemed at the time, would have to be Hegelian' (Descombes 1980: 11). One of its most fluent speakers was Jean Hyppolite. Speaking a rather more academic dialectic which has nothing of Kojève's densely impacted style, he too makes central the category of desire:

> The desire for life becomes the desire for another desire, or rather, given the necessary reciprocity of the phenomenon, human desire is always *a desire for the desire of another*. In human love, desire appears to me as the desire for the desire of the other. I need to contemplate myself in the other. Now, I am essentially desire. What I have to find in the other is the desire of my desire . . . I appear to myself in the other, and the other appears to me as myself.
>
> (Hyppolite 1971: 115)

Hyppolite has no difficulty in tracing the brief discussion of the *fort-da* game in Lacan's 'Rome Discourse' of 1953 back to its Hegelian matrix, or in asserting that it would be more profitable to relate the thesis of the 'mirror-phase' to Hegel than to the experimental protocols on which it was allegedly based (Hyppolite 1971: 218n). The point is made in a lecture delivered to the Société Française de Psychanalyse in January 1955, and published in Lacan's *La Psychanalyse* in 1957. It does not seem entirely unreasonable to suppose that it had Lacan's *imprimatur* and tacit approval. The theory of the mirror-stage is of course Lacan's first great contribution to psychoanalysis, but it would be difficult indeed to describe it as the product of a meditation on Freud's concepts alone. The chronology of its elaboration is not entirely clear; although a paper on the mirror-stage was read by Lacan to the 1936 Marienbad Congress of the IPA, he omitted to submit it for publication in the Congress proceedings. The paper included in *Ecrits* is from 1949. The 'phase' refers to the child's encounter with its image in a mirror (or equivalent). The child greets the image with jubilation; it represents a perfect whole endowed with a degree of motor control that the child has yet to achieve in reality. The image also provides a defence against the contravailing image or fantasy of fragmentation, of the 'body in pieces'. The behaviour associated with the phase is characterized by aggression towards others, and particularly towards children of the same age. The aggressivity centres around a play of mirror images: the child who hits its fellow will burst into tears. Aggression and erotically-tinged identification with an image are constituent elements of the subject. The subject is constituted as its own rival.

The 'experimental protocols' referred to by Hyppolite are supplied by child psychology and primate ethology. Thus it is claimed that, unlike a chimpanzee of similar age, the human child is captivated by its mirror image and that this captivation inaugurates an epic of alienation–identification that will structure the ego as other. The negative proofs of Lacan's thesis tend to come from the child psychology of Henri Wallon (Wallon 1947). The underlying theoretical structure, on the other hand, clearly derives from Kojève-Hegel and was one which circulated widely in the late 1940s and 1950s. Possibly the clearest formulations are from 1946 (published 1950), when Lacan ascribes to Hegel the thesis that 'man's very desire is constituted . . . under the sign of mediation; it is a desire to have his desire recognized. It has as its object a desire; that of "the other" ' (Lacan 1966a: 181), and 1948: 'Hegel . . . provided the ultimate theory of the proper function of aggressivity in human ontology, seeming to prophecy the iron law of our time. From the conflict of Master and Slave, he deduced the entire subjective and objective progress of our history' (Lacan 1977: 26).

Even after the introduction of the reference to language that generates the description of the unconscious as being 'structured like a language', the position of the subject is mapped in terms of representation and recognition. In asserting the signifier's priority over the subject, Lacan argues in 1960 that 'a signifier represents a subject for another signifier' (Lacan 1966a: 840). Here, the terminology is that of the Lacan who, from the 1950s onwards, incorporates elements of the linguistics of Saussure and Jakobson into his theoretical armoury, but the underlying thesis is still that of a relationship of recognition. As the references to ethology indicate, Lacan's theorization of the subject makes frequent reference to a key moment in the Hegelian metanarrative: that of the emergence from animality of a human desire and consciousness. It is not difficult to map this moment on to Lévi-Strauss's nature–culture transition and to the central role of the incest taboo in its negotiation (see in particular Lévi-Strauss 1969). 'The primordial Law is therefore that which in regulating marriage ties superimposes the kingdom of culture on that of a nature abandoned to the law of mating. The prohibition of incest is merely its subjective pivot' (Lacan 1977: 66). Lévi-Strauss undoubtedly owes much more to the French sociological tradition of Durkheim and Mauss, with its emphasis on the symbolic foundations of social organization, than to Hegel's chronicle of the slow emergence of absolute knowledge. Lacan, for his part, appears to insert Lévi-Strauss into his own version of the transition from animal to human consciousness described by Hegel-Kojève. It is extremely difficult to accept at face value Lacan's protestations that his reference to Hegel is 'entirely didactic . . . for the purposes of the training that I have in mind' (Lacan 1977b: 293). Quite simply, he protests too much.

Following Hegel and Kojève, Lacan makes desire (*Begierde*) a central category of psychoanalysis: '*Desidero* is the Freudian *cogito*' (Lacan 1977b: 155). This is a classic instance of making Freud's text say what it does not say. Lacan is abetted here by generations of Freud's French translators, who tend to transform, for instance, wish-fulfilment (*Wunschsefüllung*) into '*réalisation du désir*'. Freud recounts the story of the butcher's wife and her 'wish for a caviar sandwich'; the French text referred to by Lacan refers to *un désir de caviare*, and Lacan's translator renders this as a 'desire for caviar' (Freud 1900: 142; Lacan 1977a: 261). *Begierde* is not a common term in Freud. Much more common is *Wunsch*, which is usually employed in the context of dream interpretation. In introducing the much broader category of desire, Lacan is, as Laplanche and Pontalis put it, attempting to 're-orientate Freud's doctrine' (Laplanche and Pontalis 1986: 482–3). Lacan's 'desire' also blurs the specific connotations of *lust*, usefully glossed by Laplanche as referring to a desire pertaining to an action (an 'aim' in the sense that a drive has an aim) rather than an object (Laplanche 1989: 96). Freud's terminology is being translated into a philosophically charged discourse in which 'libido', 'wishes', 'drive', all tend to be subsumed within a category far wider and more abstract than any employed by Freud himself.

Desire is part of a triadic structure, the other elements being need and demand. Need refers, as in Freud, to a biological level (nutrition), demand to its expression in a request for love, and desire to a surplus irreducible to either: 'Desire begins to take shape in the margin in which demand becomes separated from need' (Lacan 1977a: 311). It is, perhaps, possible to regard this as a recasting of Freud's account in the *Three Essays on the Theory of Sexuality* of the separating out of sexual desire from the need for nutrition as the child recalls a pleasure it once enjoyed (Freud 1905), yet Lacan immediately goes on to repeat the formula 'Man's desire is the desire of the Other'. The deceptive ease with which Lacan moves from one system of reference to the other is even more apparent in a discussion of desire in the oral, anal and genital stages in the 1960–1 seminar on the transference. In the oral phases, the object does not, argues Lacan, take on its substance or erotic value from some primal hunger: 'The *eros* that inhabits it comes *nachträglich*, through retroaction. And it is in the oral demand that desire's place is hollowed out. . . . The oral phase of the libido requires this place hollowed out by demand' (Lacan 1991: 250). This is recognizably a paraphrase of Freud. Yet as he pursues his discussion of '*human* desire in the oral phase', Lacan soon begins to adopt a significantly different lexicon: 'The analytic discovery is that, in the field of the Other, the subject encounters not only images of his own fragmentation, but, already, from the outset, the objects of the desire of the Other – namely those of the mother' (Lacan 1991: 254–5, emphasis added). That the child desires the object of the desire of the mother is an Oedipal and triangular variant on Kojève-Hegel's dual structure. But it is the strikingly redundant reference to *human* desire that signals the debt to the narrative of the transcendence of animal desire. The ultimate irony is, however, that as Hyppolite notes, desire is a mode of self-consciousness (Hyppolite 1971: 114).

A general philosophical category is imposed, leading to a curiously asexual (and affectless) psychoanalysis. This may not be a purely theoretical issue. If, for instance, the Oedipal wishes and fantasies of the child are part of the same structure as the desire of the child abuser, an entire power-structure is obliterated, which leaves psychoanalysis with a rather greater problem than another debate over the alleged abandoning of the seduction theory. What has to be at stake here is not a general category of desire, but a very specific analysis of conflicting desires and power.

While it is for psychoanalysts to justify the purely analytic or clinical value of Lacan's work, it has long been such an integral part of a broad cultural field that it must also be discussed in the more general context of its reception. Indeed, in Britain the defence and illustration of Lacanian theory was largely the work of a non-analytic milieu; even today, discussion of his work is more likely to figure in academic literary journals or journals of cultural studies than in the pages of *The International Journal of Psychoanalysis* or *Psychoanalytic Quarterly*.

Lacan's theorizations raise many of the problems posed by any general theory. Marx's law of the tendency of the rate of profit to fall normally does little to explain the failure of an individual shop, and one of the difficulties with a general sociology of literature (such as that elaborated by Lucien Goldmann (Goldmann 1964)) is that it can rarely read individual texts without simply reproducing the terms of the general theory in the mode of *quod erat demonstrandum*. The broad, synthetic sweep of, say, the 'Rome Discourse' as it majestically surveys anthropology, linguistics and psychoanalysis is still, forty years after it was read to the Rome Congress of the Société Française de Psychanalyse, exciting and exhilarating. And yet it is difficult to see just how the epic of the subject's insertion into the symbolic and language, or the saga of the subversion of the subject by desire, can explain, say, a troubled adolescence. In that sense it is the very generality of the theory that is so problematic, the very abstraction of a subject which never exists 'in situation', as Sartre would say, that becomes an opaque obstacle to the understanding of concrete subjectivity.

By the mid-1960s, it was possible, at least in the French context, to see Lacan as being a member of a 'Triple Alliance' (this expression is Pêcheux's (1982: 211)), the other members of the triumvirate being Althusser and Saussure. Althusser was the most active participant in a project which Lacan himself viewed from a distance. It is Althusser who, in 1964, ascribes to Freud the realization that 'the human subject is decentred, constituted by a structure which has no "centre" . . . except in the imaginary misrecognition of the "ego", i.e. in the ideological formations in which it "recognizes itself" ' (Althusser 1971: 201). Lacan's mirror-stage now becomes the prototype for a theory of ideology seeking to avoid the Scylla of economic determinism and the Charybdis of 'false consciousness'. This eventually results in the theses on ideology of 1969: 'What is expressed in ideology is . . . not the system of the real relations which govern the existence of individuals, but the imaginary relation of those individuals to the real relations in which they live' (Althusser 1971: 155). The mechanisms of ideology are described in terms of reflections, recognition and misrecognition (Althusser 1971: 168), but are then illustrated by a rather different scene of Althusser's devising. It focuses upon the 'interpolation' of the individual by a voice that calls out 'Hey, you there'. The individual responds, is constituted as an ideological subject and is at the same time subjected to a universal Subject. Interpolation thus provides a structure for the mutual recognition of subject and Subject. As a recent commentator observes, this theory of 'all ideology' quite fails to take account of gender: the 'universal' practice of hailing an ideological subject is, she remarks, more likely to constitute women in 'unnervingly generic terms' than in terms of a universal subjectivity (Barret 1993: 174).

Althusser's attempt to use Lacan to elaborate a theory of ideology is problematic in a number of other ways. His insistence that Lacan 'thinks only Freud's concepts' is in part the result of the need to guarantee the scientificity of psychoanalysis by demonstrating that it breaks with the myths of *homo psychologicus* – just as Marx breaks with the myth of *homo economicus* (Althusser 1971: 181), but it leads him to overlook the reference to Wallon's psychology. A footnote to 'Ideology and ideological state apparatuses' observes ironically that 'Hegel is (unknowingly) an admirable "theoretician" of ideology insofar as he is a "theoretician" of Universal Recognition who unfortunately ends up in the ideology of Absolute Knowledge' (Althusser 1971: 168). The irony in fact works against Althusser himself: the mirror-stage owes a great deal to Kojève-Hegel, and Lacan successfully exploits one moment of the *Phenomenology* without subscribing to any ideology of absolute knowledge. Ultimately, Althusser ends up in an even more unfortunate position than Hegel. By positing that ideology is as eternal as the unconscious is timeless, he is forced into a timeless theory of ideology and of what might be termed 'elementary forms of the ideological life' (Macey 1994). An essay which began as an attempt to provide a materialist theory of ideology becomes a quasi-Durkheimian theory of the symbolic-religious origins of the social bond.

The existence of the Triple Alliance had one important side effect in that it provided the theoretical basis for *Cahiers pour l'analyse*, the journal published by the Ecole Normale Supérieure's 'Cercle d'épistémologie' between 1966 and 1968.

The *Cahiers* provided a platform for younger followers of both Lacan and Althusser, but its contents were rarely Lacanian or Althusserean in any classic sense. Heavily influenced by the vision of history of the sciences associated with Georges Canguilhem, which analyses scientificity in terms of its internal conceptuality rather than its objects (see the essays collected in *Collège international de philosophie* (1993)), the *Cahiers* group began to work on general theories of ideology and discourse and to move away from the specificities of psychoanalysis – and certainly psychoanalytic practice. Increasingly, formal and mathematical logic were pressed into service by a project that effectively evacuated subjectivity by arguing that the subject is merely an effect of the logic of a combinatory. *Cahiers pour l'analyse* was a relatively short-lived journal whose editorial team suddenly veered into Maoism after May 1968, but it is probable that it is one of the factors that led Lacan to adopt increasingly mathematical formulations from the 1970s onwards. While Lacan had long used quasi-mathematical 'algorithms' such as those used to transcribe the workings of metaphor and metonymy and to plot the positioning of the subject, he now began to elaborate a logic – or hyper-logic – of the signifier through the elaboration of a psychoanalytic *matheme* capable of conveying clinical knowledge in the Leibnizian form of a 'universal language' (Roudinesco 1990: 406). The editor of the *Cahiers* was Jacques-Alain Miller, author of the conceptual index appended to *Ecrits* and, subsequently, Lacan's literary executor. The theory of the *matheme* is largely the work of the so-called Lacano-Millerean tendency within the Ecole Freudienne, and it would appear to originate in the *Cahiers*. At this stage, desire and recognition begin to give way to an equally abstract universalism allegedly founded in logic.

There is little doubt that, at every stage of its evolution, Lacan's subject – so abstractly and universally human – is male (and presumably white and heterosexual), thanks to the convention that male is the unmarked term within a binary opposition. Feminist attempts – inaugurated in the English-speaking world by Juliet Mitchell and pursued by Mitchell and Rose (Mitchell 1974; Mitchell and Rose 1982; Rose 1986) – have to confront the problem that Lacan habitually speaks of a human subject that exists as a universal and prior to any gender determination. They also have to counter the claim that Lacanian discourse implies, or is even founded upon, the suppression of any female voice raised in opposition to it (Irigaray 1991: 78–104), not to mention the apparently deliberate trivialization by Lacan and his followers of any reference to feminism (Macey 1988: Chapter 6). It is often claimed that the notion of the phallus elaborated in the 1950s can be usefully appropriated by feminism and even that it offers a positive alternative to the residual biologism associated with Freud's use of 'penis' and his notorious comments about anatomical destiny. Yet it can be demonstrated that the term 'phallus' is introduced on the basis of dubious French translations of Freud (Macey 1988: 188–9). If restored to its place in the economy of intersubjective exchange, the phallus reverts to being a Kojèvean-Hegelian object of undifferentiated desire. At this level desire is neither male nor female, but human.

At his most exciting, Lacan does bring about a huge synthesis. His exploitation of Lévi-Strauss is no doubt more acceptable than Freud's speculations about 'points of agreement between the mental lives of savages and neurotics', to cite the decidedly embarrassing subtitle of *Totem and Taboo*. Lacan adds a dimension to psychoanalytic thought that makes his work more demanding, and therefore more intellectually satisfying, than any analyst since Freud. The difficulty is that the central moment of the synthesis is stubbornly Hegelian and that it is very hard to get beyond it. It is, to say the least, ironical that a phenomenology of consciousness should be so central to a theory of the unconscious.

Central to this abstract universalism is the original reference to Hegel-Kojève. If the theory of the mirror-stage and the subversive dialectic of desire are indeed central to Lacan, it has to be accepted that we are still dealing with Hegel, that at the heart of the discourse of our modernity we find the idealist so famously and so mistakenly dismissed by Marx as 'a dead dog'. It may well be the case that, as Foucault once remarked, the history of French philosophy in the post-war period has largely been the history of an unsuccessful attempt to escape Hegel (Foucault 1971: 74–5). Lacan himself seems to summarize the basic difficulty: 'I do not like talk of *transcending* beyond Hegel in the way that we talk of *transcending* Descartes. We transcend everything and we simply stay in the same place' (Lacan 1978: 91).

REFERENCES

Althusser, L. (1971) 'Freud and Lacan', in *Lenin and Philosophy and Other Essays*, trans. Ben Brewster. London: New Left Books.

Auffret, D. (1990) *Alexandre Kojève: La Philosophie l'Etat la fin de l'histoire*. Paris: Grasset.

Barret, M. (1993) 'Althusser's Marx, Althusser's Lacan', in E. Ann Kaplan and Michael Sprinker (eds) *The Althusserian Legacy*. London: Verso.

Bataille, G. (1971) *Oeuvres complètes*. Vol. 1. Paris: Gallimard.

Blanchot, M. (1963) 'Le Jeu de la pensée', *Critique*, 195–6, August–September.

Butler, J. (1987) *Subjects of Desire: Hegelian Reflections in Twentieth-Century France*. New York: Columbia University Press.

Collège Internationale de Philosophie (1993) *Georges Canqulhem: Philosophie, historien des sciences*. Paris: Albin Michel.

Descombes, V. (1980) *Modern French Philosophy*, trans. L. Scott-Fox and J.M. Harding. Cambridge, England: Cambridge University Press.

Foucault, M. (1971) *L'Ordre du discours*. Paris: Gallimard.

Freud, A. (1936) *The Ego and the Mechanisms of Defence*. New York: International Universities Press.

Freud, S. (1900) *The Interpretation of Dreams*. S.E.4–5.

—— (1905) 'Three essays on the theory of sexuality'. S.E.7.

—— (1914) 'On narcissism: An introduction'. S.E.14.

—— (1923) *The Ego and the Id*. S.E.19.

Fukuyama, F. (1992) *The End of History and the Last Man*. London: Hamish Hamilton.

Gay, P. (1989) *Freud: A Life for our Century*. London: Papermac.

Goldmann, L. (1964) *Pour une sociologie du roman*. Paris: Gallimard.

Groddeck, G. (1935) *The Book of the It*. London: The C.W. Daniel Company.

Heidegger, M. (1971) 'Building, dwelling, thinking', in *Poetry Language Thought*, trans. A. Hofstadter. New York, Harper & Row.

Hollier, D. (1979) *Le Collège de sociologie*. Paris: Gallimard.

Howells, C. (ed.) (1992) *The Cambridge Companion to Sartre*. Cambridge, England: Cambridge University Press.

Hyppolite, J. (1971a) 'La Phénoménologie de Hegel et la pensée française contemporaine', *Figures de la pensée philosophique*. Paris: PUF.

—— (1971b) 'Situation de l'homme dans la "Phénoménologie" hegelienne' (1947), in *Figures de la pensée philosophique*. Paris: PUF.

Irigaray, L. (1991) 'The poverty of psychoanalysis', trans. David Macey with Margaret Whitford in Margaret Whitford (ed.) *The Irigaray Reader*. Oxford: Blackwell, pp. 78–104.

Kant, I. (1934) *Critique of Pure Reason*, trans. J.M.D. Meiklejohn. London: Everyman's Library.

Kelly, M. (1990) *Hegel in France*. Birmingham: Modern Language Publications.

Kojève, A. (1990) *Introduction à la lecture de Hegel*. Paris: Gallimard, Collection 'Tel'.

Lacan, J. (1966a) 'Au-delà du "Principe de réalité"', *Ecrits*: Paris: Seuil.

—— (1966b) 'Réponses à des étudiants en philosophie sur l'objet de la psychanalyse', *Cahiers pour l'analyse* 3, May–June.

—— (1968) 'La Méprise du sujet supposé savoir', *Scilicet* 1.

—— (1975) *Encore*. Paris: Seuil.

—— (1977a) *Ecrits: A Selection*, trans. Alan Sheridan. London: Tavistock.

—— (1977b) *The Four Fundamental Concepts of Psycho-Analysis*, trans. Alan Sheridan. London: The Hogarth Press and the Institute of Psychoanalysis.

—— (1978) *Le Séminaire. Livre II. Le Moi dans la théorie de Freud et dans la technique de la psychanalyse*. Paris: Seuil.

—— (1979) 'Le Mythe individuel du névrosé, ou Poésie et vérité dans la névrosé', *Ornicar?* 17/18, pp. 289–307, trans. Martha Noel 'The neurotic's individual myth', *Psychoanalytic Quarterly*, 48: 386–425.

—— (1981) *Le Séminaire. Livre III. Les Psychoses*. Paris: Seuil.

—— (1986) *Le Séminaire. Livre VII: L'Ethique de la psychanalyse*. Paris: Seuil.

—— (1991) *Le Séminaire. Livre VIII: Le Transfert*. Paris: Seuil.

Laplanche, J. (1989) 'Terminologie raisonée', in André Bourguignon, Pierre Cotet, Jean Laplanche and François Robert *Traduire Freud*. Paris: PUF.

Laplanche, J. and Pontalis, J.B. (1986) *The Language of Psycho-analysis*. London: Hogarth.

Leiris, M. (1946) *L'Age d'homme*. Paris: Gallimard.

Lévi-Strauss, C. (1969) *The Elementary Structures of Kinship*, trans. James Harle Bell, John Richard von Sturmer and Rodney Needham. London: Eyre and Spottiswood. The French original was first published in 1949.

—— (1972) *The Savage Mind*. London: Weidenfeld & Nicolson.

Macey, D. (1988) *Lacan in Contexts*. London: Verso.

—— (1994) 'Thinking with borrowed concepts: Althusser and Lacan', in Gregory Elliott (ed.) *Althusser: A Critical Reader*. Oxford: Blackwell.

Macherey, P. (1990) *Á quoi pense la littérature?* Paris: PUF.

Mitchell, J. (1974) *Psychoanalysis and Feminism*. London: Allen Lane.

Mitchell, J. and Rose, J. (eds) (1982) *Jacques Lacan and the Ecole Freudienne: Feminine Sexuality*. London: Macmillan.

Nietzsche, F. (1990) *Beyond Good and Evil*, trans. R.J. Hollingdale. Harmondsworth: Penguin.

Pêcheux, M. (1982) *Language Semantics and Ideology*, trans. Harbans Nagpal. London: Methuen.

Pontalis, J.B. (1992) 'Michel Leiris, or Psychoanalysis without end', trans. D. Macey, *Yale French Studies*, 81.

Rose, J. (1986) *Sexuality in the Field of Vision*. London: Verso.

Roudinesco, E. (1990) *Jacques Lacan and Co: A History of Psychoanalysis in France 1925–1985*, trans. J. Mehlman. London: Free Association Books.

Sartre, J-P. (1936–7) 'La Transcendence de l'ego: Esquisse d'une description phénoménologique', *Recherches philosophiques*, 6.

Spinoza (1910) *Ethics*, trans. A. Boyle. London: Dent.
Stoekl, A. (ed.) (1990) 'On Bataille', *Yale French Studies*, 78.
—— (1992) *Agonies of the Intellectual: Commitment, Subjectivity and the Performative in the Twentieth-Century French Tradition*. Lincoln and London: University of Nebraska Press.
Wallon, H. (1947) *Les Origines du caractère chez l'enfant*. Paris: PUF.

Part II

The dynamics of difference

5 Individuality and difference in how women and men love

Nancy J. Chodorow

This chapter considers how women and men love. Since Freud, psychoanalysis has provided us with a normative, a theoretical, and an empirical (based on clinical observation) account of gender and sexuality. The normative story, told through the theory of the Oedipus complex, presents a model (and modal) femininity and masculinity. Clinically, psychoanalysts, as people in everyday life, have observed prevalent differences between men and women. They also observe and theorize, even if they do not critique, the connections among gender, eroticism, hetero-sexuality, and male dominance. But psychoanalytic theorists and those who draw upon psychoanalytic theory, like much of academic psychology and virtually all of the popular psychology literature, have tended to overgeneralize and universalize – to oppose all men to all women and to assume that masculinity and femininity and their expressive forms are single rather than multiple. This is a peculiar tendency in a field whose data are by necessity so resolutely and intractably idiographic – so individual and case-based.

Sexual love is a particularly useful arena for decomposing universality, for investigating the multiple intersections of gender and sexuality, and for seeing the connections of culture, ideology and psyche. In this chapter, I claim, against generalization, that women and men love in as many ways as there are women and men. Even as I do not lose insight into the psychological and cultural pervasiveness of male dominance, I suggest why it is difficult and problematic to generalize about how women and men love.

For clinicians, sexual love presents an especial challenge. It is a fulcrum of gender identity, of sexual fantasy and desire, of cultural story, of unconscious and conscious feelings and fears about intimacy, dependency, nurturance, destructiveness, power and powerlessness, and even of self-construction. It may be – along with (and of course connected to) anyone's sense of self as child (those unconscious and fantasy sequelae of individual psychobiography), men's sense of self as masculine, and women's sense of self as mother – one of the most complexly constructed of the many deeply felt, deeply conflicted issues that our patients present us, and, more generally, that people in our society experience. As with many clinical issues concerning sex and gender, a blending of culture and psyche – of cultural meaning and personal meaning – makes love complex in particular ways. These complexities entail that our typical clinical focus on intrapsychic elements, as if these can be contrasted with or considered apart from the external world and culture, misses a large part of what goes to constitute love. Any particular man or woman chooses particular objects of desire, or types of objects, and has particular types of love experiences, and in each case we need to give a cultural *and* an individual developmental story of these patterns and choices. More specifically, we need to give a story of how, among its other processes and patterns, individual development, drawing from constitutional endowment, early and later intrapsychic experience, and internal and external processes of object relationship, chooses from, reacts to, ignores, interprets, and modifies culture, to account fully for these choices.

In what follows, I suggest some very general axes of variation, or ingredients, which it behoves us as clinicians and theorists to consider as we try to unravel how particular women and men (our patients, ourselves, our friends, those we interview, those we read about in fiction or non-fiction), and women and men, more generally, love.[1] While generalization can also be useful, I believe that variation and complexity have been by and large missing ingredients in psychoanalytic accounts, as well as in psychoanalytically based feminist accounts, of normative or typical gender and sexuality (both psychoanalytic and gay and lesbian accounts of gay and lesbian sexuality, by contrast, have been more respectful of and attentive to variation).[2]

One element in love, that is, the particular sense of self and relationship that comes from the individual family in which someone grows up, and that gives any individual's love uniqueness, is familiar to us from clinical work and psychoanalytic theory. Clinicians are used to focusing on this factor, both as we reconstruct it historically and as we experience and analyse it in the transference. Through such analysis, we excavate all aspects of a particular person's psychological make-up – their prevalent defences, unconscious fantasies, projective and introjective constructions of self and objects, and so forth. We know that any particular patient comes from a particular family with a specific cultural background, but those of us who are Euro-American and middle class tend to take this background for granted if we share such a background with our patients. We find it more important to figure out how a particular mother or father was experienced, and we assume cultural setting, rather than working to elucidate, for example, how a particular parental relationship was typical, say, of a particular subculture or cultural enclave. What matters becomes not so much the cultural practice, conception or self-conception, but how the child experienced it.

Such a culturally blind strategy is in all likelihood generally problematic, but in the case of love, as in the case of gender, stopping with individual particularity especially occludes understanding.[3] Love has an added cultural resonance, especially through its link with gender, that makes stopping with personal or familial meaning singularly inadequate. As I noted earlier, in our society today no one can grow up without, from earliest childhood, shaping a sense of love from fairy tales, myths, tales of love, loss and betrayal, films, books and television. These cultural stories and fantasies are experienced directly, and they are also mediated by conscious and unconscious parental fantasies and patterns of projection, introjection, and emotional communication between child and parents, as parents read or tell stories, share films, themselves consciously or unconsciously experience such cultural fantasies in relation to sexual partners, to themselves, and to their children. Stories of passion, sexual desire and fulfilment are found in all cultures, but heterosexual erotic love as we read, see and hear about it in contemporary Euro-American culture is a specific cultural product.[4] Many cultures do not have such a concept, and in western civilization erotic love floats around historically: it is marital and heterosexual in some eras, extramarital in others, heterosexual and tied to notions of intimacy in the current period, passionately found (though questionably genital) between women in the nineteenth century, erotically found between older men and younger boys in classical Greece, normatively carnal today and normatively reserved for spiritual love of Christ in the Middle Ages. Even 'Judeo-Christian' culture splits, as Judaism finds marital sexual passion desirable and prescribed (albeit under conditions of extensive ritual control), whereas the classic Christian position holds all sexual excitement and lust to be undesirable, if unavoidable.[5]

Cultural resonance and cultural saturation ensure that sexual and romantic fantasies, mediated as they are partially through language, will incorporate cultural stories. These cultural stories and their psychological specifications often entail commonalties that allow us to label some man or woman's fantasy by gender, but, by the very fact that these fantasies are so culturally loaded, we run grave risks in saying that *this* is how men and women love – as if such fantasy is a product of biological or psychobiological endowment. In a different culture, or within different subcultures in our own, how men and women love varies tremendously.

In some cases, we can define through exclusion. The clinically observed gothic heroine, or 'Rebecca,' fantasy – involving self-devaluing or masochistically-tinged love involvements or obsessions with unavailable, angry, domineering, or distant partners, including the fantasy of transforming these partners into gentle lovers – seems a feminine form of love. When we find such a fantasy in a man (which we most certainly will), whether in relation to women or to other men, we might claim that this man loved in a feminine manner. But to claim the Rebecca fantasy as feminine does not imply that all women experience love in this way, just as it does not imply that men never do. A 'Portnoy' fantasy – obsession with a devouring, hysterical mother that pushes a man towards reserved, distant women, women with characteristics distinctly unlike that mother, or towards men – seems, generally, a masculine fantasy, but certainly not one that characterizes how all men love. These two examples both specify how some women and men love and indicate how the form of such love fantasies, partaking as they certainly do of individual familial and psychological history, takes added shape by the availability of *Rebecca*, itself perhaps an adolescent 'Beauty and the Beast' story, and *Portnoy's Complaint*, itself built on centuries of Jewish mother stories, as well as on fairy tales and other stories of terrifying and sexually or maternally engulfing women.[6] We are here in the realm of 'subjective' and 'objective' gender: these fantasies may involve unconscious or conscious identifications as feminine or masculine, and they may also more prevalently characterize how men love or how women love.[7]

We also get at the importance of the cultural input to love by comparing cultures. I draw here mainly upon women's writings, but I believe my point about cultural and individual variation holds for men as well. Two American psychoanalytic theorists and clinicians, Susan Contratto and Jessica Benjamin, articulate a prevalent theme in Euro-American psychoanalytic feminist writing on love. They draw on clinical experience and observation to describe how mothers subtly and indirectly build up and idealize fathers to their daughters, perhaps by complement effacing themselves.[8] In Lacanian and non-Lacanian French psycho-analytic writing, what American feminists criticize as indirect subtlety becomes the explicit injunction that mothers stress paternal and phallic primacy. According to Janine Chasseguet-Smirgel, children must come to recognize a genital universe which is also the 'paternal universe [of] constraints of the law'; for Joyce McDougall, sexual difference and normal heterosexuality are by necessity tied to 'the phallus, symbol of power, fertility, and life, [representing] for both sexes the image of narcissistic completion and sexual desire'.[9] Of course, we also find a protest and rejection of such a position in the writings of Helene Cixous and Luce Irigaray, but their very protest attests to the cultural and psychological power of such developmental injunctions and fantasies.[10]

US Latina writing on sexuality portrays, though critically rather than normatively, a situation similar to that invoked by French theorists, implying that male dominance is more culturally valorized and elaborated in Latino than in Anglo culture. Oliva Espín and Cherríe Moraga describe mothers who directly teach their daughters that women are inferior and men superior, that these daughters should submit to and serve their father and brothers, and that the penis is the valued genital and sexual organ.[11] My own clinical experience and cross-cultural reading suggest that variations of this directly taught sexual inequality and subservience to men may be pervasive in those cultures that the Turkish sociologist Denise Kandiyoti calls 'classic patriarchy' – North Africa, the Muslim Middle East, China and India, and perhaps in much of the circum-Mediterranean as well.[12]

At the same time, Latina writings, rather than articulating a Euro-American bewilderment about how to find 'women's desire' out of a seeming sexlessness (itself perhaps a heritage from nineteenth-century Protestant notions of women's passionlessness), describe a Mexican cultural legacy portraying women as sexual temptresses whose evil sexuality betrayed Aztec men to the Spanish conquerors – as Aztec Eves.[13] By contrast, African-American mothers do not seem to teach their daughters subservience to men. At least one survey of African-American mothers and daughters finds daughters reporting that their mothers warned them to be wary of men and marriage and stressed men's unreliability and undependability. These mothers warn of men who are sexual tempters and betrayers.[14] Such warnings about men of the same racial-ethnicity come in the context of even stronger warnings and terror about potential abuse by white men.[15] At the same time, in traditions like the blues, for instance, we find assertion of a strong black female sexuality and sexual desire.[16]

I do not mean these very brief examples to serve as generalizations about women's and men's love in these different cultures. I would not claim the cross-cultural knowledge even to begin to do so, and, as I indicate, my point in this chapter is to suggest that even such culturally-specific generalization would be highly problematic. What such examples can suggest, however, is that if even a few women from these different groups have different unconscious and conscious senses of female self, body, and sexual fantasy, and different cultural stories of male–female relations, and if a few men from these different groups have related stories, then already we have variation in how women and men love. Some middle-class Euro-American women's sexuality differs from that of some French women, who love differently from some Latinas, who experience men differently from some African-American women.

My point is that we are partially on the ground of culture, story and language when we talk about how men and women love. In turn, these stories and this language always include conceptions of gender and sexuality. For this reason, to query how women and men love yields more than a descriptive account of tendencies and patterns – that men love in particular ways, women in others. As Freud's original account of femininity suggests, we must also characterize *gendered subjectivity* in relation to love. Women and men love as psychologically and culturally gendered selves, with gender identities and sexual desires that they consciously and unconsciously experience and enact.

Understanding of these processes has been hampered by clinicians' tendencies to separate too absolutely inner and outer. Thus some clinicians and psychoanalytic theorists would argue that by looking at culture and language I am moving away from the psychoanalytic realm, with its unique focus on unconscious mental processes. But such a perspective is misguided. It does not take account of how unconscious fantasies and senses of self and identity are formed – what cultural and interpersonal experiences interact with, or are available for, those innate psychological capacities and potentialities that enable us to form a self with emotional capacities and conflicts, a particular gender identity rife with individual and cultural psychological meaning, and an organization of drive potentialities into individual erotic desire. Others believe that in the case of how women and men love we can predict from anatomical givens and the automatic psychological sequelae of these. Some, finally, rest their case on a psychoanalytic theory (for example, most Lacanian-inspired readings of psychoanalysis) that reifies 'the unconscious' as a *sui generis* autochthonous entity that is apart from culture and the symbolic. (As I suggest later, those culturalists who claim that culture predicts forms of sexuality, gender and love also have only a partial perspective.)

I argue here, by contrast, that an important ingredient in any woman's or man's love or sexual fantasies, erotic desires, and behaviour – how any woman or man loves – will be found in their particular unconscious and conscious appropriation of a richly varied, often contradictory, cultural repertoire, as this has itself been presented directly through what we think of as cultural media and indirectly, again consciously and unconsciously, through parents, siblings and other early parental figures. We remind ourselves, for example, of the Wolf Man and the Rat Man, both of whom formed their love and sexuality in important ways in relation to servant women, thereby infusing the contempt for women that Freud takes to be characteristic of the normal Oedipal resolution with images of class superiority and inferiority.[17] There are many cultural masculinities and femininities and masculine and feminine love stories, and people form their fantasies and desire for individual reasons from one or another or from none of these.

Of course, there is one consistent thread that runs in varied ways throughout many of these psychological and cultural stories: most men and women must come to psychological terms with male dominance. Men have social and familial power and cultural superiority; in the psychoanalytic view – one mirrored in most of my examples – they have sexual dominance as well. Somewhere along the line, often but not always in relation to the father, part of learning the meanings of masculinity and femininity includes not just difference but differential value and asymmetrical power and hierarchy. Family dynamics, as these reflect cultural and personal meaning, and as identity and desire are constituted, link sexuality, and particularly heterosexuality, to a psychology and culture of gender such that inequality and power difference become part of the cultural and psychological requisites that do not directly construct but that must be negotiated in sexual desire and love. One cannot find general psychoanalytic accounts of the development of heterosexuality that do not include gender inequality and male dominance.[18]

But such inequality is not monolithic. R.W. Connell suggests that we distinguish analytically between 'hegemonic' and 'subordinate' or alternate masculinities and femininities. Hegemonic masculinity organizes itself around psychological, cultural and social dominance over women (Freud's normal male Oedipal outcome), but it also organizes among masculinities, enabling dominant males to dominate subordinate males culturally, psychologically and even sexually. Tomàs Almaguer reminds us that in Latin American culture, the *activo* homosexual position is not stigmatized whereas the *pasivo* position is.[19]

Hegemonic psychological masculinity itself has many expressive forms: in the heterosexual who refuses permanent sexual commitment, moving from partner to partner in a more or less exploitative way; in the 'good' husband and father who works at a steady job to support a family. Alternate masculinities might include the new gentle feminist man and a variety of homosexualities. There is no hegemonic cultural femininity that defines itself as dominant over men, but alternate femininities can more or less emphasize subordination and compliance or sexual assertiveness and independence. Femininities can also make men more or less central. My brief account of Latina and African-American women's writing portrays such a contrast, and it seems possible that some middle- class women of today's generations are more centred – in some cases perhaps, defensively – on work identities than women of older generations.[20] Or, different femininities may substitute an emphasis on maternal love as a centre of identity for an emphasis on heterosexual femininity. There is also, as my example of black maternal teaching makes clear, often a women's culture (currently mirrored in some feminist writing and found in much nineteenth-century feminism as well) that in the context of male social domination claims personal and moral superiority over men. Parents may communicate any of these patterns covertly or overtly as a child forms her or his gendered sense of self and desire.

We now add that women and men from all groups may love people of the same gender rather than of the other gender. If we see these love relationships in gendered terms, then one partner must love according to their own gender, the other, presumably, according to the other: the 'butch' and 'femme' member of the lesbian pair, or the 'active' and 'passive' partner in the gay couple. Alternately, accounts conflate same-gender erotic choice with gender identity, claiming that lesbians love like a man – in a masculine fashion – or stressing the 'effeminacy' of boys who become gay. But if we acknowledge that some women love like men and some men like women, we are claiming that there are at least two polar opposite modes in which people of each gender can love. We hold on to a putative descriptive generalization (or prescriptive claim) concerning modes of male and female love (active versus passive, dominant versus submissive) at the expense of being able to describe how these particular, actual, men and women love. If we claim that lesbian relationships replicate mother–daughter patterns, whereas heterosexual women love as they loved their father, with ideal love, for instance, we now have three different relational stances in female love: mother of the daughter, daughter of the mother, and daughter of the father. Lewes, as we know, points to *twelve* possible Oedipal constellations and outcomes for the boy. Whereas half of these are heterosexual, only one is what we normatively think of as how men love.

We can now turn more directly back to the psychodynamics of the family, but without forgetting what we have just established: that these psychodynamics include, unconsciously and consciously, and among other elements, cultural patterns and meanings. How women and men love will be heavily influenced, if not determined, by their navigation through the relationships and fantasies of early childhood, and this is the terrain that we think of as more typically psychoanalytic.

Much of my previous writing provides an account of how girls and boys differentially negotiate these early experiences, particularly in terms of their relationship to their mother. I have argued that girls, like boys, form their first love relationship, fantasies, sense of self and gender, and modes of love and desire, through their relationship to their mother. I suggested that most girls seek to create in love relationships an internal emotional dialogue with their mother – to recreate directly the early infantile or Oedipal connection, to reconcile, rescue or repair, to attack, incorporate, or reject, to emancipate themselves or define themselves against her.[21] I have yet to come across any woman patient, or any narrative (fictional, autobiographical, biographical or poetic) written from the daughter's point of view – patients or writers of whatever sexual orientation and from any cultural group – for whom, in the broadest sense, we could say that 'love' for a daughter's mother was not central.[22] Women seek directly to reconstitute, resurrect, reshape, reimagine, an emotional relation with their mothers, fantasize and unconsciously experience internal and actual mothers even as they form relationships with men. Part of 'how women love' concerns the (never absolute, but always shifting) resolution of this desire (as well as of envy, anger, hatred, ambivalence, or whatever other strong emotions towards and internal representations of her mother a woman might have) and its 'level' of resolution –

adolescent, pre-adolescent, latency, Oedipal, pre-Oedipal or some combination –
for the individual woman.[23] I do not think that *this aspect* of female love
is necessarily subjectively gendered: women's feelings, fantasies and self-
construction in relation to their mother, coming as they do from preverbal and
pre-Oedipal preoccupations with self–other differentiation, the relation to the
breast, the managing of anxiety, and so forth, as well as from pre-Oedipal and
Oedipal subjectively gender-linked experiences, may or may not have to do with
a sense of self as female or conscious or unconscious fantasies about gendered
sexual desire. But that women are preoccupied intrapsychically with their mother
as an internal image and object, and that this intrapsychic preoccupation helps
shape their love relationships (and much else about their intrapsychic and
interpersonal life), is a near universal clinical observation.

Those aspects of men's love that grow out of their relation to their mother are
more likely than women's to be subjectively gendered; that is, to be intertwined for
a man with his sense of (cultural and personal) masculinity. Although the early
relation to the mother, coming as it does from a period before a boy can have a
subjective sense of gender, may not be gendered from the boy's subjective
viewpoint (though his mother's subjective relation to him is certainly so) this
relation is inevitably transformed by his learning (in his own idiosyncratic way,
personally charged by his own individual emotional constructions) of cultural and
personal gender. Freud argued that this personal appropriation of cultural gender
was a central outcome of the Oedipal resolution for boys, as boys learned that the
meaning of their masculinity and their penis was its superiority to femininity and
its lack of penis, but recent theorists and researchers have suggested that this
learning of the value of gender difference is an earlier developmental process, tied
more to the period of the *rapprochement* subphase in the second year.[24] Klein's
accounts of the defensive constructions of gender and of fantasies of male
superiority in boys and girls in the 'early stages of the Oedipus complex' accords
more with this contemporary developmental account.[25]

The subjective gendering of masculine love in relation to the mother is not
neutral. Subjective gendering for men means that such love defines itself negatively in relation to the mother as well as in terms of positive love and attachment:
insistent masculine superiority and asymmetry in (hetero)sexuality indicate a
defensive construction. We do not need to go far in the psychoanalytic literature
(we begin with Horney's classic statement in 'The dread of women' (1932)) or in
the popular media to read about men's fear of women, female sexuality, and the
intimacy and nurturance that evoke the early dependent relation to the mother – of
particular note in a situation of such clearly claimed and institutionally supported
cultural and psychological superiority.[26] While we may find comparable female
fear of male sexuality or power – for example, of being penetrated, violated,
attacked, or overwhelmed – this fear is in accord with rather than in opposition to
dominant cultural and social constructions of gender.

Thus, if a first ingredient in how women and men love comes more from a
personal appropriation and transformation of cultural stories and fantasies, a
second seems to arise from their negotiation of their relationship to their mother,

or to a female caretaker and primary love object. I cannot address the infinite recursiveness here: of course, the mother herself is also culturally and personally gendered, but this is not the whole aspect of her being and fantasy, and it is not the whole of what goes into the individual mother–child relationship. This relationship to the mother tends to become more pervasively tied to meanings of gender for men than for women, though it certainly becomes so for women as well. Moreover, at least in the Freudian cases, as well as in literary and theoretical writings on interracial and interclass nursing and nannies, the intrapsychic putting together of the relationship to early female caretakers can also be tied to class and racial splits in erotic love, thereby shaping active desire, avoidance, perversion, and one version of the erotic and symbolic splitting between good and bad women and erotic and idealized love that Freud first described.[27] Some writing by Euro-American lesbians (for example, Rich in *Of Woman Born* (1976)) suggests the direct connection of desire to experience with women from caretaking and servant classes that we find in men, but although many women for various reasons repeatedly choose male love objects from different racial-ethnic or class groups, I have not seen clinical or literary accounts describing racial or class splitting entering into women's heterosexual desire as a direct result of actual early experiences with men of different classes or races.[28] This is in all likelihood an artifact of my limited reading, but it may also be because men do not tend to be primary parents or because of cultural taboo.

Generally, the relation to the mother comes to symbolize for both sexes nurturance or its rejection, intimacy or its transformation, body pleasure or body shame, guilt at independence or resentment at dependence. Passivity or activity, aggression and submission, may also enter. I stress that these are *aspects* of the relationship that *tend* to be psychologically symbolized and accorded emotional meaning in later love, but that there is *no single way* in which they are worked out for women in contrast to men. Each woman and man negotiates *some* of these aspects – as well as many others – of her or his particular relation to her or his particular mother or early female love objects and caretakers.

It is thus a mistake to claim that *the* mother symbolizes or emotionally organizes something particular or generates particular kinds of fantasies, or that she must act in a particular way – that, for example, this unitary entity symbolizes castration, or that she represents 'the' pre-Oedipal oneness, 'the' holding environment, or an inevitable total dependence, or that *her* 'lack' *is* contrasted with the father's phallus, or that her baby-gestating capacities contrast with *his* lack. There is no such uniformity in early childhood experience, and as cultural summaries, these descriptions generalize and universalize without warrant and exclude emotional meaningfulness. Any individual mother's appropriation, creation and integration of her femaleness, maternality, and selfhood will have, in her development and current psychological life, the same contingent construction as that of her now-children.

To return to Freud and all analysts who reflect on Oedipus is to ask about the father – a third relational and fantasy ingredient in how women and men love. The father certainly falls under the cultural symbolizations of gender that I discussed earlier, and a large body of research suggests that he himself tends to participate actively in this cultural symbolization and placement. If we wish to understand how a man or a woman loves, insofar as gender is relevant to this loving, we would make a great mistake not to look at his or her relation to his or her father (if one is in the psychological or actual picture, and whether or not he is in the household). As it turns out, fathers are themselves intensely interested in gender and gender difference, so that if one parent can be said to 'create' gender in their children, or to help in that creation, it is the father. The research literature suggests that fathers, to put it simply, prefer boys, interact more with them, and emphasize more gender-differentiated behaviour in sons and daughters than do mothers. As marital tension increases so this differentiated behaviour increases, so that fathers become more authoritarian and rejecting of daughters as they gain less satisfaction from their wives (they are also more likely to stay in marriages with sons).[29]

Insofar as the father–daughter relationship contributes to how women love, many girls walk a kind of tightrope. Their father may wish them to be more 'feminine' (traditional psychoanalytic accounts suggest a seduction that is not a seduction to help create heterosexuality in girls), but he at the same time is likely not to be as interested in them as he is in sons, or as a mother is in daughters and sons. This leads to a feminine idealization of men and constraint on assertion of desire. The girl bargains to put up with less from him and from men than she really wants, and takes what she can get rather than what she wants in the way of attention and affection. Yet, in the absence of primary male figures, girls seem to find it hard to develop a confident sense of self in relation to men – and it would seem, whatever a girl's sexual preference, that we would prefer that she make sexual love choices as much as possible proactively rather than defensively and reactively.[30]

A primary way in which the closely intertwined cultures of gender and love may enter the family and the child's unconscious, then, is through the father. Part of any investigation of how women and men love must include, in the particular woman's and man's case, attention to how this gender, power, and paternal appreciation or lack of appreciation for a child were experienced and helped shape a self.

However, these tendencies reported in the research and theoretical literature are not universal. In my clinical experience, some women are quite comfortable excoriating their father's aggression, sexism, self-absorption and over-control, whereas it is a painful guilt more than they can bear to acknowledge any sense of maternal failure or limitation. Some women and girls, by contrast, find it easy to criticize and reject mothers – whom they are certain have the strength to survive their onslaught – whereas they protect perceived paternal inadequacy and weakness. Women's and men's fantasies and feelings about fathers also seem to be shaped, consciously and unconsciously, by cultural factors, so that, for example, women from classic patriarchal cultures tend to have a stronger sense of paternal domination and preference for sons, and/or a stronger conscious ideology of paternal perfection and desirability.

I do not here assert, as I have previously and as others have also claimed, that women fall in love rationally, putting up with flaws in male lovers as they learned to accept what love or attention they could get from fathers. I suggest, rather, that these widely observed prevalent paternally generated dynamics and fantasies should be floating through clinicians' (interviewers', readers', self-analysers', theorists') minds as potentiality, as we hear our patients express love – as, for example, our women patients may image furious, rejecting divorced fathers, whirlwinds of power and anger, rejections of their efforts to become strong and powerful, or clear paternal preference for them as latency-aged bright feminine androgynes (for years, most studies of 'successful' women indicated this sort of supportive, encouraging, seductive father behind the success: Louisa May Alcott succeeded in spite of, and Alice James may have failed because of, domineering, controlling fathers).

Nor do I suggest that men automatically or universally bask in the glory of father preference, always express gender superiority in love through paternal identification, or enter the adult world of love with an unproblematic sense of male superiority and masculine sexual aggression. Masculinity, intimacy, conflicts about sexual potency, anger, resentment, all confound how men love, and mediation by the father is *one* aspect to be investigated: did a man's father seem forever passive and unavailable as a model? Was he intensely desired for his power? Did he conform to cultural stereotypes of successful masculinity? Did he submit himself to mother and/or protect his son from her? Was he available at all or withdrawn into work, another marriage, depression, or an active single life?

In previous writing, I describe how the particular developmental pathways and resulting constellations of capacities and needs for intimacy in men and women differ and lead to prevalent tensions and strains in heterosexual relationships.[31] Many readers of that earlier writing and my own clinical experience affirm that the tensions and strains I describe reflect many men's and women's experience.[32] These asymmetries, tensions and strains in heterosexual experience have also been elaborated upon by feminist theorists, often drawing on psychoanalysis, and explained in terms of the inequality between men and women in society, culture and the family.

Recently, though, feminist theory has also taught us to be wary of generalizations about gender difference, and it is this wariness that I urge in this chapter. I do not claim that generalization is never useful clinically – I have written about gender differences, and I take the usefulness of these insights for granted. Feminist philosopher Marilyn Frye suggests the helpful concept of pattern here, and urges us towards epistemological 'strategies of discovering patterns and articulating them effectively, judging the strength and scope of patterns, properly locating the particulars of experience with reference to patterns, understanding the variance of experience from what we take to be a pattern'.[33] Patterns help give meaning to and interpretively situate particularity ('make our different experiences intelligible in different ways'). By contrast, generalizations can easily be misread as universal claims, as applying to all men versus all women and as describing an essence of gender that does not respect the very great individual and cultural differences among women and among men.

I wish to advocate caution about how to *use* generalizations and to specify what a generalization can claim. There has been within psychoanalysis, as in our everyday social and cultural world, a tendency to turn generalizations into universal claims and into polarizations – to speak of male versus female, 'the boy' or 'the man' versus 'the girl' or 'the woman' – and indeed, to search for gender differences and ignore commonalties and similarities. Such generalizations can draw our attention away from the very great similarities between some men and some women and among people in general, and from the arenas of psychological, social and cultural life in which gender or sexuality are not prominent.[34] Clinically, expectations and theories of gender difference often cloud, delimit and threaten to occlude our vision.

Alternately, we wipe out difference (and inequality): sex is sex, love is love; we can talk in general ways about how humans experience sexual love. This chapter claims that gender makes a difference, but in particular ways. Gender identity and fantasy, however we want to define these – whether you are a man or a woman, how you conceptualize yourself, your desires, and your possibilities – make an enormous difference, for our patients if we are clinicians, and for ourselves. But the fact that anyone's gender is centrally important to them, consciously and unconsciously, does not entail that we can contrast all women, or most women, and all or most men. Moreover, how people conceptualize themselves as gendered varies by a number of factors, including culture, history, and early family development – the *specifics* of their family and its meanings, as they fantasize and create this family, as they experience engulfment, separateness, destruction, threat, love, hate. What become important are not just anyone's femaleness or maleness, but the psychologically and culturally *specific* meanings that gender holds *for them*.

The problem, then, is how to consider gendered subjectivity without turning such a consideration into objective claims about gender difference. To look at *constructions of gendered experience* within the perceived relations of gender is not the same as looking at difference and similarity; subjective (conscious and unconscious) *meanings* of love and attachment are not the same as objective behavioural or clinical observations turned into generalizations and then universal claims (against which we then judge normality and abnormality, into which we then fit our particular patients).

This chapter begins to untangle the complex interactions of gender-inflected factors in sexual love and the patterns of gendered identity and meaning that can help us to interpret these specificities: male dominance as a pervasive cultural, psychological and social phenomenon; myriad cultural fantasies and stories; gender identity and identifications as subjective features of psychological life. Gender is an important ingredient in how men and women love, and all men's and women's love fantasies, desires, or practices are partially shaped by their sense of gendered self. But this sense of gendered self is itself individually created and particular, a unique fusion of cultural meaning with a personal emotional meaning that is tied to the individual psychobiographical history of any individual.

How any person's sexual orientation and organization, erotic fantasy and practices result from anatomy, cultural valuation and construction, intrapsychic solutions to conflict, family experience and gender identity, must be investigated individually. All these will enter in the individual case into how any woman or man loves. To factor out the variations I have described in order to get at what remains and 'really' differentiates how women and men love misses the point. It misses the point clinically, where we are called upon to respect individual complexity, and it misses the point theoretically as well. A variety of patterns of attachment and fear, erotic and romantic fantasy, imaging of one's own and the other's sexual anatomy and gender, specificity versus broadness of love choice and sexual aim, aggressive, reparative and intimacy seeking goals, are found in any man or woman, all themselves exhibiting varying degrees of defence or conflict-freedom and accompanying all levels of character pathology and neurosis. These patterns and processes both draw from and reshape cultural stories, and how this is done also varies in the individual case. To understand how men and women love requires that we understand how any particular woman or man loves.

NOTES

1 I note, though I cannot solve, a problem or limitation in any clinically-based consideration of love. Love is particularly difficult to study clinically because, although the clinical situation is a two-person experience, and we can study love directly through the transference and counter-transference as well as indirectly through our patients' descriptions of their lives, it is none the less the case that, as we describe 'how men and women love', we are describing this more from the point of view of one person, and not with a double lens that sees fully from the point of view of both parties to the love relationship at the same time. Inevitably, the love partner in all our case descriptions and generalizations – unless we describe our counter-transference feelings and fantasies as fully as we describe the transference feelings and fantasies of our patients – remains more object than subject, and the love relationship described does not exhibit the mutually constructed tensions, strengths, shifts and fantasies that characterize any intense two-person relationship.

2 See e.g. Golden 1987; Stein 1992; Katz 1983; and Duberman *et al.* 1989, among many writings. Among psychoanalytic writings, one has only to look at any number of case studies of 'perversion' to see careful attention to specificity and variability.

3 I have found that my by now decades-removed training as a psychological anthropologist, along with a continuing interest in cross-cultural matters, has been invaluable when I work with non-Euro-American patients (as well as in problematizing Euro-American culture and the psychological universalisms that have emerged from its theorists). I have both a continuing sense of the vast cross-cultural difference between psychological and familial practices and patterns, and some – albeit soberingly limited – concrete knowledge about a variety of non-Western cultures.

4 Particularly interesting cross-cultural studies include Gregor 1985; Levy 1973; and Herdt 1981.

5 See deRougemont 1956; Gaylin and Person 1988; Smith-Rosenberg 1985: 9–76; Katz 1990: 7–34; Duberman *et al.* 1989; and Plaskow 1990: 170–210.

6 For a remarkable discussion of such masculine fantasies in Shakespeare, see Adelman 1992.

7 Fast (1984: 77) develops the distinction of subjective and objective gender:

> Subjective definitions of masculinity and femininity must be distinguished from objective ones. Objectively defined, individuals' characteristics are masculine or feminine to the extent that they are typical of one or the other sex in a particular social group. Subjective definitions refer to personal constructs of masculinity and femininity, individuals' own notions, applied to themselves and to others, of what it is to be masculine and feminine.

So, for example, a woman's 'Rebecca' fantasy may be intertwined with her sense of womanliness or femininity, but we might also say that Rebecca fantasies are more likely to characterize women than men.

8   See Benjamin 1988 and 1991: 277–99; and Contratto 1987: 138–57.

9   Chasseguet-Smirgel 1985: 12; and McDougall 1986: 267–8.

10 See e.g. Cixous 1976: 875–93; and Irigaray 1985.

11 Espin 1984: 149–64; Moraga 1986: 173–90.

12 Kandiyoti 1988: 274–90. See also, on Morocco, Mernissi 1975; and on Italy, Parsons 1969.

13 On passionlessness, see Cott 1978: 19–36.

14 Joseph 1981: 75–126.

15 See Carby 1985: 262–77; and Collins 1990.

16 See Carby 1987: 9–22.

17 Freud 1909: 153–318, and 1918: 3–122.

18 For further discussion on heterosexuality, see Chodorow 1994, Chapter 2.

19 Connell 1987: 183–8; Almaguer 1991: 75–100.

20 In a longitudinal study of college graduates from the late 1950s – women caught between the old 1950s pattern emphasizing home and family and the emerging 1960s pattern of college graduate women having careers – Helson compares women who followed a 'feminine social clock' and those who followed a 'masculine occupational clock'. This role comparison does not directly predict or mirror personality and unconscious femininity, but it indicates that comparable psychodynamics might exist. See Helson *et al.* 1984: 1079–96.

21 See Chodorow 1978, 1989.

22 See e.g. Alarcon 1985: 85–110; Apter 1990; Chabran 1984: 161–9; Chevigny 1984: 357–79; Collins 1987: 3–10; Kikumura 1981; Moraga 1986; Walker 1977: 93–102. Particularly striking fictional accounts include Woolf 1927; Tan 1989; and Kincaid 1985 and 1990.

I have been misread previously to be claiming a universal, idealized, usually pre-Oedipally constructed mother–daughter attachment, but when I say 'love', this is not what I mean or what I described in *Reproduction*. I mean an intense, passionate attachment, which might include or be a war with envy, hatred, ambivalence. We know from psychoanalysis that intense emotions always come with their opposite. Nor do I mean that this is *all* that matters to a daughter, but it does matter, among other things, enormously.

23 I believe that we do not know nearly enough about how romantic and sexual desires are formed during adolescence, when there is a coming together of childhood, culture and pubertal development, and that as we come to know more, we will find that this period is especially crucial. Karin Martin's research on adolescent girls' and boys' senses of sexual self (1994) confirms this claim.

24 On this see Benjamin 1988; deMarneffe 1993; and Roiphe and Galenson 1981.

25 As long as we follow the Freudian tradition – as have mainstream psychoanalysts as well as Lacanians and other French theorists since Freud – there is no other possible resolution of the overwhelming fear of the mother than this repudiation and installation of male dominant heterosexuality. Pro-female psychoanalysts like Chasseguet-Smirgel, and even feminist theorists like Benjamin, can only envision this turn to the father and symbolization of paternal and phallic power and desire as the solution for women as well as for men (Benjamin emphasizes the daughter's need for accepted identificatory love in relation to her father as the solution to the potential alienation of her desire). In recently rereading Klein, it struck me that there could have been, psychoanalytically, another route. In discussing the early stages of the Oedipus complex, Klein describes clearly and forcefully the repudiation of feminine identifications and maternal dependency in both boys and girls as an ingredient in the overvaluation of the penis, but in her work on early object relations, she also makes reparation towards the mother in the depressive position into a central, perhaps *the* central, developmental goal. If Kleinians had attended to gender development and continued Klein's focus on gender

differences in the Oedipus complex, it seems to me that a solution to the fear of femininity and the maternal breast in reparation towards the mother, rather than rejection of her, would have been an alternate developmental model. On male and female development, see Klein 1928 and 1957. On reparation, see Klein's writings in general and especially 1935: 262–89 and 1937: 306–43.
26 Horney 1932: 133–46.
27 See Freud 1910: 163–75 and 1912: 177–90.
28 Rich 1976: 257–9.
29 See on fathers, gender-typing, and differential treatment, Johnson 1975: 15–26 and 1988; Kerig *et al.* forthcoming; and Cowan *et al.* 1993: 165–95.
30 On the effect of father-absence on daughters, see Hetherington 1972: 313–26.
31 See Chodorow 1976: 66–78.
32 See, e.g., Rubin 1983.
33 Frye 1990: 180.
34 See e.g. Goldner 1991: 249–72; and Thorne 1993.

REFERENCES

Adelman, J. (1992) *Suffocating Mothers: Fantasies of Maternal Origin in Shakespeare's Plays. Hamlet to The Tempest*. New York: Routledge.
Alarcorn, N. (1985) 'What kind of a lover have you made me, mother: Towards a theory of Chicanas' feminism and cultural identity through poetry'. In Audrey T. McCluskey (ed.), *Perspectives on Feminism and Identity in Women of Color*. Bloomington: Indiana University Press, pp. 85–110.
Almaguer, T. (1991) 'The cartography of homosexual desire and identity among Chicano men'. *Differences* 3: 75–100.
Apter, T. (1990) *Altered Loves: Mothers and Daughters during Adolescence*. New York: Ballantine Books.
Benjamin, J. (1988) *The Bonds of Love*. New York: Pantheon.
—— (1991) 'Identificatory love in the father–daughter relationship'. *Psychoanalytic Dialogues* 1: 277–99.
Carby, H. (1985) '"On the threshold of the woman's era": Lynching, empire, and sexuality in black feminist theory'. *Critical Inquiry* 12: 262–77.
—— (1987) 'It jus be's dat way sometime: The sexual politics of women's blues'. *Radical America*. 20: 9–22.
Chabran, M. (1984) 'Exiles'. In C. Ascher, L. DeSalvo and S. Ruddick (eds) *Between Women: Biographers. Novelists. Critics. Teachers and Artists Write about Their Work on Women*. Boston: Beacon Press, pp. 161–9.
Chasseguet-Smirgel, J. (1985) *Creativity and Perversion*. London: Free Association Books.
Chevigny, B.G. (1984) 'Daughters writing: Toward a theory of women's biography'. In C. Ascher, L. DeSalvo and S. Ruddick (eds) *Between Women*. Boston: Beacon Press, pp. 357–79.
Chodorow, N. (1976) 'Oedipal asymmetries and heterosexual knots'. In *Feminism and Psychoanalytic Theory*. New Haven: Yale (1989), pp. 66–78.
—— (1978) *The Reproduction of Mothering*. Berkeley: University of California Press.
—— (1989) *Feminism and Psychoanalytic Theory*. New Haven: Yale University Press and Cambridge: Polity Press.
—— (1991) 'Freud on women'. In J. Neu (ed.), *The Cambridge Companion to Freud*. Cambridge and New York: Cambridge University Press, pp. 224–48.
—— (1992) 'Heterosexuality as a compromise formation: Reflections on the psychoanalytic theory of sexual development'. *Psychoanalysis and Contemporary Thought* 15.
—— (1994) *Femininities, Masculinities, Sexualities: Freud and Beyond*. Lexington: The University Press of Kentucky and London: Free Association Books.
Cixous, A. (1976) 'The laugh of the Medusa'. *Signs* 1.

Collins, P.H. (1987) 'The meaning of motherhood in black culture and black mother–daughter relationships'. *Sage.* 4: 3–10.
—— (1990) *Black Feminist Thought: Knowledge, Consciousness, and the Politics of Empowering.* Boston: Unwin Hyman.
Connell, R.W. (1987) *Gender and Power.* Stanford: Stanford University Press.
Contratto, S. (1987) 'Father presence in female psychological development'. In *Advances in Psychoanalytic Sociology*, Jerome, R., Platt, G.M. and Goldman, M. (eds). Malabar, Fl: Krieger, pp. 138–57.
Cott, N. (1978) 'Passionlessness: An interpretation of Victorian sexual ideology, 1750–1850', *Signs* 4, 2: 19–36.
Cowan, P.A, Cowan, C.P., and Kerig, P. (1993) 'Mothers, fathers, sons and daughters: Gender differences in family formation and parenting style'. In *Family, Self and Society.* Hillsdale, NJ.: Lawrence Erlbaum Associates.
deMarneffe, D. (1993) 'Toddlers' understandings of gender'. Dissertation in progress, Department of Psychology, University of California, Berkeley.
deRougemont, D. (1956) *Love in the Western World.* New York: Pantheon.
Duberman, M., Vicinus, M. and Chauncey, G. Jnr (eds) (1989) *Hidden from History: Reclaiming the Gay and Lesbian Past.* New York: New American Library.
Espin, O. (1984) 'Cultural and historical influences on sexuality in Hispanic/Latin women: Implications for psychotherapy'. In G. Vance (ed.) *Pleasure and Danger: Exploring Female Sexuality.* New York: Monthly Review Press, pp. 149–64.
Fast, I. (1984) *Gender Identity: A Differentiation Model.* Hillsdale, NJ: Lawrence Erlbaum.
Freud, S. (1909) 'Notes upon a case of obsessional neurosis'. S.E.10.
—— (1910) 'A special type of choice of object made by men' (*Contributions to the Psychology of Love*, Vol. I). S.E.11.
—— (1912) 'On the universal tendency to debasement in the sphere of love' (*Contributions to the Psychology of Love*, Vol. II). S.E.11.
—— (1918) 'From the history of an infantile neurosis'. S.E.17.
Frye, M. (1990) 'The possibility of feminist theory'. In D. Rhode (ed.) *Theoretical Perspectives on Sexual Difference.* New Haven: Yale.
Gaylin, W. and Person, E. (eds) (1988) *Passionate Attachments: Thinking about Love.* New York: The Free Press.
Golden, C. (1987) 'Diversity and variability in women's sexual identities'. In Boston Psychologies Collective (eds), *Lesbian Psychologies.* Urbana and Chicago: University of Illinois Press, pp. 19–34.
Goldner, V. (1991) 'Toward a critical relational theory of gender'. *Psychoanalytic Dialogues* 1: 249–72.
Gregor, T. (1985) *Anxious Pleasures: the Sexual Lives of an Amazonian People.* Chicago: The University of Chicago Press.
Helson, R., Mitchell, V. and Moane, G. (1984) 'Personality and patterns of adherence and nonadherence to the social clock'. *Journal of Personality and Social Psychology* 46: 1079–96.
Herdt, G. (1981) *Guardians of the Flutes: Idioms of Masculinity.* New York: McGraw-Hill.
Hetherington, M. (1972) 'Effects of father absence on personality development in adolescent daughters'. *Developmental Psychology* 7: 313–26.
Horney, K. (1932) 'The dread of woman'. In *Feminine Psychology.* New York: W.W. Norton, 1967, pp. 143–66.
Irigaray, L. (1985) *This Sex Which Is Not One.* Ithaca: Cornell University Press.
Johnson, M. (1975) 'Fathers, mothers and sex-typing'. *Sociological Inquiry* 45: 15–26.
—— (1988) *Strong Mothers. Weak Wives.* Berkeley: University of California Press.
Joseph, G. (1981) 'Black mothers and daughters: Their roles and functions in American society'. In G. Joseph and J. Lewis (eds) *Common Differences.* Boston: South End Press, pp. 75–126.
Kandiyoti, D. (1988) 'Bargaining with patriarchy'. *Gender and Society* 2: 274–90.

Katz, J.N. (1983) *The Gay/Lesbian Almanac*. New York: Harper & Row.

—— (1990) 'The invention of heterosexuality'. *Socialist Review* 20: 7–34.

Kerig, P. (1989) 'The engendered family: The influence of marital satisfaction on gender differences in parent–child interaction'. Unpublished Ph.D. dissertation, University of California, Berkeley.

Kerig, P., Cowan, P.A. and Cowan, C.P. (forthcoming) 'Marital quality and gender differences in parent–child interaction', *Developmental Psychology*.

Kernberg, O. (1980) 'Boundaries and structures in love relations'. In *Internal World and External Reality*. New York: Jason Aronson.

Kikumura, A. (1981) *Through Harsh Winters: The Life of a Japanese Immigrant Woman*. Novato, CA: Chandler & Sharpe.

Kincaid, J. (1985) *Annie John*. New York: Farrar, Straus & Giroux.

—— (1990) *Lucy*. New York: Farrar, Straus & Giroux.

Klein, M. (1928) 'Early stages of the Oedipus conflict'. In *Love, Guilt and Reparation and Other Works*. New York: Delta Press, 1975, pp. 186–98.

—— (1935) 'The psychogenesis of manic-depressive stages'. In *Love, Guilt and Reparation*. New York: Delta Press, 1975, pp. 262–89.

—— (1937) 'Love, guilt and reparation'. In *Love, Guilt and Reparation*. New York: Delta Press, 1975, pp. 306–43.

—— (1957) 'Envy and gratitude'. In *Envy and Gratitude and Other Works*. New York: Delta Press, 1975, pp. 176–235.

Levy, R.I. (1973) *Tahitians: Mind and Experience in the Society Islands*. Chicago: The University of Chicago Press.

Lewes, K. (1988) *The Psychoanalytic Theory of Male Homosexuality*. New York: Simon & Schuster.

McDougall, J. (1986) *Theatres of the Mind: Illusion and Truth on the Psychoanalytic State*. London: Free Association Books.

Martin, K. (1994) 'Puberty, sexuality and the self: Gender differences at adolescence'. Ph.D. Dissertation, University of California, Berkeley.

Mernissi, F. (1975) *Beyond the Veil: Male–Female Dynamics in a Modern Muslim Society*. Cambridge, MA: Schenkman.

Moraga, C. (1986) 'From a long line of vendidas: Chicanas and feminism'. In *Feminist Studies/Critical Studies* T. de Lauretis (ed.). Madison: University of Wisconsin press, pp. 173–90.

Parsons, A. (1969) *Belief, Magic and Anomie*. New York: Free Press.

Plaskow, J. (1990) *Standing Again at Sinai*. New York: HarperCollins.

Rich, A. (1976) *Of Woman Born: Motherhood as Experience and Institution*. New York: W.W. Norton.

Roiphe, H. and Galenson, E. (1981) *Infantile Origins of Sexual Identity*. New York: International Universities Press.

Rubin, L.B. (1983) *Intimate Strangers*. New York: Harper & Row.

Smith-Rosenberg, C. (1975) 'The female world of love and ritual'. In *Disorderly Conduct: Visions of Gender in Victorian America*. Oxford and New York: Oxford University Press, 1985.

—— (1994) *Femininities, Masculinities, Sexualities: Freud and Beyond*. Lexington: The University Press of Kentucky and London, Free Association Books.

Stein, A. (1992) 'Sisters and queers: The decentering of Lesbian feminism'. *Socialist Review* 22: 33–55.

Tan, A. (1989) *The Joy Luck Club*. New York: G.P. Putnam.

Thorne, B. (1993) *Gender Play: Boys and Girls in School*. New Brunswick: Rutgers University Press.

Walker, A. (1977) 'In search of our mothers' gardens'. In S. Ruddick and P. Daniels (eds), *Working It Out*. New York: Pantheon, pp. 93–102.

Woolf, V. (1927) *To The Lighthouse*. New York: Harcourt, Brace & World.

6 Sameness and difference
Toward an 'over-inclusive' theory of gender development

Jessica Benjamin

The idea of gender development has of necessity been linked to the notion of coming to terms with difference. What has changed in contemporary psychoanalysis is the meaning of sexual difference, which is no longer equated with anatomical difference. Assimilating the meaning of sexual difference(s) and assuming a position in relation to it are no longer seen as triggered by the discovery of anatomical facts. To some degree, however, the assumptions about the character of gender difference have not been wholly liberated from the naturalizing tendency in Freud's thought, although they exist in a more covert and subtle form. This form consists of a tendency to view the realization of difference as if it were more significant than, or detached from, the realization of likeness. The implicit assumption in differentiation theory is that acknowledging difference has a higher value, is a later achievement, is more difficult than recognizing likeness. The neglected point is that the difficulty lies in assimilating difference without repudiating likeness; that is, in straddling the space between the opposites. It is easy enough to give up one side of a polarity in order to oscillate towards the other side. What is difficult is to attain a notion of difference, being unlike, without giving up a sense of commonality, of being a 'like' human being.

Some time ago Chodorow (1978) suggested that men characteristically overvalue difference and deprecate commonality because of their more precarious sense of masculinity and repudiation of the mother. Thus to conceptualize a tension between sameness and difference, rather than a binary opposition that values one and deprecates the other, is part of the effort to critique the masculinist orientation of psychoanalysis. However, to deconstruct that binary opposition between sameness and difference – rather than simply noting the overvaluing of difference or elevating sameness – requires us to address the problem of identity as well. In contemporary gender differentiation theory the use of the term identity assumes difference as equivalent to the boundary between identities. That idea of Difference has been criticized in recent feminist thought, in favour of a notion of multiple differences and unstable identifications.

To move beyond a discourse of opposites requires the notion of something more plural, decentred, than the simple axis of sameness–difference, the idea of the one Difference, implies. The notion of a singular Difference as a dividing line implies that on either side of that line is something called identity, something homogeneous with everything else on that side. It appears then as if 'identity is destiny', that like has only to identify with like, and that acknowledging difference means respecting the boundary between what one is and what one cannot be. The idea of gender identity implies an inevitability, a coherence, a singularity and a uniformity that belies psychoanalytic notions of fantasy, sexuality and the unconscious (May 1986; Goldner 1991; Dimen 1991).

While I am largely in sympathy with this critique, I believe the essential point is that one can give up the notion of identity, reified as thing, without throwing out the notion of identification, as internal psychic process. One need not assume that the process of identification always falls along one side of the axis sameness–difference. To be interested in the process of assimilating *differences* and of learning to know 'the difference', it is not necessary to privilege Difference. To define that process as reflecting the work of culture – that is, as organized by discursive systems rather than by the innate, pre-social imperatives of the psyche – does not suffice to reveal the complexity of that work. To point out the reification of gender only confronts us with its mysterious persistence as a demarcation of psychic experience that is at once firmly resilient but highly volatile in its location and content.

To begin an investigation of identifications that takes the feminist critique into account, I would like to review some current psychoanalytic thinking about gender development. I will discuss some of the prominent positions in the contemporary theory of gender differentiation, which can be traced from Stoller's work on gender identity to Fast's 'differentiation model'. I want to both make use of and critique this theory, to preserve its notable observations but push it past the notion of identity. I will follow the axis of sameness–difference and propose a brief outline of the early development of gender identifications.

In presenting this outline, I am aware that the notion of developmental order is one to which feminist theory has raised as many objections as to the idea of identity. However, it seems to me essential to review recent thinking among psychoanalysts about the sequential narrative of gender development before confronting it with such a general critique, inasmuch as many feminist thinkers still work in a circa 1933 model of how gender categories take hold in the psyche. Furthermore, analytic thinking in North America has not been consonant with that in Europe and Britain. In the last decade or so, there have been some very interesting constructions of sexual difference outside the Oedipal structure. These views allow us to formulate the many identifications and experiences, conscious and unconscious, that exceed the rigid notion of identity. In addition, I submit that it is necessary to retain a tie, however elastic, to the observational world in which, whatever we infer about the unconscious, it is apparent that children really do represent and assimilate some things before others, are preoccupied with certain conflicts at one time more than another; in short, they go through phases.[1]

One previously denied aspect of gender development that I will highlight is the coming together of likeness with difference; that is, the identification with the parent understood to be of a different sex. Recent theorizing by Fast (1984) shows how children do use cross-sex identifications to formulate important parts of their self-representations as well as to imaginatively elaborate their fantasies about erotic relations between the sexes. Fast's theory of gender differentiation (1984) argues that children are initially bisexual, reinterpreting the idea of bisexuality to mean not a constitutional, biological anlage but a position of identifying with both parents (1990). In the pre-Oedipal phase children are 'over-inclusive': they believe they can have or be everything. Initially children do not recognize the exclusivity of the anatomical difference; they want what the other has not *instead* of but in *addition* to what they have.

I will sketch an outline of how current theorizing sees gender difference as developmentally integrated, bringing together my own observations with Fast's views, Stoller's work, and some of his critics. I think a new periodization can be made, delineating four main phases in early gender development: (1) nominal gender identification formation, (2) early differentiation of identifications in the context of separation–individuation, (3) the pre-Oedipal over-inclusive phase, and (4) the Oedipal phase. The premise of this differentiation perspective, as will be evident, is virtually the opposite of the position that genital difference is the motor of developing gender and sexual identity (see Roiphe and Galenson 1981). Rather, it takes off from the position articulated by Person and Ovesey (1983) according to which gender differentiation, evolving through separation conflicts and identifications, defines and gives weight to the genital difference, which then assumes great (if not exclusive) symbolic significance in the representation of gender experience and relations. However, my scheme is 'over-inclusive', integrating many contributions of earlier psychosexual theory which are reread critically.

AN OVER-INCLUSIVE VIEW OF DEVELOPMENT

The earliest phase of gender development was conceptualized by Stoller as the formation of core gender identity in the first year and a half of life: a felt conviction of being male or female, which later expands to the conviction of belonging to one or the other group. Rather than referring to this as identity, we might call it nominal gender identification. Perhaps because the conclusions of infancy research were not available to Stoller when he postulated his notion of core gender identity, he was not sure how to formulate 'primordial representation', appropriate to the first year of life (Stoller 1973). He thought that identification or incorporation were not appropriate categories, since he went with the prevailing view that the mother was not yet seen as outside, and could therefore not be taken in. However, since Stern (1985) presented his notion of an infant who begins to differentiate its mother almost from birth, and of presymbolic interaction representation of interactions generalized (RIGs) (see also Beebe and Lachmann (1988)), we can posit a process of core gender identification, rather than a product, core gender identity; we can picture this identification developing through concrete representations of self–body and self–other body interactions which are retroactively defined as gendered.

Stoller by no means postulated core gender identity as a final achievement of masculinity and femininity. He was clear that the 'sense of belonging to a sex becomes complicated' by later conflicts and fantasies, anxiety and defence which makes of masculinity and femininity something far more ambiguous than maleness and femaleness (1973). Indeed, he argued that only if the male child separates from his mother in the separation–individuation phase, 'disidentifies' in Greenson's term, can he develop that 'non-core gender identity we call masculinity'. However, he did not offer a full picture of the pre-Oedipal period, and both his and Greenson's use of the notion disidentification seem to imply that the male child fully gives up his identification with mother. I would argue that at this point the child still identifies with both parents who are only beginning to be partially, concretely differentiated. Given this persistence of multiple identifications, the idea that the self identifies as belonging to a sex should not be equated with the idea of an unambiguous and coherent *identity*. On the contrary, the core sense of belonging does not organize all gender experience. Core gender identification, or nominal gender, only makes sense if we conceptualize it as a background for future gender ambiguity and tension, a repetitive baseline against which all the other instruments play different, often conflicting or discordant, lines.

Some time in the second year of life, and particularly with the advent of symbolic representation in the second half of the second year, begins the next phase of gender positioning at the level of identifications. Person and Ovesey (1983) refer to this as gender role identity to distinguish it from core gender identity: masculine or feminine self-image rather than male and female designations. (Again, gender role identification would be a better usage.) Gender role identity is defined as a psychological achievement occurring in the conflictual context of separation–individuation. They disagree with Stoller's theorem that boys must separate more than girls, arguing rather that conflict around separation has a gender marker for boys. Coates *et al.*'s (1991) work on gender disorder supports their critique of Stoller, disputing the notion that transsexuals have difficulty separating from maternal symbiosis. Her analysis is rather that maternal withdrawal can inspire a profound melancholic identification, which is manifested as excessive femininity in boys, as well as in girls. The upshot of this analysis is to emphasize dynamic issues like separation anxiety or envy, rather than to see disidentification from the mother as an inherently pathogenic process.

At this same point of early separation, I have proposed, we see before and alongside object love something we might call identificatory love, a love that conventionally first appears in the relationship to the *rapprochement* father (Benjamin 1986, 1988, 1991). Following Abelin (1980), I have stressed that the father (or other masculine representation) plays a crucial role in representing separation, agency and desire in the rapprochement phase. In contrast to Abelin, I have argued that ideally children of both sexes continue to identify with both parents and therefore the *rapprochement* father is as important for girls as for boys. In this phase, the parents begin to be differentiated in the child's mind, but the child continues to elaborate both identifications as aspects of self. Traditionally, the mother – the source of goodness as Klein put it – is experienced as the complementary other, a precursor of the outside love object, while the father is sought as an object to be like. The mother has represented holding, attachment and caretaking, the father has represented the outside world, exploration, freedom – a 'knight in shining armor' says Mahler (cited in Abelin 1980). This traditional parental constellation has created a distinct structural position for the father in *rapprochement*, a function that may be played by other figures who represent separate subjectivity.

The function of the father at this point, as Blos (1984) and Tyson (1986) have also recognized, is dyadic, not triadic; that is to say, not rivalrous or forbidding. He represents not so much the one who can exclusively love mother (which the child still imagines doing directly) but the desire for the exciting outside. Identification with father as a like subject serves to make the child imaginatively able to represent this desire. As a consequence, the new feature associated with this phase, its legacy to adult erotic life, is identificatory love. Identificatory love remains associated with certain aspects of idealization and excitement throughout life. This identification with the ideal has a defensive function, masking the loss of control over mother that would otherwise be felt intensely at this point. It is a way of sustaining the practising grandiosity that would otherwise be challenged. But it is not only defensive, insofar as the ideal father serves to symbolically represent longings that the child may one day hope to realize, as well as the freedom, agency and contact with the outside world of other people that compensates for loss of control.[2]

Unlike Abelin (1980), Roiphe and Galenson (1981), and others who have emphasized a girl's 'castration reaction' (Roiphe and Galenson 1981), I am convinced that the father in this position is highly important to the girl in her effort to define herself as a subject of desire, and that identificatory love of the father, 'identification with difference' (Benjamin 1991) is crucial. The girl, too, needs to use the fantasy of power to inspire efforts towards attaining a sense of autonomy regarding her own body and the ability to move into a wider world. Likewise, a girl's identification with 'masculinity' reflects not a primary reaction to a sense of castration but love and admiration of father.

I should make clear that the *rapprochement* father is a kind of first but not 'the one and only' paradigm of identificatory love. Later on, for instance, in adolescence girls often develop this sort of love for a woman who represents their ideal. And although identificatory love of the father, under traditional gender arrangements, has had this special representational meaning, of course the mother remains an important figure of identification for boys as well as girls. Furthermore, for girls (analogous to boys), although they know they are female like mother, it is an effort to become feminine like her. Insofar as the *rapprochement* phase confronts children with the difference between mother's power and their own, between grandiose aspirations and reality, 'femininity' like 'masculinity' appears as an ideal, only partly attainable.

By the same token, the son does not need to forgo identification with mother so early, unless difficulties in separation lead to an early, defensive repudiation. The child has no sense of mutual exclusivity and does not need to choose between mother and father. As Stoller pointed out (1973), the boy's pre-Oedipal love for the mother is certainly not heterosexual, it is not strictly speaking object love – love for someone different or outside. It is, however, more complementary than identificatory; that is, it is based on interlocking asymmetrical roles that can be reversed. Giver and receiver are alternating, rather than symmetrically forming 'a love of parallels', as Dinesen described her love of Finch-Hatton (Thurman 1981). It is in this sense that mother has traditionally been love object rather than like subject – an opposition, as I have reiterated, that need not devolve upon real men and women in the present. There is, furthermore, a difference between inside and outside, between the one more familiar and the one more different, the love for the security of nearness and the love that aims for the shining star. If father is identified with in a special way because he is 'different' from the primary object, a subject, not a source of goodness, then identification with mother is with 'sameness'. And as long as the primary caretaker is the mother this must be true initially for both sexes. Under traditional parenting arrangements, then, father is the outside object who represents 'Difference'. This representation of Difference has been so important, so embedded in the culture, that it usually continues to be effective as an ideal whether or not a person defined as father exists or plays this role. At most, the absence of a defined or literal father figure means that a more complex tension develops between experienced relationships and the cultural ideal.

But the relationship to father is not identical for both sexes. Identificatory love is the relational context which, for boys, not only supports separation but also confirms the achievement of masculinity as a naturalized 'male destiny'. This gives the relationship with father an additional spin, making it more crucial to the boy's representation of gender as identity, to his sense of self-cohesion (as seems implicit in Kohut's alignment of the father with the self-cohering object). Conventionally, a stronger mutual attraction between father and son is fostered by the father himself, and this promotes recognition through identification, a special erotic relationship. The practising toddler's 'love affair with the world' turns into a homoerotic love affair with the father who represents the world. The boy is in love with his ideal. This homoerotic, identificatory love serves as the boy's vehicle for establishing masculinity both defensively and creatively; it confirms his sense of himself as subject of desire. Of course, this process of identification can only be successful when it is reciprocal, when the father identifies with his son and says, You can be like me, or when the validating mother says, You are just like your dad.

The positive elaboration of those characteristics that are eventually recognized as the other's prerogative depends in part on the parental validation of the identificatory love that informs cross-sex identification. In the pre-Oedipal over-inclusive phase as denoted by Fast, children not only identify with both parents, they begin to symbolize genital meanings and assimilate unconsciously the gestural and behavioural vocabulary supplied by the culture to express masculinity and femininity. Now recognizing certain basic distinctions between masculinity and femininity, children continue to try to imaginatively elaborate both options within themselves. A 30 month old girl may imitate her older brother's play with action figures in order to assimilate symbolic masculinity, the phallic repertoire of colliding, penetrating, invading and blocking. A boy of 2 years old may insist that he has a vagina, but at 3, more aware of external anatomy, he might prefer to claim to have a baby inside his tummy, elaborating a fantasy of receiving, holding, and expelling. This phase also shows a mixing of identifications in rapid succession: a 3 and a half year old girl, jealous of the girl her older brother plays with, strides up to the girl and flexes the muscles in her raised arms, saying 'I'm stronger than you'. A few minutes later, to create yet another forceful impression, she insists that her mother dress her in her ballerina costume. Klein (1928, 1945), of all the early psychoanalysts, most clearly recognized the child's need to identify with and make symbolic use of all the organs and parental capacities, including those fantasized as part of the mother–father interaction.

To the extent that the child imaginatively identifies, without yet realizing the impossibility of acquiring certain capacities and organs, envy is not yet a dominant motive. But gradually the over-inclusive period is marked by envy and ongoing protest against increasing realization of gender difference, says Fast (1984). At this point, castration for both sexes represents the loss of the opposite sex's capacities and genitals. This protest is not completely symmetrical, since for boys the focus is usually on the capacity to bear a baby, while for girls the coveted thing is the penis (Fast 1984). But both sexes have a parallel development in their insistence on being everything, their elaboration of complementarity as opposites held within the self, and their protest against limits.

The Oedipal phase, beginning towards the end of the fourth year, might be considered gender differentiation proper, when the complementary opposites are attributed to self or other respectively. In other words, the dynamic of renunciation, giving up the hope of fulfilling identificatory love of one parent, might be seen as the road to object love, loving the object as an outside figure who embodies what the self does not. But this construction raises an important question when we consider homosexual object choice: is the parent of the same nominal gender simply experienced as 'less the same', or does a different relationship between identificatory and object love get formulated? Perhaps the delineation I have offered only fits the heterosexual child, for whom the preoccupation with complementarity becomes the Oedipal preoccupation. Thus a 3 and a half year old boy who had earlier expressed many wishes to be like his mother, began to insist on calling himself Micky and her Minnie, as in Mouse. He would say lovingly, 'Isn't this a nice day we're havin' Minnie?' He explained this himself one night at bedtime, saying, 'You're a girl and I'm a boy, but we're both mice; we're both little'. Complementarity, then, did not fully abrogate likeness; a sense of belonging to the same species compensated for the loss of being alike in gender. Another way to look at this is that the boy could not accept the 'double difference', as Chasseguet-Smirgel calls it, could only take in the gender difference by denying the generational one. By the age of 4, this piece of reality, too, was accepted and Micky Mouse was replaced by superheroes with no special female companions.

The early Oedipal phase (at and just before age 4) is usually more defensive, characterized by a rigid definition of gender complementarity and – as Freud noted in relation to boys but overlooked in girls – by scornful repudiation of the opposite sex. Again, as Freud recognized only for boys, in this phase castration anxiety refers to the loss of one's own genitals. However, as Mayer (1985) has pointed out, the fear of losing one's own genitals is crucial for girls at this point as well, and is accompanied by same-sex chauvinism, insistence that 'everyone must be just like me', fear and repudiation of the other. This chauvinism is characterized by the attitude that, to paraphrase the famous dictum about winning, 'what I have is not everything, but it is the *only thing* (worth having)'. Freud's theory of phallic monism (Chasseguet-Smirgel 1976) expressed it perfectly. As Horney (1926) rightly pointed out, his theory corresponds to the thinking of the Oedipal boy who believes that girls have 'nothing'. Envy and feelings of loss and resentment spur both the repudiation and the idealization of the opposite sex at this point. Sometimes love and longing for the lost other predominate, sometimes rivalry and repudiation.

Ideally, the later Oedipal phase allows the rigid insistence on complementarity and the repudiation of the other to be ameliorated as the fantasy of object love comes to compensate narcissistic loss. However, the Oedipal love is both a resolution and a perpetuation of mourning. One cannot yet embody the ideal of femininity or masculinity that mother and father represent, and one cannot yet 'possess' the other body in love; one cannot be or have. In my view, the unaccepted mourning for that which one will never be – for instance, the boy's inability to face the loss of not being the mother, to even acknowledge envy of the feminine – has particularly negative repercussions, more profound if less obvious than the classically recognized Oedipal frustration of not having mother. The outcome of this loss is as much a matter of cultural mediation as of object relationships. Since identification no longer devolves only on the parent but is now supplemented by secondary identifications, the mellowing out of complementarity and repudiation varies depending on the flexibility of the culture and peer group regarding cross-gender identifications.

Here I want to note an important difference between early identificatory love and later Oedipal love identifications. Identificatory love has been, wrongly I think, assimilated to the boy's negative Oedipus complex, conflating the boy's homoerotic wish to be loved by father as like him with the heteroerotic wish to be to father as the mother is. Actually, these are pretty much obverse relationships to father. The negative Oedipus, I suggest, represents a movement *from* identification *to* object love, paralleling the positive Oedipal movement from identification to object love of the opposite sex.[3] However, in the negative Oedipal case the boy renounces identification with father not because of the ineluctable dictates of gender, but because of parental impediments in the way of the identificatory paternal bond. In other words, thwarted identificatory love turns into ideal love, a submissive or hostile tie to a powerful, admired father who emasculates rather than confirms the boy's masculinity. This frequently occurs when the father is too far outside the mother–child dyad and, prematurely Oedipalizing his stance towards his son, is too rivalrous or too afraid of sadistic impulses to be tender. This transformation then presents as and is often analysed as a negative Oedipal wish for a passive relation with father.

Blos has also argued for a reinterpretation of the negative Oedipal stance in terms of the wish for the dyadic father, which he sees as requiring resolution in order to allow for heterosexual wishes to be authentic. I think his position poses an important challenge to a superficial notion of heterosexuality, which places it in opposition to homoerotic currents. The 'father hunger' shown by sons of absent fathers is primarily a reaction to lack of homoerotic love. In heterosexual men it becomes an impediment to loving women not because the role model is remote, but because the real erotic energy is tied to the frustrated wish for recognition from the father. In cultures dominated by this frustrated father–son erotic, women become valuable not as sources of inner satisfaction but as signifiers of male prowess, as currency in the exchange of power. Frequently, the thwarting of paternal identificatory love pushes the boy to deny his identificatory love of the mother on whom he depends too exclusively, and so spurs an exaggerated repudiation of femininity.

Then too, the boy's repudiation of femininity may well be linked to the mother's sacrifice of desire and early grandiosity. In her admiration of her son, she unconsciously communicates her feelings as the daughter whose identificatory love was denied. Continuing her ideal love of her father, she projects her desire and grandiosity on to her male child and casts them out of herself. The boy's gender splitting is thus also shaped by his *rapprochement* experience, when the father is inaccessible and idealized, while the mother views her son as both Oedipal object and ideal self. And so it was no accident that Freud's theory gave the woman a son to love, in his view the only unambivalent love. To the mother was granted the fulfilment of the wish for identificatory love not in relation to her father but in ideal love of her son; to the son was given the grandiosity that is mirrored by the mother who renounced it. But Freud's story also gave the son an ideal love, a forever unrequited search for identificatory love of the father who has cast him out as a murderous rival. This may be the great triangle of identificatory love, replayed endlessly in stories of women's submission to and sacrifice for heroes who leave them to follow the quest for the paternal grail, the father's recognition.

TOWARD A CRITIQUE OF GENDER COMPLEMENTARITY

The first conclusion I want to draw from the foregoing is that to the degree that the characteristics of the other have been lovingly incorporated through identification in the over-inclusive phase, loss can be ameliorated, and the sequelae of the Oedipal phase can be informed more by other-love than by repudiation/idealization. The acceptance of one's own limits and the ability to love what is different in the other are not compromised by the previous integration of opposite sex identifications; on the contrary. As Fast suggests, if the individual does not get stuck in the rigid complementarity of the early Oedipal phase, the tendency to denigrate what cannot be had may give way to an easier familiarity with opposite sex characteristics later on.

I diverge from Fast, however, insofar as she insists on the necessity of renouncing what belongs to the other, and relinquishing the narcissism of bisexuality. I would rather speculate, as Aron (1992) proposes, that the ability to continue elaborating opposite sex feelings/behaviour/attitudes under the umbrella of one's own narcissism persists as a preconscious or unconscious capacity. It includes the capacity for cross-sex identification, as well as the ability to represent and symbolize the role of the other in sexual relations. For most individuals, this may be a relatively benign form of omnipotence. Aron suggests that it may be more helpful to think of the grandiose, narcissistic aspiration to bisexual completeness as a position from which we draw creativity, hence not as something to be relinquished but rather to be maintained alongside and modified by the more differentiated positions.[4] Likewise, the wish to feel commonality and its concomitant, identificatory love, should alternate with recognizing difference, and the concomitant object love. Identification could then be used to both ratify sameness and create commonality as a bridge across difference.

The idea of renouncing the other's prerogatives in the Oedipal phase seems to misconstrue gender identity as a final achievement, a cohesive, stable system, rather than recognizing it as an unattainable, Oedipal ideal with which the self constantly struggles. As Goldner (1991) has pointed out, the tension between the ideal self-representation and actual self-experience is complicated by rigid notions of complementarity that are none the less contradictory. The maintenance of a gendered self-representation is continually taxed by conflicting identifications, requiring a capacity for living with contradiction (Goldner 1991). To remain true to the analytic posture, it is necessary to recognize these contradictions. This means, as Harris (1991) has shown, to divine the multiplicity of positions beneath the appearance of singularity in object choice or identifications, to see gender experience as both tenacious and fragile, reified substance and dissolving insubstantial. This also means, as Dimen (1991) has argued, deconstructing the reified gender dichotomies and thinking of gender in transitional terms; leaving a world of fixed boundaries with uncrossable borders for a transitional territory in which the conventional opposites create movable walls and pleasurable tension.

The use of a developmental trajectory may seem to imply a teleological view, and in this case it might be thought that identification is simply the basis for object love, that reaching an Oedipal position is still the be-all and end-all of development, that we need not look any further. Despite what I have said about the need for integrating over-inclusiveness with complementarity, the alignment of inclusiveness with early narcissism might be misconstrued to privilege later sexual complementarity and object love over early inclusiveness and identificatory love. Alternatively, this view might lead us to recognize identificatory love and object love as frequently coincident, rather than necessarily mutually exclusive. It could move us towards a positive revaluing of narcissism and a questioning of hetero-sexual complementarity as the goal of development. In fact, I believe that proposing a developmental view of differentiation is not the same as positing a normative system of sexual identity. It is not necessary to abandon all empirically based notions of development in order to avoid normative positions. If such positions are often drawn from notions of development, that is due to the acceptance of unrelated and unsupportable assumptions: that earlier is more fundamental but later is better (more developed), that development is unilinear, that it is desirable for all conflicts to be resolved and superseded, and that earlier experiences persist like geological layers unchanged by and unalloyed with later symbolic unconscious elaborations.

Perhaps psychoanalytic theory needs to decentre its account of development, such that later integrations neither seamlessly subsume earlier positions with later ones, nor replace them, but refigure them (analogous to Freud's idea of deferred action, *Nachträglichkeit* (see Laplanche and Pontalis 1973)). In this way of thinking, later integrations would retain and refine earlier positions, changing their appearance yet not obliterating them, enabling a flexible oscillation between levels of experience. When integration is confused with reductive assimilation, development is rightly suspect as a high-priced form of impoverishment – as in the world of economic development, which has already wiped out whole species and landscapes, as well as the richness and beauty of different cultures.

However, this warning against reifying gender development need not, as I said before, foreclose the efforts to formulate a dynamic perspective on the development of gender identifications. It does mean that we should be cautious about assuming that development is a simple trajectory towards heterosexual complementarity. Conventional heterosexuality does not require moving beyond the more rigidly organized complementarities of gender polarity. As Kernberg (1991) has noted, the insistence that the other be the heterosexual mirror image of the self, including intolerance of any other sexual elements, reflects a defence against envy, not an acceptance of difference. Neither heterosexual nor homosexual relationships inherently guarantee a particular stance towards complementarity or sameness; either may succumb to fixity or play around with convention and previously fixed identities. The self-conscious and ironic play with gender conventions has evolved in tension with identity politics in the homosexual community, becoming the basis for theorizing, in Butler's (1990) term, subversions of identity.

BEYOND THE OEDIPAL

Precisely such challenges to Oedipal complementarity suggest a reconsideration of the function and meaning of complementarity. What does it mean to posit the integration of the earlier over-inclusive position with the later Oedipal complementarity in the post-Oedipal phase? What would it mean to restore, at a higher level of differentiation, capacities that were excluded by Oedipal rigidity? I have proposed that object love, which has sometimes been seen as opposite to, exclusive of, or replaced by, identification, may also be seen as growing out of identificatory love. But what is the ongoing relationship between object love and identification, what becomes of identificatory love of the opposite sex later in life? Is this a simple proposition, that identification gives way to object love, a kind of reversal of the postulate that object love is replaced by identification in the ego? If not, how to conceptualize the way that identification remains part of love relationships throughout life?

These two sets of questions about the fate of identification and the integration of the over-inclusive phase are related. My answer is that the sustaining of identificatory tendencies alongside object love creates a different kind of complementarity, and a different stance towards oppositional differences. It is possible to distinguish between two forms of complementarity. The earlier Oedipal form is a simple opposition, constituted by splitting, projecting the unwanted elements into the other; in that form, what the other has is 'nothing'. The post-Oedipal form is constituted by sustaining the tension between contrasting elements, so that they remain potentially available rather than forbidden and so that the oscillation between them can then be pleasurable, rather than dangerous. While the rigid form of sexual complementarity may actually utilize a well-elaborated representation of the other's role derived from previous identification, the self repudiates and is threatened by that role as an unwanted part.

As our culture is organized, the child must traverse an Oedipal period in which complementarity is accomplished by insisting on polarity, mutual exclusivity, black and white, male and female, can and cannot. Using Kohlberg's distinction between conventional and post-conventional thinking, we could say that this Oedipal polarizing corresponds to conventional thinking about difference, which is appropriate to this stage of children's moral and cognitive development. In Kohlberg's view, post-conventional thinking does not really develop until adolescence, and this would indeed be the period when we would expect the Oedipal recrudescence to resolve with a more differentiated, flexible form of complementarity. In this vein Bassin (1991) has used the terms of genital theory to propose that the phallic phase, with its opposites have/have not, should give way in adolescence to a true genital phase, in which antithetical elements can be reunited. She proposes that the transcendence of the split unity of gender polarity is expressed through symbol formation, with its transitional bridging function. Unlike projective identification, symbolization reunites the antagonistic component tendencies (Freedman 1980; cited in Bassin 1991), for instance, active and passive. Symbolization links rather than prohibits the gratification of both aims, expressing rather than masking the unconscious oscillation between them. The key to this symbolic function is the recuperation of identification with the 'missing half' of the complementarity: in symbolization 'the familiar is found in the unfamiliar' (Freedman cited in Bassin 1991).

The familiar can be found by 'returning' to the over-inclusive position in which it was still possible to use the transitional space of communicative play to entertain wishes that reality denies: as when a 3-year-old boy said to his mother, 'I have a nipple on my penis, see, and the peepee comes out of the nipple.' To pretend the penis is the breast, or the anus is the vagina, need not serve the denial of difference, as theories of perversion have stressed; such fantasy play may also serve the symbolic bridging of difference acknowledged and enhance sexual empathy. Development thus does not require a unilinear trajectory away from the over-inclusive position but the ability to return without losing the knowledge of difference. The more differentiated post-conventional form of symbolic complementarity, which is no longer concrete and projective, requires access to the flexible identificatory capacities of pre-Oedipal life.

This notion of recapturing over-inclusive structures of identification and sublimating omnipotence is meant to incorporate the epistemological contribution of contemporary cultural theory, especially feminist theory, by decentring our notion of development and replacing the discourse of identity with the notion of identifications (plural). At the same time, this perspective lends the support of developmental theory to contemporary feminist theorizing about gender. The post-conventional relation to gender representations is not a utopian ideal drawn from theoretical speculation but a material possibility, already visible in the interstices of the gender order.

According to contemporary feminist theory, woman is not simply constructed as man's other; rather, the binary logic of male subject/female other constructs both male and female, behind the backs, as it were, of men. Woman cannot claim a position 'outside' that logic, unless by positing some essential, not yet represented femininity. As Butler (1990) has shown, to attack that logic while rejecting such essentialism requires a notion of subversion. As I have tried to show, the post-conventional complementarity, which allows the multiplicity and mutuality denied by the Oedipal form, does not exist 'outside' the gender system. It reworks its terms, disrupting its binary logic by recombining and breaking down opposites, rather than by discovering something wholly different, unrepresented or unrepresentable. It subverts the Oedipal complementarity through the leverage of its own negative tension – the impossibility of constituting a complementary system that can truly exclude from the self all identification with otherness. The post-conventional complementarity relies on the psychic capacity to symbolically bridge split oppositions as well as on pre-Oedipal over-inclusiveness.

Psychoanalytic theory has, until recently, been unable to think beyond the Oedipal level. This fixation is reflected in the prevailing theories that insist on heterosexual complementarity, that equates perversion with homosexuality and 'genital whole object relations' with heterosexuality (see Chodorow 1992). The claim that the Oedipal achievement of complementarity represents a renunciation of omnipotence and acceptance of limits – being only the one or the other – misses another dimension, the one that gives depth to the delineation of difference. It also serves to conceal the unconscious narcissism of Oedipal chauvinism – being the 'only thing' – for which Freud's theory of the girl as 'little man' *manqué* was exemplary.

The simple move, according to which 'I am the One, you are the Other', which creates the binary form of otherness, is the Oedipal move for both sexes. It is overtly hegemonic in the male form – but covertly present in its opposite form, female contempt, as Dinnerstein (1976) pointed out – because (let us abjure speculation and say for whatever reasons) men became dominant. We may speculate that this Oedipal move represents a simple reversal of the pre-Oedipal logic in which the mother seems to be everything 'generically human' (Chodorow 1979). More important, the superordinate logic that underlies both moves is that of mutual exclusivity, and it is instituted in the Oedipus complex. In this sense, the joining of heterosexual complementarity and binary opposition (Goldner 1991) in the Oedipal moment constitutes 'the' sexual Difference.

But the constitution of sexual differences in the multiple sense is not centred around one psychic complex. The reality of sexual differences is far more multifarious than the binary logic of mutual exclusivity allows. Not only does the psyche preserve unconsciously identifications that have been repudiated, but it expresses them unconsciously or consciously in sexual relations, between parents and children, lovers of whatever apparent object choices, making them far more complex than this complementarity represents. The Oedipal structure, although pervasive at one level, that of gender ideals, does not seal off other development, even when it is represented as doing so; it is not a seamless, consistent, hegemonic structure that suppresses everything else in the psyche (Goldner 1991).

By the same token, no absolute transcendence of the Oedipal is possible. To delineate the binary logic of heterosexual complementarity is not equivalent to disavowing or getting rid of Oedipal structures. It is no more possible to get rid of the omnipotent aspect of the Oedipal position than it is to get rid of the pre-Oedipal fantasy of omnipotence. (Or rather, it would only be possible in a world without loss, envy and difference – which would be a wholly omnipotent world.) Rather, the point is to subvert the concealed omnipotence by exposing it, as well as to recognize another realm of sexual freedom that reworks the Oedipal terms. To be sure, this realm depends upon the other face of omnipotence: the over-inclusive capacities to transcend reality by means of fantasy, which can be reintegrated in the sexual symbolic of the post-Oedipal phase.

The tension between the omnipotent wish for transcendence and the affirmation of limits has always found expression in the domains of aesthetic and erotic pleasure. Any effort to destabilize the fixed positions of gender complementarity depends upon the tension between limit and transgression, a limit those positions actually help to frame, a boundary in relation to which symbolic acts achieve their meaning. Both the knowledge of nominal gender identification and of the Oedipal complementarity constitute a background for the symbolic transgressions of fantasy, for the disruption of complementary oppositions and fixed identities. In fact the tension between limit and transgression suggests that each depends on the other.

The post-Oedipal complementarity also implies a different, less definite relation between object love and identification. Freud at one point described (1921) identification as the first emotional tie to the object, a way of being related to someone who is there, who is loved and not necessarily lost. He seemingly gave up that idea in favour of identification as an internal process, a precipitate of abandoned, lost and renounced objects (1923). This supercession, like other moves in Oedipal theory, gave away as much as it gained. In this instance, it probably functioned to turn attention away from identificatory love, the most important legacy of the pre-Oedipal period, which contributes to subsequent relationships of love and like. I see no reason why we cannot be inclusive, and recognize that identificatory love and object love can exist simultaneously. Likewise, the movements from identification to object love, from object love to identification are ongoing alternations throughout life. Like other oppositions, the unconscious can switch them, and the difficulty is to maintain them as tensions rather than break them down into split polarities. In other words, in post-Oedipal life, object love includes aspects of identificatory love, and vice versa. Like difference and sameness, object love and identificatory love constitute tensions that need not, and probably should not, be resolved in favour of one side.

Nor are the sides precisely what they have appeared to be within the binary logic of gender complementarity. In that logic of 'the one and the other', there is no place for 'the both or the many'. If sex and gender as we know them are oriented to the pull of opposing poles, then these poles are not masculinity and femininity. Rather, gender dimorphism itself represents only one pole, the other pole being the polymorphism of the psyche.

NOTES

1   We may wish to disrupt the idea of a phase as a self-enclosed, exclusive geological layer in favour of a notion that psychic events overlap and recur, are not merely successive but often coincident, are usually known retroactively through appearance rather than in 'pure culture'. Still, to retain a flexible idea of phase has the advantage of allowing a notion of complexes which, if they do not remain temporally organized after their initial introduction, still retain a structural connection. The idea of development has to be suspended and yet preserved – Lacan, who is often cited by critics, did no less.

2   While my conception of the pre-Oedipal father has overlapping characteristics with the imaginary father described by Kristeva (1987), the father who helps the child to 'abject' (separate from) the mother, there are important differences. Kristeva also takes up Freud's contention that identification is the first tie to the object, an immediate relation rather than an effect of lost love, and recognises that loving and being, like narcissism and object love, are not as distinct as they appear to be. She rightly sees this metaphorical object of idealization as a basis of the transference, distinct from merger or maternal satisfaction. However, her insistence on the ternary structure seems to detract from the direct relation to the father as the desired object of identificatory love, rather than something the child finds in the mother. The father represents the mother's desire for someone else besides the child, the not-I, rather than the child's desire for someone other than the mother. Thus the child is portrayed as less active, not desiring the outside or the father so much as reactive to mother's desire.

3   Here, too, the question arises as to whether 'opposite' sex means the parent whose nominal gender is different, or whether it can be the parent perceived as same. The boy's wish to be loved by the father and like mother is called homosexual, but is a heteroerotic wish. Conversely, the child's homoerotic wish to be loved as a like subject plays a role not only in male homosexuality, but in women's heterosexual love.

4   Aron points out that this notion of integration would parallel recent Kleinian interpretations that insist that the schizoid position should remain in dialectical tension with the depressive position rather than being replaced by it (see Eigen 1985; Ogden 1986).

REFERENCES

Abelin, E.L. (1980) 'Triangulation, the role of the father and the origins of core gender identity during the rapprochement subphase' in R.F. Lax, S. Bach, and J.A. Burland (eds) *Rapprochement*, New York: Aronson, pp. 151–70.

Aron, L. (1992) 'The internalized primal scene'. Unpublished.

Bassin, D. (1991) 'The true genital phase'. Unpublished.

Beebe, B. and Lachmann, F. (1988) 'The contribution of mother–infant mutual influence to the origins of self and object representations'. *Psychoanalytic Psychology*, 5: 305–37.

Benjamin, J. (1986) 'The alienation of desire: Woman's masochism and ideal love' in J. Alpert (ed.) *Woman and Psychoanalysis*. Hillsdale, NJ: Analytic Press, pp. 113–38.

—— (1988) *The Bonds of Love*. New York: Pantheon.

—— (1990) 'An outline of intersubjectivity: The development of recognition'. *Psychoanalytic Psychology*, 7, suppl.: 33–46.

—— (1991) 'Father and daughter: identification with difference – a contribution to gender heterodoxy'. *Psychoanalytic Dialogues*, 1, 3: 277–99.

Blos, P. (1976) 'Freud and female sexuality'. *International Journal of Psycho-Analysis*, 57: 275–86.

—— (1984) 'Son and father'. *Journal of the American Psychoanalytic Association*.

Butler, J. (1990) *Gender Trouble*. New York and London: Routledge.

Chasseguet-Smirgel, J. (1976) 'Freud and female sexuality', *International Journal of Psychoanalysis*, 57: 275–86.

Chodorow, N. (1978) *The Reproduction of Mothering*. Berkeley: University of California Press.

—— (1979) 'Difference, relation and gender in psychoanalytic perspective'. *Socialist Review* 9 (4): 51–70.

—— (1992) 'Heterosexuality as a compromise formation: reflections on the psychoanalytic theory of sexual development'. *Psychoanalysis and Contemporary Thought*, 15: 267–304.

Coates, S., Friedman, R. and Wolfe, S. (1991) 'The etiology of boyhood gender disorder'. *Psychoanalytic Dialogues*, I (4): 481–523.

Dimen, M. (1991) 'Deconstructing difference: Gender, splitting, and transitional space'. *Psychoanalytic Dialogues* 1 (3): 335–52.

Dinnerstein, D. (1976) *The Mermaid and the Minotaur*. New York: Harper & Row.

Eigen, M. (1985) 'Toward Bion's starting point: Between catastrophe and faith'. *International Journal of Psycho-Analysis*, 66: 321–30.

Fast, I. (1984) *Gender Identity*. Hillsdale, NJ: The Analytic Press.

—— (1990) 'Aspects of early gender development: Toward a reformulation'. *Psychoanalytic Psychology*, 7, suppl.: 105–17.

Freedman, N. (1980) 'On splitting and its resolution'. *Psychoanalysis and Contemporary Thought*, 3: 237–66.

Freud, S. (1921) 'Group psychology and the analysis of the ego'. S.E.18: 67–144.

—— (1923) *The Ego and the Id*. S.E.19: 1–66.

—— (1931) 'Female sexuality'. S.E.21: 225–46.

—— (1933) 'New introductory lectures on psychoanalysis: XXXIII, Femininity'. S.E.22: 112–35.

Galenson, E. and Roiphe, H. (1982) 'The pre-Oedipal relationship of a father, mother, and daughter' in S.H. Cath, A.R. Gurwitt, and J.M. Ross (eds) *Father and Child*. Boston: Little, Brown, pp. 151–62.

Goldner, V. (1991) 'Toward a critical relational theory of gender'. *Psychoanalytic Dialogues*, 1 (3): 249–72.

Greenson, R. (1968) 'Dis-identifying from mother: its special importance for the boy'. *International Journal of Psycho-Analysis*, 49: 370–4.

Harris, A. (1991) 'Gender as contradiction'. *Psychoanalytic Dialogues*, 1, 2: 197–224.

Horney, K. (1924) 'On the genesis of the castration complex in women' in *Feminine Psychology*. New York: Norton (1967), pp. 37–54.

—— (1926) 'The flight from womanhood', in *Feminine Psychology*. New York: Norton (1967), pp. 54–70.

Kernberg, O. (1991) 'Aggression and love in the relationship of the couple'. *Journal of the American Psychoanalytic Association*, 39: 45–70.

Klein, M. (1928) 'Early stages of the Oedipus conflict' reprinted in M. Klein *Love, Guilt and Reparation*. London: Virago, 1988.

—— (1945) 'The Oedipus complex in the light of early anxieties' reprinted in M. Klein *Love, Guilt and Reparation*. London: Virago, 1988.

Kristeva, J. (1987) *Tales of Love*. Trans. L. Roudiez. New York: Columbia University Press.

Laplanche, J. and Pontalis, J. (1973) *The Language of Psychoanalysis*. New York: Norton.

MacDougall, J. (1980) *Plea for a Measure of Abnormality*. New York: International Universities Press.

Mahler, M., Pine, F. and Bergman, A. (1975) *The Psychological Birth of the Human Infant*. New York: Basic Books.

May, R. (1986) 'Concerning a psychoanalytic view of maleness'. *Psycho-Analytic Review*, 73: 175–93.

Mayer, E. (1985) 'Everybody must be like me'. *International Journal of Psychoanalysis*, 66: 331–48.

Ogden, T. (1986) *The Matrix of the Mind*. New York: Aronson.

Person, E.S. (1988) *Dreams of Love and Fateful Encounters*. New York: Norton.

Person, E.S. and Ovesey, L. (1983) 'Psychoanalytic theories of gender identity'. *Journal of the American Academy of Psychoanalysis*, 11: 203–26.

Roiphe, H. and Galenson, E. (1981) *Infantile Origins of Sexual Identity*. New York: International Universities Press.

Stern, D. (1985) *The Interpersonal World of the Infant*. New York: Basic Books.

Stoller, R.J. (1968) *Sex and Gender*. New York: Aronson.

—— (1973) 'Facts and fancies: An examination of Freud's concept of bisexuality', in *Women and Analysis*, J. Strause (ed.), Boston: G.K. Hall, 1985, pp. 343–64.

—— (1975) *Perversion*. New York: Pantheon Press.

Thurman. J. (1981) *Isak Dinesen: The Life of a Storyteller*. New York: St. Martin's Press.

Tyson, P. (1986) 'Male gender identity: early developmental roots'. *Psychoanalytic Review*, 73: 405–25.

7 Consuming male fantasy
Feminist psychoanalysis retold

Janet Sayers

It is now twenty years since Juliet Mitchell first emphasized, in *Psychoanalysis and Feminism* (1974), the continuing importance of Freud's account of the unconscious ramifications of patriarchy. Its fantasies still abound – not least in today's backlash against feminism, as I shall explain in the first section of this chapter. Today's psychoanalytically-minded therapists however – feminist and non-feminist alike – scarcely concern themselves with such ills. Instead, as I shall recount, they are often more preoccupied with the realities of their patients' mothering. By contrast literary theorists have increasingly gone beyond Mitchell's adoption of Lacan's rereading of Freud in terms of phallic symbolism to draw attention to the centrality of male fantasy in our psychology. Illustrating, with four case examples of women's eating disorders, the relevance of Lacanian and post-Lacanian theory to clinical practice I shall conclude with the general importance of retelling feminist therapy in its terms. First though to the political ills done in patriarchy's name.

PATRIARCHAL POLITICS

Politically, male fantasy has long been deployed against those to whom it is fed; never more so perhaps than by the National Socialists in Germany in the 1930s. As the Freudian psychoanalyst Wilhelm Reich (1933) then pointed out, the Nazis ruthlessly exploited fantasies about men and their absence to draw a smoke-screen over the costs to the lower middle class of their party's alliance with big business. Their propaganda, Reich claimed, served to win this class's support by constructing in terms of emasculation their feelings about Germany's First World War defeat and subsequent economic collapse, and about the decline of this class's previously father-run businesses and farms. As a solution, the Nazis offered up the spectre of the Jew as the receptacle into which they might expel their feelings of having been unmanned, and for themselves the image of the fatherland, the Führer, and stormtrooper with which to identify. The response of the Allies was to turn this selfsame fantasy on its head – not least by crudely mobilizing their troops to risk their lives with the battle hymn 'Hitler has only got one ball'.

Nor did such deployment of male fantasy end with the war. It has since regularly been used politically by the Left as well as by the Right. Criticizing fascism, racism and the corporate state, Herbert Marcuse (1970), for instance, waxed lyrical about a time gone by when, he claimed, fathers modelled and fostered in their offspring a strong superego identification with them as theorized by Freud (e.g. 1923a) in *The Ego and the Id*. Marcuse bemoaned the demise of this strong father-based aspect of the ego. He attributed its downfall to the supplanting of nineteenth-century patriarchal authority by the development of impersonal state education and bureaucratically organized industry. As a result, he lamented, children now grew up without the personal internalized image of the father necessary to bind their aggression. It could therefore be readily channelled and unleashed against anyone their rulers chose to name – Jews in Germany, Communists in the United States.

Later, the social historian Christopher Lasch (1979) likewise berated his generation for being so supposedly supine. He too blamed the absence of strong fathers, the lack of men able and willing to be the ideal figures that psychoanalyst Heinz Kohut (e.g. 1977) implied they should be for their children to identify with and hence develop an assured sense of their own self-esteem. Without such men, Lasch complained, his contemporaries had become so unsure of themselves that they succumbed to any and every blandishment of the market provided it promised to boost their otherwise flagging narcissism.

This selfsame male fantasy – that the solution to our ills lies in restoring the supposedly ideally forceful father of yesteryear – has since been popularized in a number of self-help manuals (see e.g. Keen 1991; Lee 1991; Corneau 1991). Particularly influential in this respect has been the work of US poet Robert Bly (1990). In his book *Iron John*, Bly reiterates a folk-tale of the same name, recounted in the nineteenth century by the Brothers Grimm, about a father inducting his son into manhood, as inspiration to his peers to likewise induct each other into manhood as a means of countering its supposed wrongful undermining by feminist and other recent social developments.

A similar message is now also widely promulgated by political pundits on both sides of the Atlantic. In a celebrated *Sunday Times* article the US social commentator, Charles Murray (1990), diverts his readers' attention from the exploitation of the working class by the ruling class by attributing the former's poverty instead to rising rates of illegitimacy – to women, as he puts it, bringing children into the world without a legal father to call their own.

Nor is such rhetoric confined to the Right. Oxford's emeritus social policy professor, A.H. Halsey (1992), and other contributors to a recent Institute of Economic Affairs booklet, *Families without Fatherhood* (see also Dennis 1993), voice the selfsame outrage. They attribute youth unemployment to fathers no longer inculcating the values of work in their offspring. Disregarding the fact that the young would certainly get jobs if only they could (see e.g. Taylor-Gooby 1993), these writers blame feminism, specifically Michelle Barrett and Mary McIntosh's (1983) critique of Lasch, for undermining men's role as fathers as though, but for feminism's exposure of the harm done by patriarchy, its myths could have become reality. Still more recently the murder of 2 year old Jamie Bulger by two 10 year olds from broken homes has been laid at feminism's door (see Green 1993), as if, in recounting the ills that tear families apart, feminism had done the deed itself.

The fact is, however, that as researchers influenced by Michael Rutter's pioneering work at London's Institute of Psychiatry have long shown (see e.g. Rutter and Rutter 1972; Ferguson *et al.* 1992), it is not paternal absence but parental discord, violence and abuse that are major contributory factors to juvenile crime and delinquency. Disregarding such evidence, however, the illusion of a once ever-provident father who only has to be summoned up for such social problems to disappear has been enshrined in legislation, most recently in the 1993 Child Support Act. Diverting attention from savage cuts in welfare exacerbating the plight of what Murray calls the 'under-class', the Act conjures up the image of 'runaway fathers' whom it empowers its agencies to track down as though these men, however poor themselves, could make good the increasing shortfall in state provision for their women and children.

Nor is such mythologizing likely to fall on deaf ears. Rich and poor alike are prone to the fantasy that all can be put right if only we could have or be the ideal male figures society cracks men up to be. Arguably it is a fantasy to which the economically and emotionally dispossessed are particularly prone, so much is it bolstered by the equation of men with power and possession resulting from the political and economic ascendancy enjoyed by men in the ruling class.

Psychologically, such fantasies about men and their absence, as I have illustrated at length elsewhere (Sayers 1995), may well be first imbibed, reproduced, and ossified through the childhood fixations, acted out rebellions, and inward psychological defences theorized by Freud (e.g. 1923b) in terms of castration, and later by his follower Jacques Lacan (e.g. 1958) in terms of phallic lack.

What however has present-day psychoanalysis to say of the harm done by such fantasies and their symbolization? Precious little. Save for a few notable exceptions (see e.g. McDougall 1978, 1989; Kirshner 1992; Schachter 1993; Mann 1993), psychoanalysts, at least in their clinical practice, have virtually forgotten Freud's observations about the ill-effects of patriarchal fantasy. Instead they focus on the mother and her presence, as I shall now explain before outlining ways such fantasy, far from being forgotten, has been addressed in post-Lacanian literary theory.

FROM MOTHERING PSYCHOANALYSIS TO FEMINIST THERAPY

As I explained in my last book (Sayers 1991), the shift of psychoanalysis from exposing male fantasy to focusing on mothering and its vicissitudes was arguably pioneered by psychoanalysis's first leading women practitioners, culminating in Melanie Klein's (1957) claim that the first and most formative object of our psychological interest – both for good and ill – is not the penis but the mother's breast. She argued that the maternal body remains the primary object of fantasy, beginning with the baby's illusion that, in taking in the mother's milk, he[1] thereby incorporates her as both hated and loved, thus giving rise to paranoid–schizoid and depressive fantasies of being attacked by, or losing her.

Winnicott once complained, says his exponent Adam Phillips, on being first introduced by his analyst James Strachey to the work of Klein:

'This was difficult for me', he wrote, 'because overnight I had changed from being a pioneer into being a student with a pioneer teacher': wherever he went, he met a woman on her way back.

(Phillips 1988: 45)

Nevertheless, Winnicott provided the stamp of male approval arguably necessary to secure psychoanalysis's shift of attention from the patriarchal to the maternal factors determining our psychology that Klein and other women inaugurated.

Winnicott's (e.g. 1965) attention to mothering, together with that of Bowlby to maternal attachment (see e.g. Murray-Parkes *et al.* 1991), remains the single most popular psychoanalytic influence on today's therapy and casework. In part this is because, unlike Freud and Klein who both focused on fantasy, Winnicott instead focused, in keeping with British empiricism, on material reality – biology and the contingencies of the mother's physical presence.

Pregnancy, he claimed, instills in women the 'primary maternal preoccupation' (Winnicott 1956) necessary to their identifying with their babies once they are born. As a result, and ideally with the mothering support of their husbands, he wrote, the 'good enough' mother thereby anticipates and meets her infant's needs. In providing the breast just when her baby wants it, she gives him the comforting illusion of having created his food supply for himself.

The baby only begins to recognize her separateness, Winnicott (1969) argues, through the mother surviving his fantasy not only of creating but also of destroying her. Only then does he learn that she is outside and separate from his omnipotent control. His individuation from her also depends, Winnicott claims, on her gradually failing to meet his needs exactly as they arise. This introduces a gap between them hopefully bridged by the baby creating a 'transitional object' (Winnicott 1953) – a much-sucked rag or blanket – he suffuses with her presence such that it helps comfort, soothe and tide him over anxieties connected with her being gone.

According to this theory, the psychic birth of the baby separate from the mother, is the work of the mother and baby alone – something later re-enacted in patients' negotiation of the physical reality of their analysts' comings and goings, particularly at weekend and holiday breaks.

Given the value Winnicott, unlike Freud, attached to the work of women as mothers, as also relived in therapy, it is little surprise that feminists have found his theories particularly sympathetic, not least as developed by Nancy Chodorow (1978) and Jessica Benjamin (1990).

Adopting his account of primary maternal preoccupation, Chodorow argues that the mutual identification of mother and baby involved persists in mothers and daughters because of their shared sex. By contrast, she claims, it is quickly negated by boys in the process of their forging a separate and distinct male identity. The result is that boys develop their sense of themselves on an abstract and positional basis. This, Chodorow claims, equips them well for the instrumental roles prescribed for their sex by the structural functionalist sociologists Talcott Parsons and Robert Bales (1955), just as girls' emotional identification with their mothers adapts them for the expressive roles these sociologists prescribe for women.

But, as Chodorow also points out, this smooth-seeming 'reproduction of mothering' has several drawbacks. It serves to reproduce the social inequalities involved in relegating women to mothering while men work. It also results in men being emotionally underinvolved, and women being overinvolved and identified with others. The cure, Chodorow concludes, is for men to participate more equally with women in mothering. Only then will girls and boys grow up equally strong in their involvement with, and individuation from, others.

As far as men *qua* fathers are concerned, they are as absent from Chodorow's political agenda as they are from the Winnicottian theory on which she draws. They are almost as absent from the diagnosis of women's and men's discontents put forward by Jessica Benjamin (1990). While Chodorow attends to identification and merger in early mothering, Benjamin attends instead to individuation from the mother as described by Winnicott, as well as by Margaret Mahler (Mahler *et al.* 1975) and Daniel Stern (1985).

Chodorow argues that the baby's recognition of the mother as having a mind different and separate from his own, as Mahler and Stern claim occurred in the mother–baby pairs they observed, depends on the mother surviving the baby's fantasied attacks on her as described by Winnicott (1969). However, Benjamin adds, in male-dominated society women often suffer such chronically low levels of self-esteem that they lack the secure sense of having a mind of their own necessary to withstand their babies' onslaughts.

As a result, Benjamin suggests, toddlers often look elsewhere to have their individuality confirmed. Or they grow up, as often happens with boys, seeking to secure recognition through dominating over their lovers just as they did over their mothers as babies. Girls, on the other hand, excluded by gender stereotyping from identifying with their fathers, instead often make do with passively surrendering to men's subjugation and control with the consolation that it affords some recognition, albeit negative, in the eyes of a powerful other.

The resulting sado-masochistic pathology bedevilling relations between the sexes can only be resolved, Benjamin implies, through therapists interpreting and withstanding their patients' attacks rather than giving way to them as mothers all too often do in today's female-subordinated society. In the long term it requires strengthening women's position in society so they can better do their job of ensuring both their children's individuation from them and their initiation into the social world otherwise wrongly attributed, in Benjamin's view, by Freud and his Lacanian followers to the work of the father.

Chodorow and Benjamin are not alone in adopting Winnicott's work for feminism. So too does Susie Orbach, joint founder with Luise Eichenbaum in 1976 of London's Women's Therapy Clinic. Beginning with her book *Fat is a Feminist Issue* (1978), Orbach argues that the distress bringing women to therapy often stems from their mothers being socialized by male-dominated society into sacrificing their needs to those of others. They thereby become alienated from what they want. As a result they are often not attuned to their babies' needs, in the fashion advocated by Winnicott, at least to their baby daughters' needs insofar as, because they are biologically the same sex, mothers identify them with their own rejected needs as women.

Applying this approach to women's eating disorders, Mira Dana (1987) argues that the anorexic persists in hating her hunger just as her mother did. Meanwhile the bulimic binges only to spit out what she eats, so much does she hate herself as her mother did for being so needy. Likewise the compulsive eater stuffs herself with anything and everything in ignorance of what she wants, so much has she become alienated from her needs as a result of her mother's alienation from her own needs as a woman.

Orbach and Luise Eichenbaum (e.g. 1993) accordingly argue that therapists should attend to their women patients' feelings of unentitlement so as to make good the deprivation by their mothers that first gave rise to it. Susie Orbach (e.g. 1992) now also stresses the place of ideas about men and masculinity in our psychology. For the most part, however, such notions remain forgotten in the mother-centred psychotherapy she and other feminists initiated on the basis of Winnicott's work.

In keeping with his focus on the material contingencies of mothering – on whether the mother is physically present, and on whether she actually meets her baby's need – feminist therapists often overlook the unconscious and the psychic reality of male fantasy, crystallized according to Freud (e.g. 1923a) in the child's construction of woman's missing penis as signifying the power of the father to punish his Oedipal desire with castration, to which Lacan (e.g. 1958) returned in making the phallus pivotal to his theory.

LACANIAN AND POST-LACANIAN LITERARY THEORY

Much has occurred in Lacanian theory since Juliet Mitchell first reworked Freud's ideas, using Lacan's reformulation of them in symbolic terms, for feminism. She made much of Lacan's opposition to the sociologizing and biologizing trends of post-Freudian psychoanalysis – briefly indicated in the above outline of Winnicott's work and of its applications within feminist therapy. By contrast, Lacan insisted, as he claimed Freud also did, on the importance of focusing on language and symbolism instead.

The analyst's job, Lacan emphasized, is not to meet his patient's need. Rather his job is to expose as fantasy patients' illusions that their desires are already fulfilled – an illusion symbolized in patriarchal society, according to Lacan, by the phallus. It is, he indicated, its marks – 'the defiles of the signifier' – that the analyst should pursue. The proper province of psychoanalysis, according to Lacan, is neither biology nor society. Nor is it the analyst's job to discover what actually happened in the patient's past and current life, inside as well as outside therapy, as Winnicott and his followers imply. Rather the role of the analyst is to follow his patients' train of thought as Freud enjoined in making free association the fundamental rule of his technique.

Lacan (1956) accordingly likened the role of the analyst to that of the detective, Dupin, in Edgar Allan Poe's short story, *The Purloined Letter*. In it Dupin tracks down a compromising letter to a queen from her lover not, as the Chief of Police does, by searching high and low for the missive itself. Instead Dupin pursues the pathways indicated by its thief, one of the king's ministers, who took the letter by substituting a similar one in its place. Chances were therefore, Dupin reasons, that the minister pursued the same tack in avoiding its being found. Indeed he had. He had put the letter in an envelope similar to the one in which he first saw it. By thus following the minister's trail of substitutions, akin to the condensations and displacements pursued by Freud in analysing his patients' dreams, Dupin finds the missing epistle, in full view, in the minister's apartment.

Others have since enormously extended the application to literature of Lacan's theories. Julia Kristeva's work has been particularly important in this respect. She supplements Lacan's focus on the symbolic abstractions of language by also attending to its underlying fabric and fantasies. Specifically she focuses on what she refers to as the 'semiotic' texture of speech and writing – gesture, movement, timbre, rhythm, repetition, and so on (see e.g. Kristeva 1974). It originates, she argues, in the baby's beginning psychic separation from the mother. His individuation from her is the precondition and motive, she asserts, of his acquiring speech to fill the gap. Nor can this gap be opened up, she implies *contra* Winnicott, through the mother's doing alone.

The baby's individuation from her, even in this pre-Oedipal phase, Kristeva (1977) insists, depends on the mother diverting her attention, even if only slightly, away from herself and her child to what Freud referred to as the father of individual prehistory. Without his intervention, however notional, claims Kristeva, the baby would never be able to shift from paranoid–schizoid projective identification with the mother to depressive position recognition of her separateness as described by Klein.

Without some such paternal signifier, Kristeva (1980) goes on, the baby risks succumbing to the horror of 'abjection' – to the fantasy of disappearing back into the mother. Hence perhaps the soothing effect, eloquently attributed by Lorca to the Andalusian peasant in lulling her baby to sleep by indicating her preoccupation with an elsewhere enigmatic male other in singing:

Lullaby, lullaby
Of that man who led
His horse to the water
And left him without drink
    (Lorca 1928: 14–15)

Certainly it is to the work of men writers and artists – not to that of Lorca but to that of Giotto, Gerard de Nerval, Dostoevsky, James Joyce, Proust, Mallarmé, Céline, and others – that Kristeva applies her project of 'semanalysis'. Literary theorist Jacqueline Rose has in turn recently applied Kristeva's development of Lacanianism to the poetry of Sylvia Plath. Plath has become something of an icon within feminism, a repository of both women's and men's fantasies as Rose explains, because of both her writing and untimely death. Rose also shows how, in *Poem for a Birthday* and elsewhere, Plath eloquently recounts what psychoanalysts usually describe more prosaically, namely the child's initial fantasy of fusion with the mother – 'Mother, you are the one mouth/I would be a tongue to' – and the phallic fissure opened up between mother and child that both calls out for and makes its bridging by language possible: 'Words, words, to stop the deluge through the thumbhole in the dike' (Plath cited by Rose 1991: 31, 52).

Returning via Lacan to Freud's attention to fantasy – specifically to his claim (see e.g. Freud 1900) that thinking originates in the baby hallucinating the presence of the mother's breast in its absence – Rose shows how, in her poem *Daddy* written shortly before Plath killed herself, Plath tellingly expresses the fictions and figments of the imagination peopling men's absence. In Plath's case this was made all the more real by her husband Ted Hughes' recent departure, and by many details of her German-born father's life having been obliterated by the War, the obscenities of Nazism, and by his having died when Plath was only 8. Hence, Rose writes, her poem of self-recovery:

> Daddy, I have had to kill you.
> You died before I had time –
> Marble heavy, a bag full of God,
> Ghastly statue, with one gray toe
> Big as a Frisco seal
> . . .
> I have always been scared of you,
> With your Luftwaffe, your gobbledygoo.
> And your neat moustache
> And your Aryan eye, bright blue.
> . . .
> And then I knew what to do.
> I made a model of you,
> A man in black with a Meinkampf look
> And a love of the rack and the screw.
> And I said I do, I do.
>   (Plath 1962: 54)

Rose is by no means alone in understanding literature in terms of Lacanian and post-Lacanian psychoanalysis. It has generated an abundance of feminist scholarship. It has become the staple diet of cultural and women's studies (see e.g. Elliott 1992; Grosz 1990; O'Connor and Ryan 1993). Yet much of it is almost completely indigestible and incomprehensible so successful is its recipe, following Lacan, of rendering itself as obscure as possible.

As a result Lacanian feminist insights regarding the psychological centrality of male fantasy have exacerbated rather than reduced the already widespread hostility of feminists and others to Freud on account of his phallocentrism, immoral-seeming preoccupation with infantile sexuality, and apparently scandalous disregard for science in focusing on dreams and the unconscious (often ignored, as indicated above, in much of today's feminist and non-feminist therapy).

Writing on the occasion of Freud's death, the poet W.H. Auden was more friendly to his work and patriarchalism:

> He wasn't clever at all: he merely told
> the unhappy Present to recite the Past

like a poetry lesson till sooner
or later it faltered at the line where
long ago the accusations had begun
. . .
If some traces of the autocratic pose,
the paternal strictness he distrusted, still
clung to his utterance and features,
it was a protective coloration

(Auden 1939: 217)

Subsequent history, however, has not been so kind to Freud's memory. Many – feminists and non-feminists alike – now reject his work out of hand because of its male-centredness. Yet this is also one of its major strengths. The fantasies about men and their absence, to which Lacanian and post-Lacanian theory draws attention in his work, haunt us all. Hence the gripping power of Plath's poetry in addressing them.

We are all prey to such fictions – not least the patients of psychotherapy, as I shall now indicate by retelling in these terms four cases (in which I have of course changed all identifying details) of eating disorders in women which, as indicated above, and because they so frequently afflict our sex, are now a major focus of feminist therapy. They also illustrate four defences sustaining male fantasy – as illustrated and explained at greater length in *Freudian Tales* (Sayers 1995).

FASTING AND FEASTING: CLINICAL EXAMPLES

Negation

The earliest defence, Freud (1925) wrote, is that by which the baby affirms what gives him pleasure and negates everything unpleasant as belonging elsewhere. He went on to show how this defence is also involved in the 'oceanic feeling' stemming from the uterine fantasy of being one with the mother before anything external, represented by the father, is known (Freud 1930).

Whatever the allure of this illusion it resulted in Ann virtually starving to death. Negating and projecting everything she disliked into the men in her life – in the first place into her father – she drove herself to a shred working to keep him and all other male figures out. She rose at crack of dawn to rid her house of all invading dirt. Similarly she allowed herself virtually no food. Unconsciously she equated it too with phallic intrusion, symbolized by her feeding me chocolate fingers when I visited.

She treated me as a male authority, to be kept at a distance as she underlined by getting me to hold out my arm to shake hands with her when I left at the end of our first meeting. Subsequently she came to accept and welcome me in, as she did others, through transforming me in her mind from phallic intruder to being one with her. I thereupon found myself projectively identified with her untethered fusing–confusing mental state that Klein, as indicated above, characterizes as the baby's earliest experience of the mother. I found myself losing my way, like her, in our conversation. It lost all sense of purpose and direction.

Other times, I learnt, Ann not only ruthlessly excluded anyone she construed as a male interloper. She also often retreated to bed, and into sleep in which she nursed dreams of herself still united with her now dead grandmother to whom, as a child, she used to flee from her father. She slept so much she was in danger of choking on the very little she ate. Several times her 8 year old son, Tom, had to wake her – as a mother might her baby – lest she die a veritable cot death.

Ann would have been happy to keep him and her forever an interchangeable mother–baby couple in the belief, not unlike that propounded by Winnicott and Mahler as indicated above, that she could bring about his psychological birth through her mothering alone. Tom knew better. For want of a male figure to come between them and open up the gap necessary according to Lacan (1953) to the development of 'full speech', he remained inarticulate. He could not distance himself with words.

So he resorted to violence and running away instead. After all it was through being violent and through being imprisoned that his uncles, whom Ann had also long babied, got away. It was Tom's running that first led Ann to ask for social services help – to get him back. The social worker appointed to her case in turn became worried lest Tom get run over, and lest Ann die of self-starvation. Hence my involvement.

Repression

While Ann and Tom were at risk of fatally succumbing to her illusory absenting of men from their lives, Barbara suffered a surfeit of men – again in fantasy. In this she was akin to psychoanalysis's first patient – Anna O (see Freud 1914) – who, in the absence of her dead father kept him alive in symbolic form – in a dream image of a snake which, being repressed, could then only gain conscious expression in bodily shape – in the hysterical symptom of her arm being stiffened with paralysis in memory of the numbness Anna suffered when nursing her father through his final illness.

Repressed male fantasy was likewise expressed in bodily character in the bulimic symptoms besetting Barbara. She binged so much she virtually ate herself and her family out of house and home. Certainly she drained all their savings by spending them on food. It was this that brought her, in her mid-twenties, to therapy.

As a teenager she was sexually abused, apparently with her father's connivance, by his best friend. Later, after he had gone, she relived his abuse somatically. Urgently she indiscriminately took in anything and everything just as she once took him in to staunch her longing, which he abused, for affection from no matter whom. Having stuffed herself with food, in memory of once symbolically stuffing herself with him, it became unconsciously equated with a gross and hated version of him, whereupon she vomited into the toilet what she had eaten as though it were his disgusting ejaculate (cf. Tustin 1958).

In therapy, Barbara opened herself up to me as she had many years before opened herself up to him. Without pausing to check me out, she immediately let me know how much she needed me by letting me in on the most intimate and messy details of her life. It left me feeling I was no better than her abuser in inviting her to take me into her confidence only to abandon her when, as the clock told the end of her session, I indicated I had done.

Introjection

Barbara's bulimia illustrates the continuing toll exacted by repressed male fantasy first described by Freud in his 1909 and 1911 additions on dreamwork symbolism to his 1900 account of the unconscious in *The Interpretation of Dreams*. Charlotte's compulsive eating, by contrast, highlights the cost of yet another defence Freud also illustrated, as in the case of Anna O, in terms of male fantasy, in this case that of the woman who fends off disillusion in her husband by introjecting and identifying with an idealized version of his sex. It is this exaggerated male figure, Freud (1917) wrote, with whom the depressed housewife identifies in excoriating herself for not living up to her ideal of her husband's sex.

Depression involves being one with this figure, being so suffused with feeling there is no space to give it words, as Kristeva (1987) movingly observes in her book, *Black Sun*. Her account of depression, like Freud's, is thus quite different from that of Melanie Klein (see e.g. 1935, 1940) who attributed depression not to introjection but to its failure, at least to failed internalization of those we have lost, equated in the first place with the loved and loving mother.

Maternal loss had recently figured in Charlotte's life – her mother had died a couple of years before I started seeing her in therapy. It was not this, however, but threatened disillusion in the men in her life that caused the depression and compulsive eating that brought her to seek my help.

Like Freud's depressed housewife, she began by telling me how ashamed she was of herself: her husband had left her years before because she was no good in bed; she had never got another man; her body was lopsided; anaemia prevented her from ever completing her training as an opera singer; and now she was so incapable of following the diet prescribed for her diabetes she was already suffering devastating headaches, and would soon be crippled with arthritis and blindness as well.

In the course of recounting this sorry tale it emerged that Charlotte had even more reason to feel aggrieved and disappointed in her father and husband than in herself, given their evident shortcomings that she occasionally let slip. Or she would have been disappointed in them had she not instead lionized them in their absence and, through introjection, retained them as ideal male figures within herself. She veered from imagining herself as one with their sex, as being the heroes of the operatic world – Jose Carreras or Placido Domingo – to reviling herself for being nothing of the kind. Then, as though this male absence in herself was physical rather than mental, bodily rather than fantastical, she sought to fill it with food. Hence her compulsive eating.

In therapy she likewise looked to me to fill her – after first expressing her disappointment in me, as in herself, for not being the man she craved. Soon I found myself likewise berating myself for being so limited in what I could provide, for falling so short of Winnicott's legendary capacity for being endlessly forbearing, insightful, creative and empathic in understanding his patients.

Mania

The obverse of depressed disillusion in such legendary figures, Freud (1917) wrote, is mania. He attributed it to mourning freeing the energy otherwise bound up in idealizing and grieving those we have lost. Abraham (1924) characterized manic excitement in oral terms, as gargantuan gobbling. Klein (e.g. 1940), by contrast, emphasized its function as defence. She attributed its origin to children imagining themselves as omnipotent so as to ward off recognition of their dependence on, or fear of losing the mother through their hatred of her.

Subsequently Klein's follower Henri Rey (1986) has drawn attention to the phallic identification involved in this defence. The penis, he says, lends itself particularly well to mania because of its biological turgidity, erectile defiance of gravity, penetrative character, function in excretion and making babies, and because it both has a life of its own and is part of something greater – man. More likely its emblematic function in this respect results from the phallus in male-dominated society being a prime symbol of the grandiosity mania involves.

Nor is mania confined to men. The illusion of heroically outwitting all bodily need, of becoming all male mind, the cleverest of the clever, the thinnest of the thin, straight-up-and-down masculinity incarnate drives many an anorexic to an early grave.

Daisy survived. Several years later, however, she returned to therapy because the cracks and flaws in her continuing illusory sense of herself as embodiment of the ideals inculcated by male-dominated society threatened to break through. All too often she was in danger of letting herself down in her own eyes with hysterical shrieking at her husband and children. No wonder she shrieked. She put herself under such pressure trying to live up to an image of herself as perfect wife and mother, just as she inexorably starved herself as a teenager to become the ideal man her mother seemed to want in place of her husband, and whom she left when Daisy was 18.

Just as Daisy sought to dazzle her mother, she likewise sought to dazzle me. She let me know she wanted for nothing, that she and her son with whom she identified were brimful with artistic talent, that she only came to see me because our appointments, jotted on her kitchen calendar, happened to jog her memory. Even then she often came late.

She left me to do the wanting just as, when she was anorexic, she left it to others to want her to eat. She made me feel useless, deskilled, impotent – a reaction that all too often leads those treating anorexics to retaliate with the selfsame grandiose omnipotence. They order them to be hospitalized, kept in bed and force-fed (akin to the treatment meted out to suffragettes earlier this century; see Orbach 1986).

Such grandiosity likewise characterized – albeit to a lesser degree – not only Daisy but also Ann, Barbara, and Charlotte. They all flattered their narcissism with inflated images of manhood that, as I have sought to explain, in turn backfired to cripple them all. Hence the need to expose and in the process undo such fantasies through the methods developed by psychoanalysis and feminism as I shall now explain.

CONCLUSION: FREUDIAN THERAPY, FEMINIST POLITICS

I said good-bye
and saw his old head
as he turned,
as he left the room
leaving me alone
with his old trophies,
the marbles, the vases, the stone Sphinx,
the old, old jars from Egypt;
he left me alone with these things
and his old back was bowed
(H.D. 1934–5: 414)

Thus the symbolist poet Hilda Doolittle described the ending of her analysis with Freud – from the grandeur of classical antiquity to recognition of the frailty of this man she also called her master.

In a sense, the therapeutic voyage she described is like that of Nora in Ibsen's play *The Doll's House* in which Nora travels from self-lacerating abjection, in striving to sustain an august image of her husband and herself in his high esteem, until eventually she decides to go because, as she tells him, she realizes he is not the man she thought he was.

Her recognition that her previous inflated image of her husband was a fantasy launches her on a quest for liberation that remains an inspiration to feminism to this day. She happens on this discovery by chance. Certainly her sudden disillusion often comes as a surprise to her audience.

By contrast Freud found that such revelations could not be left to fate. His clinical work forced him to develop methods for systematically uncovering his patients' similarly inflated illusions about his sex, that so often contributed to their symptoms as they also arguably still do to women's bingeing and starving as described above.

In the first place, and in reaction to his patients questioning his patriarchal authority in seeking to make them subject to his hypnotic suggestion, he developed the technique of asking them freely to associate to their symptoms. Applying this method to the treatment of an 18 year old servant, Katharina (see Freud 1895), he enabled her to become aware of an otherwise repressed gross figure of her father (similar to that now haunting my patient Barbara) hyperventilating as he did several years before when he sexually abused her. It was an image that, as long as it remained unconscious, could only be expressed bodily, thereby preventing its conscious mental revision, in the laboured breathing that troubled Katharina for which she sought Freud's help.

Theorizing his method, Freud indicated that psychoanalysis seeks to wake patients from the illusion, beginning with the hungry baby's hallucination of the breast in the mother's absence (see Freud 1900), that they are already sexually sated and complete. In the case of his patient Dora (Freud 1905), therapy involved putting into words, in order to expose and thus undo, the fantasy of herself alias her father's mistress Frau K filling her mouth with his penis, and of Herr K's erect member pressing against her thigh as it perhaps had when he earlier tried to seduce her. It was, Freud argued, the unconscious displacement of this phallic image to Dora's throat that caused both her nervous cough and anorexic disgust at food.

Within weeks of her therapy beginning she prematurely left. Thinking it over, Freud concluded that to make unconscious fantasy conscious (and thereby dispel it by putting it into words and showing it to be a fiction) it is also necessary to verbalize its transposition or 'transference' into the patient's relation with her doctor. Unconsciously Dora had transferred on to Freud the figure of Herr K against whom she rebelled by dismissing Freud, just as Herr K's maid dismissed him.

Freud discovered that in every case the transference constitutes a major source of resistance against psychoanalysis's project of exposing and talking out our fantasies. In the case of the Rat Man (Freud 1909), for instance, analysis revealed that the young man involved was prevented from saying whatever came into his mind by the fantasy that, like his now dead father who used to beat him when he was a child, Freud too would thrash him.

As therapists now know, the transference into therapy of such fantasies often inhibits and impedes their patients' free associating talk. They are, however, also heartened by Freud's (e.g. 1912) observation that the transference also does psychoanalysis the inestimable service of bringing fantasies from the past into the present.

Freud (1937) himself however despaired at the end of his life of successfully exposing and undoing fantasy through interpreting and putting into words its transference manifestations. He anticipated that, like education and government, psychoanalysis would prove an impossible profession. Nowhere more so, he added, than when it seeks to undo the conviction of women patients that nothing short of becoming a man – through acquiring a penis – will cure them, or when faced with men, like his Wolf Man patient (Freud 1918), who refuse to submit to the analyst's treatment because they unconsciously equate passive submission to him, *qua* father-figure, with castration.

Such fantasies, Freud observed in the same essay, also mobilize the analyst's defences. Freud regarded this – the analyst's 'countertransference' – as yet another obstacle to treatment. He accordingly urged analysts to get rid of it by having further analysis themselves.

Subsequently however, analysts have drawn attention to the fact that, provided they recognize what belongs personally to their own past and present history in their response to their patients, the countertransference, like the transference, is an important communication about both the patient's fantasies and the defences sustaining them. Particularly innovatory, sympathetic and influential in this respect was the work of the sometime Kleinian analyst Paula Heimann (e.g. 1949/50).

In thus recognizing rather than repudiating the countertransference, many draw on Klein's (1946) theory of projective identification whereby, she argued, babies project their unwanted feelings into the mother with whom they then accordingly identify. Analysts have also drawn on the work of Winnicott (e.g. 1949, 1962), Bion (e.g. 1967) and others in arguing the necessity, especially where psychosis is involved, of analysts experiencing, containing and working through the feelings evoked in them by their patients, just as the mother ideally digests the feelings her baby evacuates into her so as to enable him to reintroject them in more bearable form.

In the above clinical examples I have extended to instances of male fantasy this mother-based post-Freudian development of psychoanalysis in drawing attention to the countertransference feelings elicited in me by the defences my patients used to sustain this fantasy. Where this involves aggrandizing notions about men and their absence, however, attention to their free association, transference and countertransference manifestations is not enough.

What also has to be exposed is the male dominance of our society that so massively reinforces such fantasies that, as explained above, do such harm both individually and politically. Feminists, as I briefly indicated at the beginning of this chapter, have done much to draw attention to the wishful thinking involved in the belief that, but for its exposure of the wrongs done to women (as well as men and children) by patriarchy, the solution to society's ills lies in restoring the supposedly ever-beneficent father of yesteryear.

Recently feminists have also sought to expose and undo the related fantasy, the socially received fiction, that masculinity is essentially the same the world over. It is this unitary and universalizing myth that is arguably symbolized by the phallus. Uncovering and deconstructing this symbol is crucial, as socialist feminist Lynne Segal (1992) points out in the case of men, not least because of the damage it does to the sexuality of both sexes insofar as we illusorily equate the biological penis with the symbolic phallus, and with the power (both for pleasure and pain) it represents.

In her book *Slow Motion* Segal (1990) also importantly disentangles the separate and distinct historical and political strands to masculinity as we know it in Europe and the USA. In particular she dissects out the stereotype of muscular Christianity and manhood assumed by the American and European ruling class in promoting and extending its rule in the nineteenth century through westward expansion and imperial conquest. She goes on to explain how this classic image of aggressive masculinity was in turn taken up by the working class at the beginning of this century in fighting to improve its lot. She also documents the different, but related, trajectory by which blacks exaggerate and embrace their equation with the untamed phallus – as noble or beastly savage – in opposing colonialism, slavery and racism often practised in the name of this selfsame stereotype. Thirdly she traces a distinct, but again related, set of trends by which lesbians and gays prosecute their cause by donning the spectre of absent masculinity – implied by the figure of the butch dyke, gentle femme and cruising queen – otherwise used to scourge them in today's moral panic about AIDS and, at the turn of the century, in the then interest of the dominant class in coercing its members into heterosexually reproducing themselves.

In the name of postmodernism many have made much of the plurality and instability revealed by such deconstruction. Some find it intoxicating. They revel in it. A recent example is Kaja Silverman's (1992) celebration of the erotics of men's ruination that she claims is the central motif of Henry James's novel *The Turn of the Screw*, Proust's *Remembrance of Things Past*, T.E. Lawrence's *Seven Pillars of Wisdom*, post Second World War Hollywood movies about returning veterans and their women, and the films of Rainer Werner Fassbinder.

Silverman and others come close to implying that deconstructing masculinity – and more generally gender – is the be-all and end-all of feminism. Particularly influential in this respect is cultural theorist Judith Butler's (1990) plea for women and men to make carnival of cross-dressing as though, through thus performing and dramatizing gender's arbitrary character, we could thereby do away with the male dominance of our society that is arguably its principal determinant.

But we have to do more than this. Playing havoc with the garb of patriarchy to reveal and thereby undo its fictions is only the beginning. Beyond deconstruction we also have to expose, challenge, and change the material underpinnings of male fantasy that, as indicated in this chapter's first section, is now being deployed to legitimate the dismantling of the welfare state.

Similarly with male fantasy's individual ramifications. Literary theorist Peter Middleton (1992) and many others point out that postmodern deconstructionism shows the age-old Cartesian claim, 'I think therefore I am', to be an unwarranted male conceit. Identity is not self-authenticating. But this does not entail that the project of forging a coherent identity is itself necessarily futile.

Certainly, as the clinical examples cited above indicate, this project all too readily founders through being based on dreams and fantasies about men and their absence. If we are to construct ourselves on a more secure basis, such illusory foundations to our identity do indeed have to be exposed. This means becoming conscious of, and painfully grieving for, the man who never was.

More than that, once we have thus become aware of the tatters in our male fantasies, we then have to start the laborious task of filling the gaps thereby opened up between their illusory promise and reality. Their recognition is a necessary precursor to our repairing our damaged world – the terms in which Klein recast Freud's account of the pleasure and reality principle. Only then can we begin to make it more nearly meet the wants and desires of women and men alike. It entails appreciating, confronting and painstakingly making good everyday life's manifold reverses, deprivations, losses and absences that we otherwise all too often imagine our fantasies to have already patched up. It entails repeatedly having to pick ourselves up and get going again. Or, as Stephen Frosh (1991) puts it, it means having 'to keep on keeping on'.

It is on this note that Chekhov ended his play *Uncle Vanya*. Having finally become disillusioned in the erstwhile-seeming brilliance of her uncle, the professor, Sonya urges Vanya:

We shall go on living, Uncle Vanya. We shall live through a long, long succession of days and tedious evenings. We shall patiently suffer the trials which Fate imposes on us; we shall work for others, now and in our old age, and we shall have no rest. When our time comes we shall die submissively, and over there beyond the grave, we shall say that we've suffered, that we've wept, that we've had a bitter life, and God will take pity on us. And then, Uncle dear, we shall both begin to know a life that is bright and beautiful and lovely.

(Chekhov 1897: 244–5)

Today Sonya's God is dead. Nevertheless, the destructive legacy of her nineteenth-century religion lives on. We still need to dispel the illusion of constituting and resurrecting some patriarchal heaven up above if we are to get on with the task of making this a better and more certain world for women, as well as men, here below. Hence the need to retell feminist psychoanalysis – to supplement post-Freudian therapy's insights regarding mothering (both actual and imagined) with those of Lacanian and post-Lacanian literary theory regarding phallic symbolism and male fantasy, inaugurated by Juliet Mitchell's *Psychoanalysis and Feminism* with which I began.

NOTE

1 Obviously I deplore the sexual inequality causing the generic use of the male pronoun to refer to everyone – girls and boys, women and men – alike. Nevertheless, I have followed this custom here to distinguish babies from their primary caregivers who, because of the continuing unequal sexual division of childcare, are almost always women.

REFERENCES

Abraham, K. (1924) 'A short study of the development of the libido, viewed in the light of mental disorders'. *Selected Papers on Psycho-Analysis*. London: Karnac, 1979.

Auden, W.H. (1939) 'In memory of Sigmund Freud', in *Collected Poems*. London: Faber, 1976.

Barrett, M. and McIntosh, M. (1983) *The Anti-Social Family*. London: Verso.

Benjamin, J. (1990) *The Bonds of Love*. London: Virago.

Bion, W.R. (1967) *Second Thoughts*. London: Karnac.

Bly, R. (1990) *Iron John*. New York: Addison-Wesley.

Butler, J. (1990) *Gender Trouble*. London: Routledge.

Chekhov, A. (1897) *Uncle Vanya*, in *Plays*. London: Penguin Books, 1959.

Chodorow, N. (1978) *The Reproduction of Mothering*. Berkeley: University of California Press.

Corneau, J. (1991) *Absent Fathers, Lost Sons: The Search for Masculine Identity*. Boston: Shambhala.

Dana, M. (1987) 'Boundaries', in M. Lawrence (ed.) *Fed Up and Hungry*. London: Women's Press.

Dennis, N. (1993) *Rising Crime and the Dismembered Family*. London: Institute of Economic Affairs.

Elliott, A. (1992) *Social Theory and Psychoanalysis in Transition*. Oxford: Blackwell.

Ferguson, D.M., Horwood, L.J. and Lynskey, M.T. (1992) 'Family change, parental discord and early offending'. *Journal of Child Psychology and Psychiatry*, 33 (6): 1059–75.

Freud, S. (1895) *Studies on Hysteria*. S.E.2.

—— (1900) *The Interpretation of Dreams*. S.E.4–5.
—— (1905) 'Fragment of an analysis of a case of hysteria'. S.E.7.
—— (1909) 'Notes upon a case of obsessional neurosis'. S.E.10.
—— (1912) 'The dynamics of transference'. S.E.12.
—— (1914) 'On the history of the psycho-analytic movement'. S.E.14.
—— (1917) 'Mourning and melancholia'. S.E.14.
—— (1918) 'From the history of an infantile neurosis'. S.E.17.
—— (1923a) *The Ego and the Id*. S.E.19.
—— (1923b) 'The infantile genital organization'. S.E.19.
—— (1925) 'Negation'. S.E.19.
—— (1927) 'The future of an illusion'. S.E.21.
—— (1930) *Civilization and its Discontents*. S.E.21.
—— (1937) 'Analysis terminable and interminable'. S.E.23.
Frosh, S. (1991) *Identity Crisis*. London: Macmillan.
Green, D.G. (1993) 'Forward', in *The Family: Is it Just Another Lifestyle Choice*, J. Davies (ed.). London: Institute of Economic Affairs.
Grosz, E. (1990) *Jacques Lacan: A Feminist Introduction*. London: Routledge.
H.D. (1934–5) *The Master*, in *Feminist Studies*, 1981, 7 (3): 407–16.
Halsey, A.H. (1992) 'Foreword', in *Families without Fatherhood*, H. Dennis and G. Erdos. London: Institute of Economic Affairs.
Heimann, P. (1949/50) 'On counter-transference', in *About Children and Children-No-Longer*, M. Tonnesmann (ed.). London: Routledge.
Keen, S. (1991) *Fire in the Belly: On Being a Man*. New York: Bantam.
Kirshner, L.A. (1992) 'The absence of the father'. *Journal of the American Psychoanalytic Association*, 40 (4): 1117–38.
Klein, M. (1935) 'A contribution to the psychogenesis of manic-depressive states'. *Journal of the American Psychoanalytic Association*, 40 (4): 117–38.
—— (1940) 'Mourning and its relation to manic-depressive states'. *Journal of the American Psychoanalytic Association*, 40 (4): 117–38.
—— (1946) 'Notes on some schizoid mechanisms', in *Envy and Gratitude*. London: Hogarth (1975).
—— (1957) *Envy and Gratitude*. London: Hogarth (1975).
Kohut, H. (1977) *The Restoration of the Self*. New York: International Universities Press.
Kristeva, J. (1974) *Revolution in Poetic Language*. New York: Columbia University Press (1984).
—— (1977) 'Stabat mater', in *Tales of Love*. New York: Columbia University Press (1987).
—— (1980) *Powers of Horror*. New York: Columbia University Press (1982).
—— (1987) *Black Sun*. New York: Columbia University Press (1989).
Lacan, J. (1953) 'The function and field of speech and language in psychoanalysis', in *Ecrits*. London: Tavistock (1977).
—— (1956) 'The purloined letter'. *Yale French Studies*, 48: 38–72 (1972).
—— (1958) 'The meaning of the phallus', in *Feminine Sexuality*, J. Mitchell and J. Rose (eds). London: Macmillan.
Lasch, C. (1979) *The Culture of Narcissism*. New York: Norton.
Lee, J. (1991) *At My Father's Wedding: Reclaiming our True Masculinity*. New York: Bantam.
Lorca, G. (1928) 'On lullabies', in *Deep Song and Other Prose*. London: Marion Boyars.
McDougall, J. (1978) *Plea for a Measure of Abnormality*. London: Free Association Books (1990).
—— (1989) 'The dead father'. *International Journal of Psycho-Analysis*, 70: 205–19.
Mahler, M., Pine, E. and Bergman, A. (1975) *The Psychological Birth of the Human Infant*. New York: Basic Books.
Mann, D. (1993) 'The absent father in psychotic phantasy'. *British Journal of Psychotherapy*, 9 (3): 301–9.

Marcuse, H. (1970) 'The obsolescence of the Freudian concept of man', in *Five Lectures*. London: Allen Lane.

Middleton, P. (1992) *The Inward Gaze: Masculinity and Subjectivity in Modern Culture*. London: Routledge.

Mitchell, J. (1974) *Psychoanalysis and Feminism*. London: Allen Lane.

Murray, C. (1990) *The Emerging British Underclass*. London: Institute of Economic Affairs.

Murray-Parkes, C.M., Stevenson-Hinde, J. and Marris, P. (1991) *Attachment Across the Life Cycle*. London: Routledge.

O'Connor, N. and Ryan, J. (1993) *Wild Desires and Mistaken Identities*. London: Virago.

Orbach, S. (1978) *Fat is a Feminist Issue*. New York: Paddington Press.

—— (1986) *Hunger Strike*. London: Penguin Books.

—— (1992) 'Lost boys and absent fathers', in *What's Really Going on Here?* London: Virago.

—— (1993) 'Feminine subjectivity, countertransference and the mother–daughter relationship', in *Daughering and Mothering*, J. Van Mens-Verhulst, K.J. Schreurs, and L. Woertman (eds). London: Routledge.

Parsons, T. and Bales, R. (1955) *Family, Socialization and Interaction Process*. New York: Free Press.

Phillips, A. (1988) *Winnicott*. London: Fontana.

Plath, S. (1962) 'Daddy', in *Ariel*. London: Faber (1965).

Reich, W.R. (1933) *The Mass Psychology of Fascism*. New York: Farrar, Straus & Giroux (1970).

Rey, J.H. (1986) 'The schizoid mode of being and the space-time continuum (Beyond metaphor)'. *Journal of the Melanie Klein Society*, 4 (2): 12–52.

Rose, J. (1991) *The Haunting of Sylvia Plath*. London: Virago.

Rutter, M. and Rutter, M. (1972) *Developing Minds*. London: Penguin Books.

Sayers, J. (1991) *Mothering Psychoanalysis*. London: Penguin Books.

—— (1995) *The Man who Never Was: Freudian Tales*. London: Chatto & Windus.

Schachter, J. (1993) 'The missing factor'. *Bulletin of the Anna Freud Centre*. 16: 61–72.

Segal, L. (1990) *Slow Motion: Changing Masculinities, Changing Men*. London: Virago.

—— (1992) 'Sweet sorrows, painful pleasures', in *Sex Exposed*, L. Segal and M. McIntosh (eds). London: Virago.

Stern, D. (1985) *The Interpersonal World of the Infant*. London: Basic Books.

Silverman, K. (1992) *Male Subjectivity at the Margins*. London: Routledge.

Taylor-Gooby, P. (1993) 'Poverty born in captivity'. *Community Care* no. 963, 22 April, pp. 15–17.

Tustin, F. (1958) 'Anorexia nervosa in an adolescent girl', in *Autistic Barriers in Neurotic Patients*. London: Karnac (1986).

Winnicott, D.W. (1949) 'Hate in the counter-transference', in *Collected Papers*. London: Tavistock (1958).

—— (1953) 'Transitional objects and transitional phenomena', in *Playing and Reality*. London: Penguin Books (1974).

—— (1956) 'Primary maternal preoccupation', in *Collected Papers*. London: Tavistock.

—— (1962) 'The theory of the parent–infant relationship'. *International Journal of Psycho-Analysis*, 43: 585–95.

—— (1965) *Maturational Processes and the Facilitating Environment*. London: Hogarth (1965).

—— (1969) 'The use of an object and relating through identifications', in *Playing and Reality*. London: Penguin Books (1974).

8 Mourning Freud

Madelon Sprengnether

Freud had a way of telling stories – of telling stories about others and of telling others stories about himself – that made history.

(Felman 1987)

OEDIPAL POLITICS

Suppose, for a moment, that Freud had managed to invent psychoanalysis without reference to Sophocles' *Oedipus Rex*. Or, even more radically, that a woman had created the founding concepts that underlie psychoanalytic theory and practice. How might our discussions of the relationship between psychoanalysis and feminism be different under these circumstances?

I raise these questions heuristically: in order to highlight the centrality of Freud's Oedipal construct to his entire theoretical labour, to signal the chief area of difficulty that feminism (from both sides of the Atlantic) has encountered in its critique of psychoanalytic culture, and to raise the possibility that psychoanalysis might have been conceived of differently, if not by a woman, then by Freud himself, pursuing alternate clues in his self-analysis.

An outgrowth of Freud's intense introspection following his father's death in 1896, the Oedipal construct acquired its status as the 'nuclear complex' of the neuroses when Jung began to challenge Freud's libido theory through a variety of 'complexes' of his own invention. Freud first referred to the 'Oedipus complex' in his 1910 essay, 'A special type of choice of object made by men', where he connects it to the boy's anguish at discovering his mother's sexual activity (and hence unfaithfulness) with his father. Once he had settled on this term, Freud tied it to a more ambitious project, that of explaining the evolution of human civilization. In *Totem and Taboo* (1913), Freud's rejoinder to Jung's equally ambitious *Transformations and Symbols of the Libido* (1911–12), Freud locates the Oedipus complex at the very origin of human culture.

In Freud's fanciful anthropology, there was once an all powerful father who not only dominated his sons but also claimed possession of the available women. The sons rose up against this father, killed him, and ate him. Later, filled with remorse for this deed and recognizing the necessity of making alliance with one another, they collectively atoned for their crime by forbidding the killing of a totem animal and renouncing the women they might have possessed. Freud comprehends these 'two fundamental taboos of totemism' in terms of the 'two repressed wishes of the Oedipus complex': to kill one's father and marry one's mother (1913: 143). What the sons of the primal patriarch accomplished through a voluntary act of renunciation, subsequent generations achieve by acceding to the castration complex, to the prohibition or the 'law' of the father. Systems of ethics, religion, and civilization itself, Freud claims, are built on just such a father–son dynamic.

The obvious problem in this fable is the role it accords women – as passive objects of men's fantasies and desires, as nurturers, rather than creators of human culture. Although Freud (following the lead of J.J. Bachofen) struggled to find a place for matriarchy in his scheme, the best he could do was to imagine it as a transitional stage between two father-dominated periods.[1] Freud treats mother-right as regressive, something like a dark age preceding the restoration of father-rule, which for him signals the highest level of social organization. 'The family', he claims,

> was a restoration of the former primal horde and it gave back to fathers a large portion of their former rights. There were once more fathers, but the social achievements of the fraternal clan had not been abandoned; and the gulf between the new fathers of a family and the unrestricted primal father of the horde was wide enough to guarantee the continuance of the religious craving, the persistence of an unappeased longing for the father.
>
> (Freud 1913: 149)

In Freud's rough sketch of patriarchal social organization, mother goddesses, mother-right, even mothers themselves, quietly disappear.

One reason for the success of the Oedipus complex as a structural concept is the ease with which it explains (and rationalizes) the social status quo. From this perspective, many feminists have found in Freud an ally, one who can help to elucidate the social system we hope to transform.[2] To the extent that the Oedipus complex is considered a universal and immutable phenomenon, however, it seems unlikely that any other outcome than the one Freud describes is possible. Certainly he himself did not imagine such.

While post-Freudian theorists have focused on areas Freud neglected, such as female sexual development and mother–infant relations, few have directly questioned the existence of the Oedipus complex. The pre-Oedipal researches of the early object relations theorists, for instance, were meant to supplement, rather than to displace, Freud's primary Oedipal construct. An argument could be made that contemporary psychoanalysis does not depend very heavily on interpretations based on the hypothesis of an Oedipus complex, yet the term remains intact – less as a sign of its intrinsic appeal, perhaps, than as a tribute to the founding father of psychoanalysis himself.[3] Even feminist theory, I believe, has been hampered by its assumption that the Oedipus complex must somehow be got around, rather than interrogated at its core. Ingenious arguments have been proposed for situating women differently within this general structure, yet the structure itself does not permit much flexibility. Neither Lacanian nor object relations feminism succeeds in transforming the hierarchy of Oedipal to pre-Oedipal stages (and hence the subordinate position of women) at the heart of Freud's own system of thought.

Both object relations theory and Lacanian theory incorporate the argument for cultural transcendence that informs Freud's understanding of the evolution of patriarchy and, correspondingly, the child's relationship to its mother. Just as father-right represents the highest stage of civilization for Freud, the child's renunciation of desire for its mother, under the paternal threat of castration, signals its capacity for sublimation and hence its readiness to participate in cultural activity. Like matriarchy and mother-right, the pre-Oedipal period stands in a hostile relationship to culture. Both object relations theory and Lacanian theory, though differing in almost every other respect, rely on this basic paradigm.

While focusing intently on the pre-Oedipal period, the phase that Freud forgot, so to speak, object relations theory constructs the mother–infant relationship in a way that requires the intervention of a father (or a father figure) to disrupt its claustrophobic self-enclosure. The concept of an original mother–infant symbiosis, or state of non-differentiation, from which the neonate must emerge in order to experience individual subjectivity, necessitates some such agent of separation. The mother, whose 'good enough' nurturing depends on her subordination of her own needs and desires to those of her infant, can hardly be encouraged to perform this role. So self-effacing is this figure that she appears to be devoid of subjectivity herself. Rather, it is the father who not only facilitates the child's disengagement from its primitive state of oneness with the mother, but also represents engagement with the world.

Lacan's linguistic reinterpretation of Freud would at first glance seem to offer an escape from this deterministic scheme. On closer inspection, however, it can be seen to reinscribe the function of the father and hence the valorization of patriarchy that Freud underwrites. For Lacan, the crucial dividing line between the pre-Oedipal and the Oedipal stages (renamed the imaginary and the symbolic), is the acquisition of language. Before this, the infant exists in a diffuse, boundaryless state, in which it does not clearly distinguish between itself and its mother. Her gaze (or the reflecting surface of a mirror) offers the image of a unified self, yet one which the infant does not recognize as a distortion of its actual condition of inner fragmentation. As long as the child remains fixed in this dyadic state it remains outside of the realm of symbolization and hence culture. Only the intervention of a third term, the father or the father's function, as a signifier of difference, can initiate the process by which the child enters the symbolic.

Because Lacan focuses, not on the real father, but on his name, his 'nom' (which can also be heard as 'non' or prohibition), he seems to offer a sexually neutral account of this process. Yet, like Freud, he posits a two-tier structure of relationship between the pre-Oedipal and the Oedipal, stressing the ascendance of the latter over the former and, despite many references to the arbitrariness of his terminology, couches his account of this movement in the language of sexual difference. Why, one might ask, in an otherwise ungendered linguistic system (borrowed from Saussure) must difference be assigned to the paternal function? Lacan's answer hinges on the signifying function of the phallus, a term which can never successfully be divorced from its association with the biological penis.[4] For Lacan, the phallus is 'the privileged signifier' not only because it is 'the most symbolic element in the literal (typographical) sense of the term', but also 'the most tangible element in the real of sexual copulation' and 'by virtue of its turgidity ... the image of the vital flow as it is transmitted in generation' (Lacan 1977: 287). By rewriting psychoanalysis through linguistics, Lacan only appears to disrupt the prevailing sex/gender system. In the final analysis, culture is phallocentric because language itself is phallocentric.

Freud's insertion of the Oedipus complex (and its corollary the castration complex) into the evolution of culture has had profound consequences not only for post-Freudian theory but also for the feminist uses thereof. While object relations theory remedies Freud's neglect of the pre-Oedipal mother, for instance, it does not succeed in altering her subordinate status in the Oedipal/pre-Oedipal hierarchy, nor does it appear to question the father's role as representative of culture. Lacan, while moving Freud's Oedipal construct into the linguistic register, reproduces its phallocentrism. The feminist uses of both object relations theory and Lacan, by focusing on the figure of the pre-Oedipal mother and the period of the imaginary, can act as correctives to existing theories of mother–infant relations, but they do not in themselves alter the structure which locates the pre-Oedipal period in a position prior to language and culture.

Nancy Chodorow, in *The Reproduction of Mothering* (1978), makes use of object relations theory in order to demonstrate the negative consequences of exclusive female mothering. Her account of the feminine personality structure that results from this arrangement is so appealing, however, that it partly undermines her argument for the necessity of social change.

In Chodorow's revisionary reading of object relations theory, mothers identify with their daughters in a way that inhibits the development of their autonomy. Girls' ego boundaries typically remain more fluid and permeable than those of boys, whom mothers regard as sexually other from the beginning. Under circumstances in which 'an omnipotent mother perpetuates primary love and primary identification in relation to her daughter, and creates boundaries and a differentiated, anaclitic love relation to her son, a girl's father is likely to become a symbol of freedom from this dependence and merging.' Indeed, she is likely to turn to him 'as the most available person who can help her to get away from her mother' (Chodorow 1978: 121).

According to Chodorow, daughters enter the Oedipus complex (loving their fathers while resenting their mothers) not, as Freud suggested, through penis envy, but through a desire to achieve separation from their overwhelming pre-Oedipal mothers. Such a move is never complete, however, as girls inhabit a relational triangle, looking back at their mothers even as they form new bonds with their fathers. In the long run, a girl's early experience of merging with her mother will leave its mark on her personality – in a heightened capacity for empathic identification and a special awareness of the complexity of relationship.

While softening Freud's account of female development, this use of object relations theory nevertheless preserves his legacy by reinscribing the Oedipal/

pre-Oedipal hierarchy which characterizes his thought as a whole. Here, as in Freud's texts, the mother's influence is portrayed as regressive, a dangerous undertow which threatens the achievement of individual autonomy. This reading of femininity also reproduces conventional gender roles and stereotypes. Female mothering assures that women will concern themselves primarily with relational issues, leaving men to deal with matters of abstract reasoning and justice.

The irony of Chodorow's analysis is that she herself does not subscribe to this outcome, which she attributes to the psychological configuration of the nuclear patriarchal family. Yet scores of her readers, ignoring this feature of her argument, have fastened on her account of femininity as quasi utopian. Valorizing women's diffuse ego boundaries and sensitivity to relational issues, such readers unwittingly recuperate the very categories which serve to inhibit women's progress in the social sphere.

Chodorow's object relations analysis offers a powerful (and not wholly unflattering) view of the development of femininity within patriarchy. Yet it does not provide a substantial feminist alternative. Her call for shared parenting, while laudable in itself, does not offer an adequate counterbalance to her psychoanalytic narrative, nor does it attempt to problematize the Oedipal/pre-Oedipal hierarchy at the heart of object relations theory.

French feminist theorists, working through Lacan's framework of analysis, encounter similar difficulties in dislodging the Oedipal dynamic that informs his approach. Hélène Cixous, Luce Irigaray and Julia Kristeva, though differing in their specific arguments and emphases, all focus on the pre-Oedipal mother and the period of the imaginary in their attempts to disrupt the phallocentrism of culture. While supplementing Lacan's rather sketchy treatment of this phase and its implications for the acquisition of language, they are each hampered by their failure to question the dominance and paternally organized function of the symbolic.

Cixous and Irigaray both advocate a form of 'écriture féminine' as a means of short-circuiting the categories of binary opposition (matter/spirit, nature/culture, passivity/activity) which construct woman as other. Because the existing order of language is synonymous with the symbolic order, which in turn depends on the signification of the phallus, their strategies for disruption appeal to the prelinguistic or protolinguistic imaginary, which in turn revolves around the figure of the mother. While both Cixous and Irigaray conceive of subverting the order of the sentence (a possibility open to men and women alike) as a tactic for disruption, they each invoke the pre-Oedipal mother–infant relationship as a model for such activity, hence incurring the charge of female essentialism.

Cixous finds a metaphorics for the kind of writing she proposes in the processes of pregnancy and childbirth:

> It is not only a question of the feminine body's extra resource, this specific power to produce some thing living of which her flesh is the locus, not only a question of a transformation of rhythms, exchanges, of relationship to space, of the whole perceptive system, but also of the irreplaceable experience of those moments of stress, of the body's crises, of that work that goes on peacefully for

a long time only to burst out in that surpassing moment, the time of childbirth. . . . It is also the experience of a 'bond' with the other, all that comes through in the metaphor of bringing into the world. How could the woman, who has experienced the not-me within, not have a particular relationship to the written?

(Cixous and Clement 1986: 90)

Irigaray, who bases her critique of western philosophy on its exclusion of sexual difference and its corresponding repression of the imaginary, also sees pregnancy as an analogue of the linguistic practice she promotes.

Of the two of us, who was the one, who the other? . . . A flower left to its own growth. To contemplate itself without necessarily seeking to see itself. A blossoming not subject to any mold. An efflorescence obeying no already known contours. A design that changed itself endlessly according to the hour of the day. Open to the flux of its own becoming.

(Irigaray 1981: 65–6)

Like Nancy Chodorow's object relations account of feminine personality development, these lyrical descriptions of specifically female experience have an obvious appeal. Yet they are rooted in a structure which reproduces conventional categories of sexual difference through the teleological relationship of the maternally fixated imaginary to the phallically organized symbolic. It is difficult to perceive, much less to exploit, the revolutionary potential of such a system.

Julia Kristeva's discussion of the 'semiotic' residue in language demonstrates the limits of this approach for psychoanalytic feminism. The term 'semiotic' refers to a fluid energy state on the borderline of language, which informs and disrupts the more orderly process of signification inaugurated by the symbolic. The presence of the semiotic in language attests to the existence of an even more primitive condition, which Kristeva calls the *chora*, a locus of rhythms, pressures and pulsions that 'connect and orient the body to the mother' (Kristeva 1986a: 95). Like the imaginary to which it refers, the chora must yield to the symbolic in order for the individual subject to achieve the power of signification. Hence there is no possibility of a 'pure' semiotic discourse – one that exists somewhere outside of or apart from the symbolic.

Although originally a precondition of the symbolic, the semiotic functions within signifying practices as the result of a transgression of the symbolic. Therefore the semiotic that 'precedes' symbolization is only a *theoretical supposition* justified by the need for description. It exists in practice only within the symbolic and requires the symbolic break to obtain the complex articulation we associate with it in musical and poetic practices.

(Kristeva 1986a: 118)

Kristeva's adherence to Lacan's account of language acquisition prevents her from articulating a theory of 'écriture féminine'. Like Cixous and Irigaray, however, she is drawn to the imaginary as a focus of desire and inspiration. In *About Chinese Women*, she laments the imposition of monotheistic unity which dictates a radical separation of the sexes, locating 'the polymorphic, orgasmic body [of the mother], laughing and desiring, in the other sex', in favour of 'One Law – One Purifying, Transcendent, Guarantor of the ideal interest of the community' (Kristeva 1977: 19). In 'Stabat Mater' (1986b), where she attempts a form of maternal discourse, she comes close to maintaining the possibility of redeeming this body from its mutism. More typically, however, she affirms the governing role of the symbolic.[5] 'We cannot gain access', she claims, 'to the temporal scene, i.e. to political affairs, except by identifying with the values considered to be masculine (dominance, superego, the endorsed communicative word that institutes stable social exchange).' To do otherwise simply removes one from the realm of speech and writing, placing one instead in 'a permanent state of expectation, punctuated now and then by some kind of outburst: a cry, a refusal, an "hysterical symptom"' (Kristeva 1977: 37).

Lacan's insistence on the phallocentrism of language and culture makes it impossible to locate a position from which to speak which is not already inscribed within the symbolic order. While Kristeva assents to this rigid set of conditions, she also reveals its cost to women, who must negate their primary maternal identification in order to achieve access to language and power. To refuse this course is to descend into psychosis, to become 'ecstatic, nostalgic, or mad' (Kristeva 1977: 30).

Feminist psychoanalytic theorists, while displaying considerable verve and ingenuity in manipulating Freud's Oedipal construct, have been unable to alter its bedrock implications.[6] As long as the father (or his function) remains identified with the achievement of language and culture, the position of women will be marginal to both. The Oedipus complex guarantees the perpetuation of this system (in theory at least) by requiring the submission of both men and women to its patriarchal logic.

FROM MOURNING TO OEDIPUS

'In my own case too'

I suggest that the Oedipus complex has enjoyed a privileged status in psychoanalytic theory, not because of its self-evident universality, but because of its capacity to reflect men's place in the prevailing sex/gender system in a relatively positive, even at times, heroic light. In formulating the Oedipus complex, Freud put the best possible face on his own position within a social order which served him personally and whose rightness he never questioned. That he first arrived at this hypothesis through a painful labour of introspection should not only alert us to the personal nature of this achievement but also raise the possibility of alternative constructions. What we tend to forget is the specifically autobiographical ground of Freud's foundational concepts, praising him instead for the unprecedented nature of his discoveries.

Freud's standard biographers take his self-analysis at face value, as if to do otherwise would jeopardize his entire life's work.[7] To question Freud's autobiographical effort, they imply, would raise doubts about the foundations of psychoanalysis itself. Yet this position relies on a strikingly fallible assumption – that Freud had unmediated access to the contents of his own unconscious. Freud alone, in this view, was free of the wish-fulfilling distortions of fantasy and desire. Given that psychoanalysis rests on the supposition of individual blindness in these matters, it seems contradictory, at the very least, to exempt its founder.

It makes more sense, I think, to scrutinize the process by which Freud arrived at his major insights, considering whether other self-representations might have served him (and us) as well. If, for instance, we suspend judgement about the validity of Freud's self-analysis, we may discover new theoretical prospects in the material he brought to light. Specifically, by remaining open to biographical constructions other than the Oedipus complex we may clear the way for a more fruitful alliance between psychoanalysis and feminism.

Contemporary theories of autobiography suggest that self-writing offers a means of shaping an inner world of coherence out of an inherently contradictory and unstable psychic mix.[8] They tell us that we cannot trust to memory, which is notoriously unreliable, a creator rather than a transmitter of evidence. Nor can we hope to comprehend the multitude of social factors that comprise our historical moment, giving rise to the particular vocabulary of our self-construction. Whatever narrative we arrive at will of necessity be a product of conscious artifice, partial and self-serving. As a result, the test of an autobiography lies not in its fidelity to truth, but in its use value, the extent to which it satisfies our need for meaning in the context of lived experience.

I propose that we read Freud's formulation of the Oedipus complex as autobiography, as an attempt to stabilize an unstable subject in both culturally mediated and personally invested ways.[9] From this perspective we may see how Freud's choice of the Oedipus story as a foundational myth was consonant not only with his culture's values but also with his individual needs.

Freud's fascination with Oedipus (encouraged by the preoccupation of German Romanticism with the culture of ancient Greece) predated his self-analysis, reaching as far back as his adolescence, when he made a careful study of *Oedipus Rex* in preparation for his *Matura* examination.[10] Writing to his friend Emil Fluss at this time, Freud laid out his programme of study: 'I have a good deal of reading to do on my own account from the Greek and Latin classics, among them Sophocles's *Oedipus Rex*'. Evidently his preparation paid off, as he later reported to Fluss, 'The Greek paper, consisting of a thirty-three-verse passage from *Oedipus Rex*, came off better. [I was] the only *good*. This passage I had also read on my own account, and made no secret of it' (E. Freud 1975: 4).

Not long after this, Freud formed a fantasy he revealed on the occasion of his fiftieth birthday when he was presented with a medallion bearing an image of Oedipus confronting the Sphinx accompanied by the words from Sophocles' play: 'Who divined the famed riddle and was a man most mighty.' 'When Freud read the inscription', Ernest Jones recounts, 'he became pale and agitated and in a strangled voice demanded to know who had thought of it. He behaved as if he had encountered a *revenant*, and so he had' (Jones 1955: v.2, 14). Freud offered the explanation that as a young student at the University of Vienna he used to stroll around the great arcaded court inspecting the busts of former famous professors of the institution. He then had the phantasy, not merely of seeing his own bust there in the future, which would not have been anything remarkable in an ambitious student, but of it actually being inscribed with the *identical* words he now saw on the medallion.

(Jones 1955: v.2, 14)

Early in life, it appears, Freud formed a powerful identification with Oedipus as heroic investigator. Given his attachment to this figure it is hardly surprising that he should have returned to it during the period of inner turmoil that coincided with his self-analysis. The Oedipal analogy was ready to hand, so to speak, available for Freud's creative use.

One might argue that Freud did not so much discover Oedipus in his unconscious as finally acknowledge the extent to which he had already assimilated this figure into his self-image through his daydreams of heroic achievement. Yet the psychodynamic nature of Freud's interpretation remains at issue. On this level, I believe that the Oedipus myth offered Freud a means of mediating the crisis of mourning precipitated by his father's death.

'You are requested to close the eyes'

Freud was in the midst of a profound re-examination of his professional and personal identity when Jacob Freud died in 1896. In the preceding year, Freud's last child, Anna, had been born (leading to a decline of sexual relations with his wife Martha); his patient Emma Eckstein had been operated on (with unfortunate consequences) by his friend and correspondent Wilhelm Fliess; and he himself had produced the dream of Irma's injection, the 'specimen dream' of psychoanalysis, in which he questions his efficacy as a physician of nervous diseases. While struggling to theorize the origins of his patients' neuroses, moreover, Freud was actively investigating and combating his own. He suffered variously from headaches, heart palpitations, sinusitis, fatigue, depression, and the occasional episode of impotence. During this time he, like Emma Eckstein, submitted to nasal surgery at the hands of Fliess, otherwise treating his sinus symptoms with cocaine, while anxiously attempting to calculate his 'good' and 'bad' periods according to a complex Fliessian mathematics of male and female cycles. Gloomily, he anticipated an early death.

Though fully aware of his father's failing health, Freud appears to have been devastated by his actual death. Writing to Fliess within three days of this event, he first praises his father's dignified acceptance of the inevitable: 'He bore himself bravely to the end, just like the altogether unusual man he had been', then admits to his own feelings of depression: 'All of it happened in my critical period, and I am really quite down because of it' (Masson 1985: 201). A week later, he writes with greater emotional urgency.

By one of those dark pathways behind the official consciousness the old man's death has affected me deeply. I valued him highly, understood him very well, and with his peculiar mixture of deep wisdom and fantastic light-heartedness he had a significant effect on my life. By the time he died, his life had long been over, but in [my] inner self the whole past has been reawakened by this event.

I now feel quite uprooted.

(Masson 1985: 202)

Freud describes a condition of being overwhelmed and exposed: first caught offguard by 'one of those dark pathways behind the official consciousness', then flooded by memories 'reawakened by this event', and finally left feeling 'uprooted'. This last statement stands alone, as if to emphasize Freud's sense of isolation. It also seems to mark some limit of his capacity to think along these lines, as he turns in the next paragraph to matters of professional concern.

Toward the end of this letter, Freud returns to the subject of his father's death, in a partially coded way, however, through reference to a dream. 'I must tell you about a nice dream I had', Freud states, 'the night after the funeral. I was in a place where I read a sign:

You are requested
to close the eyes.'

Freud recognizes the location of the sign as the barber's shop he visits every day. 'On the day of the funeral' he explains,

I was kept waiting and therefore arrived a little late at the house of mourning. At that time my family was displeased with me because I had arranged for the funeral to be quiet and simple, which they later agreed was quite justified. They were also somewhat offended by my lateness.

(Masson 1985: 202)

The cryptic injunction to close the eyes, Freud claims, has two meanings, both of which carry a reproach, that 'one should do one's duty to the dead (an apology as though I had not done it and were in need of leniency), and the actual duty itself' (Masson 1985: 202). Although Freud effectively chastises himself through his interpretation of this dream, he does not probe more deeply into his motives for his disappointing his family twice – first by arranging a type of ceremony they do not approve of and then by arriving late. Instead, he implies that he had good reasons for both and hence no real need to feel sorry. If there is an 'inclination to self-reproach' embedded in this dream, Freud concludes, its meaning may be found in the feeling-state 'that regularly sets in among the survivors' (Masson 1985: 202).

In *The Interpretation of Dreams* (1900) Freud offers a somewhat different analysis of this dream, where he reports it as an example of the divergent meanings contained in alternative verbal constructions. Here, he tells us that the dream occurred the night *before* his father's funeral and that the printed notice took the following form: 'You are requested to close the eyes' or 'You are requested to close an eye' (Freud 1900: 317). 'Each of these two versions' Freud maintains, 'had a meaning of its own and led in a different direction when the dream was interpreted' (318). The meaning that Freud pursues is the one that indicts him for negligence in his management of his father's funeral. 'I had chosen the simplest possible ritual for the funeral' he explains,

> for I knew my father's own views on such ceremonies. But some other members of the family were not sympathetic to such puritanical simplicity and thought we should be disgraced in the eyes of those who attended the funeral. Hence one of the versions: 'You are requested to close an eye,' i.e. to 'wink at' or 'overlook'.
>
> (Masson 1985: 318)

Reading these two dream interpretations in tandem suggests that Freud indeed felt some guilt or remorse at having settled on a simple funeral for his father. It also opens the possibility (assuming that this dream occurred *before* the ceremony) that his lateness was partly intentional, as though he were begging indulgence for an act he had yet to commit. While the 'filial duty' Freud mentions in the letter to Fliess may refer to the actual closing of the dead man's eyes, there is a further likelihood that Freud was in some sense closing his own – that is to say, not fully acknowledging his own reactions.

In consciously choosing a less than full ritual, and in (unconsciously perhaps) arriving late, was Freud expressing some reluctance to deal with his own grief? Both acts elicited his family's disapproval, as though he were slighting the occasion. In the Preface to the second edition of *The Interpretation of Dreams*, Freud refers to his father's death as 'the most important event, the most poignant loss, of a man's life' (1908: xxvi). Yet, his scanting of his father's funeral suggests a more conflicted and evasive response.[11] What might account for this?

'To be cheerful is everything!'

Freud's correspondence with Fliess in the aftermath of Jacob Freud's death deals with the symptomatology of his patients (which he continues to attribute to sexual seduction in childhood), his own physical complaints, and his darkening mood. Late in November, he writes: 'What I am lacking completely are high spirits and pleasure in living; instead I am busily noting the occasions when I have to occupy myself with the state of affairs after my death.' Freud's reference to his own death is somewhat cryptic, as if he had merged his identity with that of his father in the process of disposing of the deceased man's estate. At the very least it suggests that he is still preoccupied by the thought that he will die young, 'a topic' which, he confesses, 'one should not deal with too extensively if one loves one's friend and only correspondent' (Masson 1985: 204). However discreetly, Freud seems to be confessing to a death-wish.

In subsequent letters, Freud offers evidence from his clinical practice confirming his seduction theory, culminating in the personal observation that 'Unfortunately, my own father was one of these perverts and is responsible for the hysteria of my brother (all of whose symptoms are identifications) and those of several younger sisters. The frequency of this circumstance often makes me wonder' (Masson 1985: 231). His entire family, Freud seems to conclude, is sick.

We know, of course, that Freud abandoned the idea that every neurosis conceals a history of sexual seduction, overcoming his own nervous depression in the process of defining himself as an Oedipal subject. So triumphant, in fact, was Freud's emergence from this period of personal crisis that few have thought to question its dynamics. Yet it is not altogether clear why his formulation of the Oedipus complex should have released him from his physical symptoms, his anxiety, and his deepening melancholy.

In abandoning his seduction theory, Freud foreclosed certain lines of investigation while opening and pursuing others. The most immediate effect of his change of heart was to exonerate his father from the charge of abuse.[12] 'Then the surprise' as Freud states to Fliess on this occasion, 'that in all cases the *father*, not excluding my own, had to be accused of being perverse – the realization of the unexpected frequency of hysteria, with precisely the same conditions prevailing in each, whereas surely such widespread perversions against children are not very probable' (Masson 1985: 264). In a single stroke, Freud dispenses with the 'paternal' etiology of his siblings' hysteria – not to mention his own complex of nervous symptoms. From this perspective alone, Freud's expression of relief makes sense. 'Here I am again', Freud begins his momentous communication to Fliess, 'refreshed, cheerful, impoverished, at present without work, and having settled in again, I am writing to you first' (Masson 1985: 264).

Freud's tone elsewhere in this letter is almost jubilant. Far from being daunted by this newest discovery, he feels relaxed and confident. 'If I were depressed, confused, exhausted, such doubts would surely have to be interpreted as signs of weakness', he allows. 'Since I am in an opposite state, I must recognize them as the result of honest and vigorous intellectual work and must be proud that after going so deep I am still capable of such criticism.' He eagerly anticipates a few days' 'idyll for the two of us' in his friend's company, claims that he is 'in very good spirits' and concludes that he has 'more the feeling of a victory than a defeat' (Masson 1985: 265).

Freud's evident good humour at encountering this latest stumbling-block in his theoretical work suggests that something more than an intellectual conviction is at stake. His upbeat mood signals an emotional shift, as though the process of mourning instigated by his father's death has finally run its course, releasing him from the weight of his depressive feelings. Yet, 'cheerful and refreshed' as Freud professes himself to be, he also makes an odd allusion to Hamlet at the moment of the hero's recognition of his impending death. Adapting Hamlet's statement, 'The readiness is all' in response to Horatio's warning about Laertes, Freud pronounces '"To be in readiness": to be cheerful is everything!', hence neutralizing Shakespeare's meaning (Masson 1985: 265). Even more significantly, Freud ignores the implications of his identification with Hamlet's tragic fate.

In a draft statement included in a letter to Fliess some months before his dismissal of his seduction theory, Freud speculates on a disturbing thought process, evidently discovered in the course of his self-analysis. 'Hostile impulses against parents (a wish that they should die)' he offers, 'are also an integrating constituent of neuroses.' Pursuing this idea further, he links it with a meditation on mourning.

'These impulses are repressed' he observes,

> at periods when compassion for the parents is aroused – at times of their illness or death. On such occasions it is a manifestation of mourning to reproach oneself for their death (so-called melancholia) or to punish oneself in a hysterical fashion, through the medium of the idea of retribution, with the same states [of illness] that they have had.

(Masson 1985: 250)

Freud as much as admits that he has wished his father dead, yet in the face of his actual death turns this thought inward, punishing himself for his murderous desires through the medium of his neurotic symptoms and depression. In this way the idealized image of the father remains intact, while the guilty son gets his due.

It is tempting to speculate that if Freud was unable to sustain a theory of the neuroses that pointed the finger at a 'perverse' father it was at least in part because he could not allow himself such an act of filial impiety in the face of his father's death.[13] Trashing his father's memory in this way would be the equivalent of killing him twice over. Like Hamlet, Freud leaves his father's reputation intact, choosing to vent his hostility elsewhere.

Although Freud's comments on death-wishes against parents suggest that they emerged from his observations of his own mourning, he does not pursue this train of thought. His abandonment of the seduction theory, by curtailing the question of his father's complicity in his children's neuroses, also appears to cut off his investigation into the dynamics of the grieving process. As a result, the reasons Freud may have had for wishing his father dead remain largely opaque. By the time Freud chose to theorize them (in his Oedipal construct), he had abstracted these impulses beyond the point of individual guilt or reproach.

Freud's dream containing the injunction 'You are requested/To close the eyes' acquires even greater resonance in this regard. It is as though Freud chose to turn away, at the very moment of his father's death, from the full psychic impact of this event. Emotionally he seems to have come to an impasse until the momentous decision to jettison the troublesome seduction theory, at which point he began to emerge from mourning and to forge a new identity.

'I now feel quite uprooted'

If we examine Freud's self-analysis in the light of his grieving process, we may achieve a fresh understanding of his Oedipal identification. That Freud felt profoundly ambivalent towards his father is clear not only from his handling of the details of his funeral, but also from his self-reproach and accompanying death-wishes. That he suffered specifically from feelings of sexual rivalry with him in childhood is much less evident. Rather, Freud's early memories chiefly concern the ambiguous and disturbingly seductive behaviour of his mother and his nurse.[14] In this confusing environment, moreover, Freud's own needs for love and reassurance appear to have been overlooked. The emotional tone of these memories is primarily one of anxiety – in response to the multiple dislocations of

Freud's early life.[15] So painful was Freud's reaction to his family's departure from Freiberg, for instance, that he associated the gas jets at one of the railway stops with his nanny's description of the fires of hell. His lifelong travel anxiety was evidently due to the effects of this trauma.[16]

Freud's 'uprooted' feeling in the aftermath of his father's death refers to the period in his childhood when he was literally uprooted from his familiar family setting and perhaps similarly distraught.[17] The memories that Freud produces from this time suggest, in addition, that his mother was emotionally preoccupied or unavailable, thus compounding his feelings of anxiety and bewilderment.[18] In this way, Freud's current state of mourning appears to have touched on ancient griefs and fears. Yet these issues do not inform his Oedipal theory, which posits a passionately desiring son in relation to conventionally gendered, and otherwise idealized, parent figures.

What is missing from this formulation is an awareness of loss. As Freud later (and here implicitly) rewrites *Oedipus Rex*, for instance, no one has to die. The father's authority will prevent the son from enacting his incestuous desire, hence instilling in him the habit of renunciation necessary for participation in culture. If the mother is unavailable, moreover, it is not because of any wayward desire of her own, but rather because of the son's deference to his father's authority. In such a scenario there is no weak, ineffectual or dying old man to reckon with, no mother capable of enacting her own will.[19] From this perspective, it appears that Freud did less to uncover than to obscure the intimate dynamics of his family life. If anything, he closed the door on the earliest period of his childhood when he chose the figure of Oedipus to represent his psychic life.

THE SHADOW OF THE OBJECT

The cornerstone position of the Oedipus complex in psychoanalytic theory has made it difficult, if not impossible, for subsequent critics to examine its appropriateness to the material from which it springs.[20] Yet if we consider this construct in the light of Freud's mourning process it appears less transparently self-evident than artfully imposed. In recreating himself as an Oedipal subject, Freud clearly found relief from his personal crisis. Yet the Oedipus complex, in displacing questions of early childhood loss, occludes the most critical issues to emerge in the aftermath of Jacob Freud's death.

Freud's construction of an authoritative 'Oedipal' father not only prevented him from exploring the multiple trajectories of desire within his family system, but it also barred him from conceptualizing maternal eroticism and aggression, while rendering meaningless his childhood anxieties and ambivalences about the nature of maternal care. Perhaps most importantly, it created the illusion that social and cultural life begins with a child's recognition of his father's commanding presence in the private sphere of the family, as in the world.

While critical of Freud's reasoning, most feminist psychoanalytic theorists do not seek to dislodge the Oedipus complex *per se*.[21] Their achievements, as a result, fall short of their radical political aims. A focus on the pre-Oedipal/imaginary period, however useful in rescuing the figure of the mother from the shadowy background of Freud's theory, does not alter her position within the overall structure which absents her from culture. I believe that feminist theory will remain obstructed by this problem as long as it fails to question the foundational status of the Oedipus complex.

If, however, as I have argued, Freud's Oedipal construct serves to displace and occlude a profound crisis of mourning, then we may be free to consider other theoretical prospects in his self-analysis and hence alternate scenarios for the genesis of psychoanalytic theory. We may speculate, for instance, on how psychoanalysis might have developed had Freud chosen to theorize mourning (that is to say, the dynamics of loss), instead of Oedipus.[22] Freud himself offers hints along these lines in his essay 'Mourning and melancholia' (1917), where he picks up threads of his earlier communications with Fliess.

In 'Mourning and melancholia', Freud returns, so to speak, to the scene of mourning, probing more deeply into its painful dynamics than he was evidently capable of doing in the aftermath of his father's death. As if to signal this awareness, Freud also returns to Hamlet, referring to him this time not as an Oedipal subject, but as a classic victim of melancholy. Like the melancholic, who suffers from a disturbance of self-regard, Hamlet sees himself as 'petty, egoistic, dishonest, lacking in independence, one whose sole aim has been to hide the weaknesses of his own nature' (Freud 1917: 246). Indeed, Freud's whole interest is fixed on this syndrome, which he contrasts with so-called 'normal mourning'.

Whereas in normal mourning the ego gradually detaches itself from the lost object, releasing affective energy, the melancholic ego, according to Freud, holds on to the loved object through a process of identification.[23] This mechanism derives from 'the preliminary stage of object- choice', or the oral phase. 'The ego wants to incorporate this object into itself,' Freud explains, 'and, in accordance with the oral or cannibalistic phase of libidinal development in which it is, it wants to do so by devouring it' (1917: 249–50). 'By taking flight into the ego,' as Freud states poetically, 'love escapes extinction' (1917: 257).

Yet the love preserved in this way is full of conflict. 'The loss of a love object' Freud allows, 'is an excellent opportunity for the ambivalence in love-relationships to make itself effective and come into the open.' In melancholia, especially, 'the occasions which give rise to the illness extend for the most part beyond the clear case of a loss by death, and include all those situations of being slighted, neglected or disappointed, which can import opposed feelings of love and hate into the relationship or reinforce an already existing ambivalence.' Because the subject has incorporated the loved object, moreover, anger or hatred will be directed against the self. In this way, the melancholic's rage 'comes into operation on this substitutive object, abusing it, debasing it, making it suffer and deriving sadistic satisfaction from its suffering' (1917: 251).

Freud's understanding of melancholic identification as a psychic mechanism inherited from the oral phase suggests that he is thinking about the earliest stages of love and loss and hence the period in his own life when he was most vulnerable to disruptions of maternal care. If this is so, Freud may well have been describing the residue of his childhood reactions to his mother and his nurse, neither of whom died, yet both of whom evoked ambivalent emotions. While Freud's nurse aroused him, shamed him, and left him, his mother simply (and perhaps of necessity) turned her attentions elsewhere.[24] Although Freud does not directly address the issue of maternal loss, it hovers in the background of his description of melancholia, as a kind of shadow text.

A powerful metaphor, moreover, links Freud's discussion of melancholia with his thoughts on the same subject in 1895, indicating that Freud was preoccupied with this subject *before* his father's death and hence prior to his mourning for that loss. In a draft statement to Fliess (included in an envelope postmarked January 1895), Freud offers a neurological explanation of the dynamics of melancholia.[25] As a result of 'a very great loss in the amount of excitation' he states, 'there may come about *an in-drawing*, as it were, *into the psychic sphere*, which produces an effect of suction upon the adjoining amounts of excitation'. This giving up of excitation produces pain. Next, 'there sets in, as though through an *internal hemorrhage*, an impoverishment in excitation', which 'operates like a *wound*'. Comparing this process to neurasthenia in which excitation runs out, 'as it were, through a hole', Freud concludes that 'in melancholia the hole is in the psychic sphere' (Masson 1985: 103–4).

Freud's imagery of sucking in anticipates his description of oral incorporation in 'Mourning and melancholia', where the wound metaphor also recurs. Here he states that 'the complex of melancholia behaves like an open wound, drawing to itself cathectic energies . . . and emptying the ego until it is totally impoverished' (1917: 253). This account, while less graphic than his earlier one, portrays the same dynamic. Evidently attached to this idea, Freud repeats it towards the conclusion of his essay where he tries, rather unsuccessfully, to explain how melancholia comes to an end. 'The conflict within the ego', he suggests, 'which melancholia substitutes for the struggle over the object, must act like a painful wound which calls for an extraordinarily high anti-cathexis' (1917: 258). Whereas the mourner gradually accepts the fact that 'the object no longer exists', the melancholic must somehow manage to eject it, by 'disparaging it, denigrating it, and even as it were killing it', in order to obtain relief (1917: 255, 257).

Freud's discomfort with this explanation manifests itself in the abruptness with which he brings his essay to a close. Immediately after invoking the wound metaphor, he admits 'But here once again, it will be well to call a halt. . . . As we already know, the interdependence of the complicated problems of the mind forces us to break off every inquiry before it is completed – till the outcome of some other inquiry can come to its assistance' (1917: 258). The effect of these concluding remarks is to hold the wound metaphor in suspension, as if melancholia itself were an interminable illness.

Freud's investigation into the dynamics of melancholia at least a year and a half before his father's death suggests that more than so called 'normal mourning' is at issue. Since he (as well as his patients) suffered from depression at this time, it seems likely that his theoretical labour was autobiographically informed. Taking these suppositions together with the memories of early childhood loss that emerged in the aftermath of Jacob Freud's death and the specifically oral nature of Freud's description of melancholia in the 1917 essay, one might easily speculate that the 'open wound' metaphor he uses to convey the psychic affect of melancholia also gives expression to his feelings about the ruptures and losses of his early life.

What is most striking about the wound metaphor, of course, is its resemblance to Freud's later language about castration, a condition which he attributes literally only to females. While the boy may act to repress his desire for his mother under the *threat* of castration, only the girl *experiences* it through her awareness of phallic lack. Whereas the sight of the little girl's genitals arouses a 'terrible storm of emotion' in the boy, who feels a 'horror of the mutilated creature', as Freud states in 'Some psychical consequences of the anatomical distinction between the sexes' (1925), the girl incurs a 'wound to her narcissism' and 'develops, like a scar, a sense of inferiority' (252–3). Melancholia, in contrast, is not gender marked. Both boys and girls, men and women, may be subject to its wounding, internal haemorrhaging, and psychic scars.

Whereas Freud's concept of the castration complex acts to displace and defer the threat of wounding for the boy, his representation of melancholia as a painful hole in the psyche suggests otherwise. For the melancholic, struggling to preserve his or her love objects, castration has always already taken place. Such a construction of lack – as primary loss – not only obviates the gender imbalance of Freud's Oedipal construct, but it also avoids the problem of positing separation, or the inception of the symbolic stage, as a function of the father.[26] Only if one imagines an originary state of blissful mother–infant union, moreover, does such a step become necessary.[27]

When Freud looked back at his early childhood what he remembered was not a paradisical condition of oneness with his mother, but rather multiple contexts of pain, disappointment and loss. Although he invented psychoanalysis under the sign of mourning – for his father Jacob Freud and for the child he once was – he chose to theorize from a text which offered him more consoling images. Out of the tragic material of *Oedipus Rex*, Freud forged a hopeful, if sober, psychic construct. Perhaps more importantly he fashioned a family he could live with – one that revolved around a vigorous and commanding father, an ideally loving mother, and a lively, upstart son. Having taken this momentous step, he rarely looked back. As if in response to the dream request to close the eyes, Freud appears to have averted his gaze from the scene of mourning, effectively deferring the question of his own grief.

Yet Freud's image of pathological mourning as an open wound attests to the power of this issue in his imagination, in addition to its status as an ongoing problem. Given Freud's own depression both before and after Jacob Freud's death, one might say that psychoanalysis, insofar as it originates in his self-analysis, begins, not with Oedipus, but with the wound. One might even say that for Freud, being *in* psychoanalysis (founding it, labouring within it) was like being *in* mourning.[28]

For Freud, loss is not a foundational concept. Being in mourning, like being 'uprooted', was perhaps too painful a position for him to consider as a basis for psychoanalytic theory as a whole. From the perspective of feminism, however, it may offer a more useful starting point than the Oedipus construct, which decides one's sexual and cultural destiny with a single phallic stroke.

NOTES

1 J.J. Bachofen, in *Das Mutterrecht* (1861), postulates an early matriarchal stage of the family in which women exercised power. At the same time, he considers the emergence of the patriarchal family as a definite advance in human civilization. Many other nineteenth-century theorists accept the idea of a matrilineal phase in human history, while rejecting Bachofen's concept of matriarchy *per se*. Freud, while reluctant to posit an *initial* matriarchal phase, nevertheless tried to incorporate the notion of matriarchy as a transitional moment in the evolution from an original father-dominated primal horde to the modern form of the patriarchal family. His discomfort with the very idea of matriarchy, however, manifests itself in the confused accounts he gives of this process in *Totem and Taboo* (1913) and in *Moses and Monotheism* (1939). I treat this subject (including the complicating factor of Freud's rivalry with Jung) at greater length in *The Spectral Mother* (Sprengnether 1990).

2 Juliet Mitchell, in *Psychoanalysis and Feminism* (1974), makes a case for reading Freud in a descriptive, rather than a prescriptive sense. In this way, she argues, we may better comprehend the unconscious structure of patriarchy – as a necessary first step in dismantling it. While Mitchell reads Freud through the lens of Lacanian theory, Nancy Chodorow offers an object relations approach. In her enormously influential book *The Reproduction of Mothering* (1978), she analyses the development of masculinity and femininity within the confines of the patriarchal nuclear family. Paradoxically however, the very success of her exposition has proved an obstacle to envisioning social change, as many feminists have found her description of feminine development within patriarchy more attractive than otherwise.

3 Stephen Mitchell, in *Hope and Dread in Psychoanalysis* (1993), gives a lucid account of the developments in psychoanalytic theory since Freud which have combined to displace his drive theory model of interpretation in favour of a more interactive approach, one that recognizes the subjective situation of both analyst and analysand in the construction of meaning. Psychoanalysis, he believes, participates in the shift towards perspectivist explanation that characterizes contemporary philosophy and science. 'For Freud' he observes,

> psychoanalysis was embedded in the broad, invigorating, reassuring, scaffolding of the scientific worldview. . . . That scaffolding does not sustain us in the same way it did for Freud and his contemporaries, cannot sustain us; this fact has, in some sense, stranded psychoanalysis, unmoored it from the context that gave it its original meaning. Those who think of analysis in ways similar to our analytic ancestors seem to most of us today more like cultists than scientists.
>
> (Mitchell 1993: 21)

4 For persuasive demonstrations of this point see Jane Gallop's *Reading Lacan* (1985: 136), and David Macey's *Lacan in Contexts* (1988: 190).

5 My account of Kristeva's complex body of thought is necessarily condensed here. In my view, there are conflicting strains in her work which lead in different directions. While I see points of opening, occasionally, for a feminist appropriation of her understanding of the split subjectivity of the mother-to-be, I do not think that Kristeva herself develops this possibility. Patricia Elliott reads Kristeva in a more positive light, summarizing her position as follows:

> In order to become a human subject, according to Kristeva, something has to be given up, lost, or abandoned; the imaginary plenitude of the pleasure ego has to give way

to the reality of separation. . . . But what if the difference between the sexes is mobilized by a symbolic order intent on denying that loss by projecting it on to women? From Kristeva's perspective, even the way in which that loss is imagined – as castration – presupposes a social order already infused with patriarchal ideology.

(1991: 206–7)

While I am in sympathy with Elliott's analysis, I think that she has projected her own analysis on to Kristeva. In *The Spectral Mother*, I propose that Freud's late reformulation of castration as separation from the mother might be developed in such a way as to posit an originary loss which is not gender marked. For Elliott, Kristeva makes this case. 'An antireligious, heretical ethics' Elliott states, 'would demand an acknowledgment of separation, loss, and death rather than a denial achieved either through the idealization or the abjection of mothers' (1991: 221). Although I agree with this position, I don't believe that Kristeva articulates it as such.

6 Feminists who take psychoanalysis seriously, at one point or another, come up against the Oedipus complex. For a while during the 1970s, it seemed that an emphasis on the pre-Oedipal period might offer a theoretical avenue of escape from the imposition of Oedipal authority. The a priori definition of this phase as standing somewhere outside of the symbolic order, however, limits the possibilities for the liberation of female (and maternal) subjectivity. More recently, feminists have focused either on locating the mother–infant relationship *within* the symbolic order or on redefining the Oedipus complex in such a way as to soften its patriarchal implications. Kaja Silverman offers an example of the former strategy in *The Acoustic Mirror* (1988), where she proposes a new reading of the mother–daughter relationship. 'To situate the daughter's passion for the mother within the Oedipus complex' she argues, 'is to make it an effect of language and loss, and so to contextualize both it and the sexuality it implies firmly within the symbolic' (p. 123). Jessica Benjamin, rather than accepting the pre-symbolic/symbolic dichotomy (and hence the location of men and women on opposite sides of the cultural divide) offers a redefinition of the Oedipus complex from the standpoint of intersubjective theory. 'The three pillars of Oedipal theory,' she concludes, 'the primacy of the wish for oneness, the mother's embodiment of this regressive force, and the necessity of paternal intervention – all combine to create the paradox that the only liberation is paternal domination. . . . By going beyond Oedipus we can envisage a direct struggle for recognition between man and woman, free of the shadow of the father that falls between them' (Benjamin 1988: 181). While I am in sympathy with these (and other) efforts to reposition women in relation to the Oedipus complex, I prefer to interrogate the process by which Freud arrived at this problematic construct.

7 Ernest Jones, until recently Freud's most eminent biographer, considers Freud's self-analysis as 'his most heroic feat'. Far from questioning Freud's (or anyone's) capacity to carry out such a task, he valorizes its achievement. 'It is hard for us nowadays,' he states, 'to imagine how momentous this achievement was, that difficulty being the fate of most pioneering exploits. Yet the uniqueness of the feat remains. Once done it is done forever. For no one again can be the first to explore those depths' (1953: v.1, 319). Peter Gay, who brings Jones's work up to date, admits that 'self-analysis would seem to be a contradiction in terms', yet he excuses Freud on the grounds that he had 'no teachers but had to invent the rules for it as he went along' and he does not question its results (1988: 96, 98). While a number of demythologizing studies of Freud have appeared in recent years, none to my knowledge directly addresses this issue.

8 See, for instance, Liz Stanley's *The Auto/Biographical I* (1992), which summarizes the developments in Foucaultian and post-structuralist theory which gave rise to these assumptions. See also William Epstein's *Contesting the Subject* (1991) for reflections on how contemporary views of the self affect the writing of biography.

9 Mark Edmundson, whose argument parallels mine in certain respects, sees Freud's invention of the Oedipus complex as an act of self-creation. 'Freud's textual practice' he states, 'suggests . . . that the Oedipal complex is the negative term in a symbolic

drama of private self-recreation, the fruit of which is a new discourse, a new terminological field' (1990: 41). Edmundson regards Freud's Oedipal narrative as confining and recommends a sceptical stance towards this aspect of his achievement.

10 I am indebted to Peter Rudnytsky's *Freud and Oedipus* (1987) for this account.

11 This behaviour recurred, in a more extreme form, on the event of Freud's mother's death in 1930. Freud not only did not attend her funeral, but he also seems to have experienced more relief than grief. Given that Amalie died at the age of 95 and that her son was himself 74 at the time, it may not be surprising that Freud felt no active pain. Yet the parallel with his earlier avoidance behaviour around his father's funeral suggests otherwise. Herbert Lehmann speculates that Freud's very identification with his mother from an early age made it difficult for him to acknowledge the reality of her loss. Harry Hardin, who sees Freud's relationship with his mother as profoundly ambivalent, offers the explanation that he sent his daughter Anna as a 'mourner by proxy', because she 'could grieve without the constraints her father experienced because of his lifelong alienation from her grandmother' (1988: 85). Peter Homans observes that in Freud's 'unconscious his anxiety about his own death and his anxiety about his mother's death were probably linked, condensed, maybe even interchangeable'. He connects Freud's 'psychological sense of his own death' in later life with this profound identification (1989: 98).

12 Marianne Krüll makes this point in a different way. She reads the dream injunction 'to close the eyes' as Freud's warning to himself against exploring his father's tendencies towards perversity, among which she includes his (presumed) habit of masturbation. She concludes that 'the two central threads running through Freud's entire theoretical and therapeutic work – the subject of sexuality, which was to become the pivot of his theory of human behaviour, and the subject of guilt of the sons towards the father . . . were the very areas in which Jacob Freud himself felt beset with guilt' (1986: 101). Jeffrey Masson emphasizes Freud's conflict of allegiance between his patient Emma Eckstein and his friend Wilhelm Fliess (over the matter of Fliess's bungled operation on her nose), arguing that Freud chose to side with Fliess rather than with Eckstein when he abandoned the seduction theory (Masson 1984). For Samuel Slipp, the most important factor in Freud's repudiation of the seduction theory is his problematic relationship with his mother. He speculates that 'Freud abandoned the Seduction theory as an attempt to deny the traumatic impact of others, since he could not deal with a pre-Oedipal conflict with his mother' (Slipp 1988: 155). Larry Wolff (1988) locates the discussion of Freud's seduction theory in the context of several well-publicized trials involving child abuse at the turn of the century in Vienna, making the point that Freud would have had deliberately to ignore the questions raised by these scandals in order to relinquish his own theory.

13 Marianne Krüll believes that Jacob Freud conveyed an unspoken mandate to his son, that he 'was expected to turn his back on tradition but not on one of its most central tenets, that of filial piety on which, ultimately the entire Jewish tradition is based' (1986: 178). In the face of his father's death, Freud was unable to resist this mandate, and hence, 'dutiful son that he was, took the guilt upon his own shoulders with the help of his Oedipus theory' (Krüll 1986: 179). Although I do not agree with every point of Krüll's argument concerning Jacob Freud's transgressions, I believe that her reading of Freud's inability to point the finger of blame at his father after his death is accurate.

14 Among the flood of memories awakened by Freud's grieving process, the most striking ones relate to his mother and to his nurse from the period of his earliest childhood. The first of his startling discoveries concerns his nurse, whom he refers to as 'the "prime originator"' of his sexuality, 'an ugly, elderly, but clever woman who told me a great deal about God Almighty and hell and who instilled in me a high opinion of my own capacities' (Masson 1985: 268). This woman, Freud claims, who washed him in reddish water in which she had previously washed herself and who persuaded him to steal, 'was my teacher in sexual matters and complained because I was clumsy and unable to do

anything' (Masson 1985: 269). Elsewhere Freud reveals that as a child he believed his half-brother Phillipp to be responsible, not only for the dismissal of his nurse, but also for his mother's pregnancy with his sister Anna (1901: 51). Jacob Freud's death seems to have opened a space for Freud to explore the question of his mother's desire. Yet he glosses over these issues in his construction of the Oedipal triangle, which emphasizes a son's, rather than a mother's, guilty love.

15   Between the ages of 1 and a half and 4, Freud suffered a number of potentially tragic losses, most of which he alludes to (in condensed form) in his letters to Fliess. The first major shock was the birth, followed quickly by the death, of his brother Julius, whom Freud 'greeted . . . with adverse wishes and genuine childhood jealousy' and whose death 'left the germ of (self-) reproaches' in him (Masson 1985: 268). At the time of Julius's death in the spring of 1858, moreover, Freud's mother was already pregnant with her third child, who was born in December of that year. The following month, Freud's nanny was caught stealing and dismissed. Then in August 1859, Freud's family relocated from Freiberg to Leipzig, a move evidently prompted by the failure of Jacob Freud's business. In less than a year the family was on the road once again, this time to Vienna, where at last they set down roots. The mere chronology of these events suggests a high degree of disruption in Freud's early life: through death, the arrival of unwanted siblings, the departure of his nurse, the breakup of his extended family system and loss of their Freiberg home. The reawakening of memories from this period is more than likely to have renewed old feelings of distress.

16   Freud himself makes the connection between the sight of the gas jets and his travel phobia (Masson 1985: 285).

17   Freud's word for uprooted is '*entwurzeltes*'. Mark Edmundson notes: 'To be uprooted is to be naked, vulnerable, exposed, but also to take up a new position, unburied and unblinded, in a fresh relation to experience' (1990: 43). I am inclined to lay the emphasis on Freud's sense of vulnerability and exposure.

18   Freud's memory fragment concerning his anxiety about his mother's disappearance (near the time of her confinement with his sister Anna) is particularly suggestive. 'My mother' Freud relates, 'was nowhere to be found; I was crying in despair. My brother Phillipp (twenty years older than I) unlocked a wardrobe [*Kasten*] for me, and when I did not find my mother inside it either, I cried even more until, slender and beautiful, she came in through the door' (Masson 1985: 271). Freud evidently feared that his mother had vanished, like his nurse, who had been dismissed a short time before. In *The Psychopathology of Everyday Life* (1901), Freud explains further that he thought his brother Phillipp 'had taken his father's place' with his mother, an indication (even in fantasy form) that he felt excluded from the circle of his mother's attention (1901: 51).

19   Kathleen Woodward comments astutely:

> *The Interpretation of Dreams* may be read as a son's book of mourning for his father, albeit a strange one. But I also want to insist that to the extent the figure of the dead father dominates the book in the abstract, the figure of the infirm and aged father haunts it. It is aging, not death, which castrates the father. . . . The infirm father is all too literally present as painfully weak.
>
> (1991: 33)

20   Didier Anzieu's treatment of Freud's articulation of the Oedipus complex, though somewhat hyperbolical, is typical of the way most readers approach this subject. He writes:

> In the course of his discovery of the Oedipus myth, Freud completes the threefold process – at once subjective, objective, and self-representing – which began to get under way at the start of his self- analysis. It is the discovery of a universal truth; the discovery of himself; and the discovery of itself, by which I mean the correlative discovery of the very process through which the main discovery is made.
>
> (1986: 244)

21 One might argue that reformulating the Oedipus complex in such a way as to dissolve its primary impact constitutes an effort to abolish it, yet those whose work might be construed in this way do not make this claim. Shoshana Felman, for instance, so thoroughly rewrites the Oedipus complex in her essay 'Beyond Oedipus' (1987) that one might wonder how much of Freud's concept remains. At the same time, she does not propose changing Freud's nomenclature.

22 A case could be made that Melanie Klein's concept of the depressive position works a transformation of this sort (1987). Yet she herself does not make this claim, and her allegiance to the Oedipus complex, however reworked in her system of thought, stands in the way of a full break from Freud. Julia Kristeva's *Black Sun* (1989) comes close to such a break by emphasizing loss as the point of departure for the subject's entry into language. However, Kristeva adheres to Lacan's assumption of the necessity of third party intervention (the function of the father) in order for this development to take place, hence invoking the phallus as a privileged signifier. Peter Homans (1989) sees the invention of psychoanalysis as a work of personal and cultural mourning, but he does not critique the outcome of this process.

23 Kathleen Woodward comments on the inadequacy of Freud's account of 'normal mourning'. 'In this unequivocal distinction [between mourning and melancholia]', she observes, 'I find a peculiar kind of piety, an almost ethical injunction to kill the dead and to adjust ourselves to "reality". In "Mourning and Melancholia" Freud leaves us no theoretical room for another place, one between a crippling melancholia and the end of mourning' (1991: 116). I am very much indebted to this insight.

24 It seems that Freud's nurse treated him badly on several accounts: by sexually seducing him, casting doubt on his abilities, sexual and otherwise, taking money from him, and finally leaving him. His mother's legacy seems to have been more enigmatic and complex. Quite apart from any feelings she may have entertained for her stepson Phillipp, her loss of her second child and closely spaced pregnancies would account for some degree of emotional preoccupation or removal. Samuel Slipp argues more specifically that the multiple disappointments of Amalie Freud's early marriage (including her husband's business failure) made it difficult for her to respond fully to the needs of her firstborn son (1988: 158).

25 Freud later abandoned the attempt to blend psychology with neurology. For a full discussion of the impact of Freud's neurological training on his psychoanalytic constructs, see Frank Sulloway's *Freud: Biologist of the Mind* (1979).

26 I have argued this position more extensively in *The Spectral Mother* (Sprengnether 1990), where I make a case for regarding the ego as an 'elegiac construct'.

27 According to Daniel Stern, contemporary observations of mother–infant interactions reveal that there is no such thing as a period of mother–infant symbiosis. He states:

> Infants begin to experience a sense of self from birth. They are predesigned to be aware of self-organizing processes. They never experience a period of total self/other undifferentiation. There is no confusion between self and other in the beginning or at any point during infancy.

(1985: 10)

28 Peter Homans (1989), who regards psychoanalysis as the result of Freud's *ability* to mourn, emphasizes the success of this process. My focus, in contrast, is on the inhibited or failed aspects of Freud's mourning and his consequent *inability* to acknowledge the full impact of loss.

REFERENCES

Anzieu, D. (1986) *Freud's Self-Analysis*, trans. P. Graham. London: Hogarth.
Bachofen, J.J. (1861) *Myth, Religion and Mother-Right*, trans. R. Manheim. Princeton: Princeton University Press (1967).

Benjamin, J. (1988) *The Bonds of Love: Psychoanalysis, Feminism, and the Problem of Domination*. New York: Pantheon.
Chodorow, N. (1978) *The Reproduction of Mothering: Psychoanalysis and the Sociology of Gender*. Berkeley: University of California Press.
Cixous, H. and Clement, C. (1986) *The Newly Born Woman*, trans. B. Wing. Minneapolis: University of Minnesota Press.
Edmundson, M. (1990) *Towards Reading Freud: Self-Creation in Milton, Wordsworth, Emerson, and Sigmund Freud*. Princeton: Princeton University Press.
Elliott, P. (1991) *From Mastery to Analysis: Theories of Gender in Psychoanalytic Feminism*. Ithaca: Cornell University Press.
Epstein, W. (ed.) (1991) *Contesting the Subject: Essays in the Postmodern Theory and Practice of Biography and Biographical Criticism*. West Lafayette: Purdue University Press.
Felman, S. (1987) *Jacques Lacan and the Adventure of Insight: Psychoanalysis in Contemporary Culture*. Cambridge: Harvard University Press.
Freud, Ernst L. (ed.) (1975) *The Letters of Sigmund Freud*, trans. Tania and James Stern. New York: Basic Books.
Freud, S. (1900) *The Interpretation of Dreams*. S.E.4: 1–338.
—— (1901) *The Psychopathology of Everyday Life*. S.E.6: 1–279.
—— (1910) 'A special type of choice of object made by men'. S.E.11: 163–75.
—— (1913) *Totem and Taboo*. S.E.13: 1–161.
—— (1917) 'Mourning and melancholia'. S.E.14: 237–58.
—— (1925) 'Some psychical consequences of the anatomical distinction between the sexes'. S.E.19: 241–58.
—— (1939) *Moses and Monotheism*. S.E.23: 1–137.
—— (1986) *The Standard Edition of the Complete Psychological Works of Sigmund Freud*, ed. and trans. J. Strachey. London: Hogarth, twenty-four volumes.
Gallop, J. (1985) *Reading Lacan*. Ithaca: Cornell University Press.
Gay, P. (1988) *Freud: A Life for Our Time*. New York: Norton.
Hardin, H. (1988) 'On the vicissitudes of Freud's early mothering: Alienation from his biological mother'. *Psychoanalytic Quarterly*, 57: 72–86.
Homans, P. (1989) *The Ability to Mourn: Disillusionment and the Social Origins of Psychoanalysis*. Chicago: Chicago University Press.
Irigaray, L. (1981) 'And the one doesn't stir without the other'. *Signs*, 7: 60–67.
Jones, E. (1953–7) *The Life and Work of Sigmund Freud*. New York: Basic, three volumes (1953, 1955, 1957).
Jung, C.G. (1911–12) *Psychology of the Unconscious (Transformations And Symbols of the Libido)*, trans. B. Hinkle. New York: Moffat (1916).
Klein, M. (1987) 'A contribution to the psychogenesis of manic-depressive states', in *The Selected Melanie Klein*. J. Mitchell (ed.). New York: Free Press.
Kristeva J. (1977) *About Chinese Women*. trans. A. Barrows. New York: Urizen.
—— (1986a) 'Revolution in poetic language', in *The Kristeva Reader*. T. Moi (ed.). New York: Columbia University Press.
—— (1986b) 'Stabat Mater', in *The Kristeva Reader*. T. Moi (ed.). New York: Columbia University Press.
—— (1989) *Black Sun: Depression and Melancholia*, trans. L. Roudiez. New York: Columbia University Press.
Krull, M. (1986) *Freud and His Father*, trans. A.J. Pomerans. New York: Norton.
Lacan, J. (1977) *Ecrits: A Selection*, trans. A. Sheridan. London: Tavistock.
Lehmann, H. (1983) 'Reflections on Freud's reaction to the death of his mother'. *Psychoanalytic Quarterly*, 52: 237–49.
Macey, D. (1988) *Lacan in Contexts*. London: Verso.
Masson, J. (1984) *The Assault on Truth: Freud's Suppression of the Seduction Theory*. New York: Farrar, Straus & Giroux.

—— (trans. and ed.) (1985) *The Complete Letters of Sigmund Freud to Wilhelm Fliess 1887–1904*. Cambridge: Harvard University Press.

Mitchell, J. (1974) *Psychoanalysis and Feminism*. New York: Pantheon.

Mitchell, S. (1993) *Hope and Dread in Psychoanalysis*. New York: Basic Books.

Rudnytsky, P. (1987) *Freud and Oedipus*. New York: Columbia University Press.

Shakespeare, W. (1992) *Hamlet*, C. Hoy (ed.). New York: Norton.

Silverman, K. (1988) *The Acoustic Mirror: The Female Voice in Psychoanalysis and Cinema*. Bloomington: Indiana University Press.

Slipp, S. (1988) 'Freud's mother, Ferenczi, and the seduction theory'. *Journal of the American Academy of Psychoanalysis*, 16: 155–65.

Sprengnether, M. (1990) *The Spectral Mother: Freud, Feminism and Psychoanalysis*. Ithaca: Cornell University Press.

Stanley, L. (1992) *The Auto/Biographical I: The Theory and Practice of Feminist Auto/Biography*. Manchester: Manchester University Press.

Stern, D. (1985) *The Interpersonal World of the Infant: A View from Psychoanalysis and Developmental Psychology*. New York: Basic.

Sulloway, F. (1979) *Freud: Biologist of the Mind*. New York: Basic Books.

Wolff, L. (1988) *Postcards from the End of the World: Child Abuse in Freud's Vienna*. New York: Atheneum.

Woodward, K. (1991) *Aging and Its Discontents: Freud and Other Fictions*. Bloomington: Indiana University Press.

9 Masculine mastery and fantasy, or the meaning of the phallus

Stephen Frosh

The ambiguities of sexual difference revolve around uncertainty over the content and fixedness of the categories 'masculine' and 'feminine'. Within psychoanalysis, this is expressed by a fascination with gender divergence which has been characteristic of psychoanalytic theory since its inception, accompanied by a playful and ambivalent tradition of transgression. In the context of the transference, the analyst, whether male or female, can be related to as either masculine or feminine, whether in terms of 'whole object' identity (as mother or father), or part object attribute (breast, penis), and therefore has to have the capacity to tolerate this boundary confusion if the projections of the patient are to be understood and ameliorated. For analysands, crossing conventional gender boundaries, particularly in terms of sexual object choice, is a common phenomenon; psychoanalysis is explicit about the significance of such homoeroticism and 'bisexuality', theorized primarily in terms of sexually charged aspects of gender identity. At a more general and theoretical level, psychoanalysis struggles to find its place amongst categories which traditionally reduce to a masculine/feminine dimorphism: rational and irrational, reason and emotion, science and art, culture and nature. In the end, it becomes clear that psychoanalysis plays out both the central subjective significance of sexual division (that one experiences oneself as masculine or feminine in ways which are emotionally highly charged) and its untenability (that, because masculine and feminine are constructed categories, they never hold firm, but are always collapsing into one another). Moreover, because of the centrality of sexuality in psychoanalysis, the ambiguity of sexual difference comes to infiltrate all its domains.

Amongst psychoanalysts of the post-Freudian era, it is Lacan who has produced most outrage and energy in discussions of sexual difference, and who seems to have most self-consciously played with the divisions, appearing both to assert the ubiquity of sexual difference and to undermine it in theory and in practice. It is perhaps no surprise that an industry of competing authorities on Lacan has grown up, especially given the difficulty of his work and its availability to a range of alternative constructions. Lacan himself talks authoritatively, as if he is absolutely certain about the truth of what he says. Indeed, in a lecture given on television that supposedly offered an introduction to psychoanalysis to a mass audience, but which in fact made no concessions of any kind towards ease of understanding,

Lacan claimed, 'I always speak the truth'. The irony here is so obvious that one must assume it to be intentional, because the content of Lacanian theory seems on the face of it to be opposed to any claim that anyone can 'speak the truth' – can have a complete grasp of what is real. Authoritatively, speaking as a famous psychoanalyst who is in possession of a knowledge so deep that it cannot easily be communicated, Lacan tells us that there is no absolute authority, that the belief that anyone – any 'other' – can hold all the answers to our questions, is an illusion. There is a law, it fixes us in the symbolic order, but try to master it and all one discovers is that no one is master, no one is an absolute authority; the one 'supposed' to know does not 'really' know at all.

This can be restated more strongly and personally. Lacan's absolute certainty, his wilfulness and capriciousness, his adoption of a god-like voice, his dismissal of opponents and acolytes alike, his assumption of the right to bend the rules of analysis, all this is the most infuriating evidence of mastery. This authority, however, is used to promulgate a theory attesting to the *impossibility* of authority: no one can be master of the unconscious. Moreover, Lacan claims to let his unconscious do the work, so that when he speaks he is evoking the experience of analysis as well as discoursing upon it. The unconscious speaks for him, in very public circumstances; but by doing this it acts in 'his' service – Lacan uses his own unconscious as part of his performance. Using it, however, it ceases to be un-conscious in the simple psychoanalytic sense of something unavailable to conscious control and manipulation. Thus, in order to demonstrate that no one can master the unconscious, Lacan becomes its master.

The paradoxes of authority and power which are expressed in the form and content of Lacanian theory should not be regarded as some extraneous obstacle to understanding. Rather, these paradoxes go to the heart of the question that underpins any causal account of sexual difference: what is it that produces sexual difference and fixes the relationship between the sexes so that gender dimorphism comes to be experienced as an asymmetrical and unequivocal fact of existence? For Lacan, this question is best formulated as the question of the 'meaning of the phallus', that which is taken to be the sign of difference, privileging one sex over the other, producing divergent subjectivities. As will be described more fully below, the phallus in this theory is both something which symbolizes power and something which is empty of content, precisely paralleling the paradoxes of authority and mastery – and these paradoxes are once again enacted in the structure of the theory itself. Desiring to understand Lacan is like wanting to have the phallus; the fantasy is that it would bring in its wake everything connected with power and authority, because that is what it represents and seems to be. But just as the idea that one can own the phallus is an imaginary illusion, part of what Lacan terms the imaginary, so is the fantasy of what conquering Lacan might achieve.

It is, of course, possible that the lure of Lacan's work lies in its obscurity, that behind the veil of difficult language there is nothing of substance. If this were so, it would make his writing a kind of masquerade, something eliciting the desire to possess (understand) by virtue of its inscrutability. It would be only because its meaning (or lack of it) is so playfully veiled that it is arousing and desirable;

remove the veils and the mystery goes. Under these conditions, Lacan's reputation relies on intimidation: if people were only more willing to challenge the difficulty of his writing, they would see how apt the 'emperor's new clothes' accusation often applied to him is; once the pretence is seen through, nothing remains. The irony here, however, is that this is very much what Lacan says about desire itself, and in a different way about the pursuit of femininity as other to the male: that these enterprises refer to empty sets, that the pursuit is all there is. As the object of our desire slips away and is more and more elusive, so we desire to have it, to master it all the more.

Here, therefore, is more evidence of how one can fall into the grip of this master of manipulation and paradox. If the only thing that is interesting about Lacan's writing is its obscurity, and if behind this obscurity it is actually devoid of meaningful content, then it functions as a demonstration of the Lacanian theory of desire, so it cannot just be empty after all. Lacan wins either way: either his writing, difficult though it might be, denotes a specific theory or set of theories with which we might want or have to grapple; or its difficulty is its way of connoting the same theories, of expressing their truth in the practice of speaking and writing. In psychoanalytic thought, symptoms express something about the nature of the underlying forces from which they arise. Lacan's writing may be a kind of symptomatic enactment of his theory of the phallus; and also of the feminine object of desire.

Many people have noted Lacan's fascination and identification with femininity, his constant playing to the ladies. Clément (1983: 61) comments, 'the whole cast of characters in his early work consists of women. Not a single man is present. . . . Here is a man whose thinking is founded entirely on the study of female paranoia. A man who never stopped talking about women.' Lacan claims to know more about women than women do themselves; but he also takes on feminine poses as the performer, the hard to find, the one engaging in masquerade. Identifying himself as an hysteric, he claims to know both woman and man inside out – or at least, as in the following quotation, he can be read by others as making that claim.

> The male analyst understands the woman and speaks in her place, is the perfection of the hysteric, no symptoms, save only mistakes in gender, the misidentifications indeed, running in and out of her from *his* position, miss-taken but perfect – fear, desire, the love letter as grounding of authority.
>
> (Heath 1987: 7)

Lacan's mastery of the unconscious is what is on display, but the unconscious is also that which eludes mastery, that which is multifarious and seductive, playful and contradictory. In conventional gender terms, it lies on the feminine pole, and its associations are feminine in tone. Lacan is the master, his texts are impossible yet true. Lacan is also the one pored over, taken apart, to be desired and if possible owned, and even perhaps loved.

Reading Lacan on sexual difference can be seen to be intolerable, but unavoidable if one is to grasp the tension produced by this topic within psychoanalysis. His texts, in translation (masked) perhaps even more than in the original (masked one layer less), enact the whole problem of authority, mastery and control just as they discuss it in their content. They lay down the law and yet they play on their seductiveness; the seduction is a major element in the mastery. As part of this game, sexuality is embodied in Lacan's language, particularly in its mysteriousness; and alongside sexuality, inextricably part of it, comes sexual difference as it is played out through the dialectic of mastery and subversion that permeates Lacan's work. But sexual difference is not just implicit here, it is explicitly theorized through the Lacanian conception of the phallus, and in the account this produces of the differing positions with respect to the phallus taken up by males and females.

PHALLOCENTRIC THEORY

The Lacanian phallus has been the focus of much critical scrutiny and controversy. It has, it seems, at least one meaning; or perhaps it just, like the thing itself, signifies to excess. What is the meaning of the phallus? As 'The meaning of the phallus', it is the translation by Jacqueline Rose of a paper by Lacan, a paper which is worth taking extremely seriously as a possible source of material for unpacking the Lacanian conundrum.

In their introduction to 'The meaning of the phallus' (Lacan, 1958),[1] Mitchell and Rose (1982: 74) write that it is 'Lacan's most direct exposition of the status of the phallus in the psychoanalytic account of sexuality'. They continue,

This is perhaps the article which illustrates most clearly the problem of giving an explanation of the phallus which avoids reducing it to the biological difference between the sexes, but which none the less tries to provide a differential account, for men and for women, of its effects.

In 'The meaning of the phallus', Lacan himself locates his work on the theory of the phallus in the historical context of psychoanalytic debate on the nature and origins of femininity. One of the things that attracts him to this debate is its 'passion' (77), specifically the 'passion for doctrine' to be found in the early debates on the phallic phase. Here, 'passion' is being used in the straightforward sense of 'enthusiasm' and is employed in order to contrast the energy of that phase of psychoanalysis – its own 'phallic phase' in which the question of sexual difference is unavoidably posed – with the withering away of this energy and personal investment to be found in later developments. Lacan is 'nostalgic' for this passion particularly in the light of 'the degradation of psychoanalysis consequent on its American transplantation' (ibid.); following the early debates there has been a period in which nothing seems to have been achieved. It is tempting to see this in developmental terms. The early debates were psychoanalysis' phallic phase, struggling with incestuous wishes until castration anxiety became too great and repression intervened, with the questions of the phallus and of sexual difference left unresolved while analysts got on with the latency task of adapting (passionlessly) to the outside world. Lacan pays tribute to the diversity of positions taken up during this phase, and even acknowledges the worth of some of the contributions, although he also declares that the apparent closure produced at the end of the debate was a false one, a covering over of a problem that 'refuses to go away'. All the previous contributions had juvenile elements in them, shown for example in Ernest Jones's work as fantasies of 'natural rights' and of the maternal body. Now, however, Lacan is here to 're-open the question' (78). With the benefit of post-Freudian linguistics, something perhaps learnt during latency, Lacan can promote and face the full (genital) passion of sexuality; it is in the maturity of Lacanian thought that the early debates find their fulfilment. 'The meaning of the phallus' is the moment when passion returns, when it becomes possible to think again about sex and to face the pain as well as the excitement of sexual difference. This might also explain the element of romance which runs through the paper, its unabashed concern not just with desire, but with love. Lacan is never too much at home with humility, and here as elsewhere he takes on the burden of the whole future of psychoanalysis; he sees himself as its next important stage.

'Passion', however, is a word with a complex range of associations in 'The meaning of the phallus'. Shortly after its first use, it recurs to indicate something of the fusional force with which the unconscious operates. Translating Freud's vision of an unconscious full of physical energy into linguistic terms, Lacan manages to convey both a sexual and a religious impulse in one romantic image.

> It is Freud's discovery that gives to the opposition of signifier to signified the full weight which it should imply: namely, that the signifier has an active function in determining the effects in which the signifiable appears as submitting to its mark, becoming through that passion the signified.
>
> (p. 78)

And then, immediately,

> This passion of the signifier then becomes a new dimension of the human condition, in that it is not only man who speaks, but in man and through man that it speaks, that his nature is woven by effects in which we can find the structure of language, whose material he becomes.
>
> (ibid.)

Whose passion, or the passion of what psychic elements, is at stake in these extracts? In the first, the sense is at least ambiguous: it may be that the passion referred to is that of the 'signifiable' as it becomes the signified, or perhaps 'that passion' refers back to the 'active function' of the signifier. The second extract is clearer: the passion belongs to the signifier; but it is now not so much a process as something that 'becomes a dimension', or perhaps a phenomenon – the way in which human subjects are 'woven by effects' in which language inheres. These are the effects of the play of combination and substitution, along 'the two axes of metaphor and metonymy which generate the signified' (79), and these effects are 'determinant in the institution of the subject'. The 'passion of the signifier', then, has become that which forms the human subject; something both creative and coercive in form.

Unpacking all this is no easy task, even ignoring the exigencies of translation of Lacan's dense prose. From a position in which the signifier 'passion' seemed to refer unproblematically to sexual energy, it has become imbued both with the notion of active force and of bowing to something, of a certain transportation of subjectivity in which agency is given up and made subject to something else. This is akin to the religious sense of 'passion', the process whereby one succumbs to the other, to that 'dimension of the human condition' in which one is a tool and not a subject, in which the other speaks in one's place. In Lacan's thought, this is a process that refers to the Oedipus complex read as a formal structure of language. The apparently speaking subject is actually only able to speak by being itself positioned in a pre-existing linguistic order. The subject is thus always speaking in relation to something outside itself, some third term or 'law'. Here Lacan's immersion in phallocentrism is made explicit: this third term/law is the one to be found in the Oedipal triangle, the paternal metaphor or 'name-of-the-father'. It is in relation to this masculine term that the child becomes a speaking subject, it is in relation to it that signification continues to operate, and it is also in relation to this term that the process of analysis occurs.

The following passage from Felman (1987: 127) shows both the strength and weakness of the Lacanian claim here.

> The psychoanalytic narrative is nothing other, for Lacan, than the story of, precisely, the discovery of the third participant in the structure of the dialogue. And this dramatic, narrative and structural discovery implicitly refers to Oedipus.

Felman states that, in analysis, the analyst searches to uncover the way in which the masculinized speaking other is at work in the discourse of the analysand. But the emphatic terms 'nothing other' and 'precisely' are disturbing here. If one were a psychoanalyst, one could read Felman's emphasis as indicating uncertainty: why does she need so to italicize, so firmly to rule out alternatives? Why cannot the psychoanalytic narrative be 'both . . . and', rather than 'nothing other' than something absolutely precise, the discovery of the Oedipal third term? Writing from the position of the woman disciple of Lacan, Felman expresses with great emphasis the narrowest possible masculine rendering of the analytic experience. Analysis is about finding one's place in the law. Yet something else seems to speak in her sentences, presumably unconsciously intended, drawing attention to this narrowness. As it speaks, her discourse adopts the defence of reaction–formation, stating the narrow position more firmly, but in so doing it draws attention to its own ambivalence. The analyst's task is to find the law for the patient, but it is also the analyst's task to question that law and all that it fixes in place.

'Passion', then, has become the activity of the signifier and the submission of the signified, the force of the speaker and the subjugation of the spoken. It is a word containing tremendous tension: it is a full word; in Lacanian jargon, one is tempted to say it is a word that enacts '*jouissance*'. But despite the potential feminine energy that this suggests, and despite the passionate debate from which this all stems being that concerning feminine sexuality, the 'dimension' this passion refers to is a masculinized one, a phallocentric fascination with the Symbolic order. As will be described below, there is rather a strong tendency for this particular trajectory to be played out in 'The meaning of the phallus': that the feminine is seen as full of subversive energy and excitement, but as having no agency and nothing to say. The feminine is there, but mainly as a query, an indication that all is not quite right with the world. It slumbers, speaking only as something which is absent. Grosz (1990: 146) complains, 'If Lacan begs women to tell him in what their pleasure consists, he is not prepared to hear what they have to say'. Moore (1988: 185) perhaps grasps more clearly the colonization going on here, the sense of Lacan as trickster and fraud.

> In deciphering the language of the 'other' and then claiming it for themselves, these theoretical drag queens don the trappings of femininity for a night on the town without so much as a glance back at the poor woman whose clothes they have stolen.

The energy of femininity, fantasized as passionate and full, becomes another element in the Lacanian masquerade, as the full weight of phallic mastery is brought into play.

It is worth considering the nature of this mastery a little further. Lacan emphasizes the way paternity operates linguistically, through the 'name-of-the-father' and the prohibition its enunciation brings in its wake. In this, he is working in the biblical tradition in which the name of God is generally left unspoken because of its terrible power. In the traditional Judaic ritual, it was only on the highest of holy days and after an enormous effort of study and purification that the High Priest was allowed into the holiest part of the temple to speak this name and to use it both to expunge the people of sin and to commit them further to the law. Speaking the symbol of the highest power calls into being that power, with potentially savage effects should anything go wrong. In this tradition, the effect of speech is so potent that it dominates the material world: pronouncing the name is to enter into the mystery.

Freud, in his own way, writes from within this tradition, particularly in relation to gender. In 'Moses and monotheism' (1939), which is ostensibly an attempt to historicize the biblical figure of Moses, Freud offers an ironic and misogynistically reductionist rendering of the relationship between mastery and the symbolic, devoid of its sacred elements but none the less committed to the cultural superiority of language over the body. Discussing the supposed historical transition from matriarchy to patriarchy, he comments,

> But this turning from the mother to the father points in addition to a victory of intellectuality over sensuality – that is, an advance in civilization, since maternity is proved by the evidence of the senses while paternity is a hypothesis, based on an inference and a premise. Taking sides in this way with a thought process in preference to a sense perception has proved to be a momentous step.
>
> (Freud 1939: 361)

Explicit in this quotation is an identification of the masculine (the father) with the symbolic ('intellectuality') and the feminine with the body ('sensuality'). The former is victorious over the latter: the 'thought process' subjugates the sense. Similarly, it is by the paternal name that children are known; it is the man's name that counts. Of course, the irony here is that proof of paternity does not just require 'an inference and a premise'; it relies on the *word* of the woman – something which, in Lacanian thought, is bound to be unreliable – and, in disputed cases nowadays, on a very material genetic test.

For Lacan, as one might expect, the workings of the word are more obscure yet also more subtly controlling. It is a matter of being spoken by something absolute and also mysterious – something which, if it were not for Lacan's relentless opposition to all imaginary wholes, might again be termed religious.

> It speaks in the Other, I say, designating by this Other the very place called upon by a recourse to speech in any relation where it intervenes. If it speaks in the Other, whether or not the subject hears it with his own ears, it is because it is there that the subject, according to a logic prior to any awakening of the signified, finds his signifying place.
>
> (p. 79)

The idea that 'it' speaking is a reference to the unconscious and, through this, to something experienced as alien to the subject yet determinant of the subject's being, has become a familiar one in Lacan's work. The quotation continues: 'The discovery of what he articulates in that place, that is, in the unconscious, enables us to grasp the price of the division (*Spaltung*) through which he is thus constituted' (ibid.).

The 'Other' and the 'unconscious' are being run together here, partially differentiated from one another but both employed to communicate the idea of something outside and yet within the subject, something causal and yet somehow not owned. 'It', 'the Other', 'the unconscious': the impact of this progression is one of impersonal alienation, something abstract and impoverished, yet troubling too. Lacan chooses what are in some respects the emptiest possible terms to communicate the force of the 'division' introduced into subjectivity by language. As we speak, so we are spoken. Put crudely, language seems to speakers to be something which is used to express thoughts, yet its intractability and the *failures* of communication which so characterize speech and writing reveal that language has a life and project of its own, that it operates as a division within and between people more than as a link. In developmental terms, this division occurs at various points, but most firmly at the time of the Oedipal negation of incestuous wishes. This moment marks the entry into the subject of a repressive paternal order, making the subject 'subject to' a set of prohibitions summarizable as 'No, you may not go there'.

Given the Lacanian emphasis on the masculinity of language, its absorption in the paternal symbolic, what appears out of the mist here is an image of a domineering patriarchal structure which is both impersonal and at the heart of subjecthood. The subject is 'constituted' by division, and this division is accessed through exploration of 'what he articulates' in the unconscious, which in turn reflects a nature 'woven by effects in which we can find the structure of language' (78).

Mastery, then, is the province of the word. And this is a curiously ambiguous phenomenon. Mastery is both deathly and creative: the former because it is constituted as a prohibition – the paternal 'No' – that limits what is allowable to the subject; and the latter because it sets in motion an order of things – the symbolic order – without which there would be no communication (or miscommunication), no culture and no social organization. The pursuit of mastery may be a journey in pursuit of an (imaginary) mirage; but there is a lot of fun to be had on the way, as Lacan himself enacts. This is the master's word in action: as Lacan speaks, so the dead hand of orthodoxy reaches out to stifle dissent; but he also provides some tools to see through the fraud as well.

PHALLIC FUNCTIONS; OR, HOW MEN AND WOMEN FIND OUT WHO THEY ARE

Mastery, paternity, prohibition, 'It' speaking: Lacan has set the scene for a formal reconsideration of the phallic phase. The next sentence in 'The meaning of the phallus' following the discussion of language and the other is 'The phallus is elucidated in its function here' (79). All this speaking about otherness, then, leads to the meaning of the phallus, or at least to its function, and Lacan seems to be promising to deal fully and finally with the phallus itself, signifier of signifiers, something ultimate and profound. Unfortunately, however, but perhaps predictably, uncovering the phallus turns out to be not such an easy process.

Lacan makes a number of statements in 'The meaning of the phallus' which have the structure 'the phallus is . . .', but at first glance none of them seem to lead anywhere further than the notion that the phallus is 'a signifier', which it could hardly fail to be. Here is a selection:

> The phallus is not a fantasy, if what is understood by that is an imaginary effect. Nor is it as such an object (part, internal, good, bad, etc. . . .) insofar as this term tends to accentuate the reality involved in a relationship. It is even less the organ, penis or clitoris, which it symbolizes. (p. 79)

> the phallus is a signifier, a signifier whose function in the intrasubjective economy of analysis might lift the veil from that which it served in the mysteries. For it is to this signifier that it is given to designate as a whole the effect of there being a signified, inasmuch as it conditions any such effect by its presence as signifier. (pp. 79–80)

> The phallus is the privileged signifier of that mark where the share of the logos is wedded to the advent of desire. (p. 82)

> The phallus is the signifier of this *Aufhebung* itself which it inaugurates (initiates) by its own disappearance. (p. 82)

Considering these extracts a little more fully, however, they do begin to offer a way forward. The Lacanian phallus is neither a physical organ nor a specific fantasy, but it is a signifier with a particular function: it 'designates as a whole the effect of there being a signified'; moreover, it has a 'privileged' relationship with the 'wedding' of 'the logos' and 'the advent of desire'. It is thus generative and connecting, possessed, as one might imagine, of an aura of procreation and sexual linkage. On the other hand, it also specifically signifies an '*Aufhebung*', a cancellation – it is, therefore, not to be thought of as something positive and full of potency, but as a kind of negativity which disappears if it is held up to the light. It is in this negativity that may be found the one real definition of the phallus offered by 'The meaning of the phallus', a definition phrased in terms of the necessary conditions for the phallus to work: '[The] phallus can only play its role as veiled, that is, as in itself the sign of the latency with which everything is struck as soon as it is raised to the function of signifier' (82). The positioning of this sentence is as a response to a series of possible answers (with the structure, 'One might say . . .') to the question of why it is the phallus that should be the 'privileged signifier'. These answers are, for instance, connected with the 'turgidity' of the phallus or (relatedly) to its appearance as something which 'stands out as most easily seized upon in the real of sexual copulation' – a formulation which seems rather concrete and exact, expressing both the phallus's power and its vulnerability. Lacan, however, says that these explanations are 'veils', and what they veil is the way the phallus itself only operates as veiled; perhaps this makes the explanations themselves too phallic, referring back to the literal-mindedness of the phallic stage of development. Prior to Lacan, no one has understood that the phallus cannot be taken literally, as something to be grabbed and pulled upon. It only works if it is not seen, its message being that there is no centre to power, just the emanation of some remarkable effects. The phallus is a function, something that happens and makes things happen; it is often related to as a fantasy, like the fantasy of mastery, but no one can have it because it is not a thing to be had.

There is a considerable amount of romance and mystery in this: something operates in the world which is immensely powerful, has effects felt everywhere, and yet it can never be uncovered or known. Patriarchal emblems other than the phallus itself, particularly religious emblems, have shared these characteristics: a mystery at the heart of the human soul, both core to human life and yet always finally unknowable. Lacan continually asserts the phallus's status as signifier, as something without specific content yet with powerful effects that are sufficient to generate meanings. Amongst commentators on Lacan, there has been some attempt to understand this in ways which make it possible to free the phallus from its patriarchal context. For example, in Bowie's (1991: 128) gloss, 'The phallus is the promise of meaning organised by an organ and, equally, it is the loss or cancellation of meaning perpetually being foretold'. Moreover,

> the phallus is entitled to its extraordinary structuring and dialecticising role only if it is thought of as un-male, in a terrain that both sexes inhabit and a pivotal point for their countless mutual determinations.
>
> (Bowie 1991: 145)

Ragland-Sullivan (1991: 61) also claims a non-gendered position for the phallus by asserting that the penis is only one symbol of it. 'Other symbols of the (imaginary) phallus', she writes, 'are the breast, the voice, the gaze, fragments and slits of the body, scents, and so on . . .' – a series of feminine associations to cover over (veil?) the primary masculine one. To say that the phallus is the signifier generating the effects of meaning is therefore not necessarily a gendered statement. On the other hand, if the phallus is disconnected from its referent, it becomes the kind of fetishized ideal object which Lacanian theory is supposedly against. Gallop (1988: 128) comments, 'One of the weaknesses of the Lacanian orthodoxy is to render *phallus* transcendental, not dependent on the penis and its contingencies'. There seems to be no getting away from it: whatever veils are used, the phallus is surely a male symbol, built on the anatomical model of the penis and operating as a powerful – the primary – signifier in the lexicon of the unconscious. Despite the protestations, the injunctions not to confuse the phallus with the penis, this discourse has its roots and its emblems in masculinity. What we have here is a sexed distribution of signs, in which subjectivity is produced around a sexual divide.

The phallus cannot be known directly, it speaks its name only through its effects. And the primary function of these effects is to produce human subjects who are sexed in their essence – who are generated along a sexual divide. So the phallus is an abstract signifier and is decidedly not the penis, yet it effects a split resulting in masculinity and femininity as attributes and subjective states, each with a different relationship to the phallus itself. Put simply, masculinity and femininity are organized differently in relation to the phallus, something which comes as no surprise.

Lacan seems contradictory here. Clinical facts, he says, 'go to show that the relation of the subject to the phallus is set up regardless of the anatomical differ- ence between the sexes' (76). In particular, Lacan refers to Freud's notion that in the phallic phase of development the clitoris is 'raised to the function of the phallus' for the girl, apparently meaning that there is no difference in gendered experience until the Oedipus complex is dissolved. But he also notes that 'simply by keeping to the function of the phallus, we can pinpoint the structures which will govern the relations between the sexes' (83). The 'elucidation' of the phallus' function thus needs to be explored further, if sexual difference is to be clearly located.

Lacan identifies the differing relationship of men and women to the phallus in a relatively simple dichotomy.

> Let us say that these relations will revolve around a being and a having which, because they refer to a signifier, the phallus, have the contradictory effect of on the one hand lending reality to the subject in that signifier, and on the other making unreal that to be signified.
>
> (Lacan 1958: 83–4)

There is a good deal packed into this apparently nonchalant 'Let us say', particularly with reference to the fertility of Lacan's use of the concept of castration and the unraveling of his veiled notion of masquerade. But for the moment let us focus on the idea of being versus having, and on the function of the phallus as enabling us to 'pinpoint the structures which will govern the relations between the sexes'. On the face of it, the phallus is being referred to here as something the male has and the female has not, something which belongs to the man and is enacted and/or wished for by the woman. But it is obvious that the situation is not so simple, if only because of the impact of the imaginary dimension – let alone the empirical question of what women might actually want (as in Cixous's (1976) comment, 'I don't want a penis . . .'). The complication for men is that we might think we own something but can never be sure, because so much of that thing is a fantasy concerning potency – we never know if it is, or we are, good enough. This uncertainty and sense of distance from the ideal can then lead us into an obsessive and impossible search for the truly desirable, potent phallus to replace the one we have. In this connection, here is the rather troubled, self-conscious comment of a man.

> Belonging is a male problem in our existing system of man and woman, 'masculinity' and 'femininity'; it is the obsession of my identity as a man, getting things straight, knowing where I am and what I have and where she is and what she hasn't.
>
> (Heath 1987: 16)

'Having' the phallus attached to oneself is no guarantee of stability of identity; quite the contrary, it forces the man into an obsession with 'getting things straight' and a terror of loss which must seem comic to the penis-free woman. So much is made of it that the phallus becomes a burden to the man; living up to it becomes the necessary condition of masculinity, which is therefore always in danger of being betrayed and undermined. What is it to 'have an identity as a man'? It is, according to this view, to have everything straight and in its (intended) place.

The difficulty of sustaining a masculine identity produces and is constructed by, a number of effects. Much of the excess of masculine sexuality seems to derive from the desperate struggle to retain a conviction of phallic mastery – of potency – when what is being experienced is the impossibility of measuring up to the fantasy of the full phallus. 'The clenched fist, the bulging muscles, the hardened jaws, the proliferation of phallic symbols – they are all straining after what can hardly ever be achieved, the embodiment of the phallic mystique' (Dyer 1982: 72; quoted in Segal 1990: 89). Even in softer circles, amongst men who struggle to find themselves a place in feminism, there is a tendency to accept (or 'admire', in Heath's (1987) terminology) the force and otherness of the feminist project, only to take it over and make it into another arena for masculine competitiveness. Quoting and criticizing a statement by Terry Eagleton about the insufficiency of feminist theory, Heath (1987: 12) writes, 'None of this is written to be cleverer than or superior to Terry Eagleton . . ., even if in the reflection of writing I cannot – do not know how to – avoid the male image, the image of bettering, of asserting superiority'. In the same collection, Smith (1987: 39) writes,

> men can, – perhaps, or at least – help the effort to forestall the academic institutionalization of feminism. They may be able to take an interrogative, but sympathetic role. Indeed, from the point of their impossible – provocative, offensive, troublesome – position in or near feminism, they might be able to

help keep in view the referent which most of our current theory is all too eager to defer.

It is not difficult to see the colonizing impulse at work here again, as men find their position of mastery threatened and undermined, particularly by a system (or plurality of systems) of thought that excludes men, or can at least make do without them. The all-female world is a terrible threat, apparently offering no place within it for the third party, the man (no 'name of the father' here, it seems). What better strategy than to offer to take the position of difference, to protect feminism from the dangers of 'institutionalization' – empty narcissism – to show how much a man is needed, what umbrella he can hold up in the rain? Are these masters of the feminine any different from the flexors of muscles, all running to find a way to shore up the phallus as it becomes increasingly clear that, in itself, there is nothing predetermined and natural about it at all? (An infinite regress can creep in here too, as I write this critique of masculine strategies of power into my own masculine work on gender. Men 'find *their* position of mastery threatened' is what appears a few sentences above. But we have to go on somehow, creating hostages to fortune all the time.)

Lacan is a master of ambiguity here. On the one hand, the phallus is the primary signifier, producing difference and forcing men and women apart. The symbolic order only comes into operation when the father speaks; woman is excluded from the system, though she (in imaginary guise) has a crucial role in defining its boundaries – without the woman everything would be the same, so no specific masculinity could exist. Fascinated by castration, Lacan pretends that the phallus is not a masculine symbol; but this may be just another phallic move, veiling the particular nature of the phallus as masculine. Nevertheless, this nature is revealed in the effects of the phallus, which are to make the symbols of the male the determinants of the symbolic order as a whole. So the phallus does actually represent male mastery, despite Lacan's apparent denials. Yet the phallus is also something lost and/or losable – it reminds the boy of the threat that what he most prizes will be taken away; hence, it is a constant source of anxiety about power.

In addition to this, there is something still more fragile in the fantasy of masculine autonomy and control.

> Lacan points to the exceptional anxiety involved in taking on a masculine identification. Indeed, the figure of the male *qua* male might be called the cultural lie which maintains that sexual identity can be personified by making difference itself a position.
>
> (Ragland-Sullivan 1991: 51)

Masculinity has the appearance of being defined by something positive – that which the male has and the female lacks. However, emphasizing this, as Freud did and as Lacan appears to do, is a masculine strategy employed to deny the implications of the converse, that masculinity is defined negatively, as that which is not feminine. There are two senses in which this is the case. The concrete psychological one is the way in which the Oedipus complex operates as a division between child and mother: the boy only becomes a boy through renunciation of the feminine, not just as object of desire but also as subject of identification, and incorporation into the very general, very 'other' paternal law. More abstractly, Lacan consistently employs a structural linguistic heuristic for psychoanalysis that defines presence only in relation to difference – only in relation to that which is not also there. Laplanche and Leclaire (1966: 154) explain, 'there is no signifier that does not refer to the absence of others and that is not defined by its place in the system'. Lacan tries to exempt the phallus from this stricture, but not whole-heartedly: the phallus can only be seen as whole and positive in content when it is in the register of the imaginary; that is, this wholeness is a fantasy. So the symbolic order, the primacy of the phallic signifier and the content of masculinity, are given as a series of oppositions, as established only by comparison with what they are not. And amongst these assertions and counter-assertions about the nature of masculinity, there is even some doubt about whether the phallus is symbolized by the penis or whether something more feminine can take its place, as in the quotation from Ragland-Sullivan given earlier or as in Grosz's (1990: 119) comment that the penis 'does not have the sole right of alignment with the phallus' but can be substituted for by objects such as 'the whole of a woman's body'. Are men necessary? Living in doubt is never an easy situation.

The ambiguity of the phallus is something integral to its function: it operates both to divide the sexes and to encourage a fantasy of oneness. Grosz puts her finger on it, metaphorically at least, in the following quotation which emphasizes the way the phallus can only function in an economy of intersubjectivity, in which the 'owner' of the phallus is dependent on the recognition and desire of the other who apparently does not have it. The master depends on the slave, making the slave the master.

> As the logical or grammatical copula, [the phallus] serves to connect two terms together while disappearing or evacuating itself of any identity of its own. It functions to unite (and disappear) or to separate and divide. This fundamental ambiguity or duplicity in the term will provide a vulnerable, contradictory point within male relations and sexual domination. As signifier, the phallus is not an object to be acquired or an identity to be achieved. It is only through the desire of the other that one's own position – as either being or having the phallus – is possible.
>
> (Grosz 1990: 125)

As ever, Lacan is more elusive than this: the idea of the phallus as 'copula' is included in his 'One might say' list of those reasons why the phallus is primary signifier, which he dispatches by saying that they are 'veils'. Lacan presents his phallus, and himself, as self-sufficient. Nevertheless, to develop past the phallic phase one needs to form relationships; this means that some kind of inter-subjectivity must exist, and that 'I' and 'thou' have to be clearly differentiated and seen in relation to each other. Phallic mastery itself needs recognition and desire from the other; take that away and both phallus and man, perhaps even Lacan, dissolve into dust.

The idea of the woman as the other in the phallic economy of the symbolic order has constantly crept into these notes. It is a masculine 'other' that initiates the symbolic: the 'name of the father' places a barrier between the boy and his mother, between the self and the object of desire. But it seems to be the fantasy of the woman as something outside the symbolic which is required to keep the symbolic order in place, to set its boundaries, its inclusions and exclusions. Something ambiguous operates here too, something to do with desire and with femininity – something that again calls into question the masculine world. Ragland-Sullivan (1991: 62) writes, 'The definition of the masculine (not man *per se*) is that which believes itself to be whole. But beware the paradox: whole in relation to what *he is not* – woman. That is, man is a failed woman.' In this reading, the organization of femininity is different from that of masculinity: the latter is premised on difference, on being superior to, other than, the one-who-is-lacking; femininity, on the other hand, is built around sameness: the woman has 'identified with similarity as an identity position' (ibid.).

The possibility of such an asymmetrical situation needs to be questioned. If one side is defined by difference, can the other be absorbed in an economy of the same? This argument is akin to that of object relations theory, in which the pre-Oedipal position of the girl is taken to be one of identity with the mother, a position that produces her gender characteristics with all their struggles concerning autonomy and potency. The boy, by contrast, is constructed out of difference, out of the mother's own definition of him as 'not-I'. It is this that produces the male's unrelieved search for something which is 'same', his precarious gender identity based on differentiation from others, and his characteristic incapacity and terror when faced with demands for intimacy and mutually dependent relationships. This account has some important insights to offer when considering the trajectories of masculine and feminine development, particularly in relation to mothering and to men's fear of women. But it also reads like the imaginary picture which Lacan has identified as a fantasy of the other: that somewhere there is something whole, which needs no other, which knows itself as itself and is complete. Ragland-Sullivan writes that the woman 'knows no one is whole because she has not identified with difference as an imaginary universal, an identity fiction of autonomy' (ibid.); but in this knowledge of non-wholeness she becomes complete, she has seen and absorbed the truth. The woman again becomes idealized as phallus.

There is a great deal in 'The meaning of the phallus' which is concerned with the tensions of 'having' and 'being' the phallus, mixed in with desire and with sexual difference. Lacan devotes some space to his famous distinction between need, demand and desire – between what is required by the human subject, what becomes translated into communicable symbols, and what is left over, as an unfillable ache or gap between the hope and its realization. As needs are put into signifying form – as they become or 'are subject to' demand – so they become alienated; that is, they become converted into a message in which what is being demanded is not some specific satisfaction, but complete affirmation or recognition. 'Demand,' states Lacan (80), 'in itself bears on something other than the satisfactions which it calls for. It is a demand for a presence or an absence.' The fantasy is that the other can completely give itself up to the subject; but the actual impossibility of this means that demand is left unfulfilled, reflecting back on the subject as lack of recognition, as something still to be desired.

> Hence it is that demand cancels out the particularity of anything which might be granted by transmuting it into a proof of love, and the very satisfactions of need which it obtains are degraded as being no more than a crushing of the demand for love.
>
> (pp. 80–1)

It is in this gap between need and demand, between what can be fulfilled and what is impossible, that desire arises. In a famous if unusually reductionist (thus probably veiled) proposition, Lacan takes this as an opportunity to dictate the nature of desire:

> Thus desire is neither the appetite for satisfaction, nor the demand for love, but the difference resulting from the subtraction of the first from the second, the very phenomenon of their splitting.
>
> (p. 81)

As complete love is impossible, as each subject is split by the operations of language and the unconscious, so every human subject finds her or himself looking for proofs of love, and standing in as the cause of the other's desire. Here is the 'formula' Lacan places at the heart of sexual life: 'that for each partner in the relation, the subject and the Other, it is not enough to be the subjects of need, nor objects of love, but they must stand as the cause of desire' (ibid.).

'They must stand as the cause of desire.' Each subject strives to find the worm of desire in the other and to become it – to arouse in the other recognition of the necessity of the subject's existence. The mother's desire is for the phallus, so the child strives to become the phallus. Indeed, it is the discovery that the *mother* does not have the phallus that is taken by Lacan as decisive for the castration complex, for it both offers a way for the child to be the cause of the mother's desire, and it signifies the power of the threat of castration (or for the girl, the nostalgia for what once was). For every subject, male and female, desire is a constant reminder of incompleteness: it is always the desire of the other which has to be recognized 'meaning, the Other as itself a subject divided by the signifying *Spaltung*' (83), that is, as something split.

Becoming the cause of the other's desire creates a specific place for the woman in – or rather, outside – the masculine sexual–symbolic order. Being phallic in origin, this order is defined around the having versus not-having economy of the male, an economy different from that fantasized as characteristic of the female. Heath (1987: 21) takes up the Lacanian slogan 'there is no sexual relation' to provide the following eloquent explanation of the function of the exclusion of the woman.

> Relation, the idea of relation, depends on an imaginary other who will complement me as one, make up for the fact of division, stop the loss of identity. Women have been powerfully represented and held as 'woman' to be this other and then, the pressure of the reality of women, feared and hated and attacked as

the imaginary other of 'woman' fails and his identity is questioned – at which point she finds herself carried over into the realm of the Other, projected as an enigmatic radical alienness, the back of beyond, and then made up all over again, with talk of her mystery, her ineffable *jouissance*, her closeness to the position of God, and so on.

Heath's account here is both descriptive and explanatory, presenting Lacan's idea and employing it to make sense of the derogation of femininity, the hatred of womanhood and of specific women, which is characteristic of much male fantasy and which can also at times be seen at work in Lacan's own misogynistic musings. The split in masculinity is enforced by the prohibition encapsulated in the 'name of the father'; this creates a sensation of otherness – of the other – which exists as a fantasized place of 'true speech', of the (masculine) law, but also of (feminine) wholeness and completion. Together with narcissistic fantasies of return, this process feeds the masculine fantasy that somewhere there is a fulfilment which it is possible to achieve; given that his existence as male is structured around difference, then it is the other in the form of the not-male that comes to serve as the ideal of this Other. In this sense, the woman becomes the phallus for the man – that which holds all the answers, which stands outside the system of the symbolic, which when encountered will make him complete.

THE WOMAN FOR THE MAN

The subject is split, claims Lacan, irreparably so; the fantasy of wholeness, for instance of complete integration of the different elements of the personality, is precisely a fantasy, an element in the Imaginary order which is undermined by the symbolic. Whatever claims concerning the possibility of integration might be asserted by other schools of psychoanalysis, Lacan knows them to be false; the condition of human subjecthood is to be subject to the law which says, there is no One (no Other of the Other). But this does not prevent us searching for it: in religion, in psychoanalysis, in grand theory; in the relationship to God, in the words of the analyst, in fetishism of the cultural guru, even in Lacan. For men, one systematic element in this is the construction of a representation of the Other as woman, an idealized image drawing upon nostalgia for early infancy, but also precisely an idealization, an image made whole and good by virtue of splitting off and repressing its negative characteristics. Such idealizations are easily punctured: Lacan (1972–3: 144) states, 'There is no such thing as *The* Woman, where the definite article stands for the universal. There is no such thing as *The* Woman since of her essence . . . she is not all'. So when the woman does not deliver the goods, when the reality of women is found to be different from the fantasy of 'The Woman', this negativity floods back in. The terror of femininity returns, alongside the uncertainty produced by the masculine need for the feminine and by men's consciousness of the precariousness of gender identity in the face of feminine recalcitrance – women's unwillingness to be forced into a position in which they enact men's fantasies. At its extreme, this makes for violence, for a howl of rage from the man with no Other, with nothing to fill the vacancy that inhabits his desire.

The woman, as an image and a wish, is excluded from the masculine order but operates as its anchor, both as ideal and as a concentrated point of darkness. The rapid fluctuation from one to the other of these elements is a cliché of critical analysis: from madonna to whore, often with no boundary in between. Masculinity needs femininity, needs the feminine ideal, but dreads it and hates the impossibility of its attainment. Lacan (84) comments that even when the man 'manages to satisfy his demand for love in his relationship to the woman', he will feel dissatisfaction and look elsewhere: 'his own desire for the phallus will throw up its signifier in the form of a persistent divergence towards "another woman" who can signify this phallus under various guises, whether as virgin or as prostitute'. There is no end to it, no romance or happy ever after, only the illusion and trickery of imaginary love.

Not only is this point of view pessimistic, but it is unequivocally male: the only articulation of the position of the woman is in relation to the order and experience of masculinity. Indeed, it has been commented upon by several authors that Lacan re-enacts the dynamic his theory describes. He denigrates women ceaselessly, for instance as 'not knowing what they are saying' (1972–3: 144), or for their supposed silence on feminine sexuality; he plays seductively to them as if their desire would and should be only for him. But he also fantasizes something specific in femininity which leaves the masculine behind, something ineffable and whole, a complete experience of pleasure which always remains untranslated as '*jouissance*' – at its extreme, a self-sufficiency, a '*jouissance* wrapped in its own contiguity' (Lacan 1964: 97). Grosz (1990), in her 'feminist introduction' to Lacan notes how he 'seems to want to retain some of the allure and the mystery of the Eternal Feminine' (140) but also finds a way of doing this that itself denies women anything to call their own.

> Woman experiences a *jouissance beyond the phallus*. But if this enigmatic *jouissance* is attributed to women as the mark of her resistance to the Other, at the same time this *jouissance* is, by that fact, strictly outside of articulation and is thus *unknowable*. Lacan accords women the possibility of refusing a pleasure and desire that is not theirs, but not of claiming one that *is* theirs.
>
> (1990: 139)

Moreover, 'If Lacan begs women to tell him in what their pleasure consists, he is not prepared to hear what they have to say' (146). If one is to take seriously something articulated by Gallop (1988: 125), one of the things women might have to say is that 'it remains an open question whether there truly exists any adult sexuality, whether there is any masculinity that is beyond the phallic phase, that does not need to equate femininity with castration'. This is an accusation levelled at all men, including the one who claims to go beyond the phallic phase, Lacan; he too seems to have little place for women other than as fantasy ideal or whore.

What happens to the feminine in all this? 'The meaning of the phallus' focuses on castration; the feminine is presented as the other side of this, as that which is already castrated and therefore cannot be the subject of desire – if desire is defined in the masculine register, as Lacan appears to prefer. The woman seeks what she has not, and the way in which she seeks it is given to her by the formula mentioned earlier, that 'for each partner in the relation, the subject and the Other, it is not enough to be the subjects of need, nor objects of love, but they must stand as the cause of desire' (81). With desire organized around the phallus, and with masculinity defined in terms of a continuing struggle to 'have' the phallus – to avoid castration – 'standing as the cause of desire' for the woman means representing the phallus to the man. At its simplest, this is the process of becoming the romantic 'other', the one who will complete the man through the fact of her difference, her fantasized complementarity. In the explicit discussion of the phallus to be found in 'The meaning of the phallus', however, Lacan stresses that the woman seeks to 'be' the phallus by taking on the appearance of wholeness, of the final object of desire. As such, the woman strives to be something which in fact only *seems* to be real, and the dynamic of sexual difference becomes entwined with 'masquerade' and a descent into comedy.

> This follows from the intervention of an 'appearing' which gets substituted for the 'having' so as to protect it on one side and to mask its lack on the other, with the effect that the ideal or typical manifestations of behaviour in both sexes, up to and including the act of sexual copulation, are entirely propelled into comedy.
>
> (p. 84)

At one level, the woman acts in masquerade in the straightforward and well-documented sense that 'femininity' is a representation constructed primarily through masculine discourse, as the object of male fantasy to which individual women are asked to succumb: 'It is for what she is not that she expects to be desired as well as loved' (ibid.). Resisting this alienated construction of femininity has been a struggle long engaged in by feminists as they attempt to create a representation or set of representations of womanhood other than that given by patriarchy, including evolving modes of display that are self-consciously chosen and are not reducible to masquerade.

Lacanian ambiguity, however, puts more into this. The woman acts in masquerade in the deeper sense that, although her existence is constructed as 'other' to the phallic order of the symbolic, she must nevertheless speak from a position within that order if she is to have a voice in language and culture at all. Hence, 'when she speaks as an "I" it is never clear that she speaks (of or as) herself. She speaks in a mode of masquerade, an imitation of the masculine phallic subject' (Grosz 1990: 72). Moreover, 'The woman can be the phallus only through semblance, masquerade, or appearance, but this ensures she is also *not* the phallus. Paradoxically, to be affirmed as the phallus is to be annihilated as woman' (132). The woman's place is given in a male order; taking up the position alienates her from any possibility of being subject of her own desire, yet it is also the only way in which she can exist.

Something else happens here too, on the other side of Lacan's depreciation of women. Once again his text re-enacts the dynamic: the woman has no voice, does not exist; yet she embodies the subversion of the order that so marginalizes her. Adopting a very conventional and undeconstructed approach to gender, Lacan argues that, whereas libido is masculine, all display is feminine, even 'virile display'. The woman is presented as surface, as play, as a misleading object of desire. The female body is taken as that which can fulfil desire, but it is all masquerade; even if the man feels for a while satisfied, 'his own desire for the phallus will throw up its signifier in the form of a persistent divergence towards "another woman"' (84) – there is no end to this seeking. There are at least two ways of looking at this. The first asserts that the woman's appearance is a sham; she is fraudulent. On the other hand, this sham status actually expresses a truth: that there is no 'one', no complete other which can offer the fulfilment of desire. Femininity thus embodies the Lacanian propositions that desire is constituted precisely by lack and gap, and that the failure to accept this as the condition of human subjectivity is to live in illusion. In this sense, the woman stands as some kind of truth rooted in subversion of the masculine fantasy that complete stability and ownership of the other is possible.

Ragland-Sullivan (1991: 75–6) offers the following thought on the subversion of masculinity by masquerade.

Because the 'gift' of lack robs us of certainty and takes a bite out of ego and body – the masculine and feminine delineating different positions taken in regard to lack – the feminine masquerade automatically poses a question, while masculine identification with law, logos or authority tries to stop the question. Yet, paradoxically, *his* effort at mastery shows a lack – a lie as the basis of the symbolic – while *her* lack of position is unbearable in the real.

In this reading, masculinity closes things up, tries to deny castration, to hang on to the possession of the penis as a symbolic equivalent to possession of the phallus. It is the masculine that is engaged in masquerade here – a pretence that domination arises naturally from anatomy, that there is a biological inscription of patriarchy making resistance useless. The masculine seeks confirmation, seeks to shore up boundaries; as has been shown many times (e.g. Theweleit 1977), there is a close connection between this attribute of masculinity and authoritarian, fascist and racist modes of political action and organization. Femininity, through its play of surfaces, its multifariousness and its elusiveness, can be seen as the enemy of such confirmation; it always speaks of difference, of the impossibility of being pinned down.

This picture of masculinity suggests that it exists only by keeping the other at bay, by avoiding castration; but it also exists only in relation to the Other as desired object, as that which might confirm the male by acknowledging his ownership of the phallus. Femininity, by virtue of its otherness in the symbolic order, its position as 'already castrated', is both the desired other and a reminder of the possibility of dissolution of gender itself. In masquerade, the woman can come to represent the phallus with her whole body; but she also reveals that this process is only one of mask and display. Yet, this is also the phallic point: once again, it is worth recalling that Lacan says that 'the phallus can only play its role as veiled' (82); veils and the phallus are inextricably linked. In her masquerade, the woman not only acts as other to the symbolic order, thus defining its boundaries; she also shows that 'the phallus' is itself a process of search and play, of enigma and thus of desire; and notwithstanding its appropriation by masculine discourse, it 'belongs' to no one at all.

In the end, this seems to have brought us back to a traditional image of femininity as that which subverts the established order, as the power of a 'nature' which is always slippery and unreliable. To some extent, this simply repeats the masculine fantasy of female otherness, as something to be repudiated because of the way it upsets order and rationality ('science'), but also as something secretly longed for because of its passion and excitement ('nature'). The Lacanian algebra of phallus and Symbolic reworks this traditional image, incorporating it into a discourse on language and the unconscious that reveals the existence of something both precious and impossible – the fantasy positions of masculine and feminine constantly disrupted by desire. Femininity, most explicitly through the concepts of masquerade and *jouissance*, undermines the claims of masculinity to mastery: there is no complete master, as the phallus is not something one can ever wholly own. But this does not necessarily put an end to illusion, or to the pursuit of domination.

Moreover, there is an element here which has not yet been properly explored. Towards the end of 'The meaning of the phallus', Lacan makes a reference to the mother.

> Clinical practice demonstrates that the test of the desire of the Other is not decisive in the sense that the subject learns from it whether or not he has a real phallus, but inasmuch as he learns that the mother does not. This is the moment of experience without which no symptomatic or structural consequence (that is, phobia or *penisneid*) referring to the castration complex can take effect.
>
> (p. 83)

At its simplest, this is a conventional Freudian statement that the male subject's awareness of the existence of female genital 'insufficiency' is necessary for castration anxiety to have its effect and therefore for the Oedipus complex to be resolved, so setting into motion the patterns of identification and repression which Lacan characterizes as the symbolic order. But the explicit reference here to the *mother's* lack of phallus is a reminder of the extent to which masculinity – the status of supposedly not being castrated – is built upon the shaky foundations of distance from the mother, of being other than the mother of whom one once was part. The Oedipus complex is the structure within which the father's word is heard, denying access to the mother's body as a source of sexual gratification; but something more powerful even than that prohibition is also at work. Looking at the female 'lack', the male perceives an apparent failure to specify a limit and location for sexuality, and consequently feels a terror of dissolution, of falling back and in, of losing his precariously attained identity. It is not just *domination* that is placed in jeopardy here, but masculine *existence*. This underpins at least some of the male's idealization and terror of femininity, experienced as that which is most desired and most feared, that which at one and the same time gives and takes away. The masculine response to this, within a symbolic order constructed around difference and exclusion, is to make the woman into a goddess and then to do everything possible to keep her in chains. Thus, in the midst of approbation there is misogyny; where there is adoration there is sexual violence. Phallic uncertainty and the power of the mother: in these are the seeds of masculine sexuality sown.

NOTE

1 References to Lacan's work in this chapter are, unless otherwise specified, to 'The meaning of the phallus', translated by J. Rose in Mitchell and Rose (1982).

REFERENCES

Bowie, M. (1991) *Lacan*. London: Fontana.

Cixous, H. (1976) 'The laugh of the Medusa' in E. Marks and I. de Courtivon (eds) *New French Feminisms*. Sussex: Harvester.

Clément, C. (1983) *The Lives and Legends of Jacques Lacan*. New York: Columbia University Press.

Felman, S. (1987) *Jacques Lacan and the Adventure of Insight*. Cambridge, Mass.: Harvard University Press.

Freud, S. (1939) 'Moses and monotheism' in S. Freud, *The Origins of Religion*. Harmondsworth: Penguin, 1985.

Gallop, J. (1988) *Thinking Through the Body*. New York: Columbia University Press.

Grosz, E. (1990) *Jacques Lacan: A Feminist Introduction*. London: Routledge.

Heath, S. (1987) 'Male feminism' in A. Jardine and P. Smith (eds) *Men in Feminism*. London: Methuen.

Lacan, J. (1958) 'The meaning of the phallus' in J. Mitchell and J. Rose (eds) *Feminine Sexuality*. London: Macmillan, 1982.

—— (1964) 'Guiding remarks for a congress on feminine sexuality' in J. Mitchell and J. Rose (eds) *Feminine Sexuality*. London: Macmillan, 1982.

—— (1972–3) 'Seminar XX: Encore' in J. Mitchell and J. Rose (eds) *Feminine Sexuality*. London: Macmillan, 1982.

Laplanche, J. and Leclaire, S. (1966) 'The unconscious'. *Yale French Studies*, 48: 118–75 (1972).

Mitchell, J. and Rose, J. (eds) (1982) *Feminine Sexuality*. London: Macmillan.

Moore, S. (1988) 'Getting a bit of the other: The pimps of postmodernism', in R. Chapman and T. Rutherford (eds) *Male Order*. London: Lawrence & Wishart.

Ragland-Sullivan, E. (1991) 'The sexual masquerade: a Lacanian theory of sexual difference', in E. Ragland-Sullivan and M. Bracher (eds) *Lacan and the Subject of Language*. New York: Routledge.

Segal, L. (1990) *Slow Motion: Changing Men*. London: Virago.

Smith, P. (1987) 'Men in feminism', in A. Jardine and P. Smith (eds) *Men in Feminism*. London: Methuen.

Theweleit, K. (1977) *Male Fantasies*. Cambridge: Polity (1987).

Part III

Modern conditions, psychoanalytic controversies

10 From Hiroshima to the Gulf War and after
A psychoanalytic perspective

Hanna Segal

When psychoanalysts try to apply psychoanalytical insights to areas beyond the consulting room, such as the study of aesthetics or socio-political phenomena, there is usually an outcry that this is not the province of psychoanalysis. These are areas in which there are experts, such as literary critics, art historians, philosophers of aesthetics, etc.; the psychoanalyst is supposed to be an expert only in the field of analysing patients. In relation to socio-political phenomena, the experts are the anthropologists, sociologists, economists, politicians; in the case of military activities, such as war, the experts are generals (even though Clemenceau said that war is too important to leave to generals) and others: anyone, but not a psychoanalyst.

I, and most psychoanalysts, are on the contrary convinced that psychoanalysis aims at being the science of the human mind, and psychoanalysts have a legitimate interest in investigating, and legitimate insights to offer to all areas of human endeavour. All those endeavours are the outcome of mental processes, and subject to the influences and distortions of such processes; and they are therefore the field of psychoanalytical inquiry.

In relation to the socio-political field, Freud stated that the baby and the child relate from the beginning to other people, primarily the parents, and that the family is the prototype and the nucleus of all other social engagements. Man is a social animal. The baby depends on, and relates to, the breast from the first moments of his or her existence. The baby then relates to a mother perceived more as a whole person with her own other relationships, and to the family as a whole: father, siblings and other people immediately surrounding him or her. Very soon this extends to other groups, such as neighbours, school companions and others. We all belong to a variety of groups, some of which are chosen, some that we are born into, such as a nation, and sometimes a religion. The analyst's concern is not just with the individual, but with the interaction between the individual and his environment, starting with the family group in infancy and extending later to larger groups.

There is another reason why psychoanalysis has a particular contribution to make to the understanding of social phenomena, and that is the irrationality of group behaviour. For society to behave in such irrational ways, evident in our activities destructive to the planet we depend upon, the destruction of our own habitat by greedy exploitation and pollution, and the continuation of the insane nuclear arms race, one would assume that powerful unconscious forces are at work well beyond the rational conflicts between classes, nations and races. At times it looks as though we are just hell-bent on self-destruction.

Freud was always interested in the relation between the individual and society. He first approached this subject from an anthropological angle in *Totem and Taboo*, trying to reconstruct the origins of human civilization. In 'Group psychology and the analysis of the ego', he addresses himself more to sociology – the whole problem of group functioning. In his correspondence with Einstein (1932) he addressed himself to the topic of *Why War?*, and in 1930 he wrote *Civilization and its Discontents* which, to my mind, lays the foundation of understanding of group phenomena and the anxieties and dangers presented by our civilization.

Some of Freud's work may look very naive today. For instance, in *Totem and Taboo* he differentiates between primitive people, whom he also calls 'savages', and the civilized humanity of today, in a way that would be quite unacceptable to modern anthropology. Freud also proposed a rather untenable hypothesis, which he treats almost as a fact, that the first horde of brothers in fact combined to kill their father, and that our own sense of guilt (or what, in his later writings, he called the super-ego) is related to this original murder of the father. Nevertheless, even *Totem and Taboo* has invaluable insights. Freud states, for instance, that society is a projection of our internal world, and that our internal processes influence both our perception and our organization of the external world. He also comments that guilt can be denied if the activity is carried out by the group as a whole. (In *Totem and Taboo*, he relates this particularly to the murder of the primal father.)

In his later and more sophisticated paper, 'Group psychology and the analysis of the ego', Freud develops this theme. He contends that in a group the members project the ego-ideal into a group ideal, often represented by the leader of the group, in leaderless groups by a leading idea, and thus relieve themselves of the guilt – if the activity, however destructive, has the approval of the joint ego-ideal. And he describes two identifications that individuals make within the group: identifying their egos with the other group members and projecting the ego-ideal into the leader:

> A primary group of this kind is a number of individuals who have put one and the same object in the place of the ego-ideal and have consequently identified themselves with one another in their ego.
>
> (Freud 1921: 113)

Freud also emphasizes the importance of love (which he calls 'libidinal ties') between members of the group. He contends that even though individuals combine into groups to achieve common aims, that tie is not sufficient for the cohesion of the group, the real tie being libidinal and linked with identifications.

Freud's most weighty contribution, which does not contain the naiveties of the preceding paper, and remains, even today, the basis of the later deeper and more detailed elaboration, is *Civilization and its Discontents* (1930). In the first part of that paper, Freud speaks of the repression of sexuality imposed on us by civilization and the discontents that ensue. But he also comes to the conclusion that that factor by itself is not enough to account for the vicissitudes and discontents of our civilization. He develops his new theory of instincts, formulated in *Beyond the Pleasure Principle* in 1920. In his study of individual patients Freud also came to the conclusion that what he originally thought was the origin of neurosis, the repression of sexuality, was not a sufficient explanation; and he formulated his concept of the life and death instincts. It is this new insight which lies at the basis of his revised view of civilization. The life instinct aims at combining the subject libidinally with the object and strives for life-giving unions. The death instinct, on the contrary, aims at disintegration, and finally death. The original way of dealing with the death instinct inside is to deflect it outwards, where it becomes aggression. Applying this view to social phenomena, Freud contends that groups are formed under the aegis of the libido, to achieve harmony within the group and carry out tasks. But this process is disturbed by the continual disruptions caused by impulses and phantasies derived from the death instinct.

> In all that follows I adopt the standpoint, therefore, that the inclination to aggression is an original, self-subsisting instinctual disposition in man, and I return to my view that it constitutes the greatest impediment to civilization. At one point in the course of this inquiry I was led to the idea that civilization was a special process which mankind undergoes, and I am still under the influence of that idea. I may now add that civilization is a process in the service of Eros, whose purpose is to combine single human individuals, and after that families, then races, people and nations, into one great unity, the unity of mankind. Why this has to happen, we do not know; the work of Eros is precisely this. These collections of men are to be libidinally bound to one another. Necessity alone, the advantages of work in common, will not hold them together. But man's natural aggressive instinct, the hostility of each against all and of all against each, opposes this programme of civilization. This aggressive instinct is the derivative and the main representative of the death instinct which we have found alongside of Eros and which shares world-dominion with it.
>
> (Freud 1920: 122)

Freud was not the only person to try to apply the insights derived from the couch to observations of group behaviour and social phenomena. (Reich particularly comes to mind.) But despite all this work, somehow psychoanalysis did not seem to throw much light on actual contemporary phenomena. It is amazing to think that whilst many psychoanalysts played quite a heroic role in combating National Socialism, the organized body of psychoanalysts, the International Psycho-Analytical Association, had nothing to say on the subject, and there were no major scientific papers dealing with the Nazi phenomenon or giving a warning about its meaning, though Freud makes a passing reference to the growth of Nazism in his letter to Einstein.

It was different after the Second World War, when a number of outstanding papers and books appeared on the subject of war and fascism. I mention here only some of the studies, such as Glover's *War, Sadism and Pacifism* (1933), Fornari's *Psychoanalysis of War* (1966), and Money-Kyrle's extensive writings on psychoanalysis and politics. I think this change after the War came about for two reasons. One is that Freud and other analysts did not work directly with groups. In both *Totem and Taboo* and 'Group psychology and the analysis of the ego', Freud refers to anthropological and sociological literature, often outdated. He did not carry out anthropological or sociological research himself. During and after the Second World War analysts started carrying out group analyses and analysing groups, small and large. The argument used against psychoanalysis, that one cannot transpose directly from the couch and the individual to a group, lost much of its validity because psychoanalysts started analysing groups and specific group phenomena and characteristics of group functioning. Freud gave some hints in that direction early on: for instance, pointing out the group function of relieving the individual from guilt and also the role of the group in binding 'man's destructiveness to man'. But later analysts were able actually to study this process clinically in groups.

I think the second factor which enabled psychoanalysis to have more to say about sociological matters is the advance in our understanding of psychosis. Group functioning is often basically influenced and disrupted by psychotic phenomena. Freud said that we form groups for two reasons: one, to 'combat the forces of nature'; and the other, to bind 'man's destructiveness to man'. Groups typically deal with this destructiveness by splitting, the group itself being idealized and held together by brotherly love, and collective love of an ideal, whilst destructiveness is directed outwards to other groups. We can love one another dearly, says Freud, if we have someone to hate. Generally we tend to project into the group parts of ourselves which we cannot deal with individually and, since it is the most disturbed, psychotic parts of ourselves which we find hardest to deal with, those tend to be primarily projected into groups.

The group defence mechanisms are mainly directed against psychotic anxieties which the individual cannot contain in himself, and they use defence mechanisms in a way that if used by an individual would be considered psychotic.

In normal circumstances the constructive and realistic functioning pre-dominates and the psychotic features are kept under control. Even so, however, groups behave in a way which in an individual would be considered mad; for instance, almost invariably groups are self-idealizing, grandiose and paranoid. The French have no doubt that they are the most cultured nation in the world. The English consider themselves the only just and fair society. Poles are heroic. The Americans are just great. No sane individual, even if he has such secret beliefs about himself, would unashamedly proclaim them aloud. Groups are also free of conscious guilt. Soldiers who in their private life could not bear the guilt of killing carry out massive genocide without guilt when it is sanctioned by the group or by the authorities.

Wilfred Bion has extended Freud's hypothesis about the two functions of the group. According to him, a group fulfils two functions. One he called the work group, which is the group function of realistic joint work (to combat the forces of nature). The other he called the basic-assumption group. By that he means that the other function of the group is handling psychotic anxieties. A basic assumption, as he calls it, is a psychotic premise on which the group functions. Such psychotic premises underlie, for instance, our sense of superiority to other groups, our unwarrantable hostility or fear of them, etc. Our psychotic parts are merged into our group identity, and we do not feel mad since our views are sanctioned by the group. If the work function predominates in the group it is kept in check. Our crazy assumptions may be expressed in a fairly innocuous way.

A large group, such as a state or nation, can also delegate such psychotic functions to subgroups which are kept under control by the group as a whole, for instance, the army. The military mind and military training are based on paranoid assumptions. Our sense of dependence on omnipotence and our messianic grandiose delusions can be vested in churches or religion in general. Other subgroups of the same kind can be developed.

But what happens if the tail starts wagging the dog, and the army mentality takes over, and the realistic self-interest of the group, like a nation, becomes subjected to the megalomania and paranoia of war-lords? And what happens when the religious subgroup takes over, as in religious wars and inquisitions? Such takeovers happen only when the larger group tacitly colludes with it and obviously allows it to happen. The larger group unconsciously projects into the fanatical group or leader their own mad parts and, whilst denying it, it abdicates its own responsibilities and meekly and passively submits to an external force which they apparently may even despise.

A political grouping, such as Fascism or Communism, can combine the army mentality with the religious mentality, bringing about guiltless destruction. The same can happen when the group called the nation gets ruled by nationalism. Members of a group are brought together because they share common interests and common anxieties. Members of a group brought together by work of whatever kind have a common individual and group interest. The security of both the individual and his group is bound up with the success of the work. Rivalries are unavoidable, but tempered by the need for survival and success of the group. (As the child's security depends on the welfare of his whole family despite his jealousies and envies.) The group itself can face rivalry with other groups and this too can take a sane form (for instance of a willingness to do as well as or better than another group); or an insane, destructive form liable to destroy both parties.

Political groupings likewise are brought together by common needs and interests. Marxist analysis is not incompatible with the psychoanalytic. But what it leaves out is that like other groups political groups contain psychotic fears and mechanisms. At its simplest, the rich man or the oppressor unable to face guilt about his destructive greed or ambition joins others in denying the guilt in two ways: one is the creation of a joint group super-ego and the other is the projection of destructiveness and guilt into the poor and oppressed, creating a red monster of communism or the black-and-red monster amongst depressed coloured populations. The poor, on the other hand, feel helpless, vengeful and envious; and they too resort to projection and self-idealization – as in the Marxist idealization of the proletariat. The proletarian dictatorship would be good and constructive because the poor and oppressed are guiltless, as though that group were immune from the human factors of greed, persecution, etc.

The predominance of psychotic processes over work orientation in a group is a particular danger of political groupings, whether national or ideological. This may be so because the national or political group's work is less well defined. If a group of scientists and other workers in a laboratory were dominated not by the work function but by psychotic assumptions, the actual work could not be performed. This is not so in political groupings, which seem to embody most easily feelings of superiority, messianic mission, convictions of rightness and paranoia about others. It may be also because political groupings have to do with the search for power, which in itself is a primitive aim. I do not remember who has said that the tragedy of democracies is that in order to get to the top you must have qualities which make you unfit to be at the top. And this of course is even more true of dictatorships.

Actually, politics are involved in any sizeable groupings. It is an unrealistic ideal to think that one can have an organization or society without politics. There will always be different views about policies to be pursued, giving rise to political tensions, and there will also be more destructive tensions due to rivalries and search for power. But those politics in an ordinary, well-functioning group will be subjected to the work function of the group. One could say 'too much politicking will not be tolerated because it will disrupt the work'. Not so in a political grouping, which has no other task but politics. The group chooses its leader according to its orientation. Groups under the sway of psychotic mechanisms tend to select or to tolerate leaders who represent their pathology, for instance, Hitler or Khomeini. But not only do those groups choose unbalanced leaders. They also affect them. The groups thrust omnipotence on to their leaders, and push them further into megalomania. There is a dangerous interaction between a disturbed group and a disturbed leader, each increasing the other's pathology.

A political group may be an organization, such as a state or political party within a state. But there is a larger, undefined political group which is in fact all of us. Everybody does some political thinking, unavoidably, even those who do not bother with political parties. And our political thinking is largely controlled by the group, for instance a nation state, to which we belong. Unthinkingly we adopt the mental posture of the group to which we belong, a posture which may be quite irrational and dangerous for our survival. I think our present nuclear situation produces a constellation in which the deepest psychotic anxieties are aroused and the most primitive psychotic behaviour is used by the group.

The very existence of nuclear weapons has given a new dimension to problems of war and peace. My own interest in trying to apply psychoanalytical understanding to the socio-political scene was stimulated by my awareness of the situation. I have written papers, some published, some unpublished, on this theme since.

In my first paper on the subject, 'Silence is the real crime' (1985, published 1987), I addressed myself to the problem of the lure of destructive and self-destructive omnipotence and the terror they induce, and I argued that the very existence of the bomb arouses the most primitive psychotic anxieties about annihilation, and mobilizes the most primitive defences.

For people to accept wars, the paranoid mechanisms must be reinforced. Our group or ideas must be felt to be perfect. The enemy must be presented as an inhuman monster. In genocide another element is added – that of contempt. The victim of genocide must be presented as not only inhuman, but as subhuman. As far back as the Middle Ages, the Crusaders used to roast and eat Arabs in some crusades as a demonstration that they were not human. The Nazis called the Jews '*Untermensch*' – subhuman. The American soldiers called the Vietnamese 'Gooks'. The Japanese called the Americans 'White Devils', but the prisoners whom they used for vivisection they called 'Logs', denying them not only humanity but even animal life. Victims of genocide must be seen as completely subhuman and beneath contempt. I mention genocide because nuclear war is not only a war but a massive genocide, and we must not forget that the first atomic bomb was thrown by big white people on little yellow people. Such mechanisms as the paranoid–schizoid one of making the enemy utterly evil, or the manic one of making them totally despicable, are powerful group mechanisms against the psychic reality of guilt about destructiveness. In his book *Psychoanalysis and War* (1966), Fornari gives a detailed analysis of the use of paranoid–schizoid mechanisms as a defence against mourning and guilt as applied to war.

A new element, however, enters with the nuclear weapons. For the first time, humanity has the power of complete annihilation and self-annihilation. Glover wrote in 1947:

> The first promise of the atomic age is that it can make some of our nightmares come true. The capacity so painfully acquired by normal man to distinguish between sleep, hallucination, delusion and the objective reality of wakened life has for the first time in history been seriously weakened.
>
> (Glover 1947: 274)

I think the existence of atomic weapons mobilizes and actualizes what I would describe as the world of the schizophrenic. The obliteration of boundaries between reality and phantasy characterizes psychosis. Omnipotence has become real, but only omnipotent destruction. We can, at the push of a button, annihilate the world, but not reconstruct it. In this world of primitive omnipotence, the problem is not of death-wishes and a fear of death, which pertain to the more mature depressive and Oedipal world; it is governed by wishes for annihilation of the self and the world, and the terrors associated with it.

Lifton (1982) makes the point, very convincing to me, that atomic annihilation destroys the possibility of symbolic survival. In natural death, or even in conventional war, men die, or at least those who have acquired some maturity die, with some conviction of symbolic survival in their children, grandchildren, in their work, or in the civilization itself of which they were part. Also, mourning, reconciliation and reparation can eventually take place. Coming to terms with the prospect of one's own personal death is a necessary step in maturation and in giving full meaning to life. The existence of nuclear weapons and the prospect of nuclear war make impossible a growing acceptance of death and symbolic survival. The prospect of death in atomic warfare leaves an unimaginable void and produces terror of a different kind. Those of us who work with psychotics get an inkling of this kind of terror. In normal development, as Freud has described and Klein elaborated further, Eros, the life force, succeeds in integrating and taming destructive and self- destructive drives, and converts them into life-promoting aggression. But in the depths of our unconscious, such unintegrated wishes and terrors still exist. We are all only partly sane, and such circumstances as prevail now mobilize the most primitive parts of ourselves. The lure of omnipotence is powerful; and so, at some level, is the lure of death.

Against the anxieties and guilt about those destructive drives most powerful defences are mobilized. Splitting and projection have to be increased, creating evil empires. That in turn increases both irrational anxiety and realistic fears. Then megalomania has to be increased as a defence, and it becomes vested in the omnipotence of the bomb. Dehumanization of the enemy has to take place, making the enemy either a monster or an object beneath contempt. But not only the enemy: we also dehumanize people on our own side.

In McNamara's memorandum to President Kennedy, he states that 'The Air Force considers the loss of 50 million American lives in case of a Russian counter-strike to the first strike to be acceptable.' (A few years later, when he changed his views, McNamara said in a television interview about his memorandum: 'It scares me now even to read the damn thing.')

With dehumanization goes also a blind reliance on machines. It is well known that the computerization of nuclear weapons during the Cold War was such that, according to Joseph Weizenbaum, the leading American expert on computers, no one could understand or control the whole system. There were anxieties during the Cold War that a war could be started accidentally by a computer reaction. Fragmentation of responsibility and its projection reached a point at which there could be a nuclear war without anyone being responsible – we could attribute responsibility to the machines. It is amazing that this threatening situation did not mobilize more anxiety. Denial, or turning the blind eye, seemed to be a response to an overwhelming anxiety. Our relation to the danger of nuclear war was a disbelief: either it could not happen – nobody would be so foolish as to start it – or it would not be that bad. Speech distortion characteristic of schizophrenia contributed to the denial. A so-called nuclear 'Nuspeak' developed. The code signal for the dropping of the bomb on Hiroshima was 'Baby's Bomb'. The Hiroshima bomb was the Little Boy; the Nagasaki bomb was the Fat Man. 'Nuclear' had become 'Nuke', a nice cosy name. 'Nuclear exchange' sounds rather innocuous. At the time of the Falklands War some youngsters wore T-shirts saying NUKE BA. I doubt whether they would wear shirts saying ANNIHILATE ARGENTINIANS. 'Flexible Response', which sounds nice and flexible, simply means The First Use of Nuclear Weapons. 'Star Wars' sounds fine, like science fiction – happening in outer space and not affecting us. The worst deception, maybe, is the use of the word 'Deterrence' which over the years has completely changed its meaning. The first idea of deterrence was that the Americans had the A-bomb and could use it to deter Russia from invading Europe. Soon, of course, the Russians had the bomb as well, and 'Deterrence' changed its meaning. It came to mean 'Deter the other party from the use of nuclear weapons'. This seemed to make some sense. Since the bomb was dropped by a country possessing the bomb on a country which did not, it made some kind of sense to think that if the big powers were both armed, each would deter the other from the nuclear initiative. Even at the time, the reasoning was not very sound: how to prevent other countries from acquiring nuclear weapons; how to maintain a balance of terror as a basis for coexistence, since such balance of terror would inevitably increase the paranoia. With the increasing arms race, the system came to be known as MAD (Mutual Assured Destruction). But in later years, 'Deterrence' changed its meaning again. Already in 1950 the US National Security Document NSC 68 states:

> The only deterrent we can present to the Kremlin is evidence we give that we may make any of the critical points in the world which we cannot hold the occasion for a global war of annihilation.

It meant the threat of using atomic weapons aggressively, not to deter others from using them. It meant atomic weapons leading to a global war of annihilation whenever one nation's wishes were thwarted. The policy changed. But words do not change – they only secretly change their meaning. This change in American policy became more explicit in the 1960s and 1970s. That was when we started hearing that nuclear war could be won, that we must start to think of a 'rational nuclear war'. 'The US must possess the ability to wage nuclear war rationally' – a US Defence Advisor (1982). Again, attractive words are used to disguise a change from a purely defensive to an aggressive posture in nuclear warfare. The notion of a flexible response was introduced.

This kind of thinking was of course active on both sides of the East–West divide, producing an unstable equilibrium based on insane premises and schizoid–paranoid defences. We lived in the world of MAD (mutually assured destruction).

This system has been undermined by perestroika. The paranoid structure could no longer be maintained. We lost the enemy. Perestroika was a time of hope, a possibility of change of attitude. But it was also a time of possible new dangers and a search for a new enemy. Giving evidence to the House Services Committee in December 1990, Edward Heath said:

> Having got rid of the Cold War, we are now discussing ways in which NATO can be urged to rush to another part of the world in which there looks like being a problem, and saying 'Right, you must just put it right; we don't like those people; or they don't behave as we do; and so on; and so we are going to deal with it'.

NATO went in search of a new enemy to justify its continued military power.

George Kennan was shocked to discover, when he was visiting western capitals, that despite the disappearance of the supposed Soviet threat, our apparent reason for keeping a nuclear arsenal, the western countries could not even conceive of a nuclear disarmament, a world without the atom bomb. It was, he said, like an addiction. And though apparently much had changed with perestroika, one thing had not changed. Nuclear fire power was constantly increasing, in so-called modernization.

So what was going on? We are familiar with those moments of hope clinically when a paranoid patient begins to give up his delusions, or when an addict begins to give up the drug and get better. The improvement is genuine. But as they get better they have to face reality. With the diminishing of omnipotence (in the case of the addict, maintained by drugs) they have to face their dependence, possibly helplessness, and the fact that they are ill. With the withdrawal of projections they have to face their own destructiveness, their inner conflicts and guilt: they have to face their internal realities. Moreover they often have to face very real losses and damage brought about by their illness, in external reality. And formidable manic defences can be mobilized in defence against this depressive pain, with a revival of megalomania and, in its wake, a return of paranoia. Similarly, in the social domain, when we stopped believing in the evil empire we had to turn to our internal problems. We had to face our social problems: economic decline and unemployment, guilt about the Third World. In England and America in particular, we had to face the effect of our mismanagement of resources: the years of Thatcherism left Britain as the sick man of Europe; and the years of Reaganism left America in a complete financial mess. (Hence the financial dependence on Kuwait.) And we had to face the guilt about the waste of resources on excessive, unnecessary, mad nuclear armaments against a non-existent danger – resources which should have been turned to education, health, industrial infrastructure, etc. One of the factors in the prosperity of Germany and Japan was the fact that they were not allowed to develop weapons.

Since a very important function of the group, one of the first observed by Freud and amply confirmed both by observation and clinical experience of groups, is to defend individuals against their guilt feelings, groups find it almost impossible to face collective guilt. Fornari, in *Psychoanalysis of War* (1966), demonstrates that wars are often started as a defence against guilt about previous wars.

Faced with that possibility of facing our inner realities, we turned to manic defences: triumphalism. Perestroika was felt to be the triumph of our superior system and power. Our nuclear mentality did not change. The megalomaniac search for power, noticed by Heath, and the addiction to the bomb, noted by Kennan, was bound to create new enemies to replace Soviet Russia. Firstly, because in fact it creates new enemies; and secondly, because we need a new evil empire to justify our arrogant aggression.

Einstein has said that with the advent of atomic power, everything has changed except our way of thinking. And in a way he is of course right. It has not changed for the better. We have not come to realize that the advent of the atomic weapons made meaningless the idea of a just war, or the defence of civilised values, since the war would destroy all values. It has not changed our thinking in the direction of realizing that our national, racial, religious or political narcissisms are not only paltry but lethal, and that our concern should be with the survival of the human race. But I am afraid that the atomic bomb may have changed our thinking for the worst, producing a nuclear mentality culture based on fears of annihilation and increasing schizophrenic defences. This mentality survived the end of the Cold War, and prevented us from using constructively the collapse of the 'Evil Empire'.

I and my colleagues of the PPNW, in a number of mostly unpublished papers presented to various audiences, warned about the dangers inherent in the post-perestroika situation. But numbness and apathy had set in. Anti-nuclear war organizations lost much of their membership. Public meetings were poorly attended. There was a feeling of great relief, and a wish to believe that all was well now – and increasing denial of the dangers that were still there. Specifically, we warned that unless attitudes to the whole problem changed we were in danger of finding a new enemy. We did not think of Saddam Hussein, who at that time was the pet of both East and West, busily being armed by them; but in some way he was very appropriate, since he was in a similar position. He too had lost an enemy, Iran, and probably had to face inner socio-economic tensions. We were as well matched with Saddam Hussein as were Galtieri and Thatcher over the Falklands, but on a terrifyingly bigger scale. And then the Gulf War confirmed our predictions: not, perhaps, our worst predictions of a nuclear escalation, but certainly the prediction of an unnecessary and devastating war.

Was that war well based and necessary? What were the reasons given to us? They were dubious. The first casualty, not only of war, but of preparation for war, is the *truth*. How much truth was there in the reasons given?

To mention only a few points: we were invited to believe the war was needed to protect human rights. But was it likely? We supported Iraq to the end, knowing perfectly well about the massive genocide of Kurds, as we supported and still support Sukarno in East Timor. Equally dubious is the claim that we did it in defence of international law. Britain and America blocked sixty-nine resolutions in UNO against the invasion of East Timor. Also we ignored Iraq's invasion of Iran. The invasions of Panama, or a bit of the British Commonwealth, Grenada, were also breaking international law. It was also said that if we did wrong in not upholding international law in the past we were right to uphold it now. However, Kant established the rule about moral principles that if you apply them only when it suits you you cannot claim to be acting on moral principles at all. The same holds true of law.

Another reason given was that of our legitimate interests in oil. That is a bit nearer the truth. In the 1950s, for instance, Selwyn Lloyd reported: 'We agreed that at all costs these oil fields must be kept in Western hands.' But even that is not entirely correct. The American concern was not so much accessibility or price of oil as the financial dependence on the Gulf states.

None of the supposed causes of the war are convincing if one looks at them rationally. So what were the real reasons? Actually I think I have grounds for believing that the deepest causes had unconscious psychological roots. I think that war was the inevitable result of the mental constellation established after perestroika. We needed an enemy to project evil on to, and we wanted a new evil empire. And Saddam Hussein provided an ideal enemy. He challenged our triumphalism and this was intolerable. Our power and our righteousness had to be re-established. Hence the need to emphasize that we needed to crush him for good moral reasons: human rights, international law, etc. We needed to establish our moral ascendancy.

Looking back on the Gulf War two years after, it looks to me like a psychotic episode with rather disastrous consequences. It took most people by complete surprise. The American Intelligence reports, fairly well documented, suggested that, in the case of Iraq, sanctions would be decisively effective in a period of about six months, and probably destroy the regime. (The geopolitical and economic situation was entirely different from that in South Africa, where, anyway, sanctions were applied extremely loosely.) All sorts of compromises were possible, and comparisons with the appeasement of Hitler misleading, since Iraq did not have a fraction of Germany's power. Yet there was a violent rush into that war, a real 'desert storm', the desert being the emptiness of our minds. It had a mad feel about it. George Bush and Saddam Hussein exchanged extraordinary insults, sounding like two paranoid megalomaniacs. Both sides fed the public with horror stories about the monstrous abuses by the other side. Not that Saddam Hussein's regime did not have a record of appalling cruelties. But we had known about it for years. And it was admitted later that some of the most heart-breaking stories, like Iraqi soldiers taking premature babies out of their incubators, were totally unfounded. The 'short' war was devastating.

We were, however, invited to believe that it was a bloodless war: that our fantastic precision weapons invariably found and destroyed their targets without touching civilians. At the end, and soon after the end of the war, the triumphalism was rampant: 'We won!'. In the USA, the failure of the Vietnam War was wiped out. We were led to believe that a combination of the whole western world and the Gulf states against one small country, already exhausted by a six-year war, was a great feat and that it was bloodless. But the 'bloodless' only meant 'no casualties on our side'. For a time it was also claimed that there were not many civilian casualties. The casualties among Iraqi soldiers could not be quite concealed; and anyway hiding them would be incompatible with the fact that we heroically won some enormous battles. But that was dealt with by dehumanization of the enemy. The genocide of escaping demoralized troops was described as a 'turkey shoot'. The turkey shoot could not be concealed. It was shown on television. But other similar acts did not become known for many months.

Gradually, little by little, the truth emerged about the immediate effects of the war. We still do not know the extent of the Iraqi military casualties. General Schwarzkopf declared that he was 'not in the body-counting business'. The American estimates gradually crept up from around 100,000 to just under 200,000. Gradually we started to learn about the civilian casualties, and the 'precise' weapons. Pentagon sources now say that only 7 per cent of American explosives dropped during the war were 'smart bombs', and of these only 50 per cent found their targets. Seventy per cent of the 88,500 tons of bombs dropped on Iraq and Kuwait missed their targets completely. That, of course, meant that 'co-lateral damage', that is, civilian casualties, amounted to around 123,000.

The report of the Medical Educational Trust estimates:

In the first 19 days of the war the TNT tonnage of bombs dropped on Iraqi soil was three times that dropped in the entire second world war. The rate of tonnage dropped on Iraq was twice that of the Vietnam war and three times that of the Korean war. . . . About 90,000 tons of explosive were dropped by Coalition forces in the war, of which only 7,400 tons (7 per cent) were the so-called 'smart' precision weapons. At least 20 per cent of smart weapons missed their target.

(MET Report Background Papers, February 1992)

Those were the immediate effects of the Gulf War. But there are also long-term consequences. The combination of increased displacement of populations, the destruction of infrastructure, pollution and continuing sanctions, as well as an actual increase of abuse of human rights by both Saddam Hussein and Kuwait itself, are bringing about consequences which will last for years. To give an example, UNICEF considers that five million children will die in the area in the near future as a direct consequence of the Iraqi war. What to me is most horrifying is that now, when we can easily be acquainted with these facts, we seem to have no reaction to them.

The Gulf War is forgotten, as though it is ancient history. There is a universal denial of what we have done and what the consequences are. And those who do not remember their history are bound to repeat it. But of course facing the reality exposes us to what is most unbearable, particularly in groups: admitting that we made a mistake of vast proportions and have to take responsibility for the consequences. But unless we do that, our manic and schizoid defences will again make us blind to these realities and lead us to further disasters.

To go back to my theme of the 'nuclear mentality'. The dangers of nuclear war are no fewer than they were during the Cold War, and some experts, for instance, Professor Paul Rogers at the Peace Studies faculty in Birmingham, consider that they have increased. It is acknowledged by the Americans that they are developing now strategic nuclear weapons specifically designed for wars in the Third World. Back to the deterrence of *might is right*. Nuclear weapons used by the strong against the weak. But we know if we look at history that that kind of oppression does not produce lasting peace. This is made worse by the fact that the disintegration of the Soviet Union led to the complete fragmentation of both nuclear hardware and nuclear know-how; fragments, as it were, of the nuclear weaponry of the disintegrating empire, have now spread all over the world. And we cannot effectively enforce nuclear non-proliferation, since we not only reserve the right to keep nuclear weapons ourselves (by 'ourselves' I mean the great nuclear powers) but we also keep arming our clients, some no better than Saddam Hussein.

The dangers I was concerned with still exist, and I now think new dangers are added, through an increasing fragmentation of the nuclear know-how and nuclear resources since the breakup of the Soviet Union. To look at the situation soberly, I think we would have to face, in addition to the guilt of the whole nuclear mentality attitude, the specific guilt of the Gulf War and its consequences. Unless we can admit our part in those devastating events, the old way of paranoia and fragmentation will increase all the dangers.

I have tried to present a very short, compressed and simplified overview of the psychological constellations as I saw them developing between Hiroshima, through the Cold War, perestroika, leading to the inevitability of another war, and also to look at the aftermath of the Gulf War. What can psychoanalysts possibly offer in such a situation? I think the only remedy we can possibly offer is not to swallow lies but to try to look at the facts; and insofar as we understand them, at the underlying psychological motivations, and to help the struggle for glimmers of insight and sanity. I think psychoanalysis has something to contribute in that field.

I, and others, have been accused of being partisan – not just personally, which it is our right to be, but involving psychoanalysis and speaking as analysts. I do not agree with this viewpoint. I think psychoanalytical neutrality must not be confused with being neutered. I think we should speak, not so much of the analyst's neutrality as of his objectivity. The analyst's task is to try to understand and objectively assess the situation, and communicate this understanding to others. And there can be no neutrality, say, as between Hitler and his victims. One can only strive for the understanding of factors that produce certain situations, and we are entitled, and indeed ethically bound, to make known our views about the dangers we foresee. *Quit tacet consentire videtur.*

We have also been accused of idealism. This I do not entirely refute, but I do not consider that it is 'unanalytic'. One has to distinguish between idealization and having ideals. Idealization is a distortion of realities and a dangerous stance, since it is invariably accompanied by splitting and projection – idealizing oneself and one's ideas or groups at the expense of paranoid attitudes to others. Having ideals is very different: it is not pathological to hope for a better future: for instance, for peace, and to strive for it, whilst recognizing how hard it is to attain, and that the opposition to it comes not only from others but also has its roots in ourselves.

REFERENCES

Bion, W.R. (1962) *Experiences in Groups*. London: Tavistock.
Fornari, F. (1964) *Psicanalisi della guerra atomica*. Milan: Editione della Communita.
—— (1966) *Psychoanalysis of War*. Bloomington, In: University of Indiana Press.
Freud, S. (1913) *Totem and Taboo*. S.E.13: 1–16.
—— (1920) 'Beyond the pleasure principle'. S.E.18.
—— (1921) 'Group psychology and the analysis of the ego'. S.E.18: 67–144.
—— (1930) *Civilization and its Discontents*. S.E.21.
—— (1933) 'Why war?' S.E.22.
Glover, E. (1933) *War, Sadism and Pacifism*. London: Allen & Unwin.
—— (1947) *War, Sadism and Pacifism: Further Essays on Group Psychology and War*. Edinburgh: Hugh Paton & Sons.
Lifton, R. (1982) *Nuclear War's Effect on the Mind*. London: Faber & Faber.
Money-Kyrle, R. (1978) *Collected Papers*. Aberdeen: Aberdeen University Press.
Segal, H. (1987) 'Silence is the real crime'. *International Review of Psycho-Analysis*, 14: 3–12.
—— (1989) 'Political thinking, psychoanalytic perspectives', in Baznett, L. and Leigh, I. (eds), *Political Thinking*. London: Plato Press.

11 On racism and psychoanalysis

Joel Kovel

> [T]hat which posits itself as 'I' is indeed mere prejudice, an ideological
> hypostasization of the abstract centres of domination, criticism of which
> demands the removal of the ideology of 'personality'.
>
> (Theodor Adorno, *Minima Moralia* 1951)

THE PSYCHOANALYTIC RECAPTURE OF THE PRIMITIVE

All things flow, said Heraclitus, even psychoanalytic theory. They do not, however, flow as they please, rather according to the laws of the formation in which they find themselves. In the cases of psychoanalysis this formation happens to be the society in which it was engendered, to which it has contributed, and from which it has drawn its life's blood in concept, exchange value and legitimation. The great illusion of psychoanalysis, applying to most contemporary discourse no less than the classical Freudian theory, has been to imagine itself free from society as it goes about its work of producing putatively categorical knowledge about the psyche. Psychoanalytic propositions rarely contain the proviso that the psyche whose innards are being laid out like a patient on an operating table is no physical body but a part of a given social setting at a given time. Psychoanalysts forget, like the educators of Marx's Third Thesis on Feuerbach, that they must themselves be educated into the ways of their world, and that they everywhere exist within the prevailing framework of social relations. They tend to forget, too, what psychoanalysis itself discovered – that the psyche it studies is no free-standing entity, but rather a continually reproduced relationship between subjects which itself flows, i.e. evolves historically.

The moment of psychoanalysis came when the West could no longer contain its own otherness within the prevailing system of rationalization. The precise rupture occurred at the weakest point of repression in the system, the desire of bourgeois women. Given leisure and education, stimulated by the nineteenth-century tide of progressive thought, yet confined to idleness and forced to sit passively by while men engaged their sexual double standard, women turned their thwarted desire into hysteria and other illnesses. Enter Freud, also frustrated, seething with ambition and deeply ambivalent with respect to patriarchal authority. This would-be conquistador and emulator of Hannibal had to settle, as he put it in the Virgilian epigraph to *The Interpretation of Dreams*, for the conquest of the lower, private realms given foreclosure of the upper, political sphere.[1] Freud therefore turned to the terrain of the disordered female psyche, which he staked out for science like an explorer of aboriginal lands. As with other colonial–imperial ventures of the late nineteenth century, the escapade produced a number of unanticipated and even unwanted results. Once the opening had been made to the 'talking cure', it was only a matter of time before women would claim the power of speech and use it to define their own reality against that established by the prevailing order of things.

That story is told elsewhere. However, it expresses a relationship of wider significance. What Freud captured was also a recapture. Psychoanalysis is widely recognized as having achieved the 'decentering' of the ego, or put another way, as having broken with the self-certainty of western experience identified with the postulation of the Cartesian *cogito*. In this, psychoanalysis accomplished something genuinely subversive, undermining the claims of established reason and morality, and calling attention to a domain of longing and suffering simply not recognized by the dominant culture. Entering the territory of female desire also meant a partial appropriation of that desire, and taking the position of the other. Freud's allegiance to patriarchy may have predominated but it is not the whole story; it has to be recognized also as part of an ambivalence, the underside of which surfaces as late as 1927 in the comment that 'It goes without saying that a civilization which leaves so large a number of its participants unsatisfied and drives them into revolt neither has nor deserves the prospect of a lasting existence.'[2]

Compare this to the development of academic psychology, which may be read as a set of variations about the theme of accepting the centricity of the ego, i.e. of a coherent 'personality'. While psychoanalysis wandered into the realm of the excluded, psychology remained firmly within the bounds of Cartesianism, with its claims to positive, measurable knowledge. With nothing problematic admitted into the realm of the psyche, a way was cleared for the performance of reproducible, statistically testable and scientifically correct investigations of human behaviour. Psychoanalysis meanwhile staked its claim on the dark, unmeasurable side of things: the realm of dreams, systematically false reasonings, obscure passions and neurotic compulsions. Everything here is problematic; but in it also resided whatever hope psychoanalysis may have as an emancipatory discourse. By contrast, ego psychology – the attempt to bring psychoanalysis back into the domains of normal science and clinical respectability – however sensible in its own terms, was readily incorporated into a conservative strategy of 'adaptation'. Adorno was of course exaggerating when he claimed that nothing in psychoanalysis was true except the exaggerations. Yet if to be true means to expose that which is real but hidden, that is, the repressed, then he was also speaking the truth.

Beyond any particular truth, therefore, disclosed by psychoanalysis – the clinical theory, the insights into dreaming and child mental life, and so forth – there is a truth of psychoanalysis as a whole: the uncovering of what had been repressed by 'civilization' itself. From another angle, what Freud did was to reverse a tendency peculiar to the modern West and restore a state of affairs characteristic of the entire pre-modern history of humanity – including the humanity which had been swallowed into the West's expansion since 1492. When Freud admitted the unconscious, and later the id and super-ego, he did more than decentre the ego – he also *added* to the ego, postulating a model of psyche we may call polycentric, i.e. having more than a single organizing nucleus. Just as industrial civilization produces a simplification in ecosystems, resulting in species depletion and monocrop agriculture, so has it imposed a reduction and simplification in the notion of the self. The exigencies of modern production, with its increasing routine and bureaucracy, impose the icy hand of rationalization over human existence; thus the Cartesian identity of the self with its *cogito* became canonical because it reflected modern production and the state, and not, as it claimed for itself, for a transhistorical reason. The greatest achievement of psychoanalysis was to enrich self-understanding by recognizing the polycentric nature of mind. It is well known that Freud opted for the ego's hegemony amongst the various entities which populated the psyche.[3] This expressed his preference for patriarchy and bourgeois morality, but it did not cancel out the radical implications of a polycentric psyche, inhabited by a number of different structures and divided into distinct layers, a psyche, moreover, quite unlike the *cogito* in being problematic to itself.

In this case, what was radical meant returning to the roots of reflection about the nature of mind. Until the bourgeois West introduced its notion of a unified personality, all other societies had regarded psyche as essentially polycentric. Of course, each society gave different kinds of names to the inherent multiplicity of the psyche and saw its problematicity in a specific light. Nevertheless, whether in primitive 'state-free'[4] bands from around the world, chiefdoms like archaic Greece, the Athenian state, imperial China (from the soil of which grew Taoism), or Christian Europe until the modern era – wherever we encounter conceptualization of the psyche across an immense range of social organizations, we also find polycentrism.

Except in the Freudian rendition, polycentrism is associated with a more or less open boundary to the psyche. The capacity to see the psyche as complex and multivalent extends to a recognition of interconnection between selves, and between the self and the world; that is, to the recognition of an open psyche. Freud recognized such experience as the 'oceanic feeling', a phenomenon he hastened to explain away as an illusion based upon an infantile memory of nursing.[5] This dismissal, however, proves nothing, as there is no reason not to hold that what the baby experiences at the breast is only the first instance of interconnection and ego-unboundedness available to human beings. Freud thus has no grounds beyond prejudice for rejecting the authenticity of those mature episodes which deserve to be called 'spiritual', where spirit is defined as what happens to the self as its boundaries give way.[6] Thus the prevalence of an open view of psyche is also a way of stating the prevalence of a spiritual world-view in pre-modern societies. A spiritual world-view is therefore one in which the giving way of the self's boundaries is considered normal and not, as it is today, regressive or pathological. And if self-passage is considered normal, then those states of being which surpass the ego's boundary cannot be mere illusions but must possess some degree of reality – an acceptance of Hamlet's reminder to Horatio that there are more things in heaven and earth than are dreamt of in our philosophy.

This is consistent with the fact that spiritual practice is not done under the aegis of the Pleasure Principle, but in order to confront realities of existential significance – the ends and meaning of life and the relation of the person to the universe. A self so directed as to pass beyond itself may be called a 'soul'. The notion of the soul, another category more or less permanently eclipsed in modern discourse, conveys a degree of interiority quite beyond the ken of psychology as we know it. In this respect soul also implies a polycentrism, since other, non-soul aspects of psyche are required to mediate the interiority of soul with external reality. Again it is worth observing that psychoanalysis has succeeded in restoring a degree of soul language to psychological discourse.[7] However, it does so by eschewing existential questions and without the acceptance evinced by traditional spirituality of soul-migration and other manifestations of an open psyche. Thus psychoanalysis is no spirituality. Its major non-egoic centre, the id, is denied agency and access to consciousness; there is no question of any 'higher' form of knowing, nor of transcendent experience, arising from its domain. Freud was generally explicit on this point and future generations of analysts have continued in the same path. Meanwhile, super-ego, the other great nucleus of classical psychoanalytic polycentrism, functions quite explicitly as a this-worldly regulator. Far from having spiritual possibilities, the super-ego is a strictly interior voice calling the ego back to the tasks of the Reality Principle; that is, the productive logic of civilization. Contrast this with super-ego's precursor in Christian doctrine, the Holy Spirit. This, too, functions as a regulatory voice, but it comes from beyond the boundary of the self, and calls the self to this beyond in the kingdom of Christ.

These distinctions are compatible with the finding that the spirituality of pre-modern, especially primitive, societies, possesses an intensity quite foreign to the modern mind. Such spirituality as remains for us is generally encapsulated in the form of established religion or as a 'New Age' manifestation more or less linked to the notions of therapy, self-help or some fuzzy and unmediated encounter with nature. The manifestations are many, but they often share the common features of solace, consolation and/or relaxation. To primitives, however, spirituality involved a degree of existential depth rare in the West since the early modern period. For example, shamanism, a more or less universal practice throughout the primitive world, heals through an encounter with split-off and migratory aspects of soul that can be of truly terrifying proportions. A kind of homology can be drawn with the transference neurosis of psychoanalysis, or even with the training analysis of the future psychoanalyst who must undertake to live through the illness before embarking on a career of healing. The similarity is grounded in the common acceptance by psychoanalysis and primitive spirituality of a polycentric psyche, at odds with itself in the processes of pathology and healing itself through confrontation with its split-off otherness. The limits of this comparison need to be emphasized, however. Though psychoanalysis may reach back to the roots of human self-understanding, it never abandons its situation on thoroughly modern terrain. The essence of psychoanalytic practice remains the emphasis on verbalization and the rule of abstinence. This is grounded in the bourgeois contract in which the analyst exchanges time and attention for the patient's fee. Exchange conditions the Reality Principle for analysis with the heavy hand of rationalization, the tyranny of the clock and related phenomena. Only money can truly be sacred in capitalist society, but since money is worthless in itself, a kind of pallor enters into all transactions. By contrast, the notion that human action can be quantified and sold for money is profoundly inimical to the aboriginal, for whom the important things in life are sacred, i.e. unique and unexchangeable. This is conducive to the ecstatic character of genuine shamanistic healing (there is, it may be added, a good deal of bogus practice as well, including the operations of would-be shamans from the metropolis who think they can walk across the gulf between cultures), which frequently involves out-of-body experiences and states of terror that are deathlike in intensity.[8]

An even more radical element of primitive spirituality is the ancient and ubiquitous legend of the trickster, found 'in clearly recognizable form', according to Paul Radin, 'among the simplest aboriginal tribes and among the complex'. We encounter it among the Ancient Greeks, the Chinese, the Japanese and in the Semitic world. Trickster is a far cry from the homogeneous figure of good and evil represented by Christianity's God and devil. He comes closer, rather, to Freud's concept of the 'polymorphously perverse' – except that what psychoanalysis segregates in the forgotten eroticism of childhood, primitive spirituality promotes to a drama of the problematicity of human existence as a whole. In trickster we see the full panoply of ambivalence:

> at one and the same time creator and destroyer, giver and negator, he who dupes others and who is always duped himself. At all times he is constrained to behave as he does from impulses over which he has no control. He knows neither good nor evil yet he is responsible for both. He possesses no values, moral or social, is at the mercy of his passions and appetites, yet through his actions all values come into being. But not only he, so our myth tells us, possesses these traits. So, likewise, do the other figures of the plot connected with him: the animals, the various supernatural beings and monsters, and man.

The trickster, claims Radin, is 'a figure foreshadowing the shape of man . . . a *speculum mentis* wherein is depicted man's struggle with himself and with a world into which he has been thrust without his volition and consent'.[9] The trickster stands outside of society yet remains part of it. This reflects the refusal of the myth to submit to any rationalization of existence, its insistence on the radical problematicity of all things human. The polycentric notion of the primitive psyche is but one element in a larger refusal to simplify and boil down human existence into a metaphysics or a set of essences.

> The symbol which Trickster embodies is not a static one. It contains within itself the promise of differentiation, the promise of god and man. For this reason every generation occupies itself with interpreting Trickster anew. No generation understands him fully but no generation can do without him. Each had to include him in all its theologies, in all its cosmogonies, despite the fact that it

realized that he did not fit properly into any of them, for he represents not only the undifferentiated past, but likewise the undifferentiated present within every individual. This constitutes his universal and persistent attraction. And so he became and remained everything to every man – god, animal, human being, hero, buffoon, he who was before good and evil, denier, affirmer, destroyer and creator. If we laugh at him, he grins at us. What happens to him happens to us.[10]

The implication of this is that fully developed, the polycentric view of the psyche implies not only an open psyche, a psyche capable of wandering and interpenetrating with other beings, but an open society as well, a society open to the other.[11]

The end of the line for the trickster in western culture occurs during Greece in the classical period. In fact, Greek mythology contains two lines of the trickster myth – the god Hermes, and of special significance, the Dionysian cults. Here, as Karl Kerenyi comments, 'Dionysian ecstasy had the same function as the trickster [sic] myth: it abolished the boundaries, not least the boundaries of sex.'[12] This juncture defines what is perhaps the most harrowing of Athenian tragedies, *The Bacchae*. The nightmarish end of King Pentheus – to be torn apart and devoured by his own mother upon whose maenadic dancing he has been spying (after he incorporates the god he has denied by cross-dressing as a girl) – becomes the occasion of Euripedes's solemn warning to Athens as a modernizing state: we deny Dionysius at our doom. In terms of our discourse, the rationalizing functions of state-centred society, driving out the radical ambivalence in human nature and limiting the wandering polymorphous soul to the margins of existence, represents a repression for which we will pay dearly. From another angle, the final horror of the Bacchae is not derived from the god himself, but from that god as he is made malignant by repression, i.e. split-off, denied and mocked. For the god is only a human principle or potential, a filament of existence, unaccountable and unbounded until the King tries to rein him in.

It goes without saying that Euripedes's warning went unheeded. In the Platonic synthesis which forms the starting point for distinctively western thought, a hierarchical self is installed which banishes the 'lower' passions under the rule of reason and installs a metaphysics of essence over the unruly flow of events.[13] In Plato's ideal society, the poet and dramatist who maintain touch with the Dionysian underworld are simply banished. From this point forward, the trickster principle becomes segregated into artworks such as *The Bacchae*, that is, to an aesthetic realm distinct from the rest of social existence. The Dionysian rites themselves persist but on the margins of society, in which place they become increasingly hollowed out. They retained a status as the bacchanalia of Medieval Europe, and still live on, for example, as the Mardi Gras of New Orleans or the Halloween parades that give people a chance to dress up and cross boundaries.[14] Within the dominant culture, meanwhile, the trickster–Dionysius line was transmuted into the Christian dichotomy between God and devil, the former representing a homogeneous good manifest as pure spirit; the latter representing a homogeneous evil inhabiting flesh and matter. In this respect, Christian dualism prepares the way for the Cartesian self by clearing away the principle of ambivalence from within the conception of human nature and locating it metaphysically. The attack on paganism epitomized by the great witch-hunts of the early modern period represented the full violence inherent in this repression, for pagans, especially the witches, were more or less throwbacks to the Dionysian–Trickster tradition, with its emphasis on the erotic and the crossing of boundaries (as in the witch's Sabbath[15]). In its prodigious hatred of the body and all things carnal, [16] Christian culture succeeded – at tremendous cost – in driving out a differentiated sense of ambivalence and replacing this with a split universe divided between God and the devil, spirit and the flesh. Though the Christian self retains polycentrism and an open boundary in its relation to the Holy Spirit, as this spirit becomes increasingly purified and under the repressive sway of an imperial church, its dualism becomes ever more sharply defined, until under the pressures of advancing modernity it yields its ontological fruit in the Cartesian *cogito*.

We may summarize the argument to this point: both mind and the ways of thinking about mind are historical, the two histories being deeply intertwined. Until the modern period, mind was construed polycentrically, this being associated with an openness of the psyche to the world and, in primitive society at least, an openness of society to otherness. On the other hand, the march of historical 'progress' seems to have been inexorably associated with an attenuation of polycentrism. Major turning points in this process included the rise of Classical Athens, which, in Plato, decisively turned away from the primitive world-view; the emergence of Christian dualism (itself borrowing heavily from neoPlatonism); and the rise of modernity under the sway of Protestantism and capitalism, which effectively reduced the physical universe to, in Whitehead's term, 'scurrying matter', and constructed the mind as a homogeneous substance, stripped of all interiority and problematicity. From this perspective, the achievement of psychoanalysis becomes clear – belonging to the advancing edge of modern self-reflection and the tradition of demystification, yet doing so through a partial retrieval of what is most ancient and primary in human self-realization. Psychoanalysis therefore succeeds in being closer to the grain of primitive spirituality than does modern spirituality; it does so, however, by abandoning spiritual claims to address existential matters. This is a detail worth noting, but it is only a detail in a much larger and more fundamental pattern: that all the modern discourses are profoundly turned away from the primitive world-view.

ON RACISM

If I say that racism – by which we mean the systematic maltreatment of people because of their 'race' – is an affliction of the modern psyche I do not mean to imply that pre-modern people were without exclusionary beliefs which promoted themselves over others, whether of different tribes or nations, often with destructive consequences. Such an absurd argument – which in effect recycles the 'noble savage' mythology that is itself a product of racism – would deny a mountain of evidence as to the transhistorical capacity for irrational and destructive behaviour. From another angle, it would run contrary to the view aboriginal peoples hold of themselves and humanity in general as evinced, for example, by the trickster legends. No 'noble savage' would concoct a mythic system so expressive of the treacherous forces in the human predicament; for there is nothing noble about the trickster. Actual primitives, therefore, were quite aware that they were not uniformly capable of living up to the openness inherent in their world-view. We may safely conclude that there is no human situation free of the potential for destructiveness. This does not, however, rule out the presence of significant shifts over time in the quality as well as quantity of destructiveness. Pessimists and conservatives, in viewing the ubiquity of human aggression, often tend to join Freud in the unwarranted conclusion that this stems from a kind of primordial instinctual drive which will destroy come what may unless it is held back by repressive authority. They might as well have reduced sex and eating – two practices whose instinctual rootedness is even more established than is aggression – to similar monotony. The fact is that enormous changes exist across time and place in the way ambivalence towards the other is expressed, and it is these which must be accounted for historically. It is in this spirit that we would postulate racism as the peculiarly modern form of repressive exclusionism, and locate its pathology in the peculiar conditions of modernity.

What distinguishes modern racism from pre-modern tribalisms (and their successor nationalisms)[17] is its reliance upon an abstract essence, embodied in the notion of 'race', to become the point of splitting between peoples. Thus racism has a systematic character which belongs specifically to the modern era. In this respect it is worth considering whether the emergence of racism is related to the stripping down of the western psyche and the reduction of its own interiority and ambivalence. Could it be that as the western mentality began to regard itself as homogeneous and purified – a *cogito* – it was also led to assign the negativity inherent in human existence to other peoples, thereby enmeshing them in the web of racism?

First, some reflection concerning the nature of racism is in order. To say that racism is a systematic kind of degradation is to say that it is an entity in itself and not merely a collection of opinions or beliefs, or purely psychological processes. Racism has its own organization, with the capacity to itself evolve over time; it possesses sufficient internal coherence to enter into the evolution of the psyche. In speaking of such a structure, we might consider it schematically as a kind of triangle defined through the dynamic interaction of three constituents. See Figure 1.

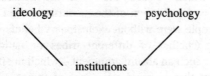

Figure 1   The structure of racism

Here 'ideology' consists of intellectual production configured about ways of accounting for reality according to prevailing relations of power (e.g. theories of racial inferiority and superiority); 'psychology' consists of prevailing patterns of mental structure and psychodynamics (e.g. 'authoritarian characters' suitably disposed to develop racial prejudice)[18]; and 'institutions' consist of materially grounded and legitimated elements of society (e.g., economy, church, family). In this view, schools of psychology such as psychoanalysis or behaviourism belong to the ideological field; while actual structures of behaviour, fantasy, etc. are part of the psychological field. The figure as a whole constitutes racism, insofar as it is disposed to the systematic degradation of one group to the advantage of another. Needless to say, each of its elements has a degree of independent derivation; yet each is also mutually defined by the others within racism. That is, ideology, psychology and institutions become constituents of racism as well as determinants of racism, and interrelate within racism. Racist institutions determine racist psychology and ideology and are defined in turn by them; the same can be said for racist psychology and ideology. In this way, racism becomes a defining feature of society itself at a certain point of development – as it has been, say, for the United States and South Africa; it becomes possible then to speak of a racist society, a society permeated by and to some degree organized around racism, whose institutions are racist, whose ideology is racist, and whose dominant psychological types incorporate and perpetuate racism.

In such a society, racism evolves in historical time; it is capable of becoming more or less racist as a whole, and also in terms of its constituent institutions, ideologies and psychologies. These may undergo a kind of uneven development. A society may come to exhibit less racist ideology, e.g. fewer theories of race superiority; and less racist psychology, e.g. fewer overtly bigoted individuals. It may even exhibit antiracist ideology, e.g. conscious efforts to overcome discrimination or to ensure equal access, as well as antiracist psychology, e.g. many individuals who consciously affirm racial equality, intermarriage and so forth. Yet such a society, because of institutional arrangements that are essentially unresponsive to good will and intentions (notably, the economy), will continue to systematically degrade individuals according to race. In other words, the existence of racism implies the possibility of 'institutional racism', a racism relatively unmediated by human agency, but inherent, rather, in impersonal market or bureaucratic forces in which racism has become sedimented.

We might add that this kind of determination of racism is not symmetrically distributed among the three elements. We would not expect racist ideology to persist on its own after institutions stopped being racist. Nor, significantly, would we expect racist psychology to endure once institutional forces no longer applied in a racist direction. No doubt, certain individuals would remain racist according to the vagaries of their particular development. But the social type would no longer apply as a dominant category. It is, after all, a racist society grounded in racist institutions (and this image tells us why we place institutions as a kind of 'base' in the triangular figure sketched in above) that generates racist ideology and, along with this, a dominant psycho-social type that may be called racist. However, although institutions such as the economy may underlie and reproduce racism, they cannot define it, precisely because of their impersonal nature. It takes sensuous, desiring human beings, organized by ideologies, to do so. Moreover, institutions are not simply the product of impersonal laws but are themselves shaped by concrete individuals and hence bear the mark of their psychology and ideology. Because of all this we are led once again to affirm that racism is a complex structure of its own, which cannot be reduced to any of its constituents.

We may now look more concretely at these relationships, using that type of racism which, more than any other, characterizes the modern West: white over black, or more simply, white racism.[19] When I speak of this kind of racism I mean to focus upon one instance of great, although not exclusive significance, namely, the racist relationship between white and black in the United States of America. But given the limits of this chapter, I mean also to use this racism as exemplary of the entire mass of racisms that have ensued from the world-historical expansion of the 'white' West over peoples of colour. Western imperialism, which begins with Columbus and is still a long way from running its course, is, along with the capitalist-industrial revolution linked to it, the principal organizing force of modern history, and white racism is its subjective reflex. There should be no expectation that a consideration of this pattern of racial dominance can be applied willy-nilly to other racisms such as anti-Semitism, or that it will provide a master key to racism as a whole. Yet there is something of special significance about white racism, for two simple reasons; first, that *whiteness* defines the centre of western identity; and second, that said whiteness came to be in the encounter with dark-skinned people. That the West defines itself as white is therefore dialectically related to the dominion established over blacks, in particular, Africans. And given the strategic importance of the United States within the West, its white racism can well be regarded as exemplary.

The institutional origin of white racism in the United States is unequivocally slavery. Slavery of course had been a well-defined practice since the beginnings of historical time; and what we know as 'civilization', could not have arisen without it. But the chattel slavery which helped form the United States was different, in two major respects.

First, it rapidly became colour coded. There is nothing inherent about slavery which would lead it to be so coded. However, once slavery did become coded by colour it exerted a decisive organizing influence upon further race relations. Within a century after the first African slaves had landed in Virginia in 1619, virtually all slaves were African in origin and virtually all African-Americans were slaves. Thus a rigid category, white = free/black = slave, arose to shape the primary productive relationship of a substantial bloc of American society. Note how the economic institution, slavery, which provided the dynamism of American white racism, was itself shaped by pre-existing attitudes concerning colour, specifically the dread of blackness which was animating the western psyche before the discovery and invasion of the New World. For example, Othello's blackness inspires considerable awe and a degree of horror in the personae of Shakespeare's tragedy, written just before Britain began major colonization of North America. Yet

Othello cannot be considered an example of white racism proper, precisely because it is the tragedy of a black *man*, indeed, a heroic and noble black man, once a slave but risen to command the armies of Venice.

This brings us to the second point, which is that American slavery was far more dehumanizing than had previously been the case. An Othello would have no place within its order. In what was to become the United States, slaves were denied any potential for manumission. Compare, for example, the potentials for freedom in societies such as Imperial Rome which had none of the emancipatory potential of the North American colonies. America's slaves were also systematically denied the benefits of European culture; at the same time every effort was made to destroy their African culture as well as family ties, in order to make them helpless and utterly dependent upon their white masters. In addition, they were systematically denied all legal rights; for example, the word of the master would automatically be assumed as true in any legal proceeding between them; the slave having no possibility of judicial recourse. In sum, whereas previous modes of enslavement had placed the chattel at the lowest end of the human scale, from which position he or she was capable of rising, that characteristic of the North American colonies took the slaves out of humanity altogether and placed them in the fixed status of animals. If slaves were well-treated in this system, it was a purely accidental occurrence, an act of human recognition against the grain of slavery as an institution; and if they were well-nourished it was out of no more intrinsic consideration than that afforded to horses and other useful beasts of burden.

When we seek to explain this extreme degree of brutalization, we encounter a remarkable contradiction. North American colonial society was on the whole no more brutal or violent than its predecessors. On the contrary, it was the cradle of democracy, along with those ideals of human rights which animate all modern progressive discourse. This contrast was not simply a case of uneven development, in which the dehumanization of North American slavery, so to speak, lags behind other features of the society. It strikes us, rather, as a case of divergent development, a peculiar dialectic between higher and lower, a dialectic in which the heights of achievement and the depths of dehumanization are part of the same processes.

The root of the dehumanization of American slavery is transparently revealed in the fact that the plantation economy for which slaves provided the labour became integrated into a capitalist world system. The slave-owner, therefore, had to regard his slave as a commodity or investment, a thing exchangeable for money. He had to do so not as a matter of desire, but simply to exist in a capitalist market. Were an individual slaveholder to drop out for reasons of moral censure or whatever, there would always be somebody waiting to replace him. The drive towards profit maximization is therefore not an instinctual drive; it is immediately linked with no desire, but simply a kind of necessity, the acceptance of which drives towards dehumanization. Needless to add, the form of desire known as greed also played a role. However, this motive is not specific for capitalist accumulation, nor was the regime of capital (especially in its early stages before circuits of commodity consumption were stimulated) a particularly favourable ground for the exercise of greed. The capitalist era was ushered in on a wave of worldly asceticism. Renunciation of immediate pleasure for long-term gain, calculation and rationalization were its hallmarks, and squandering was its bane; thus greed enters into the capitalist scheme of things but becomes transmuted into the circuits of accumulation. Capital is the realm of the ant, not the grasshopper, in the fable of the time. It is, above all, a regime in which the external world of objects, including the humans brought into the scheme of accumulation, are reduced to the level of things, emptied of quality and subjected to quantification and exchange.

And this is what happened to the slaves of capitalism. Note, to take only one example, the imperative of slave-traders to inhumanely pack their chattels aboard ship for the voyage from Africa to America. Calculate how many bodies could be jammed into the space of the ship to make the voyage profitable, allowing, of course, for a certain rate of attrition (perhaps as much as one half dying), and factor the whole by the imperative to minimize expenses for such dispensables as food – and we arrive at the infamous diagrams of human beings stacked like cordwood along the length of the slave vessel.[20]

Thus the logic of accumulation contributed to the dehumanization of blacks. So, too, did the ever-present fear of their revolt, a fear aggravated by dehumanization itself and augmented by the further threat that blacks would form alliances with Indians and poor whites on the rough and unpoliced landscape of America. There was, however, another factor, deeply ironic and peculiar to the times: the idealizing pressure stemming from the emergence of the Rights of Man. These ideals were radically incompatible with slavery and led to its moral condemnation. It was precisely because of this novel conjuncture that the objects of enslavement – black human beings – would have to be removed from the status of full human being. An age that produced the individual with democratic rights would also produce a subspecies of human beings without humanity. In this respect the true institutional origin of white racism occurs in the making of the United States Constitution. Here the necessity was to install the principle of democratic rule, and the problem was how to enumerate people for purposes of proportional representation – specifically, how to deal with the presence of black humans cut off from humanity over one half of American society. The answer – to count black chattels as three-fifths of a person for purposes of representation – solved the technical problem of democratic structure at the cost of formalizing the subhuman status of blacks. It was this device which also formally installed white racism in the United States and the rest of the western world. Thus a racism arose which derived less from persecutory hatred than from the contradiction between economic dehumanization and liberalizing ideals. Once configured, however, this structure would become capable of generating and channelling persecutory hatred to a prodigious degree. The infamous three-fifths reduction may have resolved an institutional crisis; but it aggravated an ideological one by officially confirming the loss of humanity of a substantial moiety of the population in a society which was identifying itself as dedicated to human rights. There was only one way to settle this severe contradiction, and that was to declare the blacks as inherently subhuman. Of course a simple declaration would not do; one needed a firmer foundation than that, something beyond the vagaries of personal opinion and grounded in the order of the universe itself. Here the rising scientific enterprise played its ideological role. The rage to classify that had eventuated in the Linnaean theory of speciation was readily extended to the human sphere in a theory of subspeciation. The category of race was born as a biological essence, a kind of slate upon which could be written the naturalization of a historical crime: the Negro was entitled to no more than the three-fifths share which democracy afforded because he or she belonged to an inferior race. From this gesture stems the whole history of scientific racism and all the bigotry surrounding it. The notion of 'race' should therefore be seen as the starting point of the history of racism rather than an objective category with scientific standing.[21]

THE REGIME OF THE EGO

A persistent shadow had dogged Puritanism, the dominant cultural type of the early capitalist order – a spectre of renunciation and rationalization, of the loss of sensuousness and the deadening of existence. In this context the animality projected on to the black by virtue of his or her role in slavery became suitable to represent the vitality split away from the world in Puritan capitalist asceticism. Sensuousness that had been filtered out of the universe in capitalist exchange was to reappear in those who had been denied human status by the emergent capitalist order. Blacks, who had been treated as animals when enslaved, became animals in their essence, while the darkness of their skin became suitable to represent the dark side of the body, embodying the excremental vision that has played so central a role in the development of western consciousness.[22] In this way blacks were seen as beneath whites in reasoning power and above whites in sexuality and the capacity for violence. These traits became organized into a superordinate myth of animality. In this way a kind of distorted memory of a real history is routinely activated when police encounter black males in the United States, an event with routinely horrific results. For example, in the Rodney King beatings of 1991 – an instance unusual mainly for having been videotaped – the viciousness of the clubbing administered by the Los Angeles police was justified at trial as a neces- sary measure given the extreme *wildness* of the victim, presumably high on some intoxicant. The same myth was applied in the 1920s for equipping police in the South with .38 calibre firearms instead of the standard .32 calibre issue, it being felt that a black man high on a drug like cocaine was too wild to be stopped by a lesser bullet.[23]

The splitting and projection of animality closes the logic that configures racism. Animal as beast of burden, animal as subspecies unfit for civilization, animal as bearer of instinct – racism binds the black in a net of alienation. The relationships filter into practices – judges who sentence black youths more harshly than white youths; teachers who shun or misunderstand them; employers who hire them last, fire them first and pay them less; real estate brokers and banks who perpetuate segregated, inferior housing: the list goes on and on. The result is a continuous reinstitutionalization of the material basis of racism, and a continuous reproduction of racism itself. The end result is a set of separated moral universes. This process plays a vitally important role in the establishment of what might be called the psychological economy of the West. Just as the races became segregated physically by neighbourhood, so did they come to embody segregated mental essences. And just as the common labour of subalterns is necessary for the civilization in which they are essentially unrecognized, so too does the degraded spectacle of instinct serve to connect the disembodied, despiritualized consciousness to the nature it has lost. Without the spectacle of lost nature to hate and be fascinated by, it is doubtful whether the reduction of the psyche to a homogeneous personality could be sustained.

The separation of mental essences reveals more than a superficial relationship to the nuclear psychoanalytic theory of ego and id. Freud's mapping of the psyche divided between the representative of reason, reality and self-consciousness on the one hand, and that of nature and instinct on the other, is all too often hypostatized into the discovery of a natural phenomenon like plate tectonics. It would be more accurate to say, however, that ego/id represents the titanic struggle of western 'Man' with his otherness. Since racism, with its splitting of peoples and qualities is also part of this struggle, psychoanalytic theory is not simply a return to the polycentric view of mind; it is also a reading of the specific history in which polycentrism was replaced by the singular mental substance of the ego.

By making the ego move aside, as it were, to make room for the 'primitive' id, Freud broke ideologically with a modality grounded in the imperial process that had destroyed the aboriginal, 'primitive' world. Needless to say, he did not do so consciously or wholeheartedly. Indeed, the master psychoanalyst was not what one would call a friend to the coloured peoples. Like Hegel before him, Freud, along with a considerable proportion of the psychoanalytic movement, perpetuated the essentially racist notion that primitives were basically walking ids, and at the mental level of children. Writing of the group mind, for example, he states:

> Some of its features – the weakness of intellectual ability, the lack of emotional restraint, the incapacity for moderation and delay, the inclination to exceed every limit in the expression of emotion and to work it off completely in the form of action – these and similar features . . . show an unmistakable picture of a regression of mental activity to an earlier stage such as we are not surprised to find among savages or children.[24]

'Savages', in this view, are developmentally inferior, like children. They lack the full development of bourgeois reason and give free rein to every impulse: a familiar refrain in the history of racism. And if one believes this canard about primitives, it is not too difficult to hold similar opinions about those who can be identified as their heirs.

It may be said that, partially displaced or not, the ego remains king in the bourgeois ecumene, and will do so as long as capitalism defines social relations. Hence the normalization of 'ego psychology'. In fact, one could fairly claim capitalism as the regime of the ego. A system driven by competition and self-aggrandizement is conducive to establishing in each person a principle setting the self over and against all others. The same self-aggrandizement and the non-recognition of the other comprises the nuclear attitude of racism. Of course, capitalism's ego does not automatically turn racist. It will do so only under special circumstances, when its identity is destabilized and social dislocations threaten further collapse. This is warded off by the collective banding together and expulsion of contaminating otherness on to the racially selected target – a purification through the projection of persecutory hatred which comes naturally to the ego. Here is where the two levels of primitivity are linked together and the primitive is sacrificed for the good of the higher, purer social body. There have been any number of occasions where such a turn of events has happened, from the American South (and much of its North, too), to Nazi Germany, to today's Europe as it faces economic contraction and waves of migrants, themselves the products of global crisis. The regime of capital constantly overturns community and existing social relations in its drive to submit everything to the logic of accumulation. This in turn places identity under constant threat, creating a never-ending series of breeding grounds for racist outbreak – whether of the white variety or otherwise. In this respect, racisms ironically represent a kind of protest against the abstracting logic of capital. Their splitting defines a kind of difference which is then perverted; constructing a degraded race amounts to a kind of clinging to the primitive and the polycentric, though this is recognized only negatively, as delusion and hate. Whether the capitalist system can ever control these tendencies by creating a universal identity fully adapted to the society of accumulation, and therefore immune to the collective outbursts of persecutory hatred that characterize racism, is neither to be predicted nor evaluated here.

Logically, it might seem that there are two paths out of the recurrent nightmares of racism. Either, as noted above, to submit entirely to the prevailing order, that is, to dissolve identity and individuality into universal abstraction and exchange; or, on the other hand, to have such an identity as affirms difference. In reality, the two cases often seem combined. Thus the most advanced outposts of consumerism both celebrate and inculcate difference in order to commodify desire. One thinks here of Coca-Cola, which has promoted advertisements representing the gathering together of many youths of all colours under its aegis; or most spectacularly, the Benetton sweater corporation, which deliberately promotes colour and diversity, often representing socially controversial and even taboo matters in doing so. (A recent advertisement, for example, showed a naked male torso with 'HIV Positive' stamped on it.) The intent in these instances seems to be to stir up a portion of the desire sequestered in the racial (and sexual) other, then secure it for the sales of one's own product.

These are important manifestations of the postmodern sensibility churning up all representations and traditions for its purposes. They are also pathetically inadequate means for overcoming the interlocked structure configured by institutions, ideology and psychology which is racism. In truth, a manoeuvre which does no more than stimulate channels of commodity consumption can never uproot the institutional underpinnings of racism – in fact, its aim is to reinforce them. Nor does a superficial affirmation of difference suffice. If one is to begin a confrontation with racism, it should be on the ideological front (for ideology is the part of the troika most susceptible to change), to wage mental war on racist ideology in all its forms, [25] and then to go on to confront racist institutions. Can this be waged within psychotherapeutic institutions as well? Most definitely, both in terms of ideology and actual practices, to make practitioners more antiracist in their healing work, which is to say, more affirmative of genuine difference. The war will only be won, however, when society itself is transformed. This transformation will necessarily include profound shifts in the construction of the self, shifts which would be accompanied, one would think, by a bringing of the psychoanalytic revolution to fruition.

A society/self transcendent of racism is one that has returned to an aspect of its origins. We still have a lot to learn from the so-called primitives who appreciated the extent of human ambivalence and refused the mystification inherent in the belief of a unified ego. The prevalence of this latter belief represents the closing off of the self and the closing off of society: it is the groundwork of a racist development. The admirable acceptance of the trickster as part of the self signifies, on the other hand, a real recognition of difference. Those who know the radical nature of human being and who can take the other into the self need believe in neither the devil nor racially inferior human beings. They are freed from blackness and whiteness alike as abstract signs of a false, homogeneous being. As Blake put it in the words of his little black boy:

And thus I say to little English boy.
When I from black and he from white cloud free,
And round the tent of God like lambs we joy:

I'll shade him from the heat till he can bear,
To lean in joy upon our fathers knee.
And then I'll stand and stroke his silver hair.
And be like him and he will then love me.[26]

(Blake: *dedicated to the memory of Stanley Diamond*)

NOTES

1   *Flectere si nequeo superos. Acheronta movebo* (If I can't bend the higher powers, I shall stir up Hell – defined by the River Acheron). This aspect of Freud's character is discussed by Carl Schorske, 'Politics and patricide in Freud's interpretation of dreams' in *Fin de Siècle Vienna* (New York: Alfred A. Knopf, 1979), pp. 181–207.
2   'Future of an illusion', S.E. (1961), 21, 12.
3   The story here is complex and need be no more than suggested. In fact, Freud wavered on this point depending upon how pessimistic he was feeling. In *The Ego and the Id* (1923) he portrayed the ego as a poor victim of the id, super-ego and external world. Later, in *Inhibitions, Symptoms and Anxiety*, the ego emerged as much more capable of handling itself. This text, not surprisingly, became favoured by the therapeutic establishment. In any case, however much Freud may have wavered on his prognosis for the rule of ego and its 'still, small voice' of reason, there can be no doubt that such a rule was desired by him.

4 The term 'primitive' is not much used these days, owing to the pejorative connotation of being backward and childish. This, of course, is a direct product of western ethnocentricity. We might as well think of primitive as 'primary' and original. In any case, we append the sense of 'state-free' to assert the distinguishing feature of primitive life, the absence of social class and the superordinate social regulation of the state which inevitably attend social class. See Stanley Diamond, *In Search of the Primitive* (New Brunswick, NJ: Transaction Books, 1974): Pierre Clastres, *Society Against the State*, trans. Robert Hurley and Abe Stein (New York: Zone Books, 1987).

5 'Civilization and its discontents', S.E. (1961) 21.

6 See my *History and Spirit* (Boston: Beacon Press, 1991).

7 An argument developed by Bruno Bettelheim, *Freud and Man's Soul* (New York: Alfred A. Knopf, 1983). For a critique, see *History and Spirit*, op. cit., 251–3.

8 Mircea Eliade, *Shamanism*, trans. Willard Trask (Princeton: Princeton University Press (1964) 1972).

9 Paul Radin, *The Trickster* (New York: Schocken, 1972 [1956]), pp. xxiii–xxiv. The work is mostly devoted to the trickster cycle of Winnebago Indians of what is now Wisconsin. See also Stanley Diamond, 'Job and the trickster', in *In Search of the Primitive*, 281–91.

10 Radin, op. cit., 168–9.

11 Space does not permit the discussion of this notion with respect to 'actually existing' primitive, state-free societies. Some comments about native Americans, along with further references to the very extensive literature, may be found in Chapter 10 of my *Red Hunting in the Promised Land* (New York: Basic Books, 1994).

12 Karl Kerenyi, 'The trickster in relation to Greek mythology', in Radin, op. cit., 188.

13 Joel Kovel, 'Mind and state in Ancient Greece', in *The Radical Spirit* (London: Free Association Books, 1988), pp. 208–25; Stanley Diamond, 'Plato and the definition of the primitive', in *In Search of The Primitive*, op. cit. 176–202.

14 E.R. Dodds, *The Greeks and the Irrational* (Berkeley: University of California Press, 1951), 270–82.

15 See Hans Peter Duerr, *Dreamtime*, trans. Felicatas Goodman (Oxford: Blackwell, 1985), for a discussion of the 'wandering' of the witch.

16 Jean DeLumeau, *Sin and Fear,* trans. Eric Nicholson (New York: St Martin's Press, 1991).

17 Needless to say, nationalism and racism are regularly intertwined in the real world. Further discussion here would be beyond the scope of this essay.

18 See T.W. Adorno, Else Frenkel-Brunswik, Daniel J. Levinson and R. Nevitt Sanford, *The Authoritarian Personality* (New York: Harper & Brothers, 1950).

19 Much of this argument is based upon my *White Racism: A Psychohistory* (New York: Columbia University Press, 1984 (1970)). It also constitutes. so to speak, further thoughts about the argument of that work.

20 It should be pointed out, however, that the slave society of the American South was, relative to the North, far more given over to a pre-capitalist, even aristocratic ideal. This is by way of saying that southern chattel slavery, while of the capitalist system, was backward within the terms of that system when compared to the society of the North. It flourished only because of international circuits of trade and, lacking sufficient internal markets, was eventually doomed. None the less it still contained enough elements of capitalist logic to ensure a radically dehumanized mode of enslavement.

21 For a refutation of the still very widely held idea that race connotes more than the obvious distinctions of skin colour, hair, etc., see Richard Lewontin, 'Are the races different?', in Dawn Gill and Les Levidow (eds.) *Anti-Racist Science Teaching* (London: Free Association Books, 1987), pp. 198–207. Lewontin shows that genetic differences between 'races' are far less than genetic differences between individuals of the same 'race'. In other words, there is no such thing as race except as a kind of idea or a classification of superficial distinctions. For a study of essentialism and scientific racism (particularly as applied to the study of 'intelligence'), see Stephen Jay Gould, *The Mismeasure of Man* (New York: W.W. Norton, 1981).

22 For an extended discussion, see Kovel, *White Racism*, op. cit., 107–76.
23 David Musto, *The American Disease* (New Haven: Yale University Press, 1973), p. 7.
24 'Group psychology and the analysis of the ego' (SE 18: 117). The passage also reveals, of course, Freud's hostility to collective praxis. Then there is the following, from 'On narcissism' in which Freud claims that in the mental life of primitives, 'we find characteristics which, if they occurred singly, might be put down to megalomania' (S.E.14: 75).
25 As, for example, in Gill and Levidow, *Anti-Racist Science Teaching*, op. cit., 198–207
26 David Erdman (ed.), *The Complete Poetry and Prose of William Blake* (Garden City: Doubleday, 1982), p. 9.

12 Lacan, Klein and politics

The positive and negative in psychoanalytic thought

Michael Rustin

INTRODUCTION

In Britain, at any rate, most recent political thinking influenced by the psychoanalytic tradition has been left-of-centre in its tendency. This is true of both the contrasting major currents which have influenced wider social debate – the school of Lacan, mainly influential through cultural and philosophical studies, and the Kleinian and object relations traditions, whose main basis in Britain and elsewhere has been in clinical work, both in private practice and in the National Health Service and the voluntary sector.

In the case of Lacanian ideas, a radical political orientation derives from its linkages with elements of the 'Marxisant' tradition, and with the broader positioning of the French intelligentsia through much of the post-war period as the carrier of values of authenticity and culture against a bourgeoisie of supposed conformity and materialism. The intransigence of the Lacanian psychoanalytic attitude to conventional orthodoxies and self-definitions of all kinds resonated with the insurrectionary utopianism of the May events of 1968 and won new followers from its fall-out. The sceptical, deconstructive and 'antagonistic' qualities of Lacanian practice (which did not preclude its adopting compensating forms of sectarian closure of its own) seemed to fit certain continuing attributes of French elite oppositional culture, defining itself as the inheritor of two centuries of iconoclastic struggles against the *ancien régime*. But in the 1970s, as Marxism and rational progressivism became themselves identified as oppressive orthodoxies, tainted by the catastrophic defaults of Communist practice, the deconstructive and 'postmodern' affinities of Lacanian thinking became more significant, and ensured that it remained relevant in this different political moment.

The influence of this tradition in Britain since the 1970s reflected a broader interest in Parisian ideas during this period, as the Anglo-centric cast of post-war political thinking (both of left and right) lessened and became subjected to critique. The expansion of higher education enlarged the public for critical ideas, and culture and communications in their various aspects became influential fields of study. Conventional notions of individual identity and responsibility, whose implicit assumptions about male gender, British nationality, white ethnicity and middle-class status became increasingly visible, were questioned from various critical viewpoints. The idea that a fixed and given identity could no longer be assumed – that identities were socially constructed, often coercively, and not naturally given – became central to cultural debate. Lacanian psychoanalysis provided one significant theoretical resource in the development of this critique. The intellectual milieu in which these ideas have flourished was already a leftish one. Lacanian psychoanalytic ideas provided a valuable idiom for calling into question conventional assumptions about identity.

The left-of-centre affiliations of mainstream psychoanalysis in Britain were usually much milder, from the first association of psychoanalysis with the rationalist reformers of the Bloomsbury group (progressive within its elite milieu in sexual, educational, artistic, colonial and economic matters) through to identification with the goals of social reconstruction of the post-war period, especially as these affected the family and social integration. Psychoanalysis had some influence on the development of child psychiatry in particular in the post-war period, through the development of the child guidance service (now being dismantled as a result of National Health Service and education 'reforms'), and for a time was a major influence in the development of social work. Nearly all of the psychoanalytically trained professionals who came to work in the NHS, at institutions such as the Cassell Hospital and the Tavistock Clinic, seem to have developed deep loyalty to the principles of a universal health service with a community, curative and preventive mental health dimension. Though at one stage that would have seemed a merely conventional professional commitment, it now marks its adherents as relative radicals in the post-Thatcher climate of 'full marketization'. The underlying ideas which mark this out as a 'left-of-centre' political orientation are the commitment to the application of 'scientific under-standing' to social improvement via public policy. And also, at least measured against the ultra-individualist ideological climate of Britain, the idea that social bonds and responsibilities need to be valued even where they require intervention against market forces.

The 'progressive' leanings of some sections of the British psychoanalytic movement are not, however, only explained by identification with the reforms of the welfare state. There has been a deeper tendency to define the goals of authentic personal development, whether understood ethically, emotionally or even cognitively, against the conventional norms of society and its authority structures. This amounts to the identification of psychoanalysis with a conception of 'culture' defined to some degree in opposition to the values of a merely materialist or power-seeking society. The importance attached to the arts (for example in the work of Hanna Segal and Donald Winnicott) and the significant influence of psychoanalysis on art criticism in Britain indicate the expressive values with which psychoanalysis was identified. Even in the sphere of industrial organization and consultancy, psychoanalytic ideas have mostly supported consensual and democratic approaches, in opposition to more hard-line coercive approaches to management. The development of the campaign of psychoanalysts against nuclear war in the 1980s, involving some of the most prominent members of the British

Psychoanalytical Society, is the clearest evidence of this dissenting orientation. The guiding assumption of this campaign was that the psychic structures sustaining the Cold War – even perhaps conventional forms of political organization in general – were largely paranoid–schizoid in quality. The psychoanalytic paradigm proposes an approach to conflict based on understanding of its internal and external dynamics, rather than on outward projections of destructiveness.

Facilitating this non-conforming and quietly oppositional stance was the seclusion of psychoanalytic practice in Britain within a very small professional community, which has since its beginnings in the 1920s given priority to its own 'purity' of practice over the claims of wide diffusion or popularization. (In this respect it contrasts markedly with the experience of the psychoanalytic movement in the United States.) Lacan's outspoken criticisms of the conversion of psychoanalytic ideas in America into a practice of social adaptation is implicitly echoed by the choice of the British analysts to develop the most fundamental and intractable elements of Freud's view of the unconscious, at whatever cost to comforting assumptions about the innate goodness of human nature or about the prospects of willed self-improvement. The recruitment of so significant a part of the British analytic community from refugees from Nazism not only gave it some innately radical sympathies but also impeded its complete assimilation into mainstream British society.

To identify the British and French psychoanalytic communities with a perceptibly left-of-centre orientation is to say nothing that might not also be said of Freud himself. Psychoanalysis offered rational 'scientific' ways of thinking about aspects of human nature conventionally theorized at the turn of the century in religious or prescriptively ethical terms. Freud's insistence that unconscious, irrational aspects of the mind could be brought within the scope of understanding was a (late) manifestation of the self-confidence of European rationalism, part of the Enlightenment.[1] Freud's ideas challenged the authority of the family, the church and *ancien régime* society in Europe, and supported the development of more open-ended, deliberative and non-coercive forms of social arrangement, for example in regard to the upbringing of children or the enforcement of sexual morality. While Freud was a liberal individualist, and an opponent of utopian ideologies of the left as well as of the right, his individualism in its own time if not in ours marked him as a 'progressive' figure, whose ideas were regarded as profoundly subversive by conservatives. The conception that *everything* can be properly brought into question and made the subject of rational deliberation and choice is itself a foundation of the rationalist view of progress. Hatred of this idea is evident in the current demands of conservatives in Britain and the United States to reimpose conventional morality, respect for tradition and obedience to authority in many spheres.

However, the generally progressive and rationalist orientation of the psycho-analytic movement has not prevented the emergence of deep differences in the form this radicalism has taken in the two psychoanalytic traditions of Lacan and the British object relations school. These differences are the main subject of this chapter. There has been some antagonism between these traditions, and serious difficulties in communication across their boundaries. The purpose of this chapter is to clarify their differences of approach, and to attempt to achieve, if not a reconciliation between them, at least some indication of what each can offer to a progressive social philosophy.

THE NEGATIVE AND THE POSITIVE IN PSYCHOANALYSIS

These differences can be set out in the following way. On the one hand, there is an emphasis in the Lacanian tradition on the necessarily 'negative' and 'antagonistic' aspects of psychoanalytic and other 'critical' forms of social thought. The idea of the 'negative' focuses attention on the inherent limits of human self-understanding, and the inherent distortions and falsifications involved in representation. The psychoanalytic process in this view links the idea of authenticity (itself impossible to achieve) to the questioning of the symbolic and imaginary structures by which misrecognitions are sustained. By contrast, the object relations and Kleinian traditions postulate a 'positive' core of ideas about human nature and its more benign forms of development. (By 'positive' is meant capable of being specified in empirical and logical terms, not 'morally ideal', although attached to the various developmental 'positions' and typified emotional states of this model are value implications and preferences.) The first tradition is above all adapted to the unending investigation of the inauthentic, idealized and self-regarding aspects of human consciousness. The second tradition regards psychoanalytic investigation not only as a method of recognition of illusions and self-deceptions, but also as a source of grounded understanding of 'authentic' states of feeling and object relations, conceived as the foundation of creative forms of life. The first tradition can lead, at worst, to merely nihilistic 'deconstructive' skepticism about the possibility of sustainable identities of either individual or social kinds. The second, at worst, can dogmatically enforce a prescriptive moralism which can be no less self-deceiving than the pathological states of mind it seeks to supplant. I propose to describe the construction of each of these traditions of psychoanalytic thought, as they apply to politics. The account will be highly selective, concerned not to document the whole field of relevant literature, but to clarify the central ideas of each tradition.

ALTHUSSER AND PSYCHOANALYSIS

The influence of Lacanian ideas on British political and cultural thought can be traced originally to the (brief) period of hegemony of Althusserian and more broadly structuralist ideas on the new left intelligentsia in Britain during the 1970s. At this early stage, Lacan's linguistically-centred approach to Freud was primarily of interest because it explained the self-deceiving properties of language and culture, central to the new critical interest in ideology as a form of social control. A more fully psychoanalytic interpretation of these ideas, giving due attention to emotion and phantasy, came later in the work of writers such as Žižek.

Althusser's thought was distinguished by its commitment to establishing or re-establishing the theoretical explicitness and rigour of Marxism, during a time when a grand political compromise was being sought (the attempted construction of a Catholic–Marxist *rapprochement* around a common 'humanism').[2] But also notable was Althusser's attempt to incorporate within Marxism a new recognition of the weight of cultural, ideological and linguistic forms in maintaining social domination and order. Althusser's work was 'structuralist' and 'culturalist' in its insistence on the encoding within a society dominated by the capitalist means of production of the ideology necessary for its reproduction. Institutions whose 'work' was the inculcation of social norms and beliefs (the family, schools, religion, mass communications) thus acquired an importance within Althusserian Marxism which they had not conventionally been given in the more 'economistic' versions of Marxism.

This insight gave a new implicit emphasis to institutions – such as the family – which had always been a primary site of psychoanalytic interest. Althusser was however interested at a more abstract cultural level in the mode of construction of individual and social identity. He found psychoanalytic ideas, as these had been interpreted in somewhat 'linguistic' and 'structuralist' ways in Lacan's work, of value in understanding the mechanisms of ideological transmission through which identity was constructed. It should be remembered that Althusser regarded individuals, in an extreme form of social determinism, as largely the constructions of the social order, bearers of social roles given to them by structural mechanisms. This view required some account to be given of how individuals came to recognize themselves in these roles, and thus to take on the self-definitions which would allow them to be discharged. These 'self-recognitions' were, in Althusser's view, necessarily 'misrecognitions', since they required individuals who in reality were constrained as subordinate class subjects to perceive themselves as free individual agents.

Lacan's (and Freud's) view of language as inherently self-deceptive and mystifying proved an invaluable resource in understanding this (alleged) general situation of misrepresentation and misrecognition. Lacan pointed out the parallels between the ideas of condensation and displacement that Freud used in *The Interpretation of Dreams* (1900) to explain the relationship between dreams and neurotic symptoms and unconscious desires, and the functions of metaphor and metonymy in language. This parallel between these key ideas of structural linguistics and Freud's dream theory had first been noted by Roman Jakobson in his work on metaphor and metonymy as two poles of linguistic organization.[3] The understandings that slippages and transformations of meaning were normal attributes both of language (in linguistic theory) and the mind as it was shaped by the unconscious (according to psychoanalysis) dispelled the conventional fixity of relationship between symbol and its referent. The mind was shown to be inveterately capable of using the signifying chains of language to 'hide' its desires from its internal censor, and to represent them in these disguised and metaphoric terms.

Lacan elaborated these ideas to explain the process of construction of identity in infancy as involving a kind of narcissistic illusion. This depended in part on the prior facticity of linguistic signifiers and on the encoding within language of the constituting categories of the adult world (the symbolic realm and 'the name of the father').[4] To the extent that language was learned, it imposed on to the subject the differences which constituted the world, including the differences (e.g. of gender and generational position) which constituted the subject. But the encounter with language and the other was a dynamic process, in which both the innate desires or drives of the self, and its wish to constitute itself as an ideal and complete subject (the 'mirror stage' described this moment) joined in the constituting of 'the unconscious' and its dramas. Language, which in structuralist or functionalist terms is merely the vehicle for a more or less complex set of role impositions, becomes a field of conflict and self-deception in this psychoanalytic theory, in which what is given as a representation does not correspond to reality, or is what it seems to be. Being inherently outside the symbolic realm, neither desires nor idealized images of the self (the realms of the real and the imaginary, respectively) are capable of being fully represented within it. It is this imperfect and deceptive fit between symbolic representation and psychic realities which defines the field within which psychoanalysis can work. There is, in the last resort, an irreparable schism between 'the unconscious' and the phenomena of the conscious mind. The idea of a transparency or sufficiency of representation (a self that would have no more mysteries or self-deceptions to be uncovered) is in this view merely another kind of narcissistic illusion. Incorporating Lacan's idea of an 'imaginary ideal self' as the core of an individual's identity, Althusser developed his idea of ideology as an imaginary relation to *social* identity. This idea is the key to Althusser's work on the function of ideology in society and on the construction of the individual subject through 'interpellation' as an essentially ideological (that is, mystifying) process.

At the level of the individual, Freud (and Lacan) believed neurotic symptoms to be constructed through the transposition of desires and their representations. Symptoms represented in a 'distorted' form contradictions between unconscious desires that could never be grasped, in a wholly transparent way, owing to the effects of the mechanisms of resistance. Althusser adapted this idea to explain the operations of social contradictions. He argued that conflicts ultimately based on the mode and relations of production (class conflicts) were in practice masked, elided, misrepresented and displaced in ideological forms, often manifesting themselves as conflicts of other kinds and at other levels of the social formation. The 'linguistic' mechanisms of displacement and condensation could thus also operate within the social realm.[5] Since 'society' had an irreducibly cultural dimension (the ideological definitions by which individuals defined their social roles) social determinations operated via the meanings which were assigned by 'subjects' to events and instances. Contradictory, condensed and associative structures of meaning constituted the social world. The linear simplicities of mechanistic models of causation now needed to be replaced by a model which recognized a kind of innate indeterminacy of social processes, derived from the ambiguities and multiple interpretations that were assigned to social facts by agents and subjects. Althusser's idea that despite all this the mode and relations of production remained determinant 'in the last instance' seems more like an act of faith or a wager on history's eventual outcome than a law from which empirical generalizations or predictions could be derived.

Thus, through chains of metaphoric and synecdochal association, social conflicts could now be expected to find expression in locations relatively remote from their underlying roots. While in principle Althusser believed in the possibility of understanding and predicting 'conjunctures' by which revolutionary transformations might become possible, the psychoanalytic metaphors built into his theory suggested that full understanding of such complex chains of causality were unlikely to be achieved.

The deep structure of this argument seems to deal with the classical problems of the relations of 'base and superstructure' in Marxist thought by an analogy with Lacan's theory of the relations between desire and symbolic representation. Just as the 'real' cannot be directly apprehended, except through representations which are inherently partial, and which actively shape that which they seek to represent, so, in Althusser's Marxism, the economic base is never visible as the direct determinant of the social formation. It is evident only through its effects upon a complex of other levels and instances. Ideology *necessarily* mystifies the truth of this situation, since its clarification (through the understanding of 'science') would trigger (in Althusser's view) a recognition by subordinate classes of their rational interest in an alternative social order. It is the primary objective of the ruling classes, and those identified with them, to prevent such recognition, and in this objective they are most of the time successful.

In some respects, this implicit analogy between the unconscious 'base' of psychic life, and the 'material' base of social formation, seems a surprising and invalid one. There is no reason to expect that economic interests will manifest and disguise themselves in the social and cultural system in the same way that instinctual desires represent and misrepresent themselves in psychic life.[6] But even if the drives and forces in question are quite distinct from one another, some genuine explanatory power was derived both from the linguistic analogy which linked these two fields, and from the idea that the processes of internal 'censorship' which generated an 'unconscious' mind in psychoanalysis had their equivalent in societal mechanisms of 'ideological' misrepresentation and 'repression'.

What in fact gives this analogy such persuasiveness as it has is the common 'structuralist' presuppositions which underlay both Althusser's reading of Marx and Lacan's reading of Freud. These theories are linked mainly by the priority which both of them give to linguistic structures and processes.

In the social world, the enhanced role of mass communications in maintaining consent in the affluent societies of the 1960s and 1970s justified this new emphasis on the ideological and symbolic spheres, within which indeed political conflicts in the West seemed at the time to be mostly fought out. (Later, in the Thatcher–Bush period, blunter instruments were deployed to try to put down the liberated devils of the 1960s.) The May events of 1968, crucial in defining the terms of radical politics in this period, were more a symbolic enactment of a revolutionary moment of liberation of the mind than a material struggle for institutional power. The force of the psychoanalytic metaphor in this discourse derived from the idea that ideology was most effective when its distortions, its one-sidedness, its silences, and omissions became implicit and taken-for-granted routines, not depending on overt prohibition. Control was most insidious, so the critics of ideology suggested, when it had become invisible. This situation conversely conferred a privileged role on 'intellectuals' of all kinds as the enlightened bearers of the truth.

Studies of mass communications in Britain at the Centre for Contemporary Cultural Studies in the 1970s made effective empirical use of these conceptions. The analysis of television broadcasting by Stuart Hall and others identified codes which both defined a space for legitimate and notionally open debate, but then by a variety of framing techniques marginalized opinions and attitudes which lay outside an accepted consensus. Definitions of 'good broadcasting' couched in terms of media convention and technique were shown to be the terms in which broadcasters themselves justified their day-to-day decisions. The political constraints and biases which overlay the whole system of journalism, in both its press and broadcast forms, could thus be for operational purposes 'not seen', and practitioners were able to work with idealized conceptions of freedom and impartiality which did not correspond to the deep structure of their output.

This analysis exposed a kind of 'unconscious' repression of uncomfortable and disturbing areas of conflict, and their management through the 'rationalizations' of 'professional' values and techniques. A different application of these ideas by the same group of writers identified as a specific political strategy of the right the 'displacement' and 'condensation' of social conflict into opportune kinds of populist appeal. Hall *et al.*'s *Policing the Crisis* (1978) attempted to 'decode' the focus on the crime of 'mugging' in the 1970s as a coded reference to race. It saw the implicit or explicit focus on the issue of race, in American and British politics in the period, as a displacement of attention from more pervasive and deep-seated conflicts of class and social subordination more generally, and as the 'condensation' of antagonism on to a vulnerable scapegoat group. Subsequent analysis (Edsall and Edsall 1992) of the success of the American Republicans in re-segmenting the American electorate on racial lines throughout the 1970s and 1980s has amply borne out the prescience of Hall's argument.

The main point of this appropriation of psychoanalysis was that it problematized issues of language and representation, hitherto taken as essentially unproblematic in much Marxist discourse. It had been taken as unproblematic, that is to say, in that different ideological 'discourses' were held to reflect the interests and world-views of different social classes and their representative intellectuals. The task of revolutionary politics had in this perspective been to replace 'false consciousness' with rationality. Althusser and those influenced by him saw that a simplistic relation of reflection or correspondence between material base and symbolic superstructure would no longer do. It had to be recognized that all ideological discourses were inherently deceptive, and furthermore were effective precisely *because* of their deceptive character.

The idea that societies bound their citizens through complex structures of representation led Althusser to see social conflict and upheaval as inherently contingent, more analogous to a psychic breakdown or catastrophe triggered by some traumatic event or other, than to the earlier idea of a more or less predictable mechanical collapse. Specific moments (e.g. the May events of 1968) could detonate into major explosions because of the way in which an inherently insignificant conflict (the closing of the *Cinematheque*, instances of brutality of Paris police, etc.) could become an emblem or symbolic condensation of more pervasive lines of conflict. Revolutionary outbreaks were no longer seen as the accumulation of energy finally breaking down a dam of authority relations, imagined as a concentration of physical force, but instead as a contingent conjunction of contradictions fused at the symbolic level by unpredictable events.

At a deeper level, the analogy between the psychoanalytic and historical materialist kinds of explanation depended on their common subscription to a 'realist' theory of knowledge more than on their substantive presuppositions about human nature or society. Both theoretical systems held that human behaviour needed to be understood by reference to theoretical entities whose existence had to be inferred from their empirical effects. Both held that agents' understanding of themselves and their world were not only unavoidably incomplete, but were also distorted in systematic and motivated ways. Enlightenment, for both, was interpreted as the replacement of 'distorted' by undistorted versions of reality. Clearly both systems also cast their 'scientists' or intellectuals in the role of emancipators, facilitating rational understanding in place of illusion. Of course it is a fundamental question whether such claims to the possibility of rational knowledge are valid, or whether on the contrary they depend on merely dogmatic or revelatory presuppositions, the secular successors of earlier religious versions of revealed and privileged truth.[7]

It is certainly at this abstract level of ontology and epistemology that the first encounter between structuralist Marxism and psychoanalysis took place. It was in understanding the role of the symbolic in constituting individual subjectivity and the social order, the consequences of this for causality and determination, and the relations between the illusory and the real, that Althusser found Freud to be relevant to his own theoretical project. It was in its inveterate skepticism, in its deconstruction of the everyday and the taken for granted, that Freud's and Lacan's work was found to be of exemplary interest.

ERNESTO LACLAU AND 'POST-MARXISM'

Lacan's first significant influence on socialist thinking was through his influence on Althusser and French structuralist Marxism. Ernesto Laclau's earlier work on populism (1977) had drawn on Althusser's uses of concepts of interpellation, condensation and displacement to understand how ideological definitions were constructed and rendered effective, still at this point within the framework of the Marxist idea that class contradictions remained the ultimate determinants of these structures. But in the 1980s Ernesto Laclau and Chantal Mouffe (in *Hegemony and Socialist Strategy* (1985)), broke with the orthodox Marxist foundations of their earlier position, declaring themselves to be 'post-Marxists'. They argued that whilst the recognition by Gramsci and Althusser of the relative autonomy of the political and ideological spheres had been an advance on previous formulations, their questioning of economic determinations had not gone far enough. The positing of 'objective grounds' to which ideological and political action had to be related denied the necessary contingency (perhaps an oxymoronic contradiction within Laclau and Mouffe's later thought) of political action. Social action, they argued, was inherently constituted by a process of symbolic definition and choice, and could not be derived as a 'reflection' of some prior reality. This position led them to ultra-voluntarist[8] though still radical conclusions, in that they came to define the political task as the constituting of political antagonisms through discourse. Political action was defined as the gathering together of different oppositions (for example, the various 'new social movements' and their resistances to both capitalist and authoritarian states) into a counter-hegemonic force. 'Democracy' and civil rights were seen as the potential unifying discourses of this new revolutionary politics.

Laclau, in an essay in his *New Reflections on the Revolution of our Time* (1990), discusses the relation of psychoanalysis to this new 'post-Marxist' position. He proposes the replacement of an earlier conception of the relation between psychoanalysis and Marxism, in which psychoanalysis had been viewed as supplementing an area of insufficiency within Marxism. Where Marx could be said to have identified the causal centrality of the economic level, Freud had been seen as the discoverer of another key level of determination, that of the unconscious and its instinctual drives. A psychoanalytically-informed Marxism would, according to this programme, bring to bear a commitment to rational self-understanding on both levels. It would thus free humankind from the unrecognized constraints of both material and unconscious levels of determination. Marx and Freud were thus both identified by Laclau as theorists of the rationalist Enlightenment, though of course he recognized that their respective paradigms had been much more powerful and influential in their separate versions than in their combined form.

But the distinctive interest even of Marx's work for Laclau is now in its implicit departures from a rationalist or Enlightenment form of positive knowledge, not in the respects in which it conforms to it. Understanding of the causal properties of the social world is not, for Laclau, Marxism's most important contribution to understanding. By analogy, therefore, nor is Freud's most significant contribution to be seen as his 'positive' understanding of the causal properties of the psychic or unconscious worlds. Laclau identifies two

> decisive points where Marxism breaks with the tradition of the Enlightenment. These points are (a) the affirmation of the central character of negativity – struggle and antagonism – in the structure of any collective identity; and (b) the affirmation of the opaqueness of the social – the ideological nature of collective representations – which establishes a permanent gap between the real and the manifest senses of individual and social group actions.
>
> (Laclau 1990: 94)

Laclau goes on to acknowledge that Marxism is not only a 'discourse of negativity and the opaqueness of the social'. It is also an attempt – perfectly compatible with the Enlightenment – to limit and master them. The negativity and opaqueness of the social only exist in 'human prehistory, which will be definitely surpassed by communism conceived as a homogeneous and transparent society'. Marxism, for Laclau, is thus the moment of both antagonism/negativity/ opaqueness and of mastery/transparency/rationalism. Laclau and Mouffe's project of 'post-Marxism' aims mainly to detach radicalism or socialism from its 'positive' origins in this 'rationalist half' of Marx, not least because of the distortions and oppressions to which the 'closure' of Marxism around its positive definitions of class and mode of production had led.

It is thus the 'negative' and 'antagonistic' aspects of the Lacanian psycho-analytic perspective that are of interest to Laclau from this post-Marxist perspective. Laclau argues that there is never a rational correspondence between ideological articulations and their intended objects. While they present themselves as descriptive or explanatory categories, political definitions are inherently ideological, attempting to perform by 'practice' what they ostensibly define as existent or necessary. It is the unavoidable 'gap' between symbolic definition and its objects which provides the key point of analogy between the post-Marxist concept of hegemony and the Lacanian approach to psychoanalysis. This is similar to Althusser's earlier uses of the psychoanalytic analogue to understand the misrepresentations of ideology as described earlier.

In Lacanian psychoanalysis, as Laclau points out, the category of lack is the main point of departure. Both in the modes of the imaginary (phantasy) and the symbolic (the sphere of language) the individual is doomed to misrepresent his or her desires, which have been dislocated and rendered 'impossible' at their point of infantile origin. Psychoanalysis reveals to us how this misrepresentation takes place, and uncovers the plurality of meanings and the motivating desires that underlie both symbolic and imaginary representations of ourselves and others. But since humans are divided from themselves and others both by their constitution in language itself and by the phantasied misrecognition of the self as 'ego-ideal', there is no prospect of achieving a transparency of self-recognition, or the full realization of desire.[9]

What attracts Laclau to this perspective is its dominant category of the 'impossible',[10] since his opponent in all these arguments is the 'false closure' inherent in orthodox Marxist utopias and in teleological theories of history. Laclau wishes to establish that all 'utopias' (states of desire at a social level) are in a particular sense 'impossible'. That is, they are constituted and reconstituted only by our unceasing efforts of will and do not correspond to any necessary truth about ourselves.

The link that Laclau proposes between post-Marxism and Lacanian psycho-analysis is 'around the logic of the signifier as a logic of unevenness and dislocation, a coincidence grounded on the fact that the latter is the logic which presides over the possibility/impossibility of the constitution of any identity' (Laclau 1990: 96).

In the work of Althusser and those influenced by him, psychoanalytic ideas were influential primarily as ways of understanding the properties of the symbolic sphere. As increased explanatory weight was thrown on to this domain in explaining both the persistence and the intermittent breakdown of legitimate order, so intellectual tools which seemed to explain the relation of individuals to symbolic representations became theoretically crucial.

From a psychoanalytic point of view, the idea of a libidinal investment by individuals in such representations is also essential to explain their potency as forms of control and subordination. But this idea of libidinal investment in group representations played only a small part in the theoretical system of structuralist Marxism, which always preferred a cultural to an affective or instinctual level of explanation. But its implicit presence as an explanation of the motivational energy 'locked up' in ideological belief, explaining why it *could* have such social potency, remained to be exploited by subsequent writers in this tradition such as Laclau and Žižek.

SLAVOJ ŽIŽEK

An application of Lacanian ideas to politics which is more fully psychoanalytic in its emphasis has recently been made by Slavoj Žižek (1989, 1990, 1991). His article 'East Europe's republics of Gilead' (1990) provides a succinct and politically insightful example of his method of argument.

Žižek's argument at a theoretical level is that the 'post-structuralist' account of ideology as a discursive structure fails to account for the power of ideology and the energy it is able to canalize and release. Žižek (1990) clarifies Lacan's differences with 'discursive idealism' (that is, theories of purely ideological or cultural determination). He notes that 'discursive effects' in themselves do have the power to sustain social motivations. 'The Lacanian term for the strange "substance" that must be added to enable a cause to exert its positive ontological consistency – the only "substance" acknowledged by psychoanalysis – is, of course, enjoyment.'

> A nation exists only as long as its specific enjoyment continues to be materialised in certain social practices, and transmitted in national myths that structure these practices. To emphasise, in a 'deconstructive' mode, that the Nation is not a biological or transhistorical fact but a contingent discursive construction, an overdetermined result of textual practices, is thus misleading: it overlooks the role of a remainder of some real non-discursive kernel of enjoyment which must be present for the Nation *qua* discursive–entity–effect to achieve its ontological consistency.
>
> (Žižek 1990: 52–3)

More concretely, Žižek applies this argument to the resurgence of nationalism and racism in Eastern Europe:

> To explain this unexpected turn, we have to rethink the most elementary notions about national identification – and here, psychoanalysis can be of help. The element that holds together a given community cannot be reduced to the point of symbolic identification: the bond linking its members always implies a

shared relationship towards a Thing, towards Enjoyment incarnated. This relationship towards a Thing, structured by means of fantasies, is what is at stake when we speak of the menace to our 'way of life' presented by the Other: it is what is threatened when, for example a white Englishman is panicked because of the growing presence of 'aliens'. It is this eruption of 'Enjoyment' which explains what is happening in the East just at the point when the West is narcissistically admiring the incarnation of its Ego-Ideal of democracy in a more passionate form than it usually has in the routine politics of the West.

(Žižek 1990: 51–2)

Žižek in this essay and his other works sets out to explore the phantasy identifications which are embodied in political life.[11] His argument, consistent with that of Freud, is that such phenomena need to be acknowledged as substantive dimensions of any actual political process. Failure to take account of the phantasy dimensions of political attachment to them can lead to counter-productive political practices. Žižek argued elsewhere for example that the theory of the authoritarian personality developed by Adorno and his colleagues in the 1930s represented an attack on the 'enjoyment' of working-class communities. He has suggested that the bussing of children in America in the cause of anti-discrimination in the 1960s represented an attack on the 'enjoyment' (i.e. the phantasy coherence) of black communities. The objects of antagonism in nationalist and racist xenophobias are split-off states of mind that cannot be acknowledged or incorporated within a community's own being. The lifting of prohibitions on all kinds of desires, thoughts and emotions as a result of the collapse of totalitarianism thus generates an excess of phantasy, which is thus dealt with in violent projective forms.

'Enjoyment' in this form of 'irrational' states of persecution or paranoia is analogous to the satisfaction obtained from a neurotic symptom. By Freud's definition, a symptom must give pleasure, or at least alleviate pain. The peculiar and apparently 'unpleasurable' nature of many symptoms reveals the inner conflict that is raging, making the indirect and distorted 'discharge' of the symptom the most pleasurable form of expression available. It is because of the 'unpleasurable' form that much 'enjoyment' takes that Žižek is at pains to insist on the distinction between the terms 'pleasure' and 'enjoyment'. 'Enjoyment' is much closer to Freud's idea of libidinal discharge, though parallels are complicated by the linguistic turn which Lacanian psychoanalysis has given to Freud's model of the mind.

There are many jokes in Žižek's writings, and these jokes have a characteristically East European quality to them. Freud (1905) saw jokes as forms of discharge for forbidden desires. Such desires were able to escape 'censorship' by appearing in disguise, in a narrative which 'pretended' to be one common-sensical thing whilst in fact allowing another interpretation. The sense of joy and release which arises from seeing the point of a joke comes, according to Freud, from the release of a discharge of repressed feeling. (We might now see these feelings as encompassing a broader range than did Freud, notably including sentiments of hatred as well as desire.)

Žižek's East European jokes are characteristically those of a totalitarian society, in which everything is the opposite of what it is officially claimed to be, and complete skepticism about any official definition of the world whatsoever may seem the most viable cognitive strategy for those who value the truth. Such jokes compete with one another to construct a sense of the absurd, so ludicrous is an existence in which everything that is stated publicly is liable, in one way or another, to be a lie.

The extremity of Žižek's representation of the 'symbolic' as a wholly arbitrary and constructed world, bearing little or no relation to the truth of experience, seems likely to be related to the cultural experience of Communism. The Lacanian split between the symbolic, as imposed on the self, and its inchoate, unstatable desires seems to have its most plausible embodiment when the social universe that is evoked is one which is especially authoritarian and resistant to democratic self-construction.

Conversely, the idea of an especially deep split between the real, the sphere of desire and phantasy, and its expression or representation, is given plausibility by implicit reference to a world in which all desire is socially repressed and deadened. The emergence of the imaginary from repression in the form of an excess of desire attaching itself to phantasied ideal objects, or projected negatively towards threats to a fragile new narcissistic identity, may also take its characteristic form from this post-totalitarian social experience. Thus, the distance between the real, the imaginary and the symbolic in Laclau's and Žižek's worlds reflects a specific social condition in which ideological misrepresentation and delusion have taken over. Žižek's work might be taken as one cultural direction that Freud's work can take if you build in the assumption that language is wholly unreliable as a cognitive instrument. There is a precedent for this conception of culture in Sartre's earlier characterization of inauthenticity as a prevailing social condition. It seems that the hypertrophy of language and culture in France has generated a distinctive conception of its alienating power, as well as ultra-intellectual responses to these which are themselves trapped by the forms of discourse with which they struggle. In Žižek's writing, a disruptive, modernist sensibility finds in cinema, humour, and writing itself, evidence that this oppressive carapace of authority has its cracks, and that a spirit of paradox and play can discover some space in which truth remains at least momentarily possible.

PSYCHOANALYSIS AND DECONSTRUCTION

The thrust of all of these three phases of political application of Lacanian psychoanalysis is 'deconstructive'. That is, each of them in their different ways calls into question the symbols and representations of political discourse as inherently deceptive and slippery. Žižek, whose account is by far the most fully psychoanalytic of the three writers discussed, identifies the source of misrepresentation of political discourse as the unconscious – phantasies projected on to political 'ideals' and imparting to them an 'excess' of meaning and mobilizing energy. The implication is that to be aware of this unconscious dimension of what he calls 'enjoyment' offers the possibility of dealing with its worst effects. For Laclau, the concept of the 'impossible' in Lacanian psychoanalysis – the impossibility, that is, of satisfying by representation the 'lack' which motivates symbol use – is its chief attraction for post-Marxist politics. The essential attribute of this is its refusal of positive grounding and its insistence on a self-aware discursive construction of the social world.

However, the argument that there is and should be no positive content to a psychoanalytic view of humankind is mistaken. This argument is directly parallel to Laclau's idea that there need be no 'positive' content to social or political visions, since these are self-constituting discursive entities which actively *make* rather than reflect or represent a given or possible world. But it was a central goal both of Marxism and psychoanalysis (as human sciences of the Enlightenment) to establish a 'positive' grounding of values in a 'naturalistic' view of mankind. For Marx, this 'naturalistic' view depended on the primacy of the mode of production in all existing societies. For Freud, the 'naturalistic economy' in question was a libidinal one, various needs and the barriers to their satisfaction being articulated as the psychological substructure of human existence. Laclau and others have argued, in an anti-modernist and anti-totalitarian spirit (these two tendencies are now linked) that such 'naturalistic' forms of ethics and politics should be rejected because of their propensity to function as forms of 'closure' (or in Laclau's term, 'suture'), with all the consequences we know political dogmatisms to have.

The abuse of 'positive' theories in politics does indeed have its milder equivalents in psychoanalysis, in the prescriptive use of developmental models as forms of moral judgement. The concepts of the depressive and paranoid–schizoid positions may be employed reductively, as synonyms for relative psychic health and pathology, even though these terms now refer in Kleinian theory to inherently unstable states of mind always liable to transformation into their alternate mode. The use for purposes of cultural diagnosis of terms derived from psychoanalysis such as 'narcissism' can lead to similar dead ends. There is often a significant loss of theoretical precision involved in the transposition of clinical categories to a social context. What may predominate in such applications is less a process of investigation, which calls on judgement, than moral denunciation.

But it does not follow that because 'positive terms' are used in psychoanalytic or political discourses they must unavoidably lead to authoritarian closure. It seems that without some 'positive' (that is, empirically based and rationally theorized) grounds for distinguishing different forms of social organization from one another there is no basis for a principled politics of any kind. Similarly, without some operating conception of the healthy and the pathological (based, for example, on ideas of avoidable pain to analysands and others), it is hard to see any responsible goal for psychoanalytic practice.

Freud's 'positive' model was a limited and anti-utopian one, going little further than a stoical commitment to the mitigation of suffering, and to achieving some tolerable fit between human desires and their possibilities of satisfaction. But 'positive' model it nevertheless was, an exemplary instance of a morally-engaged human science.

It is not in fact the case that Lacanian theory has no 'positive' basis; that is, that it makes no foundational empirical assumptions about human nature and development. The problem is rather that these assumptions are so bleak. A core building block of Lacanian theory is the fracturing of identity from the infant's moment of entry into social relationships. This occurs through the imaginary self-identification of the mirror stage (a version of primary narcissism as the founding principle of identity) and through the entry into an 'externally' and patriarchally determined system of language – encoding 'the name of the father' amongst its basic terms. From then on the construction of 'identity' is based on 'lack', on a kind of primary wound inflicted on the infant through the loss of sole possession of mother and through the further losses of the Oedipal stage, and incapable of repair in either the symbolic or imaginary realms. Ultimately the conception of the self which seems to regulate this model is as solipsistic and inescapably alienated as the metaphysic of Jean-Paul Sartre.[12]

The Kleinian model, by contrast, elaborates distinctions between different forms of relation to the self, to the use of language, and to others, which are of great significance in judgements of relative well-being and potentiality. Paranoid–schizoid and depressive states of mind *are* different in the recognition of the existence and needs of others they make possible. Internal objects, refracted through phantasy, can be destructive and perverse, or primarily constructive and creative. Identifications with social groups can be based on paranoid phantasies of split-off destructive aspects of the self, or on reparative impulses based on admiration and gratitude.

Of course, any model of human development can become a dogmatic system, inimical to actual development. This must also be true of 'anti-models' such as Lacan's, which seek to exist mainly in the mode of process and critique. But there is no necessary contradiction (within either Marxism or psychoanalysis) between the espousal of a 'positive' theory on the one hand, and a critical and deconstructive practice on the other, addressed no less to a self-conscious scrutiny of its own presuppositions than to the more tempting and narcissistically satisfying (or 'enjoyable', in Žižek's term) targets of opposed systems of thought.

THE 'POSITIVE' IN THE BRITISH PSYCHOANALYTIC SCHOOL

The object relations tradition in Britain has on the whole given less emphasis than the Lacanian to the negative as the key moment of psychoanalysis. It has been less inclined to characterize psychoanalysis merely as an activity of calling in question and subverting the given. While this remains a fundamental dimension of the psychoanalytic process for analysts of this tradition, as for all authentic practitioners of psychoanalysis, it has been found to be compatible with a commitment to the development of substantive theory, to ideas of causation, and to a concept of therapeutic improvement understood not as a completed state, but at least as a theoretically specifiable move towards psychic integration. Accompanying this psychic integration is understood to be an enhanced capacity for relationship with others, and for feeling responsibility towards them.

This tradition holds both that there is a 'deconstructive' process essential to psychoanalysis, which calls into question the definitions and self-descriptions offered by analysands, *and* that there exist 'deep structures' of a theoretically consistent kind whose existence and character can be inferred from clinical material, and which are amenable to transformation through interpretation, and through other kinds of experience, once a capacity for thinking has been developed. Writers in this tradition have tended, following Freud, to seek the maximum of rigour and clarity in defining these theoretical entities (of which the 'paranoid–schizoid' and 'depressive' positions are two key examples), while they have remained sensitive to ambiguity and metaphor in their understanding of psychoanalytic material. Writing in this tradition typically combines theoretical argument with clinical evidence and illustration.

A similar rigorous discipline has been developed within this school in regard to analytic technique. Again the crucial distinction is between the idea of a clear and distinct 'frame' within which analytic phenomena can be observed (and which allows the analyst's own mental phenomena and relations towards the patient to be self-monitored), and the necessarily unpredictable and chaotic events which take place and must be carefully studied within that frame. In the Lacanian tradition, by contrast, no firm boundary seems to be drawn between the protean nature of analytic phenomena and the technique and theory necessary to gain understanding of it. Attempts to insist on and impose such 'disciplines' seem to have been regarded as compromising the essential analytic process as a potential collusion with repressive kinds of symbolic authority or super-ego forces.

It is not that the object relations school and especially the Kleinians have not been attentive to what they characterize as the negative in mental life. The principal reason for antipathy to Kleinian ideas, especially in the United States, and the main line of division between the Kleinians and independents, has been the Kleinians' insistence on the constitutional role of hatred and envy in the psyche, and the need to make use of the negative as well as the positive transference if analysts are to gain access to these states of mind.

The concept of negation has various different connotations, notably that of logical contradiction or denial on the one hand, and disavowal of repressed areas of experience on the other. Freud's essay *On Negation* links the mechanism of repression with symbolic or logical negation. In thinking about objects or events defined negatively, for example as non-existing, the mind is able to think about matters which have been otherwise barred from recognition. Psychoanalytic thought has, since Freud, elaborated different ways in which the mind deals with 'unthinkable' experiences, moving from Freud's original concept of repression to ideas of splitting, projective identification, and perverse addiction to untruth in the Kleinian tradition. Wilfred Bion's work on the formation and malformation of the capacity for thought has led to a new understanding of the connections between destructive states of mind, and thinking or states of non-thinking such as occur in psychosis or autism. That is not merely to say that specific kinds of desires and their objects may be denied or excluded from thought, as Freud recognized. Bion demonstrated how the whole process of thought may be inhibited or destroyed by the pressure of unassimilable and intolerable emotional experience. An excess of unmodulated hatred and envy had the effect, he argued, of destroying the mind's capacity to function, 'attacks on linking', that is, on language and thought, being one way in which the hated and feared 'other' could be banished from the subject's awareness. The reality principle – the manifestation of a functioning apparatus of perception and reasoning – depended on a capacity to tolerate the states of mind evoked by reality. The 'negative' is perceived here as the limit or boundary condition of mental functioning, and the objective of psychoanalysis where its presence is powerful is to render this 'negative' capable of containment within some firm psychic boundaries. The development of containing mental structures is also one of the primary functions of adequate parenting in early life, by whomever it is provided (Shuttleworth 1989). Bion developed categories of minus K, minus L and minus H (negative relations to knowledge and to love and hate) to categorize these refusals of mental function, which he saw as basic or primitive forms of defence, first identified by him in work with psychotic patients (Bion 1967). But the idea of the development of mental function in Bion's work extends the Kleinian theory of the paranoid–schizoid and depressive positions, viewing them as capable of a volatile oscillation.[13] The concept of 'containment' (in some danger of becoming a cliché in contemporary psychoanalytic thought) links the psychic environment provided for infants to their development of emotional and cognitive capacities. This recent emphasis on cognitive capacities (and disorders) in Kleinian thought (and especially in Bion's contribution to this tradition) is in fact a point of convergence with the Lacanian tradition's emphasis upon the negative.[14] But the underlying assumptions and aims of the Kleinians are somewhat different, since rather than celebrating this 'negative' as an index of psychic authenticity, this perspective carries with it a commitment to the existence and growth of some 'positive' structures as the basis for mental functioning and development.

The most radical emphasis on the 'negative' in this tradition (Meltzer and Williams 1988) has developed from Bion's concept of 'catastrophic change' (Bion 1965, 1970). This approach views imaginative understanding – conceived as an 'aesthetic' experience of the beautiful and the sublime, in effect – as the true aim of psychic life. It is the encounter with the disturbance of new emotional experience – of which the infant's experience of the breast is for Meltzer the prototype – which creates the possibility of this state of aesthetic apprehension. Negation is in one sense the essence of this experience – it is the 'other' which the mind encounters. In another, more familiar sense of envy and hatred, the negative describes the desire to destroy whatever threatens the self's sense of omnipotence. The 'symbolic containments' of art and the psychoanalytic process imply a transcendence through the imagination of the 'negative' moment of disruption, understood as experienced in feeling as well as thought. There are similarities between Bion's view of the negative and its containment in symbolic terms, and Kant's theory of the aesthetic (Likierman 1989; Rustin 1991). More generally in the Kleinian tradition, especially where it is applied in clinical and preventive practice, one finds a commitment to the 'positive' in the form of framing structures, of psychological, relational, symbolic and even social kinds, as the basis of mental functioning and development.

The Kleinian and object relations traditions are constituted by a corpus of theories, an elaborated range of therapeutic techniques (not merely of classical psychoanalysis but variants developed for less intensive or more focused applications), [15] and models of psychic development which have a definite ethical cast. These have made these traditions consistent with ideas of positive social intervention. The idea that the disruptive phenomena of the unconscious can be contained in more and less destructive ways, that relatively benign relationships between the inner world and external reality can be conceived in theory and to some degree sustained in reality, has led to some commitment within the object relations tradition to projects of social improvement. Predictions can be made, from this corpus of ideas, about the conditions in which psychic development is most likely to take place, in settings which range from the neonate's family to the hospice. The idea that institutions where inner states of mind (notably anxiety) are taken seriously and as matters for reflection rather than for onward projection or punitive reprisal, has implications for various institutional designs, including those of schools, hospitals, factories, and prisons. On a more macro-social plane, the idea that mental pain and anxiety constitute valid claims on social attention has import for broader principles of social organization, qualifying and constraining the logic of markets or bureaucracies as arbiters of social life. [16]

CONCLUSION

It seems that different perspectives on unconscious aspects of mental life give rise to different political and social outlooks. Outright denial of the existence of the unconscious domain within the behaviourist psychological tradition typically generates interest-based and coercive models of social organization. Insistence, by contrast, on the repressive aspects of all symbolized social order generates a countervailing politics of resistance and 'subversion', tending to demand the revolutionary overthrow of the 'authoritarian symbolic' at the behest of the imaginary, but liable also to subsequent defaults to new structures of repression and dependency in the face of unsustainable anomie and anxiety. (This seems to have been the institutional story of the Lacanian movement.) Even Laclau's and Mouffe's concept of 'antagonism' has its problems from this point of view. It seems likely that a politics constructed largely on this principle will generate paranoid–schizoid states of mind as its normal psychic condition on both sides of any 'antagonistic' divide. This is not an argument against the acceptance of conflict in social, political, or indeed in mental life, but it does suggest that its advocates need to hold in mind its probable destructive effects. In this regard Žižek's work, with his advantage of experience of the post–1989 period, provides a significant corrective. He recognizes that social claims for recognition and self-expression are liable to assume an unconsciously motivated intensity, and can by no means be readily assumed to be reconcilable with one another even under a 'democratic' dispensation.

The view of mental life upheld by the British psychoanalytic school by contrast attempts to incorporate the idea of psychic exposure to the negative, defined by

Bion as 'learning from experience', and as a tolerated state of unknowing, [17] within forms of understanding which have a definite, 'positive' character. This perspective demands respect for and attention to the inner world, with the openness to experience (and the negative) necessary to this. Yet on the other hand it makes use of the positive corpus of concepts, theories and investigative techniques which together make up the psychoanalytic method.

The 'negative' moment in which self-definitions and self-representations are brought into question is central to all forms of psychoanalysis, which is essentially a methodology for engagement with the irrational and its impingements on the mind. The discovery that the descriptions and norms by which mental life is constituted are inherently over-determined by engagement with unconscious desires and fears, and may be least rational when they most claim rational authority, was after all the central discovery of Freud and his successors.

The British psychoanalytic tradition has tended towards scepticism and suspicion of all large-scale political practice. It has been held that engagement with the inner world, the toleration of uncertainty and the experience of intense states of feeling and intimacy can best be sustained at a micro-level, in face-to-face relationships, within psychoanalysis or through the practice of art or other creative thought. Once the world of 'large groups' is entered (of which political life is an instance), phantasy is, in this view, likely to dominate mental life. Paranoid–schizoid states of mind are the probable consequence of the mobilization of interests and anxieties in a mass political process. Freud's view that mass political life mobilizes regressive states of emotion has been shared by many of his British psychoanalytic successors.

Where projects for social intervention have been linked to this British school, they have mostly been piecemeal in character. Interventions within specific institutional spheres have been preferred to political programmes of a more 'total' kind. This reflects a preference for experience with a clinical or observational referent, the valuing of 'containment' as an institutional as well as psychological value, and no doubt the normally evolutionary climate of British political life.

The Lacanian school, by contrast with the mainstream British tradition, has defined psychoanalysis primarily through its 'negative' moment. Its influence has been for 'deconstruction'. It has attacked intellectual and professional routines, especially those of psychoanalysis itself; it has been sceptical towards all notions of the ideal or the utopian; and it has aimed to unravel and expose the forms of symbolic closure through which individuals and groups seek an unattainable or 'impossible' wholeness. This tradition frequently comes near to the celebration of the irruption of the irrational into consciousness, or rather, to the ephemeral moments of recognition in such irruptions. (The early influence of Breton and surrealism on Lacan is significant in this respect.) The ever-present risk according to this perspective is of being self-deceived by symbolic or imaginary constructions of the mind. Its protagonists are driven towards an excess of ellipsis, subtlety and paradox by their anxiety not to be themselves caught by the tail of an unrecognized positivism. The anxious questions Lacanians must address to their mirror are not about their own persecutory states of mind, but about how to sustain a genuinely psychoanalytic mode of thought and writing against innate tendencies to lapse into the positive and the banal.

The 'negative' or 'deconstructive' mode is a necessary element of political discourse. The Lacanian tradition has in recent years provided powerful resources for the critique of a number of dominant structures of identity, including those constructed around ideals of gender, race and nation. But it is less clear that within this tradition any 'positive' conceptions of theory, mind or society can be tolerated. This position seems to come near to its own form of splitting: between a 'positive' dimension which is in fact necessary to psychic and social life but is deemed to be in its essence alienated; and a 'negative' to which psychoanalysis should indeed be deeply receptive. But what kind of progressive political or social project can be built if the 'positive' – that is, concepts, theories, norms and consistent techniques – is to be refused as innately inauthentic?

The 'positive' commitments of the British psychoanalytic tradition carry their risks of moralism and intellectual rigidity. Nevertheless, the attachment of this school to both the 'negative' *and* 'positive' poles of psychoanalytic thinking does offer a more tenable basis for thinking about the psychological preconditions of a good society than a tradition concerned with the negative alone.

NOTES

1 These issues are discussed in Rustin (1993).
2 There is an affinity between the Althusserian wish to 'purify' scientific Marxist thought in the face of its apparent 'dilution' by 'bourgeois' philosophy, and the Lacanian commitment to 'rescue' the authentic thought of Freud from the dilutions of adaptive American ego-psychology.
3 Lacan's relationship to Jakobson's work is discussed briefly by Bowie (1979, 1991). Jakobson's distinctions are developed in Jakobson (1971). David Lodge has lucidly explored the relationship between these two dominant forms of linguistic organization to contrasting literary traditions in *The Modes of Modern Writing* (1977).
4 Perry Anderson's critique of this linguistic determinism in his *In the Tracks of Historical Materialism* (1983) pointed out that language was better understood as an infinitely open-ended generator of meanings, not as a rigid system of transmission and reproduction.
5 Ernesto Laclau (1977) made use of this idea, which he derived from Althusser, to explain the construction of 'populist' ideologies.
6 'Emancipatory' syntheses of Marx's and Freud's idea have attempted to make something of the analogy between desire, in Freud's sense, and rational interests in self-realization in Marx's. Economic oppression and libidinal repression were thus connected. But the philosophical anthropology (presuppositions regarding human nature and human needs) in Marx and Freud are too far apart for this analogue to be much more than an act of wishful thinking on the point of radical Freudians. The successful reconciliation of what is valid in these two world-views requires a more fundamental transformation of both.
7 On the idea of the intellectual as 'legislator' and bringer of rational enlightenment to mankind, see Zygmunt Bauman (1987).
8 I have developed this argument about *Hegemony and Socialist Strategy* in Rustin (1988).
9 These issues are very lucidly discussed in Anthony Elliott's *Social Theory and Psychoanalysis in Transition* (1992), especially chapters 4 and 5. This work explores links between Lacan, Althusser, Laclau and Mouffe and Žižek in ways parallel to the

argument presented here. Elliott's analysis provides an admirable critique of the post-Lacanian position, but does not explore the alternative British psychoanalytic tradition.

10 This concept of the 'impossible' also figures largely in the work of Jacqueline Rose (1992, 1994), whose writings on social and cultural criticism have also been greatly influenced by Lacanian ideas.

11 Žižek's (1989, 1991) writing is highly suggestive and insightful about aspects of cultural and political life, totalitarianism etc. Consistent with the Lacanian method, its strengths lie in its particulars – in instances of recognition and disclosure of paradoxical forms of control. The symbolic order in totalitarian systems may dominate through the questions that are asked, the vacancy they open in their subjects, not through the answers that are provided. Kant's moral law gains its 'surplus' unconscious investment not in spite of, but because it has no substantive content. The super-ego controls through libidinal investment in its prohibitions. Even though Žižek's writing seems to proceed by association rather than by unified theoretical argument, it is nevertheless a model of psychoanalytic reflection.

12 Lacan rejects the idea of the autonomous and free subject which Sartre in his earlier work posits as a solution to the problem of a world unavoidably constructed in alienated terms. The desires and lacks from which the self is constituted remain central to Lacan's model, which was influenced by Hegel as well as Freud. Symbolic representations remain, however, external to the self, and the coherence of the subject is for Lacan and his followers an 'imaginary' entity (i.e. based in phantasy), intended to escape lack and the fear of non-being, not a potential realization of rational mastery as it was for Sartre. Lacan's account has the merit of an extreme realism given these presuppositions, though whether these are valid is another issue. Connections between Lacan's and Sartre's ideas are discussed in Lacan (1973); Macey (1988); Brennan (1993) and Wilden, in Lacan (1968).

13 The basic grammar of these and other concepts in the Kleinian tradition is described with admirable clarity in Hinshelwood's *A Dictionary of Kleinian Thought* (1989).

14 Jacqueline Rose (1994) has explored some of these connections from a mainly Lacanian standpoint.

15 It is notable that the authoritative collection of recent Kleinian writing (Spillius 1988) has one volume devoted to theory, and another to technique. On modifications of technique for child and family mental health settings, see Szur and Miller (1991). On the Independants, see Kohon (1987) and Rayner (1991).

16 Human needs for intimate and durable relationships, especially at vulnerable phases of the life-cycle, might amount in Michael Walzer's (1983) terms to a distinct 'sphere of justice', relating to the just claims which might be made upon the larger society on behalf of infants and other dependants. On this see Rustin (1991a).

17 Winnicott's version of this (e.g. in Winnicott 1971) is his conception of a mind in contact with its unconscious processes. Play and imagination in Winnicott's model depend on the existence of a permeable membrane between conscious and unconscious process.

REFERENCES

Althusser, L. (1969) *Lenin and Philosophy and other Essays*. London: Verso.
Anderson, P. (1983) *In the Tracks of Historical Materialism*. London: Verso.
Bauman, Z. (1987) *Legislators and Interpreters*. Cambridge: Polity Press.
Bion, W.R. (1965) *Transformations*. London: Heinemann. (Maresfield reprints 1984).
——— (1967) *Second Thoughts*. London: Heinemann (Maresfield reprints 1984).
——— (1970) *Attention and Interpretation*. London: Tavistock Publications. (Maresfield reprints 1984).
Bowie, M. (1979) 'Jacques Lacan', in J. Sturrock (ed.) *Structuralism and Since*. Oxford: Oxford University Press.
——— (1991) *Lacan*. London: Fontana.

Brennan, T. (1993) *History after Lacan*. London: Routledge.

Edsall, T. and Edsall, M. (1992) *Chain Reaction: The Impact of Race. Rights and Taxes on American Politics*. New York: Norton.

Elliott. A. (1992) *Social Theory and Psychoanalysis in Transition*. Oxford: Blackwell.

Freud, S. (1900) *The Interpretation of Dreams*. S.E.5.

—— (1905) *Jokes and their Relation to the Unconscious*. S.E.8.

Hall, S. *et al.* (1978) *Policing the Crisis*. London: Macmillan.

Hinshelwood, R. (1989) *A Dictionary of Kleinian Thought*. London: Free Association Books.

Jakobson, R. (1971) *Studies on Child Language and Aphasia*. The Hague: Mouton.

Kohon, G. (1987) *The British School of Psychoanalysis: the Independent Tradition*. London: Free Association Books.

Lacan, J. (1968) *The Language of the Self: the Function of Language in Psychoanalysis*. Trans. with notes and commentary by A. Wilden. New York: Dell Publishing Co.

—— (1973) *The Four Fundamental Concepts of Psycho-analysis*, J.A. Miller (ed.), trans. A. Sheridan. Harmondsworth: Penguin.

—— (1977) *Ecrits – a Selection*. Trans. Alan Sheridan. London: Tavistock.

Laclau, E. (1977) *Politics and Ideology in Marxist Theory*. London: New Left Books.

—— (1990) 'Psychoanalysis and Marxism', in *New Reflections on the Revolution of our Time*. London: Verso.

Laclau, E. & Mouffe, C. (1985) *Hegemony and Socialist Strategy*. London: Verso.

Likierman, M. (1989) 'The clinical significance of aesthetic experience', *International Review of Psycho-Analysis*, 16 (2).

Lodge, D. (1977) *The Modes of Modern Writing: Metaphor, Metonymy and the Typology of Modern Literature*. London: Edward Arnold.

Macey, D. (1988) *Lacan in Contexts*. London: Verso.

Meltzer, D. & Williams, M.H. (1988) *The Apprehension of Beauty*. Perthshire: Clunie Press.

Rayner, E. (1991) *The Independent Mind in British Psychoanalysis*. London: Free Association Books.

Rose, J. (1992) *The Case of Peter Pan or the Impossibility of Children's Fiction*, revised edition. Philadelphia: University of Pennsylvania Press.

—— (1994) *Why War?* Oxford: Blackwell.

Rustin, M.J. (1988) 'Absolute voluntarism: critique of a post-Marxist concept of hegemony', in *New German Critique*, 42.

—— (1991a) 'Psychoanalysis and social justice', in Rustin, *The Good Society and the Inner World*. London: Verso.

—— (1991b) *The Good Society and the Inner World*. London: Verso.

—— (1993) 'Crisi di fine secolo e origine sociale della psicoanalisi', in C. Alberella and N. Pirillo (eds) *L'incognità del soggetto e la civilizzazione*. Napoli: Liguori Editore.

Shuttleworth, J. (1989) 'Psychoanalytical theory and infant development', in L. Miller, M.E. Rustin, M.J. Rustin and J. Shuttleworth (eds) *Closely Observed Infants*. London: Duckworth.

Spillius, E. Bott (1988) *Melanie Klein Today*. Vols. *1 and 2*. London: Institute of Psychoanalysis/Routledge.

Szur, R. and Miller, S. (eds) (1991) *Extending Horizons: Psychoanalytic Psychotherapy with Children, Adolescents and Families*. London: Karnac.

Walzer, M. (1983) *Spheres of Justice*. Oxford: Martin Robertson.

Winnicott, D.W. (1971). *Playing and Reality*. London: Tavistock.

Žižek, S. (1989) *The Sublime Object of Ideology*. London: Verso

—— (1990) 'East European Republics of Gilead', *New Left Review*, 183 (September–October).

—— (1991) *For They Know Not What They Do: Enjoyment as a Political Factor*. London: Verso.

Index